Books are to be returned on or before
the last date below.

DUE
1 7 MAR 2007

DUE
1 4 JUN 2007

DUE
1 8 MAR 2008

DUE
2 4 MAR 2010

LIBREX–

Computer Communications Security

Principles, Standard Protocols and Techniques

Warwick Ford

PTR Prentice Hall
Englewood Cliffs, New Jersey 07632

Library of Congress Cataloging-in-Publication Data

Ford, Warwick
   Computer communications security/Warwick Ford.
      p.   cm.
   Includes bibliographical references and index.
   ISBN 0-13-799453-2
   1. Computer security. 2. Telecommunication systesm--Security
measures. I. Title.
QA76.9.A25F65   1994
  005.8--dc20   93-11666
                                    CIP

Editorial/production supervision: *Harriet Tellem*
Cover design: *Lundgren Graphics*
Manufacturing buyer: *Alexis Heydt*

Published by PTR Prentice Hall
Prentice-Hall, Inc.
A Paramount Communications Company
Englewood Cliffs, NJ 07632

The publisher offers discounts on this book when ordered in bulk quantities. For more information contact:

   Corporate Sales Department
   PTR Prentice Hall
   113 Sylvan Avenue
   Enlgewood Cliffs, NJ 07632

   Phone: 201-592-2863
   Fax: 201-592-2249

UNIX is a registered trademark of AT&T.
Kerberos and Project Athena are trademarks of the Massachusetts Institute of Technology (MIT).

Printed in the United States of America
10 9 8 7 6 5 4 3 2 1

ISBN 0-13-799453-2

Prentice-Hall International (UK) Limited, *London*
Prentice-Hall of Australia Pty. Limited, *Sydney*
Prentice-Hall Canada Inc., *Toronto*
Prentice-Hall Hispanoamericana, S.A.,
Prentice-Hall of India Private Limited, *New Delhi*
Prentice-Hall of Japan, Inc., *Tokyo*
Simon & Schuster Asia Pte. Ltd., *Singapore*
Editora Prentice-Hall do Brasil, Ltda., *Rio de Janeiro*

To NOLA,

TERRY,

and LOUISA

CONTENTS

PART II – STANDARD PROTOCOLS AND TECHNIQUES

Foreword

Security is becoming an essential requirement of information networks. Strong security technology is required to protect users' sensitive or valuable information, both within the communication network and within information processors connected to the network. Significantly, the network itself now consists of a collection of different types of processors used to route information rapidly and to provide network support services. Reliability and integrity of the complete system are of utmost importance.

The information presented in this book represents the broadest current thinking on network security from the perspectives of end users and system architects. The end user expects a certain level of reliability from a communication network and generally wants to protect information at a level commensurate with the perceived value of, and risk to, the information. Both ubiquitous security provisions to protect the network and user selectable security mechanisms transcending the network are needed.

Users of computer networks are largely unaware of the potential threats to their information, or they choose to ignore such threats. The number of incidents of disruption or loss, on a per-user basis, is still very low. Just as residents in most of the free world are not typically concerned about terrorists or sabotage, users of networks are not typically concerned about information loss or destruction ("It won't happen to me"). However, both could happen easily. The major cause for concern is the continual rise in the number of security incidents and the costs of these incidents throughout the world.

In order for security to become a pervasive network characteristic and for information to be provided a predetermined or selectable level of protection end-to-end, standards for security are of utmost importance. Standards are developed for various reasons. We need both baseline standards to assure a uniform level of information protection and interoperability standards to assure compatibility among network components.

In the U.S. federal government, computer security standards were identified as a high-priority initiative at the National Bureau of Standards in the early 1970s. Two technology milestones, time-sharing systems and remotely accessible computers, caused leading computer science experts to become concerned about potential risks to the security of the systems and the information they processed. Other organizations, such as the U.S. Department of Defense, had recognized the need for protecting classified information in their systems in the mid-1960s but relied primarily on physical security of the stand-alone systems for the needed protection. Representatives of the two government organizations and several professional computing associations sponsored a workshop in the fall of 1972 that established a foundation for many of the computer security programs and standards that were subsequently developed.

In recent years, a large number of professional and standards-making organizations have contributed to the development of computer security programs and standards. The American Bankers Association, the American National Standards Institute, the International Organization for Standardization (ISO), and the International Telecomunication Union have led the development of voluntary industry standards in security. The U.S. Department of Defense established a series of standards and guidelines (including the *Orange Book* evaluation criteria) for its use. The National Institute of Standards and Technology (NIST; formerly the National Bureau of Standards) undertook development of Federal Information Processing Standards for protecting unclassified information (highlighted in the Computer Security Act of 1987). The NIST standards included the Data Encryption Standard (DES) and other standards supporting the application of DES. While each of these activities has contributed to a comprehensive security program, it has always been difficult for an end user or system architect to understand all aspects of the security problem, especially in a widely distributed network.

Warwick Ford has produced a thorough treatment of network security from the perspectives of end users and system architects. The content is broad enough to be used as a reference and deep enough to be used as a textbook. It takes a serious approach to a serious topic but in a readable style. The truly human nature of the computer security problem is made apparent. The fundamental desire for safety (i.e., security) and the typical unwillingness to meet the disciplinary requirements for achieving it are human characteristics that are often carried over into computer security. This book presents the big picture of network security, then elaborates on the details. It describes the elements needed for the network to exhibit and enforce the necessary discipline on a full time, automated basis.

I first met Warwick when he started participating in the NIST-sponsored Open Systems Interconnection (OSI) Implementors Workshop in the mid-1980s. I was the first chairman of the Workshop's security working group. In greeting this Australian-born Canadian I offered the Australian "G'Day." I remember the smile in response. Over the past seven years I have gotten to know Warwick well, and I responded with a similar smile when he asked me to write a foreword to his excellent book.

Warwick is an established expert in the world of commercial telecommunications security, contributing greatly to international network security standards. In addition to his individual contributions to many standards projects he has produced, in this book, a comprehensive compendium of information on the field. Both formal and informal students of the field will find this a valuable document. While security books are not intended to produce laughter I believe that, for many readers, this book will produce a smile of appreciation.

Dennis K. Branstad, Fellow
National Institute of Standards
and Technology
Gaithersburg, Maryland, U.S.A.

Preface

Computer communications security involves protecting computer networks against penetration, eavesdropping, data alteration, or disruption by unauthorized persons. Concerns in this area are currently mounting steadily. These concerns interact with another important trend — the move away from a world of incompatible vendor-proprietary networking architectures to the *open-systems* world, in which networks can be constructed by straightforward interconnection of hardware and software components from a range of vendors. The key to the open-systems world is *standardization*.

To make a heterogeneous (i.e., mixed vendor) computer network secure, it is necessary to agree to common specifications for security-related protocols implemented in communicating systems and to specifications for the security techniques that underlie these protocols. These specifications are embodied in standards of various types including international and national standards, government standards, and community (e.g., Internet) standards. Many specifications for standard security protocols and security techniques have matured in the late 1980s and early 1990s. We can now assemble a picture of how such protocols and techniques can be used together to satisfy the full communications security needs of network users.

Objectives and Organization

My objectives in this book are to create an awareness and an understanding of standardized methods for securing computer networks and their applications, focusing on intersystem, as opposed to intrasystem, security functions.

The book is designed as a tutorial/reference for any technically oriented person concerned with the design, implementation, marketing, or procurement of computer communications networks. Readers should have a basic understanding of data networking principles. No prior knowledge of security technology is needed.

The book is organized into two parts. Part I provides a technical tutorial spanning the computer communications security field. It includes an introduction to the terminology, concepts, methods, and overall architectural approaches used throughout the field. This part is intended primarily for readers without a security background. However, material on newer topics, such as non-repudiation and the placement of security in layered architectures, may be of value to the experienced security practitioner as well.

An understanding of the Part I material is a prerequisite to Part II, which describes specific security techniques and security protocols resulting from a wide range of standardization activities. Part II is targeted equally at readers with security experience and newcomers to the field.

The "roadmap" presented in this preface will assist in appreciating the organization of the material.

Stability of the Field

Is this a good time to publish a book on computer network security? Certainly, the subject is currently surrounded by its share of controversial issues, including:

(a) moves to promote encryption schemes that try to balance two conflicting interests — the interests of those seeking information privacy and the interests of law enforcement agencies which see uncontrolled information-hiding as an impediment to their functioning;

(b) the U.S. federal government move to standardize a new digital signature algorithm in competition with the worldwide *de facto* standard RSA algorithm; and

(c) the continuing competition between two "standard" network protocol development activities — the OSI and Internet protocol suites.

However, such issues do not necessarily imply instability in this field. Issues (a) and (b) simply underscore the need to adopt a "plug-in" philosophy when incorporating cryptographic algorithms into product or network designs. Recognizing that algorithm technology will continually advance, and that user needs, preferences, and biases will continually change, the wise designer will always use this philosophy.

Regarding issue (c), both the OSI and Internet suites have their strengths and weaknesses, and one would hope that the long term will bring a merging of the strong parts of both. From the security perspective, there is no significant difference in overall approach or in technological solutions for the two architectures. Consequently, the security aspects of both protocol suites can be covered in one coherent treatment of the field.

I believe this *is* a good time to publish a book on computer network security, because the field has just reached a solid ledge of stability, in terms of both technology and standards maturity. Technology-wise, the most significant factor is the bedding-in of public-key technology, which is now at the brink of large scale deployment. Standards-wise, the early 1990s have seen the completion of several important network security standards, such as the access

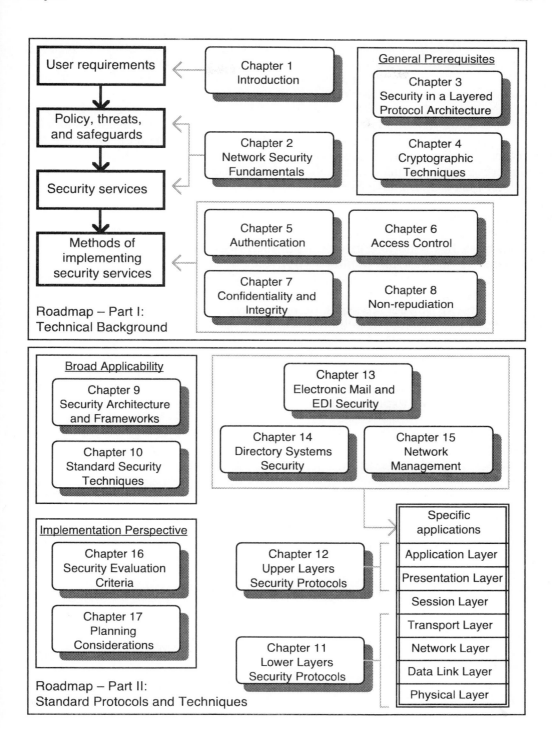

control extensions to the X.500 Directory standards, Internet network management (SNMP) security protocols, Internet Privacy Enhanced Mail, the IEEE security protocol for local area networks, and the OSI Transport and Network Layer security protocols.

There are, inevitably, some areas where the work is not stable as this book is being written. In such areas, I limit the technical coverage appropriately, to ensure that the overall accuracy of the book will be preserved into the future. The most notable area is security evaluation criteria, which is currently undergoing major change. For that reason, the coverage of this topic is much briefer than I would have liked.

Acknowledgments

This book has benefited greatly from the efforts of those who reviewed the original manuscript and provided such valuable comments. In particular, I am indebted to Vish Narayanan of General Motors and Stewart Lee of the University of Toronto for their comprehensive reviews. I also wish to thank those who reviewed the parts of the material in their respective areas of specialist expertise. These include Richard Ankney of Fischer International, Michael Ransom of NIST, Marshall Rose of Dover Beach Consulting, Bob Sharpton of Hughes, and my BNR colleagues Carlisle Adams, Sharon Boeyen, Bob Brett, Richard Thomas, Paul Van Oorschot, and Michael Wiener.

I appreciate the support of my employer, Bell-Northern Research, in this project. All views expressed, however, are entirely my own.

Warwick Ford
Ottawa, Ontario, Canada

1 **Introduction**

The importance of communications security has long been recognized in military and other environments where national security can be at stake. Mastery of communications security — and of its opposite number, cryptanalysis — is recognized as a significant factor in the winning of many of the century's major military conflicts, including the second world war. In this context, communications security is the means of hiding sensitive information and protecting it against tampering while in transit. Cryptanalysis is the means of compromising the communications security capabilities of one's enemies.

This book does not deal with national security grade communications security. Rather, it deals with the application of these same types of techniques to computer networks in commercial and *unclassified* government environments. Widespread application of such techniques in such environments has only recently become warranted. Sophisticated attacks, such as cryptanalysis, have long been considered so unlikely that the costs of sophisticated security measures were not justified. However, there are three major trends now leading to an urgent reassessment of this attitude and causing communications security concerns to escalate:

- the increasing interconnection of systems and of networks, making any system potentially accessible to a rapidly growing population of (known and unknown) users;
- the increasing use of computer networks for security-sensitive information; for example, electronic funds transfer, business data interchange, government *unclassified but sensitive* information, and corporate proprietary information; and
- the increasing ease of engineering a network attack, given the ready availability of increasingly sophisticated technology and the rapidly falling costs of such technology to a would-be attacker.

Hackers are now an ingrained element of the wide-area networking environment [STE1]. Networks of governments, financial institutions, telecommunications carriers, and private corporations have all been victims of hacker penetrations and they continue to be targets.

Network penetrations can have very wide-ranging impacts, as was apparent in the following well-documented cases:

- The sequence of hacker attacks into hundreds of U.S. military and government research facilities, described in detail by Cliff Stoll [STO1]. This was a case of successful (although not undetected) attacks over a period of many months. The objective was foreign espionage. The hacker's personal motivation was opportunistic financial gain. From Cliff Stoll's story, the most disconcerting message to network operators and users is the ease with which the penetrations were made, using very basic equipment and only a moderate level of technical expertise.

- The *Internet worm*, unleashed on the Internet in November 1988 by Cornell University student Robert Morris Jr. [SPA1]. The worm, a self-replicating penetration program, swept across the Internet, infecting and effectively disabling at least 1,200 (possibly up to 6,000) Internet computers running certain versions of the UNIX operating system.

Reliable statistics on hacker penetrations and other security incidents are difficult to obtain because of an unwillingness of many victims to publicly admit they are (or even were) vulnerable. An indication of trends can be obtained from security incident statistics maintained by the Internet Computer Emergency Response Team (CERT), which was formed in the wake of the Internet worm incident. The numbers of incidents reported in the 1989–1992 period are shown in Table 1-1. Note that an incident may involve one site or may involve up to thousands of sites, and incidents may be ongoing for long periods of time.

Year	*Incidents*
1989	132
1990	252
1991	406
1992	773

Table 1-1: Reported Internet Security Incidents 1989–1992

There are many potential motivations for attacks on commercial or unclassified government networks. They include financial fraud, theft of telecommunications resources, industrial espionage, illicit eavesdropping for financial or political gain, egotistical gratification, adventurism, and malicious attacks by disgruntled employees or wanton vandals. In addition to these *deliberate* types of attack, communications security needs to protect against *accidental* exposures. Accidental connection of a sensitive communications session to the wrong address or accidental failure to properly protect sensitive information may prove as damaging as a successful deliberate attack.

1.1 Typical Security Requirements

The hacker threat is a concern in all networks which have public network access or which use public network facilities. However, this is not the only concern. In order to assemble a picture of other network security requirements, let us consider the main security concerns in some key network application environments.

Banking

Since the 1970s, electronic funds transfer (EFT) has been the focus for applying communications security in the financial industry [PAR1]. The primary concern is ensuring that nobody tampers with electronic transactions. There is a tremendous potential for massive fraudulent financial gain through quite simple modification of a transaction, e.g., of a dollar amount or of an account number.

This is a major issue with the financial institutions which generate and process transactions, as they face the prospect of bearing the cost of such a fraud. Even if the fraud is detected, prosecution may not be practical for many reasons, one being the public exposure damage to the institution. Because the financial system constitutes such a critical element of society, protection of this system also concerns governments. A sufficiently serious attack on a major financial system network could have the effect of destabilizing a nation's economy.

The seriousness of the financial industry's concerns and the support received from government have resulted in this industry leading the application of security technology in the commercial world.

In the 1980s, the introduction of automatic teller machine (ATM) networks and of EFT at point-of-sale (EFTPOS) raised a new set of communications security concerns in the retail banking arena [DAV1, MEY1]. The use of such facilities employs plastic cards and personal identification numbers (PINs). Because cards are frequently stolen and are easily forged, the security of the systems depends upon the secrecy of the PINs. Preservation of the secrecy of PINs is complicated by the fact that multiple separately administered networks are frequently involved in the processing of a transaction.

Furthermore, banks foresee continuing cost savings in replacing paper-based transaction services by electronic services. As new electronic services are progressively introduced, network security demands grow accordingly.

Increasingly, banks need to be sure that the party claiming to originate a transaction is genuine. An electronic equivalent of a customer's paper signature is needed. Banks are also concerned with protecting the privacy of their customers' transactions.

Electronic Trading

Electronic business data interchange (EDI) began to emerge as a major telecommunications application area in the 1980s [SOK1]. The goal of EDI is to replace the whole range of paper business transactions (e.g., purchase orders, invoices, and payments) with equivalent electronic transactions. EDI can potentially provide massive reductions in the costs of doing business.

For EDI to become widely accepted in commercial trading, security is an essential element. Users must be assured that the electronic system provides them with equivalent (if not better) protection against mistakes, misinterpretations, and fraudulent activities than the protection offered by the paper-and-signature scheme to which they are accustomed.

In EDI, there is a critical need for protection against deliberate or accidental modification of data and for assurance that the source of any transaction is legitimate. Confidentiality of transactions must also be preserved because of the corporate confidential information contained therein. In these respects EDI is similar to EFT. However, EDI introduces new security challenges because the community of users is much larger and the business associations are often much more tenuous.

EDI also introduces a major new requirement. EDI transactions constitute business contracts, which means they must have electronic signatures which have the same legal significance as paper signatures. For example, they should be acceptable as evidence in resolving disputes in courts of law. While the legal standing of electronic signatures was debated for several years, that legal standing is now being recognized. For example, in 1992 the American Bar Association approved a resolution[1] to:

> recognize that information in electronic form, where appropriate, may be considered to satisfy legal requirements regarding a writing or signature to the same extent as information on paper or in other conventional forms, when appropriate security techniques, practices, and procedures have been adopted.

Because of the cost savings to users and the extensive market opportunities for equipment vendors, EDI is viewed as a massive opportunity for users and vendors alike. Technical solutions and supporting standards for EDI security are becoming of major importance to virtually all industry.

---

[1] American Bar Association Resolution number 115, August 19, 1992.

Government

Governments are increasingly using computer communications networks for information transfer. Much of this information is not of a national security nature, hence is unclassified. However, security protection is required for other reasons, such as privacy legislation. This *unclassified but sensitive* information can be conveyed using commercially available networking equipment, provided adequate security provisions are employed.

For example, in the United States the Computer Security Act of 1987 introduced the concept of "sensitive information" defined as "any information, the loss, misuse or unauthorized access to or modification of which could adversely affect the national interest or the conduct of Federal programs, or the privacy to which individuals are entitled under section 552a of title 5, United States Code (the Privacy Act) , but which has not been specifically authorized under criteria established by an Executive Order or an Act of Congress to be kept secret in the interest of national defense or foreign policy."[2] The National Institute of Standards and Technology (NIST) was assigned "responsibility for developing standards and guidelines . . . to assure the cost-effective security and privacy of sensitive information." This assignment reinforced the distinction between sensitive and classified information, the latter being the province of the National Security Agency. Many other countries have comparable policies for recognizing and handling unclassified but sensitive data.

The most prominent security concern is ensuring that privacy is maintained, i.e., that information is not disclosed, either accidentally or deliberately, to anyone not authorized to have that information. Another concern is ensuring that information cannot be entered or modified by anyone not authorized to do so.

The cost savings of electronic transactions over paper transactions, e.g., the electronic filing of tax returns, are also being rapidly realized by governments. In addition to privacy guarantees, such systems introduce the need for legally enforceable electronic signatures. In 1991, with the removal of the main legal barrier, the way was paved for U.S. federal government use of electronic signatures. A Decision of the Comptroller General stated that contracts formed using electronic signatures constitute valid legal obligations of the government, provided properly secured systems are used (federal government message authentication code or digital signature standards must be followed).[3]

----

[2] U.S. Congress, The Computer Security Act of 1987, Public Law 100-235, January 8, 1988.

[3] Comptroller General of the United States, Decision B-245714, Decisions of the Comptroller General, vol. 71 Comp. Gen. 109 (1991), December 13, 1991.

Public Telecommunications Carriers

The management of public telecommunications networks covers a broad range of functions, collectively known as operations, administration, maintenance, and provisioning (OAM&P). These management functions themselves employ substantial data networking facilities, interconnecting a vast range of equipment and having a large population of human users (operations and maintenance personnel). While access to such networks was once tightly restricted, new access paths are continually opening up. Capabilities such as *customer network management* provide for customer personnel to access the management network to perform management operations on the public network resources used by that customer organization.

Telecommunications management networks and systems are susceptible to hacker penetrations [STE1]. A common motivation for such penetrations is theft of telecommunications services. Having penetrated network management, such theft can be engineered in various ways, such as invoking diagnostic functions, manipulating accounting records, and altering provisioning databases. Network management penetrations can also be directed at eavesdropping on subscriber calls.

A major concern of telecommunications carriers is the prospect of security compromises causing network down-time, which can be extremely costly in terms of customer relations, lost revenue, and recovery costs. Deliberate attacks on the availability of the national telecommunications infrastructure can even be viewed as a national security concern.

In addition to external penetrations, carriers are concerned about security compromises from internal sources, such as invalid changes to network management databases on the part of personnel who are not authorized to make such changes. Such occurrences may be accidental or deliberate, e.g., actions of a disgruntled employee. To protect against such occurrences, access to every management function needs to be restricted to only those individuals who legitimately require it. It is important to know correctly the identity of an individual attempting to access a management function.

Corporate/Private Networks

Virtually all private corporations have requirements to protect sensitive proprietary information. Disclosure of such information to competitors or other external entities can severely damage business, to the extent of winning or losing major contracts and possibly impacting corporate survival. Networks are being increasingly used for conveying proprietary information, e.g., between individuals, office locations, corporate subsidiaries, and/or business collaborators. Closed corporate networks are now a concept of the past — the growing trend of working at home (*telecommuting*) has ensured that.

Protection of proprietary information is not the only concern. Many organizations are entrusted with information about other organizations or individuals, for which they are obliged to provide privacy protection. Examples are the health-care and legal sectors.

Requirements for ensuring the authenticity of messages also arise in corporate networks. A sufficiently important electronic message always needs to be authenticated, in the same way that an important paper document requires a signature.

Until recently, corporations have operated under the assumption that comparatively simple protection mechanisms will satisfy their security requirements. They have not been concerned about technologically sophisticated penetrations, as might concern the government classified arena. However, there is increasing evidence that the resources of some foreign government intelligence agencies are now being used for industrial espionage purposes.[4] Commercial industry can no longer be complacent about the strength of security protective measures employed to protect sensitive proprietary information.

1.2 Security and Open Systems

While *network security* and *open systems* may appear to be contradictions in terms, this is not necessarily the case. The open-system concept represents the buyer's reaction to many years of lock-in to individual computer and communications hardware and software vendors. It is seen as the path to open choice of vendor for separate system components, with confidence that components from separate vendors will readily work together to satisfy a buyer's needs. The open-systems drive is tied to the establishment and widespread implementation of standards.

Computer networking and open systems go hand in hand. The flagship open-systems initiative — Open Systems Interconnection (OSI) — has been progressing since the 1970s, developing internationally agreed computer communications protocol standards. In addition to the formal OSI standards, open-system networking protocols have been established by other groups — notably the Internet community, with its TCP/IP protocol suite.   Through these open-system networking activities, it is becoming possible to interconnect

---

    4 See, for example, the purported disclosures of the former head of the French Secret Service organization, DGSE [MAR1]. These disclosures indicate that the French Secret Service has a policy of supplying French industry with industrial espionage information gained through its international telecommunications interception facilities, and that such information has been successfully used by French corporations in procuring major international contracts.

equipment from many vendors, using virtually any communications technology and satisfying the needs of virtually any application.[5]

The incorporation of security protection into open-system networks is a comparatively recent endeavor. It has proven to be a complex task, largely because it represents a marriage of two technologies — security technology and communication protocol design. To provide open-system network security, it is necessary to employ *security techniques* in conjunction with *security protocols*, the latter being integrated with conventional network protocols.

Needed are compatible and complementary standards which span three broad fields:

- security techniques;
- general-purpose security protocols; and
- specific application protocols, e.g., banking, electronic mail.

Relevant standards for these fields are from four main sources[6]:

- international standards on information technology, developed under the International Organization for Standardization (ISO), the International Electrotechnical Commission (IEC), the International Telecommunication Union (ITU), and the Institute of Electrical and Electronics Engineers (IEEE);
- banking industry standards, developed either internationally under ISO or in the United States under the American National Standards Institute (ANSI);
- national government standards, especially those of the U.S. federal government; and
- Internet standards, developed by the Internet community.

Security-relevant standards from all of these sources are described in this book.

Summary

Network security is no longer a specialized requirement of military and national security environments. Network security requirements have emerged in

---

5 The open systems concept has also spread beyond networking into areas such as database models and languages, computer operating system interfaces, and application software interfaces [NUT1]. However, the scope of this book is restricted to networking.

6 Appendix A provides an overview of relevant standardization groups, including the organizations identified here, and describes the way they operate.

virtually all network application environments, including banking, electronic trading, government (unclassified), public telecommunications carriers, and corporate/private networks. A collection of typical requirements of these environments is summarized in Table 1-2.

Network security needs to be implemented in concert with the move to open-system (i.e., vendor-independent) networking. This means that the basic components of network security — security techniques and security protocols — need to be reflected in appropriate open-systems standards.

In Chapter 2, we use the collection of security requirements in Table 1-2 as an illustration of how such informally stated requirements translate to *threats*, and how *security services* can be used to counter these threats. Subsequent chapters describe methods of implementing these security services.

Application Environment	Requirements
All networks	Prevent outside penetrations (hackers)
Banking	Protect against fraudulent or accidental modification of transactions Identify retail transaction customers Protect PINs from disclosure Ensure customers' privacy
Electronic trading	Assure source and integrity of transactions Protect corporate privacy Provide legally binding electronic signatures on transactions
Government	Protect against unauthorized disclosure or manipulation of unclassified but sensitive information Provide electronic signatures on government documents
Public telecommunications carriers	Restrict access to administration functions to authorized individuals Protect against service interruptions Protect subscribers' privacy
Corporate/private networks	Protect corporate/individual privacy Ensure message authenticity

Table 1-2: Typical Network Security Requirements

REFERENCES

[DAV1] D.W. Davies and W.L. Price, *Security for Computer Networks*, Second Edition, John Wiley and Sons, New York, 1989.

[MAR1] P. Marion, *La Mission Impossible à la tête des Services Secrets*, Calmann-Lévy, France, 1991 (French language).

[MEY1] C.H. Meyer, S.M. Matyas, and R.E. Lennon, "Required Cryptographic Authentication Criteria for Electronic Funds Transfer Systems," *Proceedings of the 1981 Symposium on Security and Privacy*, Oakland Ca., IEEE Computer Society Press, 1981.

[NUT1] G.J. Nutt, *Open Systems*, Prentice Hall, Englewood Cliffs, NJ, 1992.

[PAR1] D.B. Parker, "Vulnerabilities of EFTs to Intentionally Caused Losses," *Communications of the ACM*, vol. 22, no. 12 (December 1979), pp. 654–660.

[SOK1] P.K. Sokol, *EDI: The Competitive Edge*, Intext Publications, McGraw-Hill Book Company, New York, 1988.

[SPA1] E.H. Spafford, "The Internet Worm: Crisis and Aftermath," *Communications of the ACM*, vol. 32, no. 6 (June 1989), pp. 678-687.

[STE1] B. Sterling, *The Hacker Crackdown: Law and Disorder on the Electronic Frontier*, Bantam Books, New York, 1992.

[STO1] C. Stoll, *The Cuckoo's Egg*, Doubleday, New York, 1989.

PART I

TECHNICAL BACKGROUND

2   Network Security Fundamentals

Traditionally, information security has been considered to have three fundamental objectives:

- *Confidentiality*: Ensuring that information is not disclosed or revealed to unauthorized persons.
- *Integrity*: Ensuring consistency of data; in particular, preventing unauthorized creation, alteration, or destruction of data.
- *Availability*: Ensuring that legitimate users are not unduly denied access to information and resources.

In contemporary computer network environments, there is one further fundamental objective which is not covered by the above:

- *Legitimate use*: Ensuring that resources are not used by unauthorized persons or in unauthorized ways.

To support these objectives, a network administration needs to have a *security policy* and needs to put in place a range of security measures to ensure that the goals of the security policy are met. Security measures fall into several categories. The two categories addressed in this book are *communications security* and *computer security*.[1] Communications security is the protection of information while it is being communicated from one system to another. Computer security is the protection of information within a computer system, and it embraces such subcategories as operating system security and database security. Communications security and computer security measures need to interwork with security measures in other categories, such as physical security and personnel security. The term *security service* is used to describe technology-based security functions provided in network systems and network products.

This chapter introduces the following fundamental concepts:

---

[1] This book deals mainly with communications security, but also addresses some aspects of computer security, e.g., the communication of management information between systems as needed to support computer security.

(1) security policy;
(2) threats and safeguards;
(3) the five generic security services: authentication, access control, confidentiality, data integrity, and non-repudiation; and
(4) intrusion detection and security audit.

Consideration of mechanisms for implementing network security is left to later chapters.

2.1 Security Policy

A *security policy* is a set of rules to apply to all security-relevant activities in a *security domain* (a security domain is typically the set of processing and communications resources belonging to one organization).   The rules are established by an *authority* for that security domain.

Security policy is a very broad concept, and the term is used in many different ways in the literature and in standards. Some recent analyses of this issue [CHI1, STE1] have concluded that there are several different levels of security policy, such as:

- *Security policy objectives*: Statements of an organization's intent with respect to protecting identified resources.
- *Organizational security policy*: The set of laws, rules, and practices that regulate how an organization manages, protects, and distributes resources to achieve security policy objectives.[2]
- *System security policy*: Statements as to how a specific information technology system is engineered to support organizational security policy requirements.

In this book, use of the term *security policy* usually means the system security policy level, but readers should bear in mind that this forms part of the broader policy concept.

The following subsections identify some key aspects of security policy which impact network system and component design. Security policy models are discussed further in Chapter 6. For a more detailed coverage of the subject, see [NAT1].

---

[2] Organizational security policy may have implications upon the full range of safeguard categories, including communications security, computer security, physical security, and personnel security.

Authorization

Authorization is a fundamental part of a security policy. Authorization is the granting of rights — it amounts to establishing who may do what to what. Examples of authorization statements (at the organizational security policy level) are:

(a) File *Project-X-Status* can only be modified by person *G. Smith*, and can only be read by persons *G. Smith*, *P. Jones*, and members of the *Project-X* project team.
(b) A personnel record can only be created or modified by personnel division staff; it can be read by personnel division staff, by executive managers, and by the individual to whom it refers.
(c) Information classified within the hierarchy *confidential-secret-top secret* can only be disclosed to an individual with a clearance level equal to or greater than the classification level.

These policy statements place demands on various safeguard categories, e.g., personnel security for determining peoples' clearances. In the computer and communications categories, the main demands are reflected in a type of system security policy called *access control policy*.

Access Control Policies

Access control policies are system security policies which drive the automated enforcement of authorization in computer systems and networks. The example authorization statements (a), (b), and (c) above map to different types of access control policy, respectively:

(a) *Identity-based policy*: A policy that permits or denies access to explicitly identified individuals or groups of individuals;
(b) *Role-based policy*: A variation of an identity-based policy that assigns roles to individuals and applies authorization rules based on these roles; and
(c) *Multi-level policy*: A policy employing general rules, based on broad levels of the sensitivity of information and corresponding levels of clearances of people.

Access control policies are sometimes categorized as being *mandatory access control* or *discretionary access control* policies [DOD1]. Mandatory policies are imposed by the security domain authority and cannot be circumvented by individual users. Mandatory policies are most common in military and other government classified environments; policy (c) above is an example. Discretionary policies provide particular users with access to resources (e.g., information), then leave it to these users to control further access to the resources. Policies (a) and (b) above are examples of discretionary policies. In classified environments, discretionary policies are used to enforce the *need-to-know* concept.

Access control policies are discussed further in Chapter 6.

Accountability

A fundamental principle underlying any security policy is *accountability*. Individuals taking actions which are governed by security policy need to be accountable for their actions. This provides an important link to personnel security. Some network security safeguards, involved with authenticating human identities and linking actions with such identities, contribute directly to support of this principle.

2.2   Threats and Safeguards

Basic Concepts

A *threat* is a person, thing, event, or idea which poses some danger to an asset, in terms of that asset's confidentiality, integrity, availability, or legitimate use. An *attack* is an actual realization of a threat. *Safeguards* are physical controls, mechanisms, policies, and procedures that protect assets from threats. *Vulnerabilities* are weaknesses in a safeguard, or the absence of a safeguard.

Risk is a measure of the cost of a realized vulnerability that incorporates the probability of a successful attack. Risk is high if the value of a vulnerable asset is high, and the probability of a successful attack is high. Conversely, risk is low if the value of the vulnerable asset is low and the probability of a successful attack is low. Risk analysis can provide a quantitative means of determining whether expenditure on safeguards is warranted.

Threats can sometimes be classified as being deliberate (e.g., hacker penetration) or accidental (e.g., message sent in error to the wrong address). Deliberate threats may be further classified as being *passive* or *active*. Passive threats involve monitoring but not alteration of information (e.g., wiretapping). Active threats involve deliberate alteration of information (e.g., changing the dollar amount of a financial transaction). In general, passive attacks are easier and less costly to engineer than active attacks.

There is no universally agreed way to identify, classify, or interrelate threats. The existence and significance of different threats varies from environment to environment. However, in order to explain the role of network security services, we can assemble a picture of the threats typically encountered in contemporary computer networks. We do this in three stages — we identify *fundamental threats*, then *primary enabling threats*, then *underlying threats*.

Fundamental Threats

The four fundamental threats directly reflect the four security objectives identified at the start of the chapter:

- *Information leakage*: Information is disclosed or revealed to an unauthorized person or entity. We shall later see how this might involve direct attacks, such as eavesdropping or wiretapping, or more subtle types of information observation.
- *Integrity violation*: The consistency of data is compromised through unauthorized creation, alteration, or destruction of data.
- *Denial of service*: Legitimate access to information or other resources is deliberately impeded. This might involve, for example, making a resource unavailable to legitimate users through a heavy load of illegitimate, unsuccessful access attempts.
- *Illegitimate use*: A resource is used by an unauthorized person or in an unauthorized way. Examples are an intruder penetrating a computer system and using that system either as the basis of theft of telecommunications services or as a staging point for penetrating another system.

Primary Enabling Threats

The primary enabling threats are significant because a realization of any of these threats can lead directly to a realization of any of the fundamental threats. These threats therefore *enable* the fundamental threats. The primary enabling threats comprise *penetration* threats and *planting* threats. The main penetration threats are:

- *Masquerade*: An entity (person or system) pretends to be a different entity. This is the most common way of penetrating a security perimeter, e.g., a computer's *login perimeter*. An unauthorized entity convinces a perimeter guard that he is an authorized entity and thereafter assumes the rights and privileges of the authorized entity. Hackers succeed largely through the use of masquerade.
- *Bypassing controls*: An attacker exploits systems flaws or security weaknesses (e.g., system "features" whose existence was intended to be kept secret), in order to acquire unauthorized rights or privileges.

- *Authorization violation*: A person authorized to use a system or resource for one purpose uses it for another, unauthorized purpose. This is known as an *insider* threat.

The main planting threats are:

- *Trojan horse*: Software contains an invisible or apparently innocuous part which, when executed, compromises the security of its user. An example of a Trojan horse is a software application which has an outwardly legitimate purpose, e.g., text editing, but which also has a surreptitious purpose, e.g., copying user documents into a hidden private file which is read later by the attacker who planted the Trojan horse.
- *Trapdoor*: A feature is built into a system or system component such that the provision of specific input data allows security policy to be violated. An example is a login-processing subsystem which allows processing of a particular user-identifier to bypass the usual password checks.

Planting threats are usually realized by the planting party only after the planted capability has been left dormant for a period of time.

Underlying Threats

If we analyze any of the fundamental threats or primary enabling threats in a given environment, we can identify particular *underlying threats*, any of which may enable the more fundamental threats. For example, if we consider the fundamental threat of information leakage, we might find several underlying threats (apart from the primary enabling threats), such as:

- eavesdropping;
- traffic analysis;
- indiscretions by personnel; and
- media scavenging.

Figure 2-1 illustrates typical threats, and their interrelationships. Note that the path can become convoluted. For example, masquerade is a threat which can underlie all fundamental threats. However, masquerade can itself have information leakage as an underlying threat (because information leakage might reveal a password, which can enable masquerade). Table 2-1 lists the threats identified.

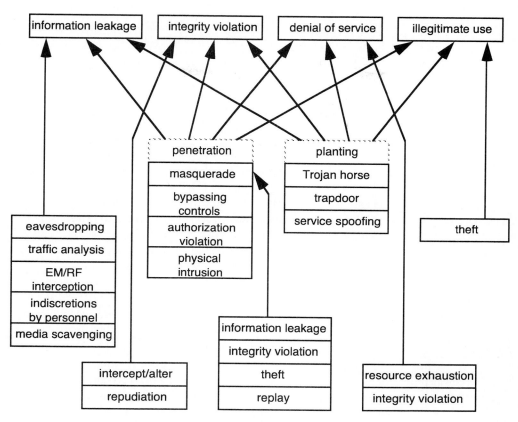

Figure 2-1: Threats Underlying Threats

An indication of the real-life significance of such threats can be obtained from [NEU1]. In a sampling of a collection of over 3,000 cases of computer system abuse, drawn from the media and personal reporting, the following threats were the most predominant (in order of decreasing frequency):

- authorization violation;
- masquerade;
- bypassing controls;
- Trojan horse or trapdoor; and
- media scavenging.

Threat	*Description*
Authorization violation *	A person authorized to use a system for one purpose uses it for another, unauthorized purpose.
Bypassing controls	An attacker exploits system flaws or security weaknesses.
Denial of service *	Legitimate access to information or other resources is deliberately impeded.
Eavesdropping *	Information is revealed from monitored communications.
EM/RF interception	Information is extracted from radio frequency or other electromagnetic field emanations from electronic or electromechanical equipment.
Illegitimate use	A resource is used by an unauthorized person or in an unauthorized way.
Indiscretions by personnel	An authorized person discloses information to an unauthorized person, e.g., for money or favors, or through carelessness.
Information leakage *	Information is disclosed or revealed to an unauthorized person or entity.
Integrity violation *	The consistency of data is compromised through unauthorized creation, modification or destruction of data.
Intercept/alter *	A communicated data item is changed, deleted, or substituted while in transit.
Masquerade *	An entity (person or system) pretends to be a different entity.
Media scavenging	Information is obtained from discarded magnetic or printed media.
Physical intrusion	An intruder gains access by circumventing physical controls.
Replay *	A captured copy of a legitimately communicated data item is retransmitted for illegitimate purposes.
Repudiation *	A party to a communication exchange later falsely denies that the exchange took place.
Resource exhaustion	A resource (e.g., access port) is deliberately used so heavily that service to other users is disrupted.
Service spoofing	A bogus system or system component aims to dupe legitimate users or systems into voluntarily giving up sensitive information.
Theft	A security-critical item, e.g., a token or identity card, is stolen.
Traffic analysis *	Information is leaked to unauthorized entities, through observation of communications traffic patterns.
Trapdoor	A feature is built into a system or system component such that the provision of specific input data allows security policy to be violated.
Trojan horse	Software that contains an invisible or apparently innocuous part which, when executed, compromises the security of its user.

* Threats that computer communications security can counter.

Table 2-1: Typical Network Threats

The Internet worm [SPA1] employed a combination of bypassing controls and masquerade attacks. Bypassing controls involved exploiting known flaws in the Berkeley UNIX system. Masquerade involved password cracking (this is pursued further in Chapter 5).

Safeguards

There are several categories of threat safeguard. *Communications security*, the primary subject of this book, and *computer security* were introduced at the start of this chapter. Other categories include:

- *Physical security*: Locks or other physical access controls; tamper-proofing of sensitive equipment; environmental controls.
- *Personnel security*: Identification of position sensitivity; employee screening processes; security training and awareness.
- *Administrative security*: Controlling import of foreign software; procedures for investigating security breaches, reviewing audit trails, reviewing accountability controls.
- *Media security*: Safeguarding storage of information; controlling marking, reproduction, and destruction of sensitive information; ensuring that discarded paper or magnetic media containing sensitive information are destroyed securely; scanning media for viruses.
- *Emanations security*: Radio frequency (RF) and other electromagnetic (EM) emanations controls (called TEMPEST protection).
- *Life cycle controls*: Trusted system design, implementation, evaluation, and endorsement; programming standards and controls; documentation controls.

A security system is only as strong as its weakest link. For effective security, countermeasures from the different categories need to be used together. For example, a technically sound password system, designed to counter masquerade, will be ineffective if users leave written passwords in an unsecured place or can be duped into revealing a password to an unknown telephone caller.

Safeguards can be provided against most threats, but every safeguard has a cost. A network user or procurer needs to carefully consider whether the potential cost of a successful attack warrants expenditure on safeguards. For example, in commercial networks, countermeasures are not normally provided against EM/RF interception, because the risks are very small and the countermeasures are very costly (in a classified environment, the analysis may produce a different conclusion). The field of *risk management* assists in making such decisions. Various qualitative and quantitative risk management tools have been developed; for further information see [COX1, GIL1, HOF1, MIG1, PFL1].

Viruses

A virus is a piece of executable program code that can "infect" other programs by modifying them to include a (possibly evolved) copy of itself. A virus generally contains two functions — a function which causes the "infection" of other programs, plus another function which is usually either a damage-causing function or a planted attack capability.

    While there is little that can be done to totally eliminate viruses in "open" environments, their spread can be readily controlled through rigid software and media management practices in conjunction with some technological support. The technological support involves both proactive and reactive "antiviral" software.

    Viruses are a computer security problem, not limited to network environments. Nevertheless, network environments can foster the spread of viruses, by facilitating transfer of executable program code between systems. Access controls to executable program resources are therefore particularly important. In countering viruses, the benefits of network environments should be exploited, e.g., by providing centrally initiated virus scans of distributed computers.

    For an excellent study of the fundamental nature of viruses, see [COH1]. For a more recent insight into the practicalities of the virus problem, see [KEP1].

2.3 Security Services

In the computer communications context, the main security safeguards are known as *security services*. There are five generic security services[3]:

- *Authentication service*: Provides assurance of the identity of some entity (a person or a system).
- *Access control service*: Protects against unauthorized use or manipulation of resources.
- *Confidentiality service*: Protects against information being disclosed or revealed to unauthorized entities.

---

[3] The security service concept and the five generic security services are from the OSI Security Architecture standard ISO/IEC 7498-2.

- *Data integrity service*: Protects against data being changed, deleted, or substituted without authorization.
- *Non-repudiation service*: Protects against one party to a communication exchange later falsely denying that the exchange occurred.

Security policy for a security domain will govern whether any security service is used within that domain or in communications between that domain and other domains. It will also govern under what circumstances a security service is used, and what constraints are placed upon any variable parameters of such a service.

None of the generic security services was conceived specifically for data communications environments or even electronic environments. All of these services have non-electronic analogs, which employ supporting mechanisms familiar to most readers. Table 2-2 provides some examples.

Security Service	Non-electronic Mechanism Examples
Authentication	Photo-identification card Knowledge of mother's maiden name
Access Control	Locks and keys; master key system Checkpoint guard
Confidentiality	Sealed letter; opaque envelope Invisible ink
Integrity	Indelible ink Hologram on credit card
Non-repudiation	Notarized signature Certified or registered mail

Table 2-2: Non-electronic Security Mechanisms

In the following subsections, the purposes of the five security services are spelled out in more detail. The means of providing them are addressed in Chapters 5 through 8.

Authentication

Authentication services provide assurance of the identity of someone or something. This means that when someone (or something) claims to have a particular identity (e.g., a particular user name), an authentication service will provide a means of confirming that this claim is correct. Passwords are a well-known way of providing authentication.

Authentication is the most important of the security services, because all other security services depend upon it to some extent. Authentication is the means of countering the threat of masquerade which can directly lead to compromise of any of the fundamental security objectives.[4]

Authentication applies in a particular context, i.e., the context in which the identity is presented. Two important cases are:

- An identity is presented by a remote party participating in a communication connection or session. The authentication service in this case is known as *entity authentication*.
- An identity claiming to be that of the originator of a data item is presented along with that data item. The authentication service in this case is known as *data origin authentication*.

Note that data origin authentication can be used to authenticate the real source of a data item, regardless of whether that source is involved in current communications activities. For example, the data item may have been relayed through many systems whose identities may or may not have been authenticated.

Both types of authentication services have significant roles in meeting the fundamental security objectives. Data origin authentication is a direct means of ensuring part of the integrity objective, i.e., ensuring that the true source of a data item is known. Entity authentication contributes in various ways to meeting security objectives:

- As a necessary support for access control services, the operation of which depends upon assured knowledge of identities. (Access control services contribute directly to meeting confidentiality, integrity, availability, and legitimate use objectives.)
- As a possible means for providing data origin authentication (when used in conjunction with a data integrity mechanism).
- As a direct support for the accountability principle, e.g., providing assured identities associated with actions, for recording in audit trails.

An important special case of entity authentication is *personal authentication*, that is, authentication of a person at a network termination point. It requires special recognition for two reasons. The first is that different people can very easily replace each other at a termination point. The second is that special technologies may be applicable in identifying individual people.

The provision of authentication services is discussed in Chapter 5.

---

[4] Note also that, as masquerade is the number-one tool of the hacker, authentication is the primary countermeasure against hacker attacks.

Access Control

The goal of access control is to protect against unauthorized access to any resource (e.g., computing resource, communications resource, or information resource). The term *unauthorized access* includes unauthorized use, unauthorized disclosure, unauthorized modification, unauthorized destruction, and unauthorized issuing of commands. Access control contributes directly to achieving the security goals of confidentiality, integrity, availability, and legitimate use. The contribution to confidentiality, integrity, and legitimate use goals is obvious. The contribution to the availability goal lies in controlling:

- who can issue network management commands which may impact network availability;
- who can tie up resources in a way which does not productively use them; and
- who can learn information which may be used subsequently in a denial-of-service attack.

Access control is a means for enforcing authorization. It is as much a computer security (operating system) issue as a communications security issue. However, it places significant requirements on communications protocols, because of the need to communicate access control information between systems.

The general model for access control assumes a set of active entities, called *initiators*, or *subjects*, which attempt to access members of a set of passive resources called *targets*, or *objects*. While the subject/object terminology is used extensively in the literature, the term *object* can be confusing because of overloading of this term in modern computer and communications technologies. For this reason, the initiator/target terminology is being increasingly used, especially in security standards (and is favored in this book).

Authorization decisions govern which initiators may access which targets for which purposes and under which conditions. These decisions are reflected in an access control policy. Access requests are filtered through an access control mechanism which enforces the access control policy.

An access control mechanism can be modeled as comprising two conceptual components — an *enforcement function* and a *decision function*. The OSI access control model (in standard ISO/IEC 10181-3) uses these concepts; it is illustrated in Figure 2-2. In practice, the physical configurations of these components may vary widely. Typically, some are co-located. However, there is generally a need to communicate access control information between these components. The access control service provides for this communication.

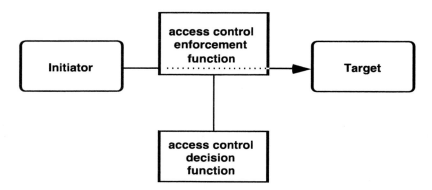

Figure 2-2: Access Control Model — Basic Conceptual Components

Another aspect of access control is preventing sensitive information from being transmitted through environments where it might be at risk. This involves the enforcement of *routing control* of network traffic or messages.

Further discussion of access control services depends on two factors: the type of access control policy and the configuration of the components. Such discussion is deferred to Chapter 6.

Confidentiality

Confidentiality services protect against information being disclosed or revealed to entities (e.g., people or organizations) not authorized to have that information.

At this point it is worthwhile emphasizing the difference between *information* and *data*. Information has semantics, or meaning. A data item is a string of bits, commonly used to store or communicate an encoded representation of a piece of information. Hence, a data item in storage or communication constitutes one form of *information channel* [DEN1]. However, this is not the only information channel in a computer communications environment. Other information channels include:

- observing the existence or non-existence of a data item (regardless of its contents);
- observing the size of a data item; and
- observing dynamic variations in data item characteristics (data item contents, existence, size, etc.).

For example, the information "the missile has been launched" may be communicated (intentionally or unintentionally) in any of the following ways:

- a one-bit data item, value 1 indicating "the missile has been launched" and value 0 indicating "the missile has not been launched";
- the existence or non-existence of a file called "missile launch report" in some file directory;
- the fact that the size of a data item containing a list of missile launch records is greater than it was after the preceding missile launch; or
- the fact that a counter of missile flight miles can be observed to be continually incrementing.

Achieving a confidentiality objective ideally requires protecting against disclosure of information through any such information channel.

In computer communications security, this leads to the recognition of two types of confidentiality service. A *data confidentiality service* makes it infeasible to deduce sensitive information from the content or size of a given data item (e.g., using encryption). A *traffic flow confidentiality service* makes it infeasible to deduce sensitive information by observing network traffic flows.

Considering data confidentiality services, there are several variations, depending on their granularity, i.e., to what data item(s) confidentiality is to apply. Three different cases are significant. The first, known as a *connection confidentiality* service, applies to all data transmitted on a connection.[5] The second, known as a *connectionless confidentiality* service, applies to all the data comprising one connectionless data unit. The third is a *selective field confidentiality* service, which applies only to nominated fields within a data unit (either a data unit sent on a connection or a connectionless data unit).

The means of providing confidentiality services are discussed in Chapter 7, building on the discussion of cryptographic techniques in Chapter 4.

Data Integrity

Data integrity services (or simply *integrity services*)[6] act as safeguards against the threat that the value or existence of data might be changed in a way inconsistent with the recognized security policy. Changing the value of a data item includes inserting additional data or deleting, modifying, or reordering parts of the data. Changing the existence of a data item means creating or deleting it.

---

[5] The terms *connection* and *connectionless* are explained in Section 3.1.

[6] The wider subject of information integrity has been expounded in the *Clark-Wilson Model* [CLA1]. This model defines integrity as those qualities which give data and systems both internal consistency and a good correspondence to real-world expectations for the systems and data. Controls are needed for both internal consistency and external consistency. Communications data integrity cannot help with external consistency. It helps with internal consistency of data by ensuring that a data item maintains its value while in communication.

Depending on the environment, any of the above forms of threat may be serious. Consider, for example, a (hypothetical) automatic teller machine (ATM) communicating with its controlling bank. If adequate consideration is not given to integrity, it is conceivable that any of the following attacks might be perpetrated by someone inserting his or her own equipment in the communications link:

- *Modifying* the dollar amount on a withdrawal-request message from ATM to bank (say from $500 to $50), then modifying the amount on the approval message from bank to ATM (back to the original $500), causing the ATM to pay out much more than was recorded for debit at the bank.
- *Repeating* the physical motions of an earlier withdrawal at the ATM, but passing nothing to the bank and replaying to the ATM all the responses recorded from the earlier transaction. The ATM pays out again, but nothing is debited at the bank.
- *Creating* a "cancel transaction — cash dispensing failed" message from ATM to bank in the dispense phase, even though the cash has been dispensed successfully.
- *Deleting* all black-list notifications from bank to ATM (used by those ATMs which sometimes operate in an off-line mode), then making a withdrawal with a voided (black-listed) card at an off-line time.

Similar to confidentiality, an important characteristic of a data integrity service is its granularity, i.e., to what data item(s) it is to apply. Three cases are significant. The first, known as a *connection integrity* service, applies to all data transmitted on a connection. The second, known as a *connectionless integrity* service, applies to all the data comprising one connectionless data item. The third is a *selective field integrity* service, which applies only to nominated fields within a data unit.

All data integrity services counter attempts to create or modify data. However, they do not all necessarily counter attempts to duplicate or delete data (which are harder to detect). Duplication can result from a replay attack. Connectionless and selective field integrity services, which are primarily concerned with detecting modification of individual pieces of data, may or may not detect replay. A connection integrity service is required to protect against replay of data within a connection. However, there may still be a vulnerability, as it might be possible for an intruder to *replay an entire connection*. Detecting deletion of pieces of data (e.g., one connectionless data unit, one selective field, or possibly one complete connection) is at least as difficult as detecting replay and may require special attention in specifying any data integrity service.

A connection integrity service may also offer the option of *recovery*. If so, when an integrity violation is detected within a connection, the service will attempt to recover. For example, the communications will be rolled back to some checkpoint and restarted.

The means of providing data integrity services are discussed in Chapter 7, building on the discussion of cryptographic techniques in Chapter 4.

Non-repudiation

Non-repudiation is fundamentally different from the other security services. Its primary purpose is to protect communications users against threats from other legitimate users, rather than from unknown attackers. Repudiation was earlier defined to be a threat, whereby a party to a communication exchange later falsely denies that the exchange took place. Non-repudiation services counter this type of threat.

The word *non-repudiation* is not, in itself, very helpful. This service does not eliminate repudiation. It does not prevent any party from repudiating another party's claim that something occurred. What it does is ensure the availability of irrefutable evidence to support the speedy resolution of any such disagreement.

The motivation for non-repudiation services is not just the possibility that communicating parties may try to cheat each other. It is also a reflection of the reality that no system is perfect, and that circumstances can arise in which two parties end up with different views of something that happened.

Consider first some of the problems that can arise in the world of paper business transactions. Paper documents, such as contracts, quotations, bids, orders, invoices, and checks play a critical role in the conducting of business between organizations. However, many problems can occur in their handling, such as:

- document lost in the mail;
- document lost by recipient before processing;
- document generated by a person with insufficient authorization;
- document accidentally corrupted within an organization or while in transit between organizations;
- document fraudulently modified within an organization or while in transit between organizations;
- forged document; and
- disputed filing time of a document.

To aid in systematically dealing with such problems, various mechanisms are employed, such as signatures, countersignatures, notarized signatures, receipts, postmarks, and certified mail. If good business practices are followed, there will usually be an adequate paper trail to make dispute resolution straightforward. If necessary, evidence will be available in the form of records held by the disputing parties plus third parties such as the post office, courier agents, and notaries. With the help of such evidence, parties may be able to resolve their differences themselves or, in some cases, may need to settle their dispute under arbitration, e.g., in a court of law.

With electronic business transactions, the problems that can arise are analogous to those for paper transactions. Non-repudiation services provide the protective mechanisms. In some respects the problems with electronic transactions are more difficult to resolve than those with paper transactions. There are fewer humans involved in the handling of documents (interrogating these humans assists greatly in resolving paper transaction problems). Also, original paper documents are not generally available for reference (another key basis for resolving paper transaction problems). However, in other respects, problems with electronic transactions are easier to solve. This results from the availability of sophisticated technologies such as digital signatures (which are described in Chapter 4).

In principle, non-repudiation can apply to any of a variety of events which affect two or more parties. In general, disagreements relate to whether a particular event occurred, when it occurred, what parties were involved with that event, and what information was associated with that event. If we restrict our concerns to data networking environments, repudiation scenarios can be separated into two distinct cases:

- *Repudiation of origin*: There is disagreement as to whether a particular party originated a particular data item (and/or disagreement as to the time this origination occurred).
- *Repudiation of delivery*: There is disagreement as to whether a particular data item was delivered to a particular party (and/or disagreement as to the time this delivery occurred).

These scenarios lead to two distinct variants of non-repudiation service.

The mechanisms for providing non-repudiation services are discussed in Chapter 8.

Application Examples

Chapter 1 (Table 1-2) identified typical security requirements of some important network application environments. That discussion can now be taken two steps further — mapping the requirements to threats and identifying security services which can constitute safeguards. Table 2-3 shows typical threats associated with the identified requirements (considering only those threats pertinent to computer communications security). Table 2-4 indicates the security services used to counter the threats identified in Table 2-3.

Requirements (Informal)	Threats
All Networks: Prevent outside penetrations (hackers)	Masquerade
Banking: Protect against fraudulent or accidental modification of transactions Identify retail transaction customers Protect PINs from disclosure Ensure customers' privacy	Integrity violation Masquerade, repudiation Eavesdropping Eavesdropping
Electronic Trading: Assure source and integrity of transactions Protect corporate privacy Provide legally-binding electronic signatures on transactions	Masquerade, integrity violation Eavesdropping Repudiation
Government: Protect against unauthorized disclosure or manipulation of unclassified but sensitive information Provide electronic signatures on government documents	Masquerade, authorization violation, eavesdropping, integrity violation Repudiation
Public Telecommunications Carriers: Restrict access to administration functions to authorized individuals Protect against service interruptions Protect subscribers' privacy	Masquerade, authorization violation Denial of service Eavesdropping
Corporate/Private Networks: Protect corporate/individual privacy Ensure message authenticity	Eavesdropping Masquerade, integrity violation

Table 2-3: Typical Threats in Particular Application Environments

2.4 Intrusion Detection and Security Audit

Intrusion detection is a general term for automated methods which, based on the analysis of real-time event sequences and/or accumulated records, can alert a security administrator to possible security violations. The main goal of these methods is to detect unusual activity, such as a large number of unsuccessful login attempts from one terminal or a large number of attempts to access a computer's password file. The methods used are typically based on statistical

Threat	*Security Service*
Masquerade	Authentication
Authorization violation	Access control
Eavesdropping	Confidentiality
Integrity violation	Integrity
Repudiation	Non-repudiation
Denial of service	Authentication, access control, integrity

Table 2-4: Security Services to Counter Typical Threats

analysis or, increasingly, on rule-based expert systems. Intrusion detection is a particularly powerful security tool because of its ability to counter attacks from insiders who misuse their privileges and attacks resulting from such events as lost or stolen passwords or cryptographic keys.

A *security audit* is an independent examination and review of system records and procedures. Its purposes include testing the adequacy of security policy, confirming compliance with security policy, recommending changes in security policy, assisting in the analysis of attacks, and gathering evidence for use in prosecuting an attacker.

A *security audit trail* is a journal of security-related events collected for potential use in intrusion detection and/or security audits.

A *security alarm* is a real-time indication of a situation which suggests a security violation. It involves sending a message to a system operator, administrator, or manager. Its purpose is to alert relevant staff so that damage from a security violation may be minimized, further violations may be prevented, and/or evidence may be gathered for use in prosecuting an attacker.

None of the above concepts is identified as a security service in the OSI Security Architecture standard. However, security audit trail and security alarm are recognized as *pervasive security mechanisms* which supplement the basic security services identified in Section 2.3. This distinction is moot. Security audit trail and alarm functions provide their own types of service to a system or network administrator — services to aid detection of weaknesses in security policy, procedures, and mechanisms, and to gather evidence. They also constitute a safeguard in their own right, by acting as a deterrent to would-be attackers.

Security audit trail and alarm functions are driven by *intrusion detection policy* and *audit policy*, which are elements of security policy. A vast range of security-related events occurs in a system, e.g., every request to establish a connection or to access a sensitive information item. Intrusion detection policy and audit policy govern which of these events cause an audit trail record to be generated and which cause an alarm to be signaled. Such decisions may be based on complex intrusion detection procedures. The response to an event may depend on criteria such as the time of day, a threshold counter, the event type, and/or the event source. Audit policy further governs the type of post-event analysis to be systematically applied to an audit trail.

Protocols supporting the communications needs of security audit trail and alarm functions are addressed in Chapter 15. For further reading on intrusion detection and security audit see [LUN1, MCA1, SCH1, WIN1].

Summary

Information security has four fundamental objectives — confidentiality of information, integrity of data, availability of information and resources, and legitimate use of resources. To support these objectives, a network administration needs to have a security policy, and needs to put in place a range of security measures to ensure that the goals of the security policy are met. A security policy is a high-level set of rules typically applied across the set of communications resources belonging to one organization. Access control policy is the part of a security policy governing who may access information or other resources.

The determination of security requirements is based on assessing threats. Four fundamental threats follow directly from the above objectives: information leakage, integrity violation, denial of service, and illegitimate use. Primary enabling threats, which can directly enable any of the fundamental threats, involve either penetration (e.g., masquerade, bypassing controls, or authorization violation) or planting (e.g., Trojan horse or trapdoor). In a given environment, any threat can be considered to have underlying threats. Such threats include eavesdropping, intercept/alter, traffic analysis, and repudiation. Safeguards protect assets from threats. Safeguards fall into several categories, including communications security and computer security.

In the computer communications arena, safeguards are described in terms of security services. The five basic security services are authentication, access control, confidentiality, data integrity, and non-repudiation. Authentication services provide assurance of the identity of someone or something. Access control services protect against unauthorized access to resources, by enforcing an access control policy. Confidentiality services protect against information being disclosed or revealed to people who are not authorized to have it. Data integrity services counter the threat that the value or existence of data might be changed (in a way inconsistent with the recognized security policy). Non-repudiation services protect against a communications user falsely denying that an earlier communication exchange took place.

Intrusion detection denotes a method which, based on the analysis of real-time event sequences and/or accumulated records, alerts a security administrator to a possible security violation. A security audit is an independent examination and review of system records and procedures. A security alarm is a real-time indication of a situation which suggests a security violation.

Exercises

1. List seven threats for which network security services can act as safeguards. Give a real-life example of each. For each threat identified, name the security service (or services) which may be used to counter it.

2. Describe:
    (a) the differences between entity authentication and data origin authent-ication;
    (b) the different variations of confidentiality services;
    (c) the different variations of data integrity services; and
    (d) the relationship between authorization and access control.

3. Suppose a password-based authentication system on a small network is managed by storing all user passwords on a password-server system. When a user wants to change his password, he does this through a short communications session with the password-server. When a host wants to authenticate a user, it does so by obtaining the user's password from the password-server and comparing it with that presented by the user. Identify the primary threats to such a system, and briefly describe how authentication, confidentiality, data integrity, and access control services might contribute to countering these threats.

REFERENCES

[CHI1] D.M. Chizmadia, "Some More Thoughts on the Buzzword 'Security Policy,'" *Proceedings of the 15th National Computer Security Conference*, October 1992, Baltimore, MD, pp. 651-660.

[CLA1] D.D. Clark and D.R. Wilson, "A Comparison of Commercial and Military Security Policies," in *Proceedings of the 1987 IEEE Symposium on Security and Privacy*, Oakland, CA, IEEE Computer Society Press, 1987, pp. 184-94.

[COH1] F. Cohen, "Computer Viruses: Theory and Experiments," *Computers and Security*, vol. 6, no. 1 (February 1987), pp. 22-35.

[COX1] R. Cox, M. O'Neill, and W. Price, "Risk Management of Complex Networks", *Proceedings of the 15th National Computer Security Conference*, October 1992, Baltimore, MD, pp. 544-553.

[DEN1] D.E. Denning, *Cryptography and Data Security*, Addison-Wesley, Reading, MA, 1982.

[DOD1] U.S. Department of Defense, *Department of Defense Trusted Computer System Evaluation Criteria*, DOD 5200.28-STD, National Computer Security Center, Fort Meade, MD, December 1985.

[GIL1] I.E. Gilbert, *Guide for Selecting Automated Risk Analysis Tools*, NIST Special Publication 500-174, U.S. Department of Commerce, National Institute of Standards and Technology, 1989.

[HOF1] L. Hoffman, "Risk Analysis and Computer Security: Bridging the Cultural Gap," *Proceedings of the 9th National Computer Security Conference*, October 1986, Baltimore, MD.

[KEP1] J.O. Kephart, S.R. White, and D.M. Chess, "Computers and Epidemiology," *IEEE Spectrum*, vol. 30, no. 5 (May 1993), pp. 20-26.

[LUN1] T.F. Lunt, "Automated Audit Trail Analysis and Intrusion Detection: A Survey", *Proceedings of the 11th National Computer Security Conference*, October 1988, Baltimore, MD, pp. 65-73.

[MCA1] N. McAuliffe, *et al.*, "Is Your Computer Being Misused? A Survey of Current Intrusion Detection System Technology," *Proceedings of the Sixth Annual Computer Security Applications Conference*, IEEE Computer Society Press, Los Alamitos, CA, December 1990, pp. 260-272.

[MIG1] J. Miguel, "A Composite Cost/Benefit/Risk Methodology," *Computer Security: A Global Challenge, Proc. IFIP Conference*, 1984, pp. 307-312.

[NAT1] National Research Council (U.S.), *Computers at Risk: Safe Computing in the Information Age*, National Academy Press, Washington, DC, 1990.

[NEU1] P.G. Neumann and D.B. Parker, "A Summary of Computer Misuse Techniques," *Proceedings of the 12th National Computer Security Conference*, October 1989, Baltimore, MD, pp. 396-407.

[PFL1] C.P. Pfleeger, *Security in Computing*, Prentice Hall International, Inc., Englewood Cliffs, NJ, 1989.

[SCH1] S.I. Schaen, "Network Auditing: Issues and Recommendations," *Proceedings of the Seventh Annual Computer Security Applications Conference*, IEEE Computer Society Press, Los Alamitos, CA, December 1991, pp. 66-79.

[SPA1] E.H. Spafford, "The Internet Worm: Crisis and Aftermath," *Communications of the ACM*, vol. 32, no. 6 (June 1989), pp. 678-687.

[STE1] D.F. Sterne, "On the Buzzword 'Security Policy,'" *Proceedings of the 1991 Symposium on Security and Privacy*, Oakland, CA, IEEE Computer Society Press, 1991, pp. 218-230.

[WIN1] J.R. Winkler and L.C. Landry, "Intrusion and Anomaly Detection: ISOA Update," *Proceedings of the 15th National Computer Security Conference*, October 1992, Baltimore, MD, pp. 272-281.

Standards

ISO/IEC 7498-2:   *Information Technology — Open Systems Interconnection — Basic Reference Model — Part 2: Security Architecture* (Also ITU-T Recommendation X.800).
ISO/IEC 10181-3: *Information Technology — Security Frameworks in Open Systems — Access Control Framework* (Also ITU-T Recommendation X.812) (Draft).

3   Security in a Layered Protocol Architecture

Layered protocol architectures are fundamental to modern computer networking. They allow network designs to accommodate unlimited applications, unlimited underlying media technologies, and unlimited interconnection techniques. The primary purpose of layering is to modularize the protocol specification problem, such that separate pieces of the protocol puzzle can be developed independently and mixed and matched in different ways to give a "complete" protocol. To some extent, this modularization can also flow into implementation, such that different protocol components can be realized in different software modules or hardware products. This chapter addresses the important issue of how the provision of network security relates to architectural layering.

The Open Systems Interconnection (OSI) architecture is the recognized basis of protocol layering. The first OSI standard, the Basic Reference Model (ISO/IEC 7498-1), establishes this architectural model. Other OSI standards define specific protocols to fit into this model. Other protocol architectures, notably the Internet TCP/IP suite, define protocols which constitute alternatives to formal OSI protocols at some layers, but nevertheless fit into the same overall layering scheme.

This book requires a basic understanding of the OSI architecture and some knowledge of the internal structures and protocols of certain of the layers. To assist the reader in this respect, this chapter commences with an overview of the basic OSI concepts. Applicable international standards references are given. Relevant Internet protocol standards are also identified, and their relationships to the OSI architecture noted. For readers requiring tutorial coverage of these areas, the following texts are recommended. For a complete coverage of OSI, see [BLA1, DIC1]. For a more detailed coverage of the upper layers, see [HEN1]. For a more implementation-oriented perspective on OSI, see [ROS1]. For coverage of the Internet protocol suite, see [COM1].

This chapter also describes the issues underlying mapping of security services to architectural layers, and presents ground rules for making such mapping decisions. A four-level security architectural model is introduced as a simpler, more pragmatic, substitute for the OSI model when focusing on security placement issues. This four-level model is used throughout the book when discussing layer placement of security services.

The chapter is organized into sections addressing:

(1) general principles of protocol layering and associated terminology, as introduced in the OSI Basic Reference Model;

(2) the structures, services, and protocols of specific OSI layers;

(3) the Internet TCP/IP protocol suite and its relationship to the OSI architecture;

(4) the architectural placement of security services, including the four-level model; and

(5) the way management of security services relates to architectural layers.

3.1   Protocol Layering — Principles and Terminology

In the real world, communication occurs between *real systems*. For the purposes of defining protocols, the OSI standards introduce the concept of a *model* of a real system, known as an *open system*.[7] The model system is considered to be structured in layers. This does not necessarily require implementations of real systems to be structured in the same way — they can be constructed any way the implementor chooses, provided the resultant behavior of the complete implementation conforms to the behavior defined using the model. For example, an implementation may merge the functions of multiple adjacent layers into one piece of software, without interlayer boundaries needing to be apparent.

History

The OSI initiative was launched in 1977 by ISO Technical Committee TC97 (Information Processing Systems).[8] Subcommittee TC97/SC16 (Open Systems Interconnection) was established, with the goal of developing a model and identifying protocol standards to support the needs of an unlimited range of applications over multiple underlying communications media technologies. The project captured the attention of the International Telecommunication Union (ITU), which develops Recommendations used internationally by telecommunications carriers (until April 1993, these were called *CCITT* Recommendations). A collaborative arrangement was set up between ISO and the ITU to work

---

[7] Note that ISO/IEC 7498-1 applies this specific interpretation to the term *open system*, as distinct from the term's common usage.

[8] The organizations and committees mentioned here are described in more detail in Appendix A.

together to produce aligned ISO International Standards and ITU Recommendations on OSI.

The first significant output of this activity was the OSI Basic Reference Model. This was published in 1984 by ISO as international standard 7498 and by the ITU as Recommendation X.200. This document describes a seven-layer architecture, to be used as the basis for independently specifying individual layer protocols. Standards for the first protocols were published soon after the Basic Reference Model, and further standards have appeared in a steady stream since.

Layering Principles

The OSI model lays out certain principles for constructing communications protocols out of multiple layers. Some important concepts are illustrated in Figure 3-1.

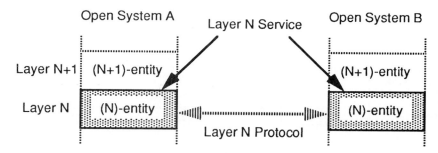

Figure 3-1: OSI Layering Concepts

Consider some middle layer, say layer N. Above it is layer $N+1$ and below it is layer $N-1$. In both open systems there is functionality supporting layer N. This is denoted the *(N)-entity* in each open system. The pair of communicating (N)-entities provide a *service* to $(N+1)$-entities in their respective systems. This service includes carrying data for the $(N+1)$-entities.

The pair of (N)-entities communicate with each other. They use an *(N)-protocol*, which embraces the syntax (format) and semantics (meaning) of data exchanged between them, plus rules for procedures to be followed. The (N)-protocol is conveyed by making use of a service provided by $(N-1)$-entities. Each message sent in an (N)-protocol is known as an *(N)-protocol-data-unit* (PDU).

An important principle underlying this layering concept is *layer independence*. The intention is that an (N)-layer service can be defined and can then be used in defining protocols for the $(N+1)$-layer, without any knowledge of the (N)-protocol used in providing that service.

The Seven OSI Layers

The OSI reference model defines seven layers, as shown in Figure 3-2. Protocols from each of the layers are grouped together into what is known as an OSI layer stack. An OSI layer stack fulfills the communication needs of an *application-process*, which is the part of a real system which performs information processing for a given application purpose.

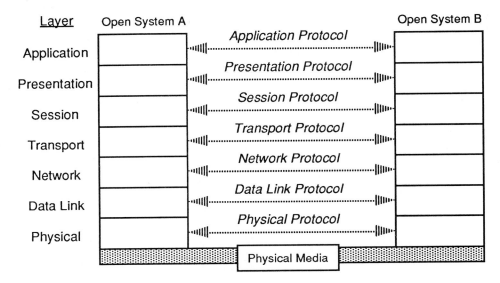

Figure 3-2: The Seven OSI Layers

The layers and their main functions are as follows:

- The *Application Layer* (Layer 7) provides a means for the application-process to access the OSI environment. Application Layer protocol standards deal with communications functions which apply to one particular application or a family of applications.
- The *Presentation Layer* (Layer 6) provides for the representation of information that application layer entities use or refer to in their communication.
- The *Session Layer* (Layer 5) provides the means for higher-layer entities to organize and synchronize their dialogue and to manage their data exchange.

- The *Transport Layer* (Layer 4) provides transparent transfer of data between higher-layer entities and relieves them from any concern with the detailed way in which reliable and cost-effective data transfer is achieved.
- The *Network Layer* (Layer 3) provides transmission between higher-layer entities, with independence from routing and relay considerations. This includes the case where multiple subnetworks are used in tandem or in parallel. It makes invisible to higher layers how underlying communications resources (i.e., data links) are used.
- The *Data Link Layer* (Layer 2) provides for transferring data on a point-to-point basis, and for establishing, maintaining, and releasing point-to-point connections. It detects and possibly corrects errors which may occur in the underlying Physical Layer.
- The *Physical Layer* (Layer 1) provides mechanical, electrical, functional, and procedural means to activate, maintain, and deactivate physical connections for bit transmission between data-link entities.

Figure 3-3 illustrates the OSI architecture, taking into account the significance of subnetworks in the Network Layer. It shows how multiple subnetworks (possibly using different interconnection or media technologies) may be used in tandem to support one application communication session.

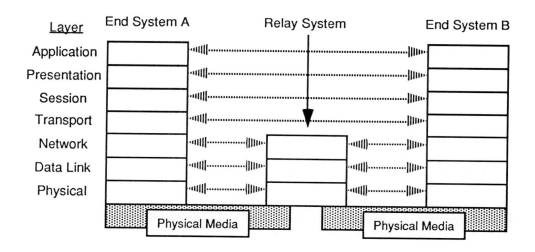

Figure 3-3: OSI Layering with Multiple Subnetworks

Upper Layers and Lower Layers

From a practical perspective, the OSI layers can be considered in terms of:

(a) application-dependent protocols;
(b) protocols associated with particular media; and
(c) a bridging function between (a) and (b).

The application-dependent protocols comprise the Application, Presentation, and Session Layers — the *upper layers*. Realizations of these layers are closely tied to the application being supported, and are entirely independent of the underlying communications technology or technologies.

The remaining layers, which span categories (b) and (c) above, are known as the *lower layers*. The media technology-dependent protocols are in the Physical and Data Link layers, and the lower (*subnetwork-dependent*) sublayers of the Network Layer.

The bridging function is provided by the Transport Layer and the upper sublayers of the Network Layer. The upper sublayers of the Network Layer enable a consistent network-service interface to be presented to the layer above, although the *quality-of-service* will be variable, dependent on the subnetwork(s) used. The Transport Layer makes the layers under it transparent to the upper layers. It either obtains network-connections of adequate quality-of-service, or upgrades the quality-of-service as necessary, e.g., by providing error detection and recovery in the transport protocol if the error performance of the Network Layer is inadequate.

Layer Services and Facilities

The service provided by any layer is described in terms of *service primitives*, which are atomic events at the (abstract) service interface. A layer service is divided into a number of *facilities*, each of which involves a collection of related primitives. A facility generally relates to the generation and processing of one or more particular protocol-data-units (PDUs).

For example, in the transport service, there is a T-CONNECT facility, which establishes a transport-connection. It involves four primitives (two at the end that initiates connection establishment and two at the other end) and two PDUs (one sent in each direction). The relationship between the primitives and PDUs is illustrated in Figure 3-4 as a time-sequence diagram.

The above type of sequence, involving two PDUs and four primitives, is very common, and is known as a *confirmed service*. Another common case, known as an *unconfirmed service*, involves only one PDU and two primitives. It is basically the same as the first half of the sequence shown in Figure 3-4.

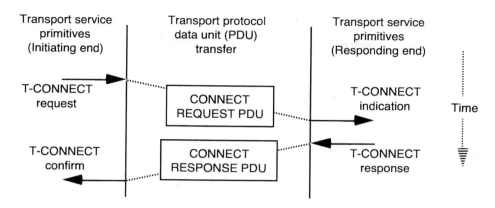

Figure 3-4: Layer Service Facility and Primitives

Connection-Oriented and Connectionless Services

There are two distinct modes of service at any layer:

- The *connection-oriented* mode is based on (*N*)-connections provided by the (*N*)-layer. A connection is an association between two (*N*)-entities, having an establishment phase, transfer phase, and release phase. During the transfer phase, a stream of data units is conveyed on behalf of higher-layer users of the service.
- The *connectionless* mode involves the conveyance of single data units, without any requirement to interrelate them. The service may route data units independently, provides no acknowledgment of receipt, and does not guarantee delivery in the same order as sent.

The main reason for the two types of service is that some underlying communications technologies are inherently connection-oriented (e.g., packet switching networks) and some are inherently connectionless (e.g., local area networks). The bridging function at the Network and Transport Layers includes supporting the operation of connection-oriented upper layers over connectionless communications technologies.

With connection-oriented upper layers, the connections at the individual layers map directly to each other. An application-association (which is the Application Layer's equivalent of a connection) maps directly to a presentation-connection, which maps directly to a session-connection. However, at layers below this, there is not necessarily this one-to-one mapping. For example, a transport-connection can be serially reused for multiple session-connections, and a network-connection may convey several multiplexed transport-connections at the same time.

3.2 The OSI Layer Structures, Services, and Protocols

Application Layer

The Application Layer can include a wide variety of functions, which may need to be defined by different standardization groups. A modular approach has therefore been taken to defining Application Layer protocols. The structure of the Application Layer is described in standard ISO/IEC 9545. This standard defines concepts used to describe the internal structure of an application-entity, plus concepts used to describe active relationships between invocations of application-entities.

The most basic building block of an application-entity is called an application-service-element (ASE). (An ASE can be thought of as a piece of protocol specification which can be conveniently specified in one standard document.) The more general structuring component of an application-entity is an application-service-object (ASO), which is built up from ASEs and/or other ASOs. The structuring principles relating to application-entities, ASEs, and ASOs are discussed further in Chapter 12.

Two important concepts describing relationships between communicating application-entities are:

- *Application-association*: A cooperative relationship between two ASO-invocations which governs their bilateral use of the presentation service for communication purposes. This is the Application Layer's equivalent of a *connection*. It can also be considered the Application Layer view of a presentation-connection.
- *Application-context*: A set of rules shared by two ASO-invocations in order to support an application-association. This is effectively the complete Application Layer protocol in use on an application-association.

One ASE of special significance is the *Association Control Service Element* (ACSE). This ASE supports establishment and termination of application-associations, and it is required in all application-contexts. A practical view of ACSE is that it defines the Application Layer information conveyed in the protocol exchanges for establishing and terminating presentation-connnections and session-connections. The ACSE service is defined in standard ISO/IEC 8649, and the protocol in ISO/IEC 8650.

Several standard OSI-based applications have been defined. The standards include specifications of Application Layer protocols, plus supporting material such as definitions of information models and procedures to be followed within systems. The main applications addressed in this book are:

- *Message Handling Systems (MHS)*: This application supports electronic messaging, including interpersonal electronic mail, EDI transfer, and voice messaging. MHS was a leading OSI application in incorporating security features. This application and its security features are discussed in Chapter 13.
- *Directory*: This application provides the basis for interconnecting information processing systems so as to provide a logically integrated but physically distributed directory system, with a variety of potential uses. The Directory application and its security features are discussed in Chapter 14.
- *File Transfer, Access, and Management (FTAM)*: The FTAM application provides support for reading or writing of files in a remote computer system, accessing components of such files, and/or managing (e.g., creating or deleting) such files. FTAM is defined in ISO/IEC 8571.

The OSI network management facilities also constitute an OSI application. They are discussed in Chapter 15.

The OSI Application Layer standards include an important protocol modeling and construction tool called the *Remote Operations Service Element* (ROSE). ROSE is based on a general client-server model, in which one system (the client) invokes specified operations in the other system (the server). The protocol can be expressed in terms of arguments that accompany the invocation, and results or an error indication that can be returned from the operation. For an application which fits this model, use of ROSE can greatly facilitate protocol specification. ROSE is used in the MHS, Directory, and OSI network management protocols. The ROSE model, service, and protocol are defined in the ISO/IEC 9072 multi-part standard.

Presentation Layer

The Presentation Layer deals with how application information is represented (as a bit string) for purposes of transfer. An overview of the operation of this layer is provided in Chapter 12.

The standards for the presentation service and protocol are ISO/IEC 8822 and 8823 respectively.

Another pair of Presentation Layer standards, which are particularly important, are the standards ISO/IEC 8824 and ISO/IEC 8825 dealing with Abstract Syntax Notation One (ASN.1). ASN.1 is used heavily by OSI and non-OSI applications alike, for defining application layer information items and corresponding bit-string encodings for them. A brief introduction to ASN.1

is given in Appendix B. Readers unfamiliar with ASN.1 should read this appendix before starting Part II of this book. For a more detailed ASN.1 tutorial, see [STE1].

Session Layer

The Session Layer performs such functions as dialogue management and resynchronization, under the direct control of the Application Layer. Dialogue management supports full-duplex and half-duplex operational modes for applications. Resynchronization supports the insertion of synchronization marks in a data stream and the resynchronization back to an earlier mark in the event of an error condition. The standards for the session service and protocol are ISO/IEC 8326 and 8327, respectively.

Later discussion on security architecture will conclude that the Session Layer has virtually no role to play in providing security, hence readers unfamiliar with this layer can safely ignore it.

Transport Layer

The transport service is defined in ISO/IEC 8072. It supports end-system to end-system transparent transfer of data. It provides its (upper layers) users with independence from underlying communications technologies and with the ability to nominate a *quality-of-service* (in terms of such characteristics as throughput, residual error rate, and failure probability). If the quality-of-service of the available underlying network services is inadequate, the Transport Layer will upgrade the quality-of-service to the requisite level by adding value (e.g., error detection/recovery) in its own protocol. The transport service has both connection-oriented and connectionless variations.

The Transport Layer protocols to support the connection-oriented service are specified in ISO/IEC 8073. There are five different *classes* of protocol, as follows:

- *Class 0* adds no value to the network service.
- *Class 1* supports error recovery, upon detection of an error by the Network Layer.
- *Class 2* supports multiplexing of transport-connections on one network-connection.
- *Class 3* provides error recovery and multiplexing.
- *Class 4* provides error detection (checksum), error recovery, and multiplexing.

Using its error recovery features, the Class 4 protocol can operate over a connectionless network service, to provide a connection-oriented transport service.

The protocol to support the connectionless transport service is specified in ISO/IEC 8602.

Network Layer

The Network Layer is one of the more complex OSI layers, because it needs to accommodate a variety of subnetwork technologies and interconnection strategies. It has to deal with the problems of relaying between subnetworks of different technologies, and it has to deal with the problem of presenting a common service interface to the Transport Layer above. The existence of both connection-oriented and connectionless styles of operation contributes significantly to the complexities of the Network Layer standards.

The standards that best explain the working of the Network Layer are ISO/IEC 8880, ISO/IEC 8648, and ISO/IEC 8348. Figure 3-5 illustrates the relationships between these standards.

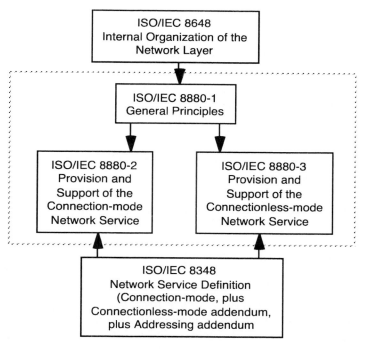

Figure 3-5: General Standards for the Network Layer

ISO/IEC 8648 introduces some important terms and concepts and describes how the OSI modeling concepts in this layer map to *real* network components. The concept of an *end system* (introduced in the OSI reference model) models a piece of equipment, or a collection of pieces of equipment, which implement a full seven-layer stack. The concept of an *intermediate system* is introduced in the Network Layer. An intermediate system performs only functions allocated to the lowest three OSI layers. An end system can communicate with another end system either directly or through one or a series of intermediate systems.

A *real subnetwork* is a collection of equipment and physical links used to interconnect other real systems, e.g., a public packet-switching network, a local area network (LAN), or an interconnected set of other real subnetworks. An interworking unit is a piece of equipment (or part of a piece of equipment) which realizes a network relay function. The term *intermediate system* can refer to the abstraction of any of:

(a) a real subnetwork;
(b) an interworking unit, connecting two or more real subnetworks (e.g., a router); or
(c) a combination of a real subnetwork and an interworking unit.

Many different Network Layer protocols may be defined. The internal structure of the layer takes into account that subnetwork protocols may or may not have been designed to specifically support OSI. Hence, the basic protocol of a subnetwork does not necessarily have to support all the functions required by the Network Layer service. If necessary, further sublayers of protocol can be provided above a subnetwork protocol to provide the necessary functionality.

In any particular interconnection scenario, a Network Layer protocol performs one or more of three *roles*:

- *Subnetwork-independent convergence protocol (SNICP)*: Provides functions to support the OSI network service over a well-defined set of underlying capabilities which are not specifically based on any particular subnetwork. This role commonly applies to an internetworking protocol used, for example, to convey addressing and routing information over multiple interconnected networks.
- *Subnetwork-dependent convergence protocol (SNDCP)*: Operates over a protocol providing the SNAcP role in order to add capabilities needed by a SNICP protocol or needed to provide the full OSI network service.
- *Subnetwork access protocol (SNAcP)*: A protocol which is inherently part of a particular type of subnetwork. It provides a subnetwork service

at its end points, which may or may not be equivalent to the OSI network service.

One of the more important Network Layer protocols is the Connectionless Network Protocol (CLNP) defined in ISO/IEC 8473. This protocol is generally used in a SNICP role, for providing the connectionless-mode network service. The ISO/IEC 8473 standard also defines how this protocol can operate over X.25 packet switched subnetworks or LAN subnetworks.

Subnetwork Technology Functions

OSI is designed to operate over a virtually unlimited range of underlying subnetwork technologies. These technologies have their own subnetwork-dependent (SNAcP and SNDCP role) Network Layer protocols, and Data Link Layer and Physical Layer protocols. Many standards have been developed for specific subnetwork technologies, including:

- local area networks (LANs) — the ISO/IEC 8802 series;
- packet switched data networks (PSDNs) — ITU-T Recommendation X.25, and international standards ISO/IEC 8208, 8878 and 8881;
- circuit switched data networks (CSDNs);
- point-to-point subnetworks;
- integrated services digital networks (ISDNs); and
- public switched telephone networks (PSTNs).

The LAN protocols, including bridging functions, are all considered to be located in the Data Link layer. X.25 spans two layers. The X.25 packet-level protocol is a subnetwork-dependent Network Layer protocol, while the X.25 link access protocol is in the Data Link Layer.

As open-system networks typically span multiple subnetwork technologies, security features linked to a specific technology are of limited value. This part of the OSI architecture is therefore of lesser relevance to this book than higher layers. Security for LANs and for X.25 packet switched data networks is addressed in Chapter 11.

3.3 **Internet (TCP/IP) Protocol Suite**

The Internet protocols have evolved since the mid-1970s, when the U.S. Defense Advanced Projects Research Agency (DARPA) started funding the development of packet switched network facilities for interconnecting universities and government research institutions across the United States. A complete suite of protocols has been specified, spanning virtually the same range of functionality as the OSI reference model. The protocol suite is often known as the TCP/IP suite, named after two of the most important constituent protocols. These protocols are being rapidly deployed in many networks worldwide, especially the collection of interconnected networks known as the DARPA Internet.

The Internet protocol suite is sometimes seen as a head-to-head competitor with the OSI protocol suite. However, it is becoming increasingly apparent that both sets of protocols have their strengths and weaknesses, and a great deal can be gained by mixing member protocols of both families to provide complete networking solutions. Protocol layering makes this possible.

The Internet protocol suite can be modeled using the same layering approach as the OSI architecture and, although not all seven layers are apparent in the Internet suite, the protocols map readily to the OSI model. There are effectively four Internet layers. For the purposes of this book, we shall call them:

- *Application Layer*: This layer combines the functionalities of the OSI Application, Presentation, and Session Layers, i.e., the OSI *upper layers* as defined in Section 3.2.
- *Transport Layer*: This layer is functionally equivalent to the OSI Transport Layer.
- *Internet Layer*: This layer is functionally equivalent to the subnetwork-independent part of the OSI Network Layer. (Unless further qualified, the term *Network Layer* used in the remainder of this book should be taken to include the Internet Layer.)
- *Interface Layer*: This layer is functionally equivalent to the OSI subnetwork technology functions discussed in Section 3.2.

Assuming this mapping, it is possible to consider security architecture in terms equally applicable to the OSI and Internet suites. The upper layers architectural differences prove inconsequential because, from the security perspective, there is no need to separate out the OSI upper layers into Application, Presentation, and Session Layers. Similarly, in the lower layers, there is no need to separate out the subnetwork technology functions into constituent layers.

Application Layer Protocols

There are numerous Internet Application Layer protocols, some important ones being:

- *File Transfer Protocol (FTP)*: A protocol which allows users to log into a remote system, identify themselves, list remote directories, and copy files to or from the remote machine.
- *Simple Mail Transfer Protocol (SMTP)*: An electronic mail protocol based on [POS1, CRO1]. Internet electronic mail and related security features are discussed in Chapter 14.
- *Simple Network Management Protocol (SNMP)*: A protocol supporting network management. SNMP and related security features are discussed in Chapter 15.
- *TELNET*: A simple remote terminal protocol which allows a user at one site to establish a connection to a login server at another site, passing keystrokes and responses between them.

Transport and Network Layer Protocols

There are two primary Internet Transport Layer protocols:

- *Transmission Control Protocol (TCP)*: A connection-oriented transport protocol designed for operation over a connectionless network service [POS2]. This protocol is comparable to the Class 4 OSI transport protocol.
- *User Datagram Protocol (UDP)*: A connectionless transport protocol [POS3]. This protocol is comparable to the OSI connectionless transport protocol.

The primary Internet Network Layer protocol is the *Internet Protocol* (IP), which is a connectionless network protocol [POS4]. This protocol is comparable to the OSI connectionless network protocol (CLNP).

3.4 Architectural Placement of Security Services

The provision of security services in a layered communications architecture raises some significant issues. Protocol layering results in data items being embedded within data items and connections being carried within connections, potentially with multiple layers of nesting. Hence, there are major decisions to be made as to the layer(s) at which data-item or connection-based protection should be provided.

The first formal standard addressing layer assignment of security services was the OSI Security Architecture (ISO/IEC 7498-2), published in 1988. This standard (which is discussed in Chapter 9) provides guidance as to which OSI layers are appropriate for providing the various security services. However, it does not provide all the answers, leaving many options open. Some services may need to be provided in different layers in different application scenarios; some may even need to be provided in multiple layers in the same scenario. One reason for the apparent inclusiveness of ISO/IEC 7498-2 is the approach taken of trying to assign fourteen security services to seven architectural layers. This can be crystallized into a much simpler and more pragmatic four-level model, based on the *real* security implications in *real* networks.

Figure 3-6 illustrates how a pair of end systems communicate with each other via a cascaded series of subnetworks. An end system is usually one piece of equipment, anywhere in the range from personal computer to workstation to

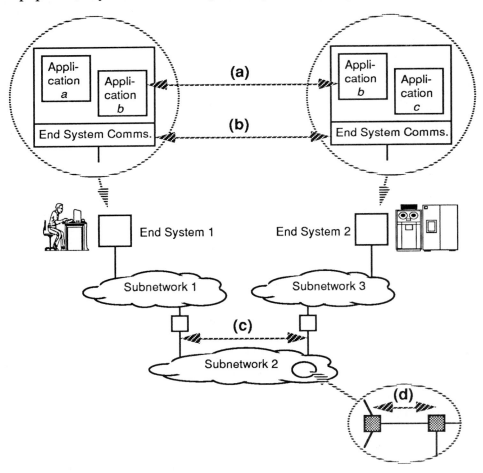

Figure 3-6: Basic Communications Architecture

minicomputer to mainframe computer. One characteristic that can be reasonably assumed for an end system is that, for security purposes, it has one policy authority.

A subnetwork is a collection of communications facilities employing the same communications technology, e.g., a particular local area network (LAN) or wide area network (WAN). It is also reasonable to assume that, for security purposes, any subnetwork has one policy authority. However, distinct subnetworks will often have different security environments and/or different policy authorities. An end system and the subnetwork to which it connects may or may not have the same policy authority. A typical scenario is an end system connecting to a LAN on one corporation's premises, with the LAN having a gateway to a public WAN. After possibly traversing multiple separately administered WANs, communications pass via another LAN to the other end system.

Another aspect introduced in Figure 3-6 is that of an end system simultaneously supporting multiple applications, such as electronic mail, directory access, and file transfer, for one or more users simultaneously. Another simultaneous application may be network management services for the system administrator. The security requirements of these applications often differ considerably.

We also need to recognize that security requirements may vary *within* a subnetwork. Subnetworks generally comprise multiple links connecting multiple subnetwork components and different links may pass through different security environments. Therefore, protection of individual links may need to be accommodated.

Figure 3-6 indicates four levels at which distinct requirements for security protocol elements arise:

(a) *Application level:* Security protocol elements that are application-dependent.
(b) *End-system level:* Security protocol elements providing protection on an end-system to end-system basis.
(c) *Subnetwork level:* Security protocol elements providing protection over a subnetwork which is considered less trusted than other parts of the network environment.
(d) *Direct-link level:* Security protocol elements providing protection internal to a subnetwork, over a link which is considered less trusted than other parts of the subnetwork environment.

From the communications protocol perspective, these four levels are all that need to be distinguished. An approximate mapping of these levels to the OSI architectural layers is illustrated in Figure 3-7.

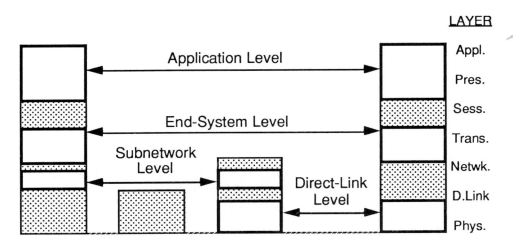

Figure 3-7: The Four Basic Architectural Levels for Security

What are the ramifications of locating security services at higher as opposed to lower levels? Before discussing each level individually, we can identify some general properties that vary between higher and lower levels:

- *Traffic mixing*: As a result of multiplexing, there is a greater tendency at lower levels to have data items from different source/destination users and/or applications mixed in a data stream than at higher levels. The significance of this factor varies with the type of security policy. If the security policy tends to leave it to individual users and/or applications to specify the protection required for their data, placing security services at a higher level tends to be better. With security at lower levels, the individual users/applications have inadequate control, and there is likely to be a cost in unnecessarily protecting some data because of the security requirements of other data sharing the data stream. On the other hand, if the security policy is such that an organization wants to ensure that all organizational traffic is protected to a certain degree, regardless of user or application, this is more easily achieved with security services at lower levels.

- *Route knowledge*: At lower levels, there tends to be more knowledge of the security characteristics of different routes and links. In an environment where such characteristics vary significantly, placing security at lower levels can have effectiveness and efficiency benefits. Appropriate security services can be selected on a subnetwork or direct-link basis, while eliminating security costs entirely on subnetworks or links where protection is unnecessary.

- *Number of protection points*: Placing security at a very high level (i.e., application level) requires security to be implemented in every sensitive application in every end system. Placing security at a very low level (i.e., direct-link level) requires security to be implemented at the ends of every network link. Placing security closer to the middle of the architecture (i.e., end-system or subnetwork level) will tend to require security features to be installed at significantly fewer points, which may significantly reduce costs.

- *Protocol header protection*: Security protection at higher levels cannot protect protocol headers of lower levels which, in at least some environments, may be sensitive. This tends to encourage placing security services at a low level.

- *Source/sink binding*: Some security services, such as data origin authentication and non-repudiation, depend upon associating data with its source or sink. This is most effectively achieved at higher levels, especially the application level. However, it can sometimes be achieved at lower levels, subject to special constraints, e.g., binding of a message originator to a particular end system through the use of trusted hardware and/or software.

Taking all the above considerations together, it becomes apparent why there is no simple answer to the question of the "best" architectural placement for security services. In the following subsections, the characteristics of each of the four levels are discussed further, in a service-independent way. Subsequent chapters discuss architectural placement of specific security services with reference to these four levels.

Application Level Security

In terms of the OSI architecture, application level security relates to the upper layers. (In OSI protocol terms, this means the Application Layer, possibly assisted by Presentation Layer facilities; the Session Layer does not contribute to the provision of security. The division of functions between Application and Presentation Layers is addressed in Chapter 12.)

For most security services, it is *possible* to locate the service at the application level. In many cases, lower-level alternatives are also available and frequently have advantages (e.g., lower equipment or operational costs). However, there are two situations in which the application level is the *only* viable level for locating a security service:

(a) Where security services are application-specific, either semantically or by virtue of being built into a particular application protocol.

(b) Where security services traverse application relays.

Some security requirements are inextricably linked to application semantics. For example, a file transfer application may need to deal with file access control, e.g., reading or updating access control lists attached to files. In other cases, the granularity of security protection is reflected in application protocol fields. This is very common with selective field confidentiality, selective field integrity, and non-repudiation services. Examples are giving confidentiality protection to a PIN field in a financial transaction, or digitally signing individual retrieval requests in a directory protocol. In all of these cases, the security services must be located at the application level, as layer independence prevents lower layers from having knowledge of the requisite semantics or the protocol boundaries.

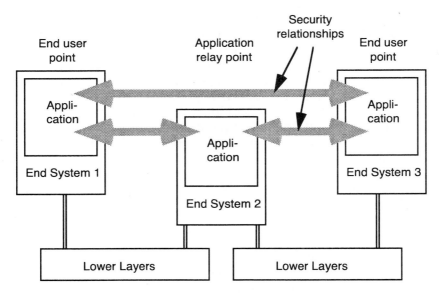

Figure 3-8: Application Relay Scenario

The other situation demanding an application level solution is an application relay scenario. Some applications inherently involve more than two end systems, as illustrated in Figure 3-8. Electronic mail systems are an example. A message originating at one end system may pass through multiple relay systems before arriving at a recipient in another end system. There may be a requirement to protect the *content* part of the message on an end-user to end-user basis, i.e., the keying relationship rests with the end-user systems, and the relay systems do not know the key(s) used. However, other parts of the message, e.g., address fields and trace fields, are not protected this way, as the relay systems need to use, and possibly update, such fields. In such a scenario, all security services in the end-user to end-user security relationship need to be at the application level.

When deciding if a security requirement should be dealt with at the application level, or at a lower level, the above factors should be considered first. If none apply, consideration should be given to using lower levels.

End-System Level Security

The following types of security requirements point to an end-system level solution:

- requirements based on the assumption that the end systems are trusted, but that all underlying communications network(s) are untrusted;
- requirements dictated by the end-system authority, that are to be enforced upon all communications regardless of the application; and
- requirements relating to network connections (or all traffic thereon), that are not linked to any particular application, e.g., confidentiality and/or integrity protection of all traffic on a connection.

Some services, such as confidentiality and/or integrity protection of all user information on an end-system to end-system basis, could potentially be provided at either the application level or the end-system level. In deciding which level, there are several factors to be taken into account. Factors tending to favor an end-system level solution over a comparable application level solution include:

- the ability to make protection services transparent to the applications;
- superior performance of bulk data protection services, owing to the ability to operate on larger data units and to process the data of multiple applications in a common way;
- placing management of the security facilities in the hands of one end-system administrator, rather than in separate applications (supports a consistent security policy); and
- ensuring that the protocol headers of mid-layer protocols (i.e., Transport, Session, and Presentation Layer protocols) receive protection.

In OSI terms, end-system level security relates to either Transport Layer or subnetwork-independent Network Layer protocols. The decision between these two options has been the subject of ongoing debate in the standards forums for several years. There has been no real resolution to this debate, in that standards have been developed supporting both options (standards ISO/IEC 10736 and ISO/IEC 11577 respectively).

Factors favoring the Transport Layer approach include:

- extension of the protection right to the end system, thereby protecting against vulnerabilities in local-access or front-end communications facilities; and
- the possibility of providing different grades of protection to different transport-connections multiplexed on a network-connection.

Factors favoring the Network Layer approach include:

- the ability to use the same solution at the end-system and subnetwork levels;
- the ease of transparently inserting security devices at standardized physical interface points, e.g., X.25 or LAN interfaces; and
- the ability to support *any* upper-layer architecture, including OSI, Internet, and proprietary architectures.

The irreconcilability of such factors explains why there is no simple resolution of this issue. Profiling groups and user communities need to make their own decisions, based on their own requirements.

Subnetwork Level Security

The difference between end-system level security and subnetwork level security is that the latter provides protection across one or more specific subnetworks only. There are two very important reasons for distinguishing this level from the end-system level:

- It is very common that subnetworks close to end-systems are trusted to the same extent as the end-systems themselves, since they are on the same premises and administered under the same authorities.
- In any network, the number of end systems usually far exceeds the number of subnetwork gateways. Therefore, equipment costs and operational costs for subnetwork level security solutions may be much lower than those for end-system level solutions.

Subnetwork level security should therefore always be considered as a possible alternative to end-system level security.

In OSI, subnetwork level security maps to the Network Layer or, in the case of LANs, to the Data Link Layer (where LAN protocols are located).

Direct-Link Level Security

The appropriate situations for using direct-link level security are those with comparatively few untrusted links in an otherwise-trusted environment. On a given link, a high level of protection can be provided at a low equipment cost. Provision of security at this level can be transparent to all higher communications layers, including network-protocols, hence it is not tied to any particular network architecture (e.g., OSI, TCP/IP, or proprietary). Security devices can be easily inserted at common standardized physical interface points. However, operational costs may be high, because of the need to independently manage devices on a link-by-link basis. It is important to realize that direct-link level security cannot protect against vulnerabilities *inside* subnetwork nodes, e.g., hubs, bridges, or packet switches.

In terms of OSI layers, direct-link level security usually relates to the Physical Layer. Protection is provided at the bit-stream level and is transparent to all higher-level protocols. For example, encryption processes can be applied to the bit-streams passing at any interface point. Protection transmission technologies, such as spread-spectrum or frequency hopping techniques, can also be employed [TOR1]. Direct-link level security can potentially relate to the Data Link Layer, e.g., if protection is provided at the frame level.

Human User Interactions

Some network security services involve direct interaction with a human user. Such interactions do not fit cleanly into any of the architectural options presented above. The most important case is *personal authentication*. The user is external to the communication facilities, i.e., beyond one of the end systems. Communications supporting personal authentication are either local (i.e., between the human user and his local end system) or they involve protocol elements at the application level, or they combine both of the above. Examples of these three cases are:

- The human user authenticates to his or her local end system. That end system then authenticates itself to the remote end system, and advises the user identity, which the remote end system accepts as authentic.
- The human user passes authentication information (e.g., a password) to his or her local end system, which conveys it on to the remote end system which performs the user authentication.
- The human user enters a password to his or her local end system, which this system uses to obtain an authentication certificate from an on-line authentication or key server. The certificate is passed to the remote end system which uses it as the basis of authenticating the user.

Personal authentication is addressed further in Chapter 5.

Figure 3-9 illustrates the relationship between human user interaction protocols and the application level architectural option.

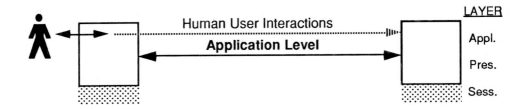

Figure 3-9: Human User Interactions

3.5 Management of Security Services

Security services need the support of management functions, such as:

- key management for cryptosytems used in providing a security service (this is discussed in Chapters 4 and 7);
- distribution of required information to decision-making points, e.g., for use in making authentication or access control decisions — this includes information enabling a positive decision to be made and notifications of the withdrawal of previously distributed information;
- central accumulation of information for purposes such as archival (for subsequent non-repudiation purposes) or security audit trail or alarm generation;
- operational functions, such as service activation and deactivation; and
- special security management functions, such as remotely invoking virus scans on network workstations or monitoring systems for illegitimate software.

Such management functions usually employ communications capabilities of the same network they are helping to protect. In this case it is essential that these management communications be protected to the maximal extent available. Any vulnerability in security management communications will translate to an equivalent or magnified vulnerability in protected communications generally.

In architectural terms, security management functions are generally provided through network applications. These can include applications dedicated to network management (some examples are discussed in Chapter 15) or applications with other primary purposes. Exceptions to this level of placement can occur, e.g., when key management exchanges are closely linked to cryptographic processing at lower layers. The latter issue is taken up in Chapters 4 and 7.

Summary

Layered protocol architectures allow network designs to accommodate unlimited applications, unlimited underlying media technologies, and unlimited interconnection techniques. The OSI architecture provides a general model on which layering can be based. There are seven layers, which can be separated into the upper layers (Application, Presentation, and Session Layers) and lower layers (Transport, Network, Data Link, and Physical Layers). Other OSI standards define layer services and specific protocols for the seven layers. The Internet TCP/IP protocol suite defines alternative protocols, which can be mapped straightforwardly to the OSI model.

In providing security services, there are significant issues in deciding the layer(s) at which protection should be located. To assist in making these decisions, four security architectural levels can be identified — the application level, the end-system level, the subnetwork level, and the direct-link level. The application level involves security protocol elements which are application-dependent, and require support in upper layers protocols. Certain security requirements demand a solution at this level. The end-system level involves security protocol elements providing protection on an end-system to end-system basis. This can employ security protocols at either the Transport or Network Layer; both options are available, and there are various factors favoring each. The subnetwork level provides protection over particular subnetworks within the Network Layer or (in the case of LANs) the Data Link Layer. The direct-link level provides protection on a link-by-link basis over parts of a subnetwork environment; this level relates to the Physical or Data Link layer. Interactions with human users (especially for authentication purposes) do not fit fully into the above four levels, and require special consideration.

Management of security services involves various functions, most of which are provided through network management applications.

Exercises

1. When unprotected data exists within network switching equipment (such as bridges, routers, or packet switches), this equipment may need to be

physically secured to maintain adequate protection. Such physical security can be costly. To minimize this cost, at what security architectural level(s) should protection be located?

2.   In an on-line financial transaction message, a PIN is to be conveyed encrypted while the other transaction details are transferred unprotected. Which of the four security architectural level(s) is (are) involved and why?

3.   If sensitive information can be gleaned by monitoring the addressing information in a connection establishment exchange or in a connectionless data unit, which security architectural level(s) could be employed to ensure adequate protection?

4.   A large corporation has a network which spans several sites. At the discretion of individual users, the traffic includes a substantial amount of corporate proprietary information. The corporation wants to apply blanket protection to vulnerable parts of the network to protect against disclosure of proprietary information to outsiders. In each of the following configuration scenarios, what appears the most appropriate architectural level for applying a confidentiality service, and why?

(a)   The network involves local area networks within corporate locations, with a public wide area network interconnecting these locations.

(b)   The network involves local area networks within corporate locations, with a small number of leased lines interconnecting LAN gateways at these locations.

(c)   The network involves a wide variety of communication links, trusted to varying extents, with the end user having no control over the security of the route used for any communicated item.

REFERENCES

[BLA1] U. Black, *OSI: A Model for Computer Communications*, Prentice Hall, Englewood Cliffs, NJ, 1991.

[COM1] D.E. Comer, *Internetworking with TCP/IP: Principles, Protocols, and Architecture*, Prentice Hall, Englewood Cliffs, NJ, 1988.

[CRO1] D.H. Crocker, *Standard for the Format of ARPA Internet Text Messages*, Request for Comments (RFC) 822, Internet Activities Board, 1982.

[DIC1]   G. Dickson and A. Lloyd, *Open Systems Interconnection*, Prentice Hall, Englewood Cliffs, NJ, 1991.

[HEN1]   J. Henshall and S. Shaw, *OSI Explained: End-to-End Computer Communication Standard*, Second Edition, Prentice Hall, Englewood Cliffs, NJ, 1990.

[POS1]   J.B. Postel, *Simple Mail Transfer Protocol*, Request for Comments (RFC) 821, Internet Activities Board, 1982.

[POS2]   J.B. Postel, *Transmission Control Protocol*, Request for Comments (RFC) 793, Internet Activities Board, 1981.

[POS3]   J.B. Postel, *User Datagram Protocol*, Request for Comments (RFC) 768, Internet Activities Board, 1981.

[POS4]   J.B. Postel, *Internet Protocol*, Request for Comments (RFC) 791, Internet Activities Board, 1981.

[ROS1]   M.T. Rose, *The Open Book: A Practical Perspective on OSI*, Prentice Hall, Englewood Cliffs, NJ, 1990.

[STE1]   D. Steedman, *Abstract Syntax Notation One (ASN.1): The Tutorial and Reference*, Technical Appraisals Ltd., Isleworth, England, 1990.

[TOR1]   D.J. Torrieri, *Principles of Secure Communication Systems*, Second Edition, Artech House, Inc., Norwood, MA, 1992.

Standards

ISO/IEC 7498-1:   *Information Technology — Open Systems Interconnection — Basic Reference Model* (Also ITU-T Recommendation X.200).

ISO/IEC 7498-2:   *Information Technology — Open Systems Interconnection — Basic Reference Model — Part 2: Security Architecture* (Also ITU-T Recommendation X.800).

ISO/IEC 8072:   *Information Technology — Open Systems Interconnection — Connection Oriented Transport Service Definition* (Also ITU-T Recommendation X.214).

ISO/IEC 8073:   *Information Technology — Open Systems Interconnection — Connection Oriented Transport Protocol Specification* (Also ITU-T Recommendation X.224).

ISO/IEC 8208:   *Information Technology — Data Communications — X.25 Packet Level Protocol for Data Terminal Equipment.*

ISO/IEC 8326:   *Information Technology — Open Systems Interconnection — Basic Connection Oriented Session Service Definition* (Also ITU-T Recommendation X.215).

ISO/IEC 8327:   *Information Technology — Open Systems Interconnection — Basic Connection Oriented Session Protocol Specification* (Also ITU-T Recommendation X.225).

ISO/IEC 8348:   *Information Technology — Data Communications — Network Service Definition* (Also ITU-T Recommendation X.213).

ISO/IEC 8473:   *Information Technology — Data Communications — Protocol for Providing the Connectionless-Mode Network Service.*

ISO/IEC 8571:   *Information Technology — Open Systems Interconnection — File Transfer, Access and Management (FTAM).*

ISO/IEC 8602:   *Information Technology — Open Systems Interconnection — Protocol for Providing the Connectionless-Mode Transport Service.*

ISO/IEC 8648: *Information Technology — Data Communications — Internal Organization of the Network Layer*.

ISO/IEC 8649: *Information Technology — Open Systems Interconnection — Service Definition for Association Control* (Also ITU-T Recommendation X.217).

ISO/IEC 8650: *Information Technology — Open Systems Interconnection — Protocol Specification for the Association Control Service Element* (Also ITU-T Recommendation X.227).

ISO/IEC 8802: *Information Technology — Local and Metropolitan Area Networks*.

ISO/IEC 8822: *Information Technology — Open Systems Interconnection — Connection Oriented Presentation Service Definition* (Also ITU-T Recommendation X.216).

ISO/IEC 8823: *Information Technology — Open Systems Interconnection — Connection Oriented Presantation Protocol Specification* (Also ITU-T Recommendation X.226).

ISO/IEC 8824: *Information Technology — Open Systems Interconnection — Specification of Abstract Syntax Notation One (ASN.1)* (Also ITU-T X.680 series Recommendations).

ISO/IEC 8825: *Information Technology — Open Systems Interconnection — Specification of ASN.1 Encoding Rules* (Also ITU-T X.690 series Recommendations).

ISO/IEC 8878: *Information Technology — Data Communications — Use of X.25 to Provide the Connectionless-mode Network Service*.

ISO/IEC 8880: *Information Technology — Data Communications — Protocol Combinations to Provide and Support the OSI Network Service*.

ISO/IEC 8881: *Information Technology — Data Communications — Use of the X.25 Packet Layer Protocol in Local Area Networks*.

ISO/IEC 9072: *Information Technology — Open Systems Interconnection — Remote Operations*.

ISO/IEC 9545: *Information Technology — Open Systems Interconnection — Application Layer Structure* (Also ITU-T Recommendation X.207).

ISO/IEC 10736: *Information Technology — Telecommunications and Information Exchange Between Systems — Transport Layer Security Protocol* (Also ITU-T Recommendation X.824).

ISO/IEC 11577: *Information Technology — Telecommunications and Information Exchange Between Systems — Network Layer Security Protocol* (Also ITU-T Recommendation X.823) (Draft).

ITU-T Recommendation X.25: *Interface between data terminal equipment (DTE) and data circuit-terminating equipment (DCE) for terminals operating in the packet mode and connected to public networks by dedicated circuit* (ISO/IEC adaptation in ISO/IEC 8208).

4   Cryptographic Techniques

Cryptographic techniques, such as encipherment and digital signatures, are important building blocks in the implemention of all security services. This chapter introduces the major cryptographic techniques used in securing contemporary computer networks.

The most basic building block is called a cryptographic system (or *cryptosystem*). A cryptosystem defines a pair of data transformations. The first transformation is applied to an ordinary data item, known as *plaintext,* and generates a corresponding (unintelligible) data item called *ciphertext*. The second transformation, applied to ciphertext, results in the regeneration of the original plaintext. The two transformations are most commonly called *encryption* and *decryption,* respectively. The alternative terms *encipherment* and *decipherment* are also used, and are generally preferred in international standards.[1]

An encryption transformation uses as input both the plaintext data and an independent data value known as an *encryption key*. Similarly, a decryption transformation uses a *decryption key*. These keys are seemingly random bit-vectors.

An obvious use of a cryptosystem is for providing confidentiality. The plaintext is unprotected data. The corresponding ciphertext may be transmitted in untrusted environments because, if the cryptosystem is a good one, it will be infeasible for anyone to deduce the plaintext from the ciphertext without knowing the decryption key. Cryptosystems also have uses other than confidentiality, as will become apparent later in the chapter.

There are two basic types of cryptosystems — *symmetric* systems (sometimes called private-key or secret-key systems) and *public-key* (or asymmetric) systems. These have distinct characteristics and are used in different ways to provide security services.

This chapter is organized into sections addressing:

(1) symmetric cryptosystems;
(2) public-key cryptosystems;
(3) integrity check-values or seals (also known as message authentication codes);

---

[1] This is because "encryption" and "decryption" become confused with more traditional interpretations of "burying" and "digging up" in some languages.

(4) digital signatures;

(5) general principles for managing cryptographic keys;

(6) methods of distributing secret keys; and

(7) methods of distributing keys for public-key cryptosystems.

The coverage here is limited to aspects of immediate practical concern and does not extend to describing the mathematics underlying cryptography. For detailed coverage of cryptographic systems generally, see [BRA1, DEN1, MEY1, SEB1], and for a specialized coverage of public-key cryptography, see [NEC1]. Chapter 10 provides full details of standards publications relating to the described techniques.

4.1 Symmetric Cryptosystems

Symmetric cryptosytems are characterized by the fact that the *same* key is used in the encryption and decryption transformations (see Figure 4-1). To provide confidentiality, a symmetric cryptosystem works as follows. Two systems, *A* and *B*, decide they want to communicate securely. By some process (discussed later) they both obtain knowledge of a data value to be used as a key. The key is kept secret from all parties other than *A* and *B*. This enables either *A* or *B* to protect a message sent to the other party by encrypting it using the agreed key. The other party can decrypt the message, but outside parties cannot.

Symmetric cryptosystems have been in use in commercial networks since the early 1970s. The U.S. Data Encryption Standard (DES) is the only cryptosystem of this type which has had its full specification published as a public standard.

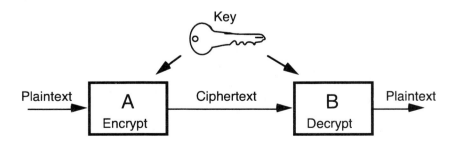

Figure 4-1: A Symmetric Cryptosystem

Data Encryption Standard (DES)

In 1973 and 1974, the U.S. National Bureau of Standards (NBS) — since renamed the National Institute of Standards and Technology (NIST) — issued solicitations for an encryption algorithm for use by U.S. federal agencies for protecting sensitive information. From the proposals submitted, the algorithm chosen was one submitted by IBM. It was subjected to a public review period beginning in 1975, then adopted as Federal Information Processing Standard FIPS PUB 46 in 1977, with the name Data Encryption Standard (DES). In 1981, the same specification was adopted by the U.S. commercial standards organization, ANSI, as American National Standard ANSI X3.92 *American National Standard Data Encryption Algorithm* (leading to the alternative acronym DEA). The algorithm was rapidly deployed for confidentiality purposes in government, and for integrity purposes in the financial industry, and has since been widely adopted in other application areas.

DES *almost* became an international standard. In 1986, it was approved within ISO as International Standard 8227 (*Information Processing — Data Encipherment — Specification of Algorithm DEA 1*). However, last-minute intervention by national representations at the ISO Council level led to a resolution that ISO should not standardize cryptography. The DES international standard was never published. For a complete description of the history of DES, see [SMI1].

The DES algorithm employs a 56-bit key and operates on 64-bit blocks of data. The encryption process applies an initial permutation to the plaintext bits, passes the result through 16 rounds of a key-dependent computation, then applies a final permutation to give the ciphertext. The key-dependent computation involves dividing the 64-bit data input into two 32-bit halves. One half is used as input to a complex function, and the result is exclusive-ORed to the other half. The complex function includes passes through eight nonlinear table-specified substitutions known as *S-boxes* (substitution-boxes). After one iteration, or round, the two halves of the data are swapped and the operation is performed again. The output of the entire process displays no correlation to the input. Every bit of the output depends upon every bit of the input and on every bit of the key. The security of DES depends primarily upon the S-boxes, which are the only non-linear components.

The decryption process is of the same form as the encryption process, except that the selected portions of the key used internally for the 16 rounds are in reverse order.

The effective key size of DES can be increased by using a multiple encryption approach [TUC1]. Triple-DES involves an initial encryption of a 64-bit block using key *a*, followed by a decryption of the result using key *b*, followed by an encryption of that result using key *c*. The same value can be used for keys *a* and *c*, with a reduction in cryptographic strength [MER1,

VAN1]. Hence, the triple-DES approach has both two-key and three-key variations.

The original FIPS PUB 46 required DES to be implemented in hardware, although this restriction was eased with NIST's 1993 reaffirmation of the algorithm. ANSI X3.92 has been less restrictive, always recognizing that software implementations may be acceptable in some environments. Some guidance to DES implementors is provided in FIPS PUB 74. Two NIST special publications are also worthy of note — [NIS1] describes validation procedures for DES devices, and [NIS2] describes a DES maintenance test suitable for use, for example, in an equipment self-test run at system start-up.

Modes of Operation

As cryptographic processes need to be applied over messages or streams of data of arbitrary size, the concepts of *block ciphers* and *stream ciphers* are important. A block cipher breaks the data to be protected into blocks of the same size as the cryptosystem block size (64 bits in the DES case). A stream cipher breaks the data into a sequence of characters.

The standardization of DES was accompanied by a specification of four *modes of operation* of the basic algorithm.[2] The four modes of operation are:

- *Electronic Codebook (ECB) mode*: A codebook-style process for encrypting a single 64-bit block. When a data item larger than 64 bits is to be protected, it is split into blocks, and each block is encrypted and decrypted independently of other blocks. The ECB mode has the limitation that, for a given key, the same plaintext always produces the same ciphertext. It is easier to attack than other modes and is unsuitable for use in applications where recognizing repetitions or commonly used sequences is a threat. The other three modes do not have this limitation.

- *Cipher Block Chaining (CBC) mode*: A block cipher process in which each plaintext block in a stream of data is exclusive-ORed with the preceding ciphertext block before encrypting. For the first block, the plaintext of the block is exclusive-ORed with an independent 64-bit input quantity known as the initialization vector (IV). In the event of a bit-error in the ciphertext stream, the CBC mode is self-synchronizing after two blocks (i.e., the block in error and the following one will not decrypt correctly, but subsequent blocks will). A message being encrypted needs to be padded out to be a multiple of 64-bit blocks.

- *Cipher Feedback (CFB) mode*: A stream cipher process in which the plaintext stream is divided into k-bit characters, $1 \leq k \leq 64$. The

---

2 This specification was published originally as FIPS PUB 81. Commercial standards have appeared subsequently; see Chapter 10 for details

ciphertext for each character is obtained by XORing the plaintext character with a key character derived by encrypting the preceding 64 bits of ciphertext (e.g., with the preceding 8 ciphertext characters, when using 8-bit characters). At the start of the process, a 64-bit initialization vector (IV) takes the place of ciphertext. The CFB mode is also self-synchronizing in the event of a bit error. For example, with 8-bit characters, loss or corruption of a ciphertext character during transmission will result in an error propagated forward for 8 characters, but the decryption resynchronizes by itself after 8 correct ciphertext characters.

- *Output Feedback (OFB) mode*: A stream cipher process in which the DES algorithm is used to generate a random key stream that is exclusive-ORed with a plaintext stream. Like CFB, it operates on k-bit characters. It also requires an IV to start. However, unlike CFB and CBC, it does not chain cipher. A one-bit error in ciphertext causes only one bit of the decrypted plaintext to be in error. This mode, unlike CBC and CFB, is unsuitable for providing a data integrity service. It is not self-synchronizing; if cryptographic synchronization is lost, then a new IV must be established between both ends.

The IV used in starting the chaining and feedback modes should be a random number. While it is not essential that IVs be kept secret, public knowledge of an IV can facilitate cryptanalytic attacks on the start of a message. Hence, IVs are often communicated in an encrypted form. In any case, a system should ensure that the IV is different on each use of a given mode with a given key.

Strength of DES

The strength of DES has been a controversial issue, ever since the first call for comments on the proposed standard in 1975. Underlying the controversy have been two main issues:

- the key size being set at an unnecessarily small value (56 bits); and
- the classification by the U.S. National Security Agency (NSA) of the design of the S-boxes (upon which the security of the algorithm primarily depends).

This has led to continuing debate on the susceptibility of DES to exhaustive attack, i.e., an attack based on simply trying all keys (about 7×10^{16} of them) until one is found to work. There has also been speculation that DES may have built-in "trapdoors" known only by the NSA, and there has been concern about the comparative strengths of different keys. Some keys are identified in the standard as being weak or semi-weak[3]; however, the varying strengths of the remaining population of keys are not spelled out.

The extensive debate on this subject through the period 1975 to 1990 was well summarized by Dorothy Denning [DEN2]. Her conclusion was:

> DES has been in active field use for over a decade. No instances of successful attack, brute force or otherwise, have yet been published. This is a remarkable pragmatic validation. Although the DES is potentially vulnerable to attack by exhaustive search, the public literature suggests that such attacks can be successfully avoided with triple encryption, especially if three independent keys are used. Thus, the DES with triple encryption may provide adequate protection for its intended application for many years to come.

There can be no doubt that the useful life of single-DES is running out. DES can be broken by exhaustive attack by anyone prepared to spend enough money on the required equipment. For example, Eberle [EBE1] estimates that DES can be broken in an average of 8 days using equipment costing around $1 $1 million, constructed from 1992-technology DES chips. (This compares with the estimate in [GAR1] that DES can be broken in a week for $500,000 using equipment available in the year 2000.) In fact, if someone were to custom-design chips specifically for breaking DES, the above estimates would likely be reduced by 1-to-2 orders of magnitude, i.e., with equipment costing $1 million, DES could be broken in a few hours. If such an investment could enable someone to compromise multiple high-value financial transactions, it is clear that such attacks are not far fetched.

On a separate front, the recent publication of details of a cryptanalytic approach called differential cryptanalysis [BIH1, BIH2] has raised new questions on the strength of DES and other symmetric algorithms. Differential cryptanalysis can result in an attack on DES which is slightly less computationally intensive than an exhaustive key search. However, this attack requires 2^{47} *chosen* plaintext-ciphertext pairs to be available to the cryptanalyst, hence does not represent a practical threat to the use of DES for commercial purposes.[4] Nevertheless, this development does highlight the need to continually track progress in the attacking of cryptographic algorithms.

Inexpensive silicon chip implementations of DES are readily available. Data rates up to 1 gigabit-per-second can be achieved [EBE1].

---

[3] See [MEY1] for a detailed discussion.

[4] DES proved quite resistant to differential cryptanalysis, because its designers knew of this possible type of attack. Other algorithms proved much weaker in the face of differential cryptanalysis.

DES is reviewed with respect to suitability for U.S. federal government use every five years. It was reaffirmed in 1983, 1988, and 1993. The 1993 reaffirmation was accompanied by an indication that alternative algorithms for government use were being actively considered.

U.S. Government DES Replacement

In April 1993, the U.S. government announced a new proposal for providing information confidentiality through communications encryption, while simultaneously preserving the ability of law enforcement agencies to eavesdrop upon such communications when lawfully authorized to do so. This announcement included release of limited information about a new symmetric cryptosystem called SKIPJACK.

This new algorithm is a 64-bit block cipher like DES. A significant difference from DES is that it employs an 80-bit (compared with 56-bit) key, adding many orders of magnitude to the cryptographic strength. It involves 32 rounds of computation (compared with 16 rounds for DES). It can be used in conjunction with the same modes of operation as DES. Unlike DES, the full specification of the new algorithm is classified, hence not publicly available. In due course, the algorithm is destined to replace DES for the protection of government unclassified but sensitive information.

The April 1993 announcement also described an implementation of the SKIPJACK algorithm on a chip designed to support *key escrowing technology*. This chip, designed by the NSA, supports law enforcement needs by having the encryption process generate, along with the ciphertext, a Law Enforcement Field. This field is sent with the ciphertext to a decrypting chip. Subject to release of two independent 80-bit secret key-information items from two independent escrow agents, operating under stringent controls, the Law Enforcement Field is able to reveal the encryption key to an agency authorized to intercept the communications.

4.2 Public-Key Cryptosystems

The technology of public-key cryptography was introduced in 1976 by Whitfield Diffie and Martin Hellman of Stanford University [DIF1]. Since then, the technology has followed an extremely interesting development path [DIF2] and can now be considered mature.

In contrast to symmetric cryptosystems, public-key cryptosystems use complementary pairs of keys to separate the functions of encryption and decryption. One key, the *private key*, is kept secret like a key in a symmetric cryptosystem. The other key, the *public key*, does not need to be kept secret. The system must have the property that, given knowledge of the public key, it

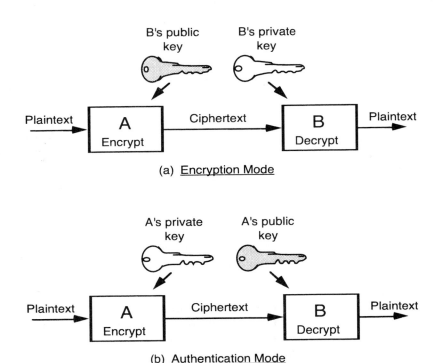

Figure 4-2: A Public-Key Cryptosystem

is not feasible to determine the private key. This two-key approach can simplify key management, by minimizing the number of keys that need to be managed and stored in a network, and can enable keys to be distributed via unprotected systems such as public directory services.

Potentially, there are two modes of use of public-key cryptosystems, depending on whether the public key is used as an encryption key or decryption key (see Figure 4-2). Suppose there exists a public directory that contains the public keys for a set of communicating parties. Using these keys as encryption keys, any party can send a confidential message to any other party. The sender simply looks up the recipient's key and uses it to encrypt the message. Only the holder of the corresponding private key can read the message. This is the *encryption mode*.

By using the published key as a decryption key, public-key cryptography can be used for data origin authentication and for ensuring the integrity of a message. In this case anyone can obtain the decryption key from the directory and can therefore read the message. The reader also knows that only the holder of the corresponding private key could have created the message. This is the *authentication mode*.

A public-key cryptosystem that can operate in both of these modes is called a *reversible public-key cryptosystem*. Some public-key cryptosystems can operate in the authentication mode but not the encryption mode. They are known as *irreversible public-key cryptosystems*.

Public-key cryptosystems present a much greater challenge to the algorithm designer than symmetric cryptosystems, because the public key represents additional information which can be used in attacking the algorithm. Public-key systems in current use rely for their strength on the underlying assumption that a particular, known mathematical problem is difficult to solve.

RSA Algorithm

RSA is a reversible public-key cryptosystem, named after its inventors, Rivest, Shamir, and Adleman, from MIT. Its description was first published in 1978 [RIV1]. It makes use of the fact that, while finding large prime numbers is relatively easy, factoring the product of two such numbers is considered computationally infeasible.

An RSA key pair is created as follows. An integer e is chosen, to be the *public exponent*. Two large odd prime numbers, p and q, are then randomly selected, satisfying the conditions that $(p - 1)$ and e have no common divisors, and $(q - 1)$ and e have no common divisors.[5] The *public modulus* is the value $n = pq$. The values of n and e together form the public key. A *private exponent*, d, is then determined, such that $(de - 1)$ is divisible by both $(p - 1)$ and $(q - 1)$. The values of n and d (or p, q, and d) together constitute the private key.

The exponents have the important property that d functions as the inverse of e, that is, for any message M, $(M^e)^d \bmod n = M \bmod n$. For details of the mathemetics leading to this conclusion, see [RIV1].

The encrypting process for message M involves calculating $M^e \bmod n$. This can be carried out by anyone who knows the public key, i.e., n and e. Decrypting of message M' involves calculating $M'^d \bmod n$. This requires knowledge of the private key.

The strength of RSA has sometimes been questioned. It has a very obvious way of being broken — which is to factor the modulus n, using any of several known factoring methods. The strength therefore depends upon the time required and the cost of equipment that could perform the factoring. The continually decreasing cost of equipment has to be taken into account in

---

[5] Other constraints may also be warranted in order to avoid "weak" keys; see, for example [GOR1]. However, such constraints are likely to change as the state of the art in cryptanalysis advances.

considering RSA's strength into the future. The state of the art in factoring in 1990 was demonstrated by a well-publicized experiment by M. Manasse and A. Lenstra which, using a loosely coupled network of 200 engineering workstations, succeeded in factoring a 116-digit modulus in a month.

What can give us good confidence that RSA will maintain its strength into the future is the fact that a very small increase in the size of the modulus results in a tremendous increase in the effort required to factor it. (As a rule of thumb, with current factoring algorithms, increasing the size of the modulus by three digits doubles the difficulty of factoring it.)

Suppose, for example, we advance the technology of Manasse and Lenstra a little and assume a 150-digit modulus can be factored in a month. If we then make a comparatively modest extension of the modulus size to, say, 200 or 250 digits, the times required to perform the factoring with the same technology are as shown in Table 4-1. It can be seen that tenfold, hundredfold, or even thousandfold improvements in technology can be easily countered by a simple increment in modulus size. Hence, in order for RSA to be secure, now or in the future, one simply has to make a sensible choice for the modulus size.

Number of digits	Time to factor
150	1 month
200	100 years
250	500,000 years

Table 4-1: Times to Factor an RSA Modulus

There is, of course, a possibility of a major breakthrough in factoring methods. However, mathematicians have been seeking fast factoring algorithms for many years without success. The main attestation as to the strength of RSA is that it has withstood so many years of continuing attempts by experts to crack it.

A major shortcoming of RSA, in comparison with symmetric cryptosystems like DES, is a much higher processing overhead for encryption and decryption. Hence, RSA is rarely used for bulk data encryption. However, RSA has some important applications — these are discussed under digital signature, key management, and authentication topics later. RSA is being extensively used in products today, in various forms including specialized silicon chips, digital signal processor (DSP) programs, and conventional software.

Efficient implementation of RSA depends largely upon having modular arithmetic code suitable for the processor used. There are many publications which will assist an implementor. Some useful starting points are [BRI1, SHA1] if considering a hardware implementation, or [DUS1] for a software implementation.

ElGamal Algorithm

In 1985, ElGamal [ELG1] proposed an alternative public-key cryptosystem, based on a different underlying mathematical problem to RSA. This algorithm depends upon the difficulty of computing discrete logarithms over finite fields. The ElGamal proposal included both encryption-mode and authentication-mode schemes. While the encryption-mode scheme has not been exploited, the authentication-mode scheme has attracted much interest and has formed the basis of the proposed U.S. Digital Signature Standard (DSS). The DSS algorithm is discussed in Section 4.4.

For a detailed comparison of the RSA and ElGamal cryptosystems, see [VAN2].

4.3 Integrity Check-Values (Seals)

The utility of cryptographic techniques extends far beyond the provision of confidentiality services. We next consider how these techniques can provide the basis for data integrity and data origin authentication services.

Data integrity and/or data origin authentication for a message can be provided as follows. The originator of the message generates, using all data bits of the message contents, an *appendix* which is transmitted along with the message. The message recipient checks that the received message content and appendix are consistent before accepting the message content as being genuine. This is similar to common error-detection procedures, such as attaching a cyclic redundancy check (CRC) to a message. However, there is one major difference. The prospect of a deliberate attack has to be taken into account. If an active attacker changes a message, there is nothing to prevent him from recalculating and replacing the CRC on a message, so the recipient will not detect that data modification occurred. To protect against such attacks, the process for generating the appendix employs a secret key. The recipient of a message can be confident that, if message contents and appendix are consistent on receipt, the appendix was generated by someone who knows the key. Hence, message modification by an intruder will almost certainly be detected.

This *integrity-checking* procedure is known by many names. In the banking field it is called *message authentication*. In OSI security standards, it is often called *sealing*. The appendix is variously known as a seal, integrity check-value (ICV), message authentication code (MAC), or message integrity code (MIC).

The general mechanism is illustrated in Figure 4-3. At the originating system, a cryptographic appendix-generation process is applied across a message, to yield a (usually shorter) appendix string which accompanies the message in transit. At the recipient system, the same appendix-generation process is applied to the received message, using the same key, and the result is compared with the appendix value received with the message.

Banking industry standards (e.g., ANSI X9.9 and ISO 8730) specify a particular appendix-generation process to apply to message authentication codes for financial transactions. This process, which uses a symmetric cryptosystem such as DES, is illustrated in Figure 4-4. It involves padding the message as necessary to be a multiple of the cryptosystem block size (64 bits for DES), then applying the encryption process in CBC mode to generate an appendix. For a discussion of variations of this technique, see [JUE1].

Other appendix-generation processes exist, such as that discussed in [TSU1] and used with the Internet SNMP protocol (described in Chapter 16).

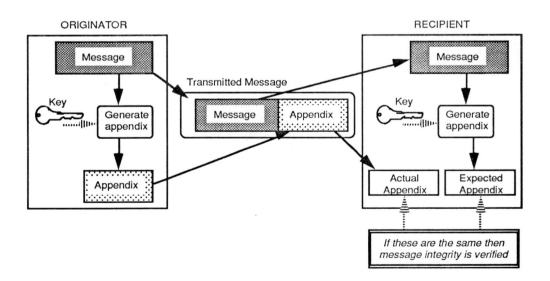

Figure 4-3: General Sealing Scheme

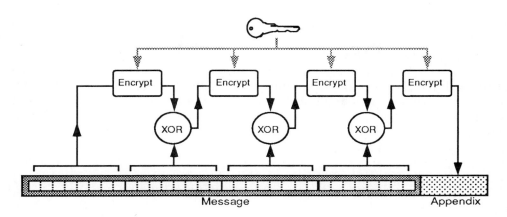

Figure 4-4: Appendix Generation Using a Symmetric Block Cipher

This approach, illustrated in Figure 4-5, does not require use of a symmetric cryptosystem, but instead employs a *hash function*. A hash function is a one-way function which maps values from a large (possibly very large) domain into a comparatively small range[6]. (Hash functions are discussed further in Section 4.4.) The appendix-generation process involves either prefixing or suffixing a secret key to the message data string, then applying the hash function to this concatenation. The output of the hash function provides the appendix.

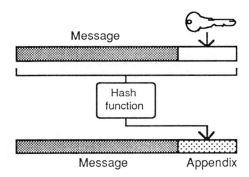

Figure 4-5: Appendix Generation Using a Hash Function

---

[6] There are sometimes considered to be two types of hash function — *unkeyed* hash functions, which always generate the same output data from the same input data, and *keyed* hash functions, which employ a cryptographic key as a secondary input. In this book, use of the unqualified term *hash function* should be taken to indicate an unkeyed hash function.

4.4   Digital Signatures

A *digital signature* can be considered a special case of a seal. It is used where there needs to be sufficient confidence in the source of a message (as verified through the seal) that it can be considered at least as good as verifying the source of a written message on the basis of a written signature. The digital signature may need to be used as the basis of resolving a dispute between the originator and the recipient of a message (e.g., a check or business document). The party with most to gain by falsifying the message will very likely be the recipient. Hence, the recipient must not be able to generate a digital signature which is indistinguishable from one generated by the originator.

For this reason, a sealing process like the DES-based or hash-based processes described above is usually inadequate for this purpose. The recipient knows the key used to generate the seal. The only way to use such a process for digital signature purposes is in conjunction with a secure hardware device which is under the control of a trusted third party. The recipient is provided with a tamperproof device which is capable of verifying that a seal is correct but is not capable of generating a seal for the same key. The key is stored within the device where the recipient cannot access it; its management is under the control of a trusted third party.

Public-key cryptosystems provide more powerful digital signature capabilities, and do not require that the verification key be kept secret from the recipient.

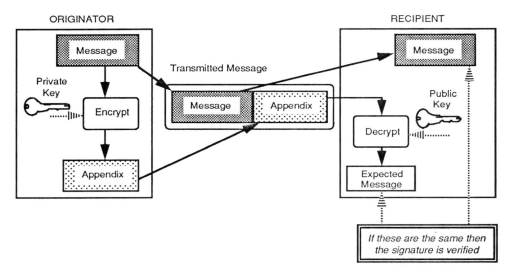

Figure 4-6: Simplistic Digital Signature Scheme

A simplistic digital signature technique employing a reversible public-key cryptosystem such as RSA is illustrated in Figure 4-6. The originator of a message generates an encrypted version of the message, using the public-key system in the authentication mode (i.e., the encryption key is the private key of the originator). This encrypted version of the message is sent as an appendix, along with the plaintext message. The recipient, who needs to know the corresponding decryption key (the public key of the originator), can decrypt the appendix and compare it with the plaintext contents. If the two are the same, the recipient can be assured that the originator knew the encryption key, and that the message contents were not changed en route.

A public-key-based digital signature scheme like the above has the valuable property that *any* potential message recipient will have the ability to check the signature, because the decryption key (the originator's public key) can be made publicly known without compromising security.

An objection to the above scheme is its cost in terms of processing and communications overheads. Encryption and decryption have to be applied to the entire message contents, and the volume of data sent is at least double the basic message size. The scheme also has cryptographic weaknesses which can be overcome with the modification we are about to describe [DEN3].

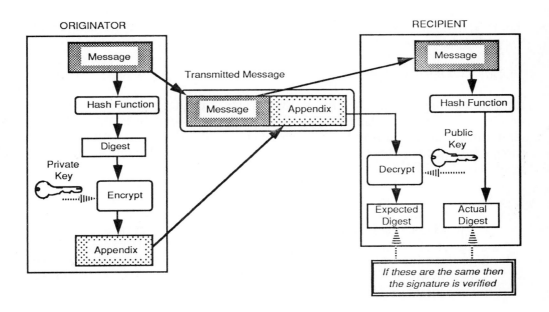

Figure 4-7: Digital Signature Scheme Using Encrypted-Hash Appendix

To improve the scheme, a hash function is introduced into the processing, as shown in Figure 4-7. The hash function is used to generate, from the message content requiring protection, a much smaller data item known as a *message digest*. The digest has the property that, in general, any change to the message will result in a different digest.

With this scheme, the originator applies the hash function to obtain the digest, then encrypts the digest to give the appendix which is transmitted with the message. On receiving the message, the recipient recomputes the digest, and also decrypts the appendix. It then compares these two values. If they match, then the recipient is assured that the originator knew the encryption key, and that the message contents were not changed en route.

When using RSA this way, the padding convention for the value being encrypted is important. For example, if the hashed digest is much shorter than the RSA modulus, and it is padded out by adding 0-bits to the left-hand end, this results in applying RSA to a very small integer value. This has certain cryptographic weaknesses. If the padding is with 1-bits, these weaknesses are overcome. More complex padding schemes are recommended by some researchers.

Other techniques for providing digital signatures have been devised — see [MIT1] for a full coverage. Two specific techniques are addressed below — the ISO/IEC standard for digital signatures giving message recovery, and the U.S. Digital Signature Standard (DSS). Both of these techniques are important, by virtue of being embodied in recognized standards.

Digital Signature with Message Recovery

International standard ISO/IEC 9796 defines a digital signature technique, which may or may not use the appendix-based digital signature approach. The technique is designed for signing messages of limited length, with a minimal resource requirement for verification. It uses a reversible public-key cryptosystem, usually RSA.

There are two ways of using ISO/IEC 9796:

- As a method for signing very small messages. No hash function is involved, and the plaintext content of the signed value is recovered as part of the verification process (the signed value is effectively transferred in an encrypted form via the signature process). These characteristics are well suited to signature requirements encountered in authentication and key management protocols.
- As a signature algorithm applied to a hashed digest of a larger message. This amounts to applying a sophisticated padding convention to the digest. (The ISO/IEC 9796 technique is used this way in the ANSI RSA signature standard, Part 1 of X9.31.)

To explain the ISO/IEC 9796 process, assume that the reversible algorithm employed is RSA. The length of the message to be signed must be no greater than half the RSA modulus size. The signing process involves the following steps:

- The message bits are padded with 0-bits, if necessary, to give an integral number of octets.
- The resultant string is extended, if necessary, by repeated self-concatenation to give a string with length at least half the RSA modulus size.
- Artificial redundancy is added by interleaving the extended message octets with redundancy octets, the values of which are derived from corresponding extended message octets.
- The signature is obtained by performing an RSA encryption on the result.

The corresponding signature verification process involves performing an RSA decryption on the signature, extracting the message octets, and checking the correctness of the redundancy octets.

The U.S. Digital Signature Standard

In August 1991, the U.S. National Institute of Standards and Technology (NIST), issued an annoucement of a proposed Digital Signature Standard (DSS), with a request for comments thereon [NIS3]. In conjunction with this announcement, a technical specification for the proposed standard was made available, describing the Digital Signature Algorithm (DSA). The public review of the proposed DSS resulted in substantial negative comment (see [RIV2] for a good sampling). The main areas of negative comment were technical and performance concerns, objections to introducing DSA in competition with the *de facto* signature standard RSA, and patent issues. The NIST response is in [SMI2]. The negative comment resulted in some small technical changes to the proposal, which is subsequently being progressed by NIST towards publication as a FIPS PUB standard. It is also being progressed as Part 1 of ANSI standard X9.30.

DSA employs an irreversible public-key system, based on the ElGamal approach, as modified by Schnorr [SCH1]. Its security depends upon the difficulty of calculating discrete logarithms. Let:

$$y = g^x \bmod p$$

where p is a prime and g is an element of suitably large order[7] modulo p. It is simple to calculate y, given g, x, and p, but it is extremely difficult to calculate x, given y, g, and p. This gives a basis for a public-key system where x is a private key and y is a public key.

The system uses three integers, p, q, and g, which can be made public and common to a group of users. p is a prime modulus, of a size in the range 512 to 1024 bits.[8] q is a 160-bit prime divisor of p - 1. g is chosen as follows:

that:

$$g = j^{[(p - 1)/q]} \bmod p, \text{ where } j \text{ is any random integer with } 1 < j < p \text{ such}$$

$$j^{[(p - 1)/q]} \bmod p > 1.$$

For a given originator, private key x is selected randomly, with $1 < x < q$. Public key y is calulated as indicated above.

The process of signing and verifying a message is illustrated in Figure 4-8. To sign a message which has digest h, the user chooses a random integer k (with $0 < k < q$) and computes, using the private key x, the two numbers:

$$r = (g^k \bmod p) \bmod q$$

$$s = (k^{-1}(h + xr)) \bmod q$$

where k^{-1} is the multiplicative inverse of $k \bmod q$; i.e., $(k^{-1} k) \bmod q = 1$ and $0 < k^{-1} < q$. The pair of values (r, s) constitutes the signature appendix for the message.

To verify a received signature (say r', s') accompanying a message with digest h', the recipient first checks that $0 < r' < q$ and $0 < s' < q$. If either condition is violated, the signature is rejected. Otherwise, the recipient then computes from s' and h' a value v. For the signature to verify correctly, this value needs to be the same as the value r' sent in the signature. The calculation of v is as follows:

$$w = (s')^{-1} \bmod q$$

$$u1 = (h'w) \bmod q$$

---

[7] This means that the smallest positive integer i, such that $g^i \bmod p = 1$, is sufficiently large.

[8] The modulus size is an algorithm parameter, which can take values from 512 to 1024 bits in 64-bit increments.

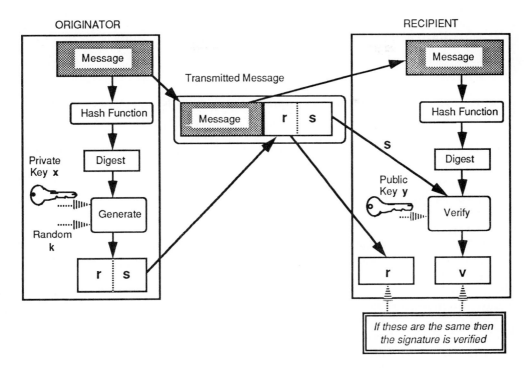

Figure 4-8: DSA Digital Signature Scheme

$u2 = ((r')w) \bmod q$

$v = ((g^{u1}\ y^{u2}) \bmod p) \bmod q$

For a mathematical proof of the validity of these formulae, and the infeasibility of generating a valid r, s pair without knowing the private key x, see appendices to the DSA specification.

Note that an implementation of DSA does not provide any capability to encrypt data for confidentiality purposes. While this may appear a deficiency, it can also be a benefit, because it can be harder to obtain export approval for equipment capable of encryption. Another characteristic of DSA is that its verification process is much more processing-resource-intensive than its generation process.

The RSA and DSA digital signature schemes are likely to be seen as competitors for some time to come. In terms of the function provided (for digital signature purposes) and the cryptographic strength, the schemes seem essentially equivalent. The choice between them will therefore rest on factors such as performance, licensing issues, and political acceptability.

Hash Functions

Hash functions used in sealing or digital signature processes need to have the following properties:

- The function must be truly one-way, i.e., it must be computationally infeasible to construct an input message which hashes to a given digest.
- It must be computationally infeasible to construct two messages which hash to the same digest.

Any weakness in these properties may result in a weakness in the sealing or digital signature process which uses the hash function. For example, if an active attacker can examine a message and its digest and deduce another message content with the same digest, he can substitute that message content. The substitution will not be detected, regardless of the strength of the cryptosystem used in generating the appendix.

The design of good hash functions has proven a difficult task. Many different hash functions have been proposed, and the majority of them have subsequently been shown to have weaknesses of some sort (see [MIT1] for further details). At the time of publication, the most credible hash functions used in open-system networks are:

- Hash functions based on block cipher algorithms such as DES [MER2]. Two particular DES-based functions, known as MDC2 and MDC4, have been promoted by IBM [MAT1].
- The series of hash functions known as MD2, MD4, and MD5 [KAL1, RIV3, RIV4]. These all generate 128-bit outputs. MD2 is the oldest, having been included in the original Internet Privacy Enhanced Mail proposal in 1989. MD4 is much faster, especially on 32-bit processors, and can be coded quite compactly. MD5 is a little slower than MD4 and is probably no stronger cryptographically (in fact, it is currently thought to be weaker).
- The U.S. government Secure Hash Algorithm (SHA), specified in FIPS PUB 180 and Part 2 of ANSI X9.30. SHA is an adaptation of MD4, which generates a 160-bit output (for compatibility with the DSA algorithm). Given the longer output size, SHA appears more powerful than MD2, MD4, or MD5 and can be expected to gain widespread acceptance.

4.5 Introduction to Key Management

The cryptographic techniques described above all depend upon cryptographic keys. Management of these keys is itself a complex subject and a crucial aspect of providing security. Key management includes ensuring that key values generated have the necessary properties, making keys known in advance to the parties that will use them, and ensuring that keys are protected as necessary against disclosure and/or substitution. The methods of key management vary substantially depending on whether the keys being managed are those of symmetric cryptosystems or of public-key cryptosystems.

All keys have limited lifetimes. This is necessary for two reasons:

- Cryptanalysis is facilitated by having large amounts of ciphertext on which to work; the more a key is used, the greater the opportunity for an attacker to gather ciphertext.
- Given that a key can conceivably be compromised, or an encryption/decryption process with a particular key cryptanalyzed, limiting the lifetimes of keys limits the damage that can occur.

The period for which use a particular key is authorized is called the *crypto-period* for that key.

In general, the life cycle of a key includes the following phases:

- key generation and, possibly, registration;
- key distribution;
- key activation/deactivation;
- key replacement or key update (sometimes called *re-keying*);
- key revocation; and
- key termination, involving destruction and, possibly, archival.

Key *generation* needs to take into account the recognized constraints for the specific cryptosystem (e.g., avoiding weak keys for RSA). Generation also has to ensure that an adequately random process is involved. If there is any known bias in a key selection process, an attacker using an exhaustive approach may benefit tremendously from trying the more likely candidates first. The task of providing a suitable random number generator for this purpose should not be underestimated. A truly random process, such as a (hardware) random noise source, is preferable. A pseudorandom software process operating upon a secret random initial seed may be adequate, but the full characteristics of such a system need to be analyzed carefully before assuming it is suitable for key generation.

Key *registration* involves binding a generated key with its particular use. For example, a key to be used in authenticating a digital signature needs to be bound with the identity to which the signature will be attributed. This binding has to be securely registered with some authority.

Key *distribution* is addressed in Sections 4.6 and 4.7. Key *activation/de-activation* and key *replacement/update* are associated with key distribution.

Key *revocation* may be necessary in exceptional circumstances. Reasons for key revocation include removal of a system with which a key was associated, suspicion that a particular key may have been compromised, or changes in the purpose for which the key was being used (e.g., increased security classification).

Key *destruction* involves obliterating all traces of a key. The value of a key may persist long after it has ceased to be actively used. For example, an encrypted data stream recorded now may contain *information* which will still be confidential several years into the future; the secrecy of any key used for confidentiality purposes needs to be maintained until the protected information no longer needs to be considered confidential. Also, the ability to prove the legitimacy of a digital signature in a legal test (possibly several years hence) will depend upon ensuring that the key or keys involved remain protected throughout the entire intervening period. This makes it important to securely destroy all copies of sensitive keys after their active use terminates. For example, it must not be possible for an attacker to determine old key values by examining old data files, memory contents, or discarded equipment.

Archival of a key and its binding is required if an assured copy of a key might be required in the future, e.g., as evidence of the validity of an old digital signature for non-repudiation purposes. Such archiving must be very well protected, as both the integrity and the confidentiality of the key will usually need to be maintained.

In general, protection of a key needs to be enforced throughout its entire lifetime, from generation to termination. All keys need to be protected for integrity purposes, as the possibility of an intruder modifying or substituting a key can compromise the protection service for which the key is being used. Additionally, all keys, except for public keys in public-key cryptosystems, need to be protected for confidentiality purposes. In practice, the safest way to store a key is in a physically secure location. When physical security of a key is impractical (e.g., when it needs to be communicated from one place to another), the key must be protected by other means, such as:

- assignment to a trusted party, e.g., a bonded courier, who will guarantee protection of items held or carried;
- use of a dual-control system, whereby a key is split into two parts with each part being entrusted to a separate person and/or environment for purposes of communication or intermediate storage; or

- protection during communication, by confidentiality (e.g., by encryption under another key) and/or integrity services.

The latter item introduces the concept of layers of cryptographic protection (and layers of keys) in network security. This concept arises frequently in key management.

4.6 Distribution of Secret Keys

Key Distribution Using Symmetric Techniques

Substantive commercial use of symmetric cryptosystems started in the early 1980s, especially in banking, following the standardization of DES and the banking industry's equivalent — the ANSI Data Encryption Algorithm (DEA). The prospective widespread application of DES raised the issue of how to manage DES keys [GRE1]. It resulted in the development of the ANSI X9.17 standard on *Financial Institution Key Management (Wholesale)*, which was completed in 1985 [BAL1].

An early conclusion of the work on financial institution key management was that multiple layers of keys were needed. Keys used for encrypting bulk data would need to be changed quite frequently (e.g., on a per-session or daily basis). Clearly, this could not be accommodated through manual key distribution systems, because of the high costs of such systems. This led to the recognition of two distinct types of key — *primary keys*, used to protect bulk data, and *key-encrypting keys* used to protect primary keys when they need to be communicated from system to system. A primary key, when used to protect data during a communication session, is sometimes known as a *session key*. A key-encrypting key is sometimes known as a *master key*.

ANSI X9.17 went further in adopting a three-level hierarchy of keys:

- (manually distributed) master keys (KKMs);
- (on-line distributed) key-encrypting keys (KKs); and
- primary keys, or data keys (KDs).

Basically, KKMs protect KKs or KDs in transit. KKs protect KDs in transit.

Master keys form the basis for a long-term keying relationship between two communicating parties. There are two basic types of configuration. The first, a point-to-point configuration, is illustrated in Figure 4-9. The two communicating parties share a master key, and no other parties are involved. In this configuration, either party generates new KKs or KDs as necessary, and communicates them to the other party under the protection of the master key or a KK.

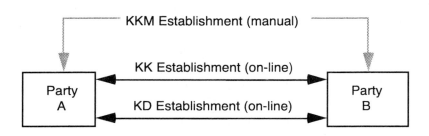

Figure 4-9: Point-to-Point Configuration

A major problem with this type of configuration is that, if there is a community of *n* parties all wishing to communicate with each other, the number of manually distributed master keys needed is of order n^2. With a large network, the manual key distribution problem becomes intractable. This problem is alleviated greatly with the introduction of a *key center* into the configuration, as illustrated in Figure 4-10. In this configuration, communicating parties need to each share a master key with the key center, but not with each other. Hence, for a community of *n* parties, the number of manually distributed master keys needed is *n*.

There are two variations of key center configurations — *key distribution centers* and *key translation centers*. With a key distribution center, when party *A* wishes to establish a key with party *B*, it requests a key from the key center. The key center generates the desired key and returns it to *A*. It is returned in two forms — the first protected under the master key shared between *A* and the center, the second protected under the master key shared between *B* and the center. *A* retains the first for its own use, and passes the second to *B* for its use.

A key translation center is similar, except that one of the parties generates the required key, rather than having the center generate the key. When party *A* wants to use a locally generated key to communicate with party *B*, it generates the key and sends it to the center, protected under the master key shared between *A* and the center. The center decrypts the primary key, re-encrypts it under the master key shared between *B* and the center, and returns it to *A* who, in turn, passes it to *B* for use.

A key management protocol to support such key transfers also has to provide protection against replay of old key transfers. Failure to do so may result in an intruder being able to substitute keys, e.g., repeatedly reuse an old key that was compromised some time in the past. Ways of countering replay attacks include:

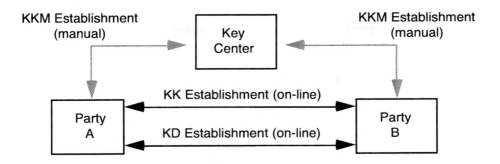

Figure 4-10: Key Center Configuration

- *Key counters*: Every key transfer message has a sequence number sealed with it. The number is incremented on each message between a pair of parties using the same key-encrypting key.
- *Key offsetting*: The sequence count associated with a key-encrypting key is exclusive-ORed with that key before it is used to encrypt another key for distribution. The receiver also *offsets* the key-encrypting key with the same count before decrypting.
- *Time-stamps*: Every key transfer message has a time-stamp sealed with it. Messages with time-stamps that are too old are rejected by the receiver.

The ANSI X9.17 standard defines a key management protocol, in terms of formats for messages known as Cryptographic Service Messages (CSMs). These are messages exchanged between a pair of communicating parties to establish new keys and replace old keys. They may carry encrypted keys and also initializing vectors for chaining and feedback modes of operation of symmetric cryptosystems. The messages have integrity checking based on ANSI X9.9.

In ANSI X9.17, the key-encrypting keys may actually be key pairs, supporting triple encryption (encrypt with first key, then decrypt with second key, then encrypt with first key). This increases the strength of the algorithm substantially.

The above approach of using symmetric techniques for the distribution of symmetric keys is still used in many environments. Increasingly, however, it is being replaced by new approaches for distributing symmetric keys, which use public-key techniques and/or the Diffie-Hellman key derivation method (discussed later in this chapter).

Key Usage Control

In modern network security implementations, there are many different keys which are used for many different purposes. For example, primary keys are used to encrypt and decrypt data, while key-encrypting keys are used to protect other keys during distribution. In addition to preserving secrecy of keys, it is sometimes very important for key distribution processes to ensure that a key intended for one purpose is not interchanged with a key intended for another purpose. This leads to the requirement to seal, together with a key value, an indication of the key's legitimate usage.

As an example of this requirement, consider the distribution of primary and key-encrypting symmetric keys. Suppose it were possible for an active attacker to replace a primary key with a key intended for key-encrypting purposes. A cryptographic device can be expected to have a mode whereby it will use a primary key to decrypt a piece of ciphertext and return the result externally to the device. However, as a protective measure, the same device will likely not have a mode where it returns externally the result of decrypting with a key-encrypting key (the result will normally be retained in physically secure storage internal to the device). If an attacker can convince the device that a key-encrypting key is actually a primary key (e.g., by tampering with the key distribution protocol), he can now use the device to decrypt (and deliver externally) values of keys protected by that key-encrypting key.

For further discussion of this subject, see [MAT1].

Key Distribution via Access Enforcement Key Server

The ANSI X9.17 type of key distribution system is designed for establishing keys to enable systems to conduct protected pair-wise communication activities. In the typical enterprise computer network, another type of key distribution requirement can arise. This requirement can also be satisfied using symmetric cryptographic techniques, in conjunction with authentication and access control mechanisms.

It is often necessary to protect a file such that a limited set of users may read it, while the rest of the user community may not. Such files may need to be distributed via various unprotected means, such as posting on public file servers. This can be achieved by the originating user encrypting the file then distributing the file by unprotected means. The decryption key is lodged with a trusted key server, together with a statement of who is authorized to receive that key and decrypt the file. (This statement is an access control statement, such as an access control list; Chapter 6 discusses access control in detail.)

Any user is entitled to request the key from the server, but the server will only supply the key after authenticating the requesting user and checking that the access control statement permits that user to have that key. Communications between users and the key server need to be confidentiality-protected using independently protected communications sessions.

The package of information containing a key and access control statement (plus other information such as algorithm identifier, parameters, and lifetime information) is sometimes called a *key package*.

Key Distribution Using Reversible Public-Key Techniques

Public-key cryptosystems can facilitate key management, especially for indefinitely large networks. With purely symmetric systems, it is necessary to maintain many pair-wise keying relationships and to deploy trusted on-line key centers or servers. With public-key systems, far fewer keying relationships need be maintained, and the public keys can be distributed without confidentiality protection (this subject is discussed in Section 4.7). Countering these advantages of public-key systems, symmetric systems have an important advantage, namely a far lower processing overhead than public-key systems. This makes them particularly attractive for the bulk encryption of large volumes of data.

To benefit from all the advantages, a hybrid approach can be employed. For encrypting bulk data, symmetric cryptosystems are used, i.e., the primary keys are symmetric keys. However, the system of symmetric key-encrypting keys is replaced by a reversible public-key cryptosystem. For example, if party *A* wants to establish a symmetric primary key with party *B*, using RSA, it can do so as follows. Party *A* first obtains a copy of party *B*'s public key (using the methods described in Section 4.7). Party *A* then generates a random symmetric key and sends it to Party *B*, encrypted under Party *B*'s public key. Only Party *B* can learn the symmetric key value, as only Party *B* knows the private key needed to decrypt the message. Hence the two parties establish shared knowledge of the symmetric key and can proceed to use it for protecting data communicated between them.

This scheme, which requires neither on-line servers nor interparty negotiations, is well suited to such applications as encrypting electronic mail.

Diffie-Hellman Key Derivation

An alternative approach to establishing a symmetric primary key, which has some advantages over the above public-key-encryption approach, was devised by Whitfield Diffie and Martin Hellman [DIF1]. This is known as Diffie-Hellman key derivation, or exponential key derivation. It works as illustrated in Figure 4-11.

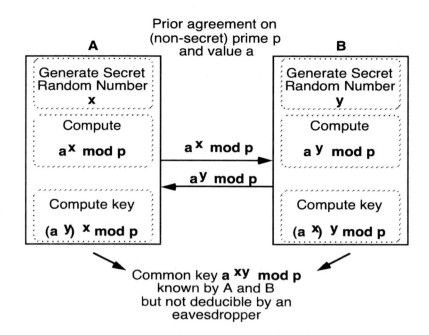

Figure 4-11: Diffie-Hellman Key Derivation

Parties *A* and *B* agree, in advance, upon a prime number p and a primitive element a in GF(p).[9] Prime p should be such that (p - 1) has a large prime factor. This agreement could be on the basis of published systemwide constants or could result from previous communications (note, though, that the values must be known reliably by both parties). As the first step in deriving a key, party *A* generates a random number x, $2 \leq x \leq p$ - 2. It then calculates a^x mod p and sends this value to party *B*. Party *B* generates a random number y, $2 \leq y \leq p$ - 1, calculates a^y mod p, and sends this value to party *A*. Then party *A* calculates $(a^y)^x$ mod p and party *B* calculates $(a^x)^y$ mod p. Both parties now know a common key, $K = a^{xy}$ mod p.

While this exchange was occurring, an eavesdropper could easily have learned both a^x mod p and a^y mod p. However, because of the difficulty of

---

[9] In modular arithmetic, when the modulus is a prime p, the set of integers mod p, together with the arithmetic operations, is a finite field, i.e., a finite integral domain in which every element besides 0 has a multiplicative inverse. This set of integers is known as the Galois field GF(p). A primitive element of GF(p) is an integer a, $1 \leq a \leq p$, such that a, a^2, ... a^{p-1} are, in some order, equal to 1, 2, ... p - 1. For example, with p = 7, a primitive element is a = 3, since a = 3, a^2 = 2, a^3 = 6, a^4 = 4, a^5 = 5 and a^6 = 1. Such primitive elements always exist.

computing discrete logarithms, it is not feasible for him to calculate x or y, hence not feasible for him to calculate K.

For this key derivation approach to be useful, it must be done in conjunction with an entity authentication process. (There is little point in establishing a key with another party if you are not entirely sure who that party is!) This aspect is pursued later in the book, in discussing authentication, confidentiality, and data integrity services and their interactions.

The main reason why Diffie-Hellman key derivation is better than public-key encryption of primary keys is that it limits the impact of a cryptosystem compromise. With public-key encryption, if the cryptosystem is broken or if the private key is compromised, all primary keys protected under that system, and all traffic protected under those primary keys, are compromised. If a Diffie-Hellman derivation is compromised, only the traffic protected under the one primary key is compromised. Compromise of authentication, which employs a different cryptographic technique, is unaffected by a Diffie-Hellman compromise, and vice versa.

4.7 Distribution of Public-Key Cryptosystem Keys

The key distribution requirements for public-key cryptosystems are inherently very different from those for symmetric cryptosystems. With a symmetric cryptosystem, it is necessary to place copies of one key in the hands of two parties who will use it to protect communications between them, while keeping knowledge of the key secret from all other parties. With a public-key cryptosystem, it is necessary to place one key (the private key) in the hands of one party, keeping knowledge of it secret from all other parties. At the same time, an associated key (the public key) is made public knowledge to anyone who wishes to communicate securely with the holder of the private key.

Public-Key Distribution

When distributing a public key, confidentiality is not required. However, it *is* essential that the *integrity* of the public key be maintained. There must not be any opportunity for an attacker to substitute some other value for what party B believes to be the public key of party A. Otherwise, the following type of attack might succeed. An attacker forges a message purporting to come from party A, and generates a digital signature using his or her own private key. The attacker then substitutes his or her own public key for what party B believes to be party A's public key. Party B's check of the digital signature (using the wrong public key) will indicate that all is well, i.e., the attacker has succeeded in masquerading as party A.

Hence, distribution of public keys is *not* as simple as publishing them in a telephone directory (unless users have a high level of trust in that directory, which can be difficult to achieve).

This leads to public keys being distributed in the form of *certificates*. A certificate, generally speaking, is a data structure which is digitally signed by some party which users of the certificate will trust. A *public-key certificate* is a data structure which binds the identifier of some party (the *subject*) with a public-key value. The certificate data structure is digitally signed by some other party known as a *certification authority*. Figure 4-12 illustrates a possible structure for such a certificate.

CERTIFICATE

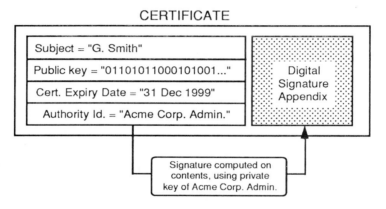

Figure 4-12: Sample Structure of a Public-Key Certificate

Public-key certificates can be stored and distributed in an unprotected way, including publication in a directory whose services are not necessarily trusted. Provided a user knows in advance the authentic public key of the certification authority, that user can check the validity of the signature on the certificate. If this checks correctly, the user can be confident that the certificate carries a valid public key for the identified party.

In a self-contained network (e.g., a corporate network) this constitutes an easily realizable system. Initially, all prospective user sytems are given, via some reliable means (e.g., manual distribution), a copy of the public key of the network's certification authority. They can then use this key to verify public-key certificates for all other network users, hence reliably obtain the public key of any such user.

This certification approach also extends to an environment where multiple certification authorities need to be involved, i.e., where it is not practicable for a single certification authority to know of and certify all public keys of all potential communicating parties. Suppose party *B*, who is in the domain of certification authority CA_2, wants to obtain a reliable copy of the public key of party A, who is in the domain of certification authority CA_1. Provided authorities CA_1 and CA_2 adequately trust each other, CA_2 will be prepared to issue a certificate which certifies the public key of CA_1, and CA_1 will do likewise for CA_2's public key. Given this certificate, plus the public-key certificate of party A issued by CA_1, party B can reliably obtain a copy of party A's public key. B does this by first obtaining (from CA_2's certificate of CA_1's public key) a reliable copy of CA_1's public key. B then uses this key to verify CA_1's certificate of party A's public key.

The above arrangement generalizes to the scenario where there is any *chain of trust* through multiple certification authorities linking parties A and B. Provided a complete certificate chain is made available, and provided party B has sufficient cause to trust the issuers of the certificates in the chain, party B can reliably obtain a copy of the public key of any party A reachable through such a chain of trust.

To simplify the construction of such chains and limit their length, certification authorities may be organized in a hierarchy, e.g., as illustrated in Figure 4-13. This can even be extended to a global scale, i.e., there is an international certification authority which issues certificates for national certification authorities, which in turn issue certificates to national entities (government agencies, corporations, or other organizations), and so on.

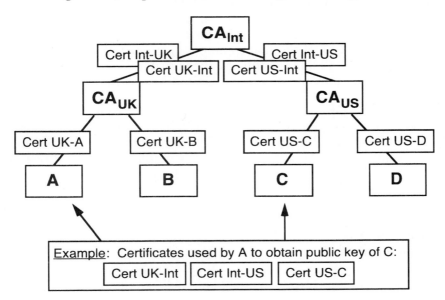

Figure 4-13: Example of a Hierarchical Certification Authority Structure

Suppose that, in Figure 4-13, CA_{Int} is an international certification authority and CA_{UK} and CA_{US} are national certification authorities for the United Kingdom and United States respectively. Suppose organization A in the United Kingdom wants a certified public key of organization C in the United States. This might be achieved using a certificate chain comprising three certificates:

- *Cert-UK-Int* (the U.K. authority's certificate for the international authority's public key): As A knows *a priori* the public key of the U.K. authority, A can confirm it has a reliable copy of the international authority's public key.
- *Cert-Int-US* (the international authority's certificate for the U.S. authority's public key): Using the public key from the previous certificate, A can confirm it has a reliable copy of the U.S. authority's public key.
- *Cert-US-C* (the U.S. authority's certificate for organization C): Using the public key from the previous certificate, A can confirm it has a reliable copy of C's public key.

With such a scheme, it is important to note that checking of the certificate chain is not just a matter of mechanically checking the signatures, but also of checking the identities of the certification authorities to ensure that they are adequately trusted for the current purpose. For example, there may be nothing preventing generation of a certificate chain in which the international certification authority certifies the public key of the national certification authority of a tiny third-world state, and the latter authority certifies the public key of the President of the United States. While all the signatures may check correctly, it may be unwise for someone, say, in the United Kingdom to blindly trust such a chain.

Another very important point to note about such a scheme is the criticality of the security surrounding the authorities at the upper levels of the hierarchy. Suppose, for example, an attacker compromises the security of the U.S. certification authority, to the extent the attacker is able to forge certificates from that authority (e.g., the attacker learns the authority's private key). This will enable the attacker to:

- forge digital signatures from anybody in the United States and generate certificate chains that will convince anybody in the world the signatures are legitimate; *and*
- forge digital signatures from anybody outside the United States and generate certificate chains that will convince anybody in the United States the signatures are legitimate.

For the international certification authority, the risk can be even higher. If we assume that any chain up the tree and down again is usable, then a compromise of the international authority could devastate the entire system. An attacker at this level can potentially forge digital signatures from anybody in the world and convince anybody else in the world that the signatures are legitimate.

This risk is alleviated somewhat by forbidding redundant certificate chains. For example, we can require that certification chains involving pairs of end systems within the domain of the U.S. authority must not extend above that authority, i.e., when *D* verifies *C*'s public key, the single-certificate chain *Cert-US-C* is acceptable but the (redundant) three-certificate chain of *Cert-US-Int*, *Cert-Int-US*, *Cert-US-C* is not acceptable. This at least means that domestic U.S. communications cannot be compromised by an attack on the international certification authority.

For high-risk environments, the form of a certificate can be extended to include two signatures, generated independently by separate agents of the certification authority, using separate cryptographic devices possibly at separate sites. This greatly reduces the vulnerability to an attack on a certification authority's system, which could prove catastrophic by potentially compromising the protection of all users of that authority.

Key Pair Generation

Let us now consider the generation of a private/public key pair, and the means of ensuring the secure despatch of:

(a) the private key to its *owner* system; and
(b) the public key to a certification authority.

To minimize vulnerabilities, the key generation process is best carried out either within the owner system or within the certification authority system, thereby necessitating only one protected key transfer. Generation within the owner system is simplest, as the subsequent transfer of the public key to the certification authority system requires only integrity protection (not confidentiality protection). This arrangement is also the best from the security perspective, as it is possible to construct a tamperproof piece of equipment which generates its own key pair and which subsequently uses the private key of the pair. The private key need *never* leave that tamperproof enclosure.

If keys are generated within the certification authority system, transfer of the private key to the owner system will require both integrity and confidentiality protection. In either case, if key archiving is required, reliable copies of both keys will need to be sent to an archiving system (which may be co-located with the certification authority system), and protection measures for such transfers will require very careful consideration.

Certificate Revocation

There are various reasons for needing to revoke previously issued certificates. One reason is that the key needs to be revoked (for reasons as identified in Section 4.5). However, there are other reasons for revoking certificates. For example, if there is a change in the relationship between a public-key owner and a certification authority (e.g., the owner leaves the employ of the organization which had issued a certificate), it may be necessary to revoke a certificate, even though the key itself is not revoked (the owner may take the key with him to his new employer and have a new certificate issued there). Therefore, the more general issue with public-key systems is certificate revocation rather than key revocation.

Certificate revocation is important, and potentially impacts all public-key implementations. Suppose, for example, a certification authority issued a certificate for user U, certifying a public-key value and stating a certificate validity period of six months. This certificate was freely distributed throughout an unbounded user community and cached in various systems. Subsequently, user U suspects his or her private key to have been compromised and requests that the corresponding public key be revoked. The problem is that nobody can be sure who needs to be informed of the revocation. There may well be some unsuspecting user, a long way off, who is verifying signed messages as coming from U when they are actually coming from an intruder in possession of a long-compromised key. Hence, the onus for checking on possible revocation of certificates needs to rest with certificate users.

Certificate revocation is typically accomplished by posting, in a directory, a certificate revocation list (a *CRL*, also known as a *hot-list* or *blacklist*). A revocation list is itself a certificate, signed by the same authority who signed the original certificate(s). Dependent upon factors such as certificate age, value of transaction being processed, etc., a user of a public-key certificate should decide whether or not he should first obtain and check a revocation list before accepting the original certificate at face value.

Because certification authority keys may also need to be revoked from time to time, a user of a certificate chain potentially needs to check revocation lists pertaining to all certificates in the chain (although different criteria may be used for different certificates in deciding whether or not to check for revocations). Appropriate revocation lists always need to be available to users of certificates.

Care has to be taken to avoid having an attacker interfere with the distribution of revocation lists. It is generally adequate to have a fixed procedure whereby revocation lists are updated on a regular basis, even if there are no changes to the revocation information. Also, each revocation list should contain a time-stamp. An entity requiring a revocation list can then be sure it has both a valid list (by checking the certificate signature) and an up-to-date list (by checking the time-stamp).

Case Study: PEM Certification Infrastructure

Internet Privacy Enhanced Mail (PEM) is a security option for Internet electronic mail, which uses a public-key system for authentication and symmetric-key distribution purposes. PEM includes a specification of a supporting public-key certification infrastructure [KEN1]. The overall PEM system is described in Chapter 13 of this book. Here, we consider only the general form of the certification infrastructure, which provides a valuable practical illustration of many of the principles discussed above.

The structure is hierarchical, as illustrated in Figure 4-14. The PEM specification defines the form of the upper levels, and certain rules regarding lower levels. There are three types of certification authority:

- *Internet Policy Registration Authority (IPRA)*: This authority, operated under the auspices of the Internet Society, acts as the root of the certification hierarchy at level 1. It issues certificates only for the next layer of authorities, PCAs.
- *Policy Certification Authorities (PCAs)*: PCAs are at level 2 of the hierarchy, each PCA being certified by the IPRA. A PCA must establish and publish a statement of its policy with respect to certifying users or subordinate certification authorities. Distinct PCAs aim to satisfy different user needs. For example, one PCA (a "regular organizational" PCA) might support the general electronic mail needs of commercial organizations, and another PCA (a "high-assurance" PCA) might have a more stringent policy designed for satisfying legally binding signature requirements.
- *Certification Authorities (CAs)*: CAs are at level 3 of the hierarchy and can also be at lower levels. Those at level 3 are certified by PCAs. CAs represent, for example, particular organizations, particular organizational units (e.g., divisions, departments), or particular geographical areas.

The structure is a tree, with only minor variations. One variation is that a CA at level 3 may be certified by more than one PCA (e.g., CA4 in Figure 4-14). This enables different trust semantics to be applied to different certificate chains which include that CA.

Three main types of policy are identified for certification authorities at the PCA or CA level:

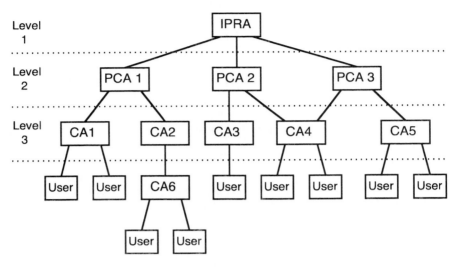

Figure 4-14: PEM Certification Authority Structure

- An *organizational CA* issues certificates to individuals affiliated with an organization, such as a corporation, government body, or educational institution. *Affiliation* might mean employment by a corporation or government body, or being a student of an educational institution.
- A *residential CA* issues certificates to individuals on the basis of geographical address. It is envisioned that civil government entities will assume responsibilities for such certification in due course.
- A *PERSONA CA* is a special case, in which the certification does not claim to link the name in the certificate with a particular physical person or entity. It is established to accommodate users who wish to conceal their identities while making use of PEM security features.

The certificate verification process assumes that every user has a copy of the IPRA's public key. Every certificate chain starts at the IPRA, then proceeds through a PCA, then CAs as necessary.

The IPRA and PCAs are required to generate certificate revocation lists and make them publicly available. PCAs are required to state the revocation list issuing policies for CAs subordinate to them.

The PEM certification structure constitutes a special case of the general hierarchical structure illustrated in Figure 4-13, in which cross-certificates were employed up and down the hierarchy. In the PEM model, there are no upward-directed certificates. The IPRA is considered to be universally trusted by all users for all communications. While this is satisfactory in the PEM environment, it constitutes a trust relationship restriction which may not be acceptable in other environments (In the international example discussed earlier, it was noted that U.S. entities might wish to trust the U.S. certification authority *more* than they trust the international authority; therefore, the tree root is not always the most trusted point.) The PEM structure has the advantages of requiring fewer certificates than the general structure and of leading to straightforward procedures for verifying certificate chains.

A major contribution of the PEM design is the establishment of common technical and procedural conventions by which certification authorities are expected to abide. The PCA concept is particularly interesting as it provides a systematic means of dealing with different trust scenarios. Much valuable experience in practical certification infrastructures will undoubtedly be gained from the PEM project through the 1990s.

Summary

Cryptographic techniques are important building blocks in the implementation of any security service. A cryptosystem defines encryption and decryption transformations, which depend upon the values of keys. A symmetric cryptosystem uses one key for both transformations. A public-key cryptosystem uses separate keys for each transformation.

The only publicly-standardized symmetric cryptosystem is the U.S. Data Encryption Standard (DES), which has been widely used since the 1970s. Due to technological advances, the useful life of single-encryption DES is running out. However, use of multiple-encryption DES systems may provide adequate protection for many applications for many years to come.

Public-key cryptosystems can have an encryption mode and an authentication mode. The RSA algorithm is a reversible algorithm, i.e., it can operate in both modes. The strength of RSA depends upon the difficulty of factoring the product of two large prime numbers. Selection of an appropriate modulus size can make RSA arbitrarily strong. The ElGamal algorithm is an altenative public-key algorithm, the strength of which depends upon the difficulty of computing discrete logarithms.

Integrity check-values or seals are a means of generating an appendix to a transmitted message, using a secret key. This enables a recipient knowing the key to check that the message source and contents are genuine. In banking protocols, the appendix is known as a message authentication code, and the most common appendix generation process employs the DES algorithm. An alternative appendix-generation process can employ a hash function.

A digital signature is an electronic equivalent of verifying the source of a written message on the basis of a written signature. A digital signature is stronger than a seal in that the recipient must not be able to generate a digital signature which is indistinguishable from one generated by the originator. Digital signatures usually employ public-key cryptosystems, often in conjunction with a hash function. The international standard ISO/IEC 9796 defines a digital signature procedure for use with the RSA algorithm. The U.S. proposed Digital Signature Standard uses an alternative approach based on the ElGamal algorithm. The design of suitable accompanying hash functions is a difficult task, and a limited set of credible options exists.

Application of all cryptographic techniques depends upon management of cryptographic keys. All keys have limited lifetimes. The life cycle of a key involves several phases such as generation, distribution, activation/deactivation, revocation , and termination.

Distribution of secret keys can be accomplished using symmetric cryptosystems. Primary keys are distributed encrypted under key-encrypting keys. The ANSI X9.17 standard allows for three such levels of encryption. To keep numbers of keys manageable, on-line key distribution centers or key translation centers are required. Secret keys for symmetric cryptosystems can also be distributed encrypted under a reversible public-key system such as RSA. Another alternative is the Diffie-Hellman technique, which enables two parties to derive on-line a secret key known only to them.

In managing keys for public-key cryptosystems, it is necessary to distribute public keys such that a user is assured he has the correct public key. Public keys are therefore distributed in the form of certificates, signed by a trusted certification authority. In general, multiple certification authorities are required. Certification authorities can certify each others' public keys, leading to certificate chains linking signing and verifying parties. This approach can potentially be extended to a global scale, with a hierarchy of certification authorities. The Internet Privacy Enhanced Mail (PEM) project provides a valuable case study for the construction of such certification authority hierarchies.

Exercises

1. Describe the basic differences between symmetric and public-key cryptosystems. For what purposes are symmetric cryptosystems best suited? For what purposes are public-key cryptosystems best suited?

2. In providing a data integrity service, how can the chaining and feedback modes of DES contribute to protecting against data item replay or re-ordering?

3. What roles can a hash function play in sealing or digital signature techniques? What are the necessary characteristics of such a function?

4. Briefly describe roles that the cryptographic techniques of encryption/decryption, sealing, and digital signature might play in providing the following security services:

    (a) confidentiality;
    (b) data integrity;
    (c) data origin authentication;
    (d) access control; and
    (e) non-repudiation with proof of origin.

5. What are the main events that may occur in the life cycle of a key, and what is their significance, in the cases of:

    (a) a key used for encryption; and
    (b) a key used for digital signature.

6. What are the principal differences between managing the keys of symmetric cryptosystems and managing those of public-key cryptosystems?

7. Party B wants to use a public key of party A to check the signature on a message from Party A. The only certification authority party B trusts is Z. Party A's public key is certified by authority X. Certification authority Y is prepared to certify X's public key, and Z can certify Y's public key. What certificates will party B need? What checks on these certificates should party B perform?

8. Given the scenario of Question 7, if attacker E learns the private key of certification authority Y and wants to forge party A's signature on a message to party B, what certificate chain might E generate to accompany the forged signature?

9. Suppose Party A wants to send a large confidential file to multiple recipients — Parties B, C, and D — all of whom have RSA key pairs. The file is to be sent encrypted, such that no party other than A, B, C or D can determine its contents by monitoring the transmission. Rather than send separate messages to each of B, C, and D, A wants to generate only one message containing only one encrypted version of the file contents. How can this be accomplished?

REFERENCES

[BAL1] D.M. Balenson, "Automated Distribution of Cryptographic Keys Using the Financial Institution Key Management Standard," *IEEE Communications Magazine*, vol. 23, no. 9 (September 1985), pp. 41-46.

[BIH1] E. Biham and A. Shamir, "Differential Cryptanalysis of DES-like Cryptosystems," *Journal of Cryptology*, vol. 4, no. 1 (1991), pp. 3-72.

[BIH2] E. Biham and A. Shamir, "Differential Analysis of the Full 16-round DES," in E. Brickell (Ed.), *Advances in Cryptology — CRYPTO '92 (Lecture Notes in Computer Science)*, Springer-Verlag, Berlin, 1993 (in publication).

[BRA1] G. Brassard, *Modern Cryptology: A Tutorial (Lecture Notes in Computer Science 325)*, Springer-Verlag, Berlin, 1988.

[BRI1] E.F. Brickell, "A Survey of Hardware Implementations of RSA," in G. Brassard (Ed.), *Advances in Cryptology — CRYPTO '89 (Lecture Notes in Computer Science 435)*, Springer-Verlag, Berlin, 1990, pp. 368-370

[DEN1] D.E. Denning, *Cryptography and Data Security*, Addison-Wesley, Reading, MA, 1982.

[DEN2] D.E. Denning, "The Data Encryption Standard Fifteen Years of Public Scrutiny", *Proceedings of the Sixth Annual Computer Security Applications Conference*, Tucson, AZ, December 1990, IEEE Computer Society Press, Los Alamitos, CA, 1990, pp. x-xv.

[DEN3] D.E. Denning, "Digital Signatures with RSA and Other Public-Key Cryptosystems," *Communications of the ACM*, vol. 27, no. 4 (April 1984), pp. 388-392.

[DIF1] W. Diffie and M. Hellman, "New Directions in Cryptography," *IEEE Transactions on Information Theory*, vol. IT-22, no. 6 (1976), pp. 644-654.

[DIF2] W. Diffie, "The First Ten Years of Public Key Cryptology," in Gustavus J. Simmons (Ed.), *Contemporary Cryptology: The Science of Information Integrity*, IEEE Press, New York, 1992, pp. 136-175.

[DUS1] S.R. Dusse and B.S. Kaliski, Jr., "A Cryptographic Library for the Motorola DSP56000," in I.B. Damgård (Ed.), *Advances in Cryptology — EUROCRYPT '90 (Lecture Notes in Computer Science 473)*, Springer-Verlag, Berlin, 1991, pp. 230-244.

[EBE1] H. Eberle, "A High-Speed DES Implementation for Network Implementations", in E. Brickell (Ed.), *Advances in Cryptology — CRYPTO '92 (Lecture Notes in Computer Science)*, Springer-Verlag, Berlin, 1993 (in publication).

[ELG1] T. ElGamal, "A Public Key Cryptosystem and a Signature Scheme Based on Discrete Logarithms," *IEEE Transactions on Information Theory*, vol. IT-31, no. 4 (1985), pp. 469-72.

[GAR1] G. Garon and R. Outerbridge, "DES Watch: An Examination of the Sufficiency of the Data Encryption Standard for Financial Institution Information Security in the 1990's," *Cryptologia*, vol. XV, no. 3 (July 1991), pp. 177-193.

[GOR1] J. Gordon, "Strong RSA Keys," *Electronics Letters*, vol. 20, no. 5, pp. 514-6.

[GRE1] M.B. Greenlee, "Requirements for Key Management Protocols in the Wholesale Financial Services Industry," *IEEE Communications Magazine*, vol. 23, no. 9 (September 1985), pp. 22-28.

[JUE1] R.R. Jueneman, S.M. Matyas, and C.H. Meyer, "Message Authentication," *IEEE Communications Magazine*, vol. 23, no. 9 (September 1985), pp. 29-40.

[KAL1] B. Kaliski, *The MD2 Message-Digest Algorithm*, Request for Comments (RFC) 1319, Internet Activities Board, 1992.

[KEN1] S. Kent, *Privacy Enhancement for Internet Electronic Mail: Part II: Certificate-Based Key Management*, Request for Comments (RFC) 1422, Internet Activities Board, 1993.

[MAT1] S.M. Matyas, "Key Handling with Control Vectors," *IBM Systems Journal*, vol. 30, no. 2 (1991), pp. 151-174.

[MER1] R.C. Merkle and M.E. Hellman, "On the Security of Multiple Encryption," *Communications of the ACM*, vol. 27, no. 7 (July 1981), pp. 465-67.

[MER2] R.C. Merkle, "One-Way Hash Functions and DES, in G. Brassard (Ed.), *Advances in Cryptology — CRYPTO '89 (Lecture Notes in Computer Science 435)*, Springer-Verlag, Berlin, 1990, pp. 428-446.

[MEY1] C.H. Meyer and S.M. Matyas, *Cryptography: A New Dimension in Computer Data Security*, John Wiley and Sons, New York, 1982.

[MIT1] C.J. Mitchell, F. Piper, and P. Wild, "Digital Signatures," in G.J. Simmons (Ed.), *Contemporary Cryptology: The Science of Information Integrity*, IEEE Press, New York, 1992, pp. 325-378.

[NEC1] J. Nechvatal, "Public Key Cryptography," in G.J. Simmons (Ed.), *Contemporary Cryptology: The Science of Information Integrity*, IEEE Press, New York, 1992, pp. 178-288.

[NIS1] U.S. Department of Commerce, National Institute of Standards and Technology, "Validating the Correctness of Hardware Implementations of the NBS Data Encryption Standard," NIST Special Publication 500-20.

[NIS2] U.S. Department of Commerce, National Institute of Standards and Technology, "Maintenance Testing for the Data Encryption Standard," NIST Special Publication 500-61.

[NIS3] U.S. Department of Commerce, National Institute of Standards and Technology, "A Proposed Federal Information Processing Standard for Digital Signature Standard (DSS)," *Federal Register*, August 30, 1991.

[RIV1] R.L. Rivest, A. Shamir, and L. Adleman, "A Method for Obtaining Digital Signatures and Public-Key Cryptosystems," *Communications of the ACM*, vol. 21, no. 2 (February 1978), pp. 120-126.

[RIV2] R.L. Rivest, M.E. Hellman, and J.C. Anderson, "Responses to NIST's Proposal," *Communications of the ACM*, vol. 35, no. 7 (July 1992), pp. 41-52.

[RIV3] R.L. Rivest, *The MD4 Message-Digest Algorithm*, Request for Comments (RFC) 1320, Internet Activities Board, 1992.

[RIV4] R.L. Rivest, *The MD5 Message-Digest Algorithm*, Request for Comments (RFC) 1321, Internet Activities Board, 1992.

[SCH1] C.P. Schnorr, "Efficient Signature Generation by Smart Cards," *Journal of Cryptology*, vol. 4, no. 3 (1991), pp. 161-174.

[SHA1] M. Shand, P. Bertin, and J. Vuillemin, "Hardware Speedups in Long Integer Multiplication," *Proceedings of the 2nd ACM Symposium on Parallel Algorithms and Architectures*, Crete, July 2-6, 1990.

[SEB1] J. Seberry and J. Pieprzyk, *Cryptography: An Introduction to Computer Security*, Prentice Hall, Englewood Cliffs, NJ, 1989.

[SMI1] M.E. Smid and D.K. Branstad, "The Data Encryption Standard: Past and Future," *Proceedings of the IEEE*, vol. 76, no. 5 (May 1988), pp. 550-559.

[SMI2] M.E. Smid and D.K. Branstad, "Response to Comments on the NIST Proposed Digital Signature Standard," in E. Brickell (Ed.), *Advances in Cryptology — CRYPTO '92 (Lecture Notes in Computer Science)*, Springer-Verlag, Berlin, 1993 (in publication).

[TUC1] W. Tuchman, "Hellman Presents no Shortcut Solutions to the DES," *IEEE Spectrum*, vol. 16, no. 7 (July 1979), pp. 40-41.

[TSU1] G. Tsudik, "Message Authentication with One-Way Hash Functions," *Computer Communication Review*, vol. 22, no. 5 (October 1992), ACM Press, New York, pp. 29-38.

[VAN1] P.C. van Oorschot and M.J. Wiener, "A Known-Plaintext Attack on Two-Key Triple Encryption," in I.B. Damgård (Ed.), *Advances in Cryptology — EUROCRYPT '90 (Lecture Notes in Computer Science 473)*, Springer-Verlag, Berlin, 1991, pp. 318-325.

[VAN2] P.C. van Oorschot, "A Comparison of Practical Public Key Cryptosystems Based on Integer Factorization and Discrete Logarithms," in G.J. Simmons (Ed.), *Contemporary Cryptology: The Science of Information Integrity*, IEEE Press, New York, 1992, pp. 289-322.

Standards

ANSI X3.92: *American National Standard, Data Encryption Algorithm*, 1981.

ANSI X9.9: *American National Standard for Financial Institution Message Authentication (Wholesale)*, 1986.

ANSI X9.17: *American National Standard for Financial Institution Key Management (Wholesale)*, 1985.

ANSI X9.30: *American National Standard, Public Key Cryptogrphy Using Irreversible Algorithms for the Financial Services Industry* (Draft).

ANSI X9.31: *American National Standard Public Key Cryptogrphy Using Reversible Algorithms for the Financial Services Industry* (Draft).

FIPS PUB 46: U.S. Department of Commerce, *Data Encryption Standard*, Federal Information Processing Standards Publication 46, 1977 (republished as FIPS PUB 46-1, 1988).

FIPS PUB 74: *Guidelines for Implementing and Using the NBS Data Encryption Standard*, Federal Information Processing Standards Publication 74, 1981.

FIPS PUB 81: U.S. Department of Commerce, *DES Modes of Operation*, Federal Information Processing Standards Publication 81, 1980.

FIPS PUB 180: U.S. Department of Commerce, *Secure Hash Algorithm*, Federal Information Processing Standards Publication 180, 1993.

ISO 8730: *Banking — Requirements for Message Authentication (Wholesale)*.

ISO/IEC 9796: *Information Technology — Security Techniques — Digital Signature Scheme Giving Message Recovery*.

5   Authentication

Authentication is the most important of the security services, because all other security services depend upon it. It counters the threat of masquerade — the threat which can enable all of the fundamental threats identified in Section 2.1.

Authentication gives *assurance of identity*. It is the means of gaining confidence that people or things are who or what they claim to be. The legitimate owner of an identity is known as a *principal*. Principals of various physical forms may need to be authenticated, for example, people, pieces of equipment, or running applications in computer systems.

There are many different methods for providing authentication. Some depend upon cryptographic techniques and some do not. This chapter discusses a range of authentication methods, their strengths, and their vulnerabilities. No distinction is made between authenticating persons and authenticating inanimate objects, unless there is some particular characteristic pertaining to one of these. The chapter is organized into sections addressing:

(1) some basic authentication concepts;
(2) password mechanisms;
(3) other authentication mechanisms which do not use cryptographic techniques;
(4) authentication mechanisms which use cryptographic techniques;
(5) authentication protocol subtleties, which take into account some of the less obvious attack possibilities;
(6) some specific authentication schemes, including Kerberos, the X.509 public-key-based authentication exchanges, and an authenticated Diffie-Hellman exchange;
(7) data origin authentication;
(8) communication protocol requirements; and
(9) architectural placement of authentication services.

5.1   General Concepts

Authentication relates to a scenario where some party (a *claimant*) has presented a principal's identity and claims to *be* that principal. Authentication enables some other party (a *verifier*) to gain confidence that the claim is legitimate. Authentication methods are based upon any of the following principles:

(a) The claimant demonstrates knowledge of something, e.g., a password.
(b) The claimant demonstrates possession of something, e.g., a physical key or card.
(c) The claimant exhibits some required immutable characteristic, e.g., a fingerprint.
(d) Evidence is presented that the claimant is at some particular place (possibly at some particular time).
(e) The verifier accepts that some other party, who is trusted, has already established authentication.

Reliance on any one of the principles (a) through (d) alone is often considered inadequate. It is therefore common to base an authentication system on a combination of these principles.

Authentication applies in a particular *context*. Two distinct contexts encountered in computer networks are:

* *Entity authentication*: An identity is presented by a remote party participating in a communication connection or session.
* *Data origin authentication*: An identity is presented along with a data item. It is claimed that the data item originated from the principal identified.

Entity authentication may be either *unilateral* or *mutual*. With unilateral authentication, just one party to a communication activity authenticates to the other. With mutual authentication, the parties at both ends authenticate to each other. The importance of mutual authentication is often underestimated. When a roving user connects to a major facility, the need for the user to be authenticated is rarely questioned. But, should the major facility authenticate itself to the roving user? An important reason for doing so is to prevent an intruder from setting up a spoofing system, which emulates the major facility just long enough to capture the user's password or other sensitive information.

5.2 Passwords

Passwords, or personal identification numbers (PINs), are a mechanism on which most practical authentication systems depend to some extent.

There have been innumerable reports of password systems failing to be effective. The majority of these failures could have been avoided if appropriate procedures had been followed by the administrators, operators, and legitimate users of the systems involved.

Password systems have many vulnerabilities, which need to be understood. The two most serious vulnerabilities are *external disclosure* and *password guessing*. Other vulnerabilities are *line eavesdropping*, *verifier compromise*, and *replay*.

Countering External Disclosure and Password Guessing

External disclosure refers to a password becoming known to an unauthorized person by a means outside normal network or system operation. There are many ways this might happen. A user may write down a password in an insecure place (on an identity card or on the wall) in order not to forget it. A user may store the password in unprotected command files or program it into a programmable terminal key. Passwords may be obtainable by browsing through discarded printouts from hard-copy terminals. An attacker may learn a password through a telephone call to a system administrator, in which he successfully passes himself off as a legitimate user. External disclosure vulnerabilities are compounded if more than one user share a password, as the password is more likely to be written down or spoken publicly and protection is harder to control.

Measures to help prevent external disclosure include:

- providing user and administrator education;
- establishing strict organization policies and enforcement procedures;
- ensuring that passwords are changed regularly, hence limiting the exposure if external disclosure should occur;
- having passwords associated with single individuals only;
- ensuring that typed-in passwords are never echoed on terminals (overprinting is not effective); and
- using passwords which are easy to remember.

Password guessing is also a serious vulnerability. If there is any tendency for particular character strings to be used as passwords more commonly than others, an attacker may gain advantage by trying these more common strings first. A system in which very short passwords are permitted is particularly vulnerable, as there is a smaller population of short passwords for an attacker to try, and the short passwords are more likely to be selected by users. A particularly serious problem can arise with default passwords for standard user/account names established at system installation (which is not an uncommon practice). If the system administrator is not properly educated or diligent, he may fail to change all such passwords immediately, leaving a simple entry path for a password-guessing intruder. This was a common ploy used in gaining illicit system access to U.S. military computers in the attacks documented by Cliff Stoll [STO1]. Another tendency is to use a password that is the same as or systematically related to a user name, account name, or other user characteristic such as birth date. Password-guessing attacks may take advantage of such relationships. Furthermore, any use of dictionary words or common names or acronyms as passwords can facilitate password-guessing attacks.

The proliferation of the Internet worm depended upon its password-cracking algorithm [SEE1]. This was a three-pronged process, applied to a discovered account name, as follows:

- First, a check was made for a null password, the account name, the account name concatenated with itself, the user's first and last names (available from the account file), and the account name reversed.
- Second, a check was made against a fixed list of 432 favorite passwords, most of which were real English words or proper names.
- Third, a check was made against words in the UNIX on-line dictionary (trying lower case variants of capitalized words as well).

The worm limited the amount of time spent on any account, as its resources might be better spent elsewhere. The WANK/OILZ worms [LON1] used a much simpler password-cracking algorithm — just a null password and a password identical to the username of a given account — but even this algorithm proved adequate for these worms to successfully proliferate.

General measures to help prevent password guessing include:

- providing user and administrator education;
- severely limiting the number of invalid authentication attempts that can be made from a given terminal or access path;
- incorporating a substantial real-time delay in password verification procedures, to hamper the productivity of a computer-automated password guesser;
- implementating provisions which prevent a user from choosing a password which is too short, which is related to user/account name or other user characteristic, or which is contained in a dictionary of strings considered to be common password candidates at a given site;
- ensuring that passwords are changed regularly, hence limiting the exposure if password guessing should succeed;
- avoiding default passwords at system installation; and
- using machine-generated rather than user-chosen passwords.

Unfortunately, a conflict can arise between the measures to protect against external disclosure and those to protect against password guessing. The methods to protect against password guessing tend to result in users having less user-friendly passwords than they might like. If passwords are harder to remember, there is a greater tendency to write them down. Designers and administrators of password systems should bear this in mind and ensure that a reasonable trade-off occurs. Some aids exist, e.g. [LIN1].

Further advice on password management procedures can be found in the U.S. government standard FIPS PUB 112 or the U.S. Department of Defense password management guideline [DOD1].

Note that there are several measures identified above which may need to be taken into account in the design of network equipment which employs passwords for authentication purposes.

Countering Line Eavesdropping

After external disclosure and password guessing, the next most serious vulnerability of password systems is *line eavesdropping*. It is frequently neither difficult nor expensive for a passive wiretapper to monitor a login sequence of a legitimate user. If that sequence contains an unprotected password, or data from which the unprotected password can be deduced, it is a simple matter for the attacker to then masquerade as the legitimate user at an ordinary terminal. Mechanisms called *protected password* mechanisms can counter this type of attack.

Without resorting to cryptography, protection can be provided using a *one-way function*. This is a function $y = f(x)$, with the property that, if x is given, it is easy to compute y, but, if y is given, it is infeasible to calculate $x = f^{-1}(y)$. The details of the one-way function may be made publicly known, and no secret key is required.

A simplistic protected password scheme is illustrated in Figure 5-1(a). Suppose the correct password for identity *id* is *p*. At the terminal where an authentication request originates, identity *id* and a password *p'* are entered. The value $q' = f(p')$ is calculated and is sent along with *id* to the verifier. The verifier's system holds, for each *id*, the value *q* which is the value of *q'* which would be generated for the correct password *p*. The verifier compares *q* and *q'*. If they are the same, it concludes that the correct password was entered, hence the identity is authenticated. The mechanism has the protective qualities that, even if an attacker determines *q* by monitoring a successful authentication exchange or by reading the file in the verifier's system, the attacker is unable to (easily) determine *p*. Hence, the attacker cannot obtain the password needed to masquerade as principal *id* at an ordinary terminal.

This simplistic scheme has a major weakness. It is very easy for a would-be attacker to construct a table of values of *q* corresponding to values of *p*, ensuring especially that the table contains the most likely expected values for *p*. Having constructed a sufficiently good table, he can then passively monitor large numbers of authentication attempts and, with reasonably high probability, obtain some passwords for some principals.

This weakness can be substantially overcome with the simple modification shown in Figure 5-1(b). The only change is to make $q = f(p,id)$ and $q' = f(p',id)$, e.g., apply the one-way function to a string comprising the password and identity concatenated. With this variation, it is still possible to prepare a table of *q* values for *p* values, but only for one particular *id*. Hence, the potential gain from a table-based attack is greatly reduced.

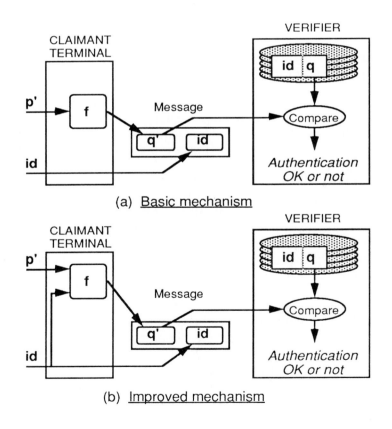

(a) Basic mechanism

(b) Improved mechanism

Figure 5-1: Protected Password Mechanisms

Countering Verifier Compromise

Another potential threat to a password system is the compromise of a verifier's password file or database through an internal attack. Such an attack can potentially be devastating, because it may instantly compromise all passwords that system is capable of verifying.

The protected password mechanism described above gives a certain measure of protection against such an attack, as the values stored are one-way transformed passwords — not unprotected passwords. Learning a value of q does not give an attacker a password p that can be used for masquerading at an ordinary terminal.

However, if we take the attacker's technology one step further, and assume an ability to generate an authentication request message *on the wire*, it is clear that an attacker knowing q can easily generate the required message to successfully masquerade to the verifier.

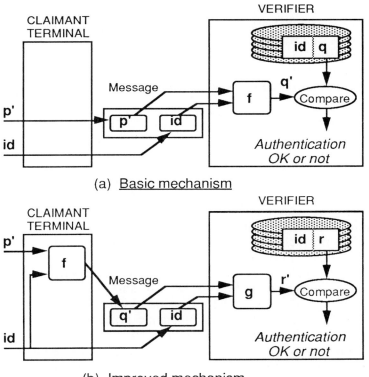

(a) Basic mechanism

(b) Improved mechanism

Figure 5-2: Mechanisms with Improved Resistance to Verifier Compromise

To counter this vulnerability, we can move the one-way function from the claimant system to the verifier system as shown in Figure 5-2(a). This is essentially the UNIX password scheme. (The UNIX scheme adds a further value, a random seed associated with an identity, as input to the one-way function. This addition further improves protection against table attacks, given that common values for *id* may find widespread use throughout the community of UNIX systems.)

The scheme in Figure 5-2(a) has an obvious shortcoming. As the unprotected password is transferred over the network, the scheme is highly vulnerable to line eavesdropping. Addition of a further one-way function, as in Figure 5-2(b), alleviates this exposure while maintaining good resistance to verifier compromise. It effectively combines the beneficial characteristics of the schemes in Figures 5-1(b) and 5.2(a). The verifier stores $r = g(q,id)$, where $q = f(p,id)$. One-way functions $f(x)$ and $g(x)$ may be the same function or may be different.

Protected password mechanisms of this type also present an opportunity for forcing a delay onto a password verification process, thereby making exhaustive or password-guessing attacks more costly. The verifier-end one-way function is deliberately chosen to require substantial processing resources. This is done in the UNIX password algorithm, which is based on DES [SEE1]. Of course, a potential weakness with such an approach is the tendency for natural technology advances (e.g., faster processors) to counteract such protection.

Countering Replay

The mechanisms described above do not protect against an active attack on a communications line which involves the recording and later replaying of a legitimate authentication exchange. An attacker with equipment which can operate this way can easily masquerade as any user whose successful authentication exchange he has observed, provided the user's password has not changed. The protected password scheme can be extended to provide some protection against replay attacks. This is illustrated in Figure 5-3. One-way function $g(x)$, which may or may not be the same function as $f(x)$, is added. The terminal calculates q' as before, then q' and another value, *nrv*, are both input to function $g(x)$ to generate the value r' which is sent along with *id* and *nrv* to the verifier. The verifier calculates $r = g(q,nrv)$ and compares this with r' to decide if the authentication checks correctly.

The value *nrv* is intended to be a non-repeating value (sometimes known as a *nonce* or a *time-variant parameter*). The verifier should examine *nrv* and attempt to establish that the same *nrv* has not been used before. If the verifier believes *nrv* has been used previously, the authentication request should be rejected as a possible replay. Non-repeating values can be realized in various ways, e.g., time-stamps, synchronized counts maintained between the two communicating systems, or random numbers for which the verifier remembers all previously used values (non-repeating values are discussed further in Section 5.5).

Note that this mechanism may still have a vulnerability with respect to verifier compromise. If an attacker knows the value q for id, and can generate an acceptable nrv, that attacker can fabricate an authentication sequence which will be verified correctly.

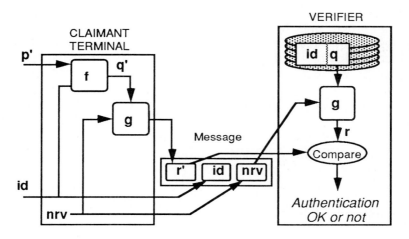

Figure 5-3: Protected Password Mechanism with Replay Protection

5.3 Other Non-cryptographic Mechanisms

One-Time Passwords

One-time password mechanisms are related to the protected password mechanisms with replay protection described above. The main goal is to ensure that a different password is used on each authentication, in order to counter replay attacks. Ways to determine the password to use on any occasion include:

(a) reference to a list of random passwords known to the two ends, with both ends keeping synchronized as to position in the list;

(b) use of a pseudo-random sequence generator known to the two ends, with both ends keeping synchronized as to the sequence generator state; and

(c) use of a time-stamp, with both ends maintaining synchronized clocks.

While the utility of (a) is limited to manually controlled environments, (b) and (c) are potentially useful in modern network environments.

A very effective *personal* authentication mechanism can be built using these methods, in the form of a personal one-time password generator. Suppose we take the "terminal" functions described in the preceding subsection, and package them into a hand-held personal authentication device. The device generates, as output on a display, the value r'. This value is then re-entered by the user as the "password" to be conveyed over an untrusted network to a verifier system. As far as network communication is concerned, this is a one-time password system. This can also be a means of combining the "something known" and "something possessed" principles of authentication.

A possible mechanism is illustrated in Figure 5-4. A user has a personal authentication device, with a character-entry pad and a display. A secret device-specific value *dsv* is stored internally in the device. It is assumed that physical tampering with the device will not reveal *dsv*. The device maintains clock synchronization (within an agreed time granularity) with one or more verifier systems with which it may be used. When the device-holder wants to authenticate to a verifier, he or she enters password p' to the device. The device displays a value r', computed by applying one-way functions f and g to the values p', *dsv*, and *ts* (a current time-stamp) as shown. The value r' is sent along with the user's identity *id* to the verifier's system. The verifier's system holds, for each *id*, the value *dsv* and a value $q = f(p, dsv)$. On receipt of the authentication request, the verifier calculates $r = g(q, dsv, ts)$. Comparison of r and r' determines if authentication is accepted.

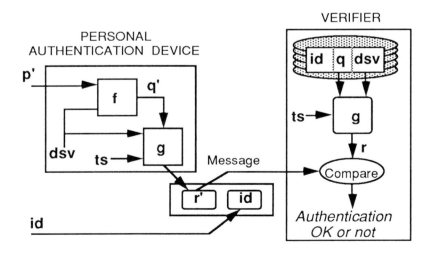

Figure 5-4: Personal One-time Password Generator

This mechanism has the following strengths:

- Knowledge of password p, without possessing the device, does not lead to a simple attack.
- Possession of the device, without knowing password p, does not lead to a simple attack.
- Replay of earlier (id, r') messages is not a simple attack (unless an attack is also made on time synchronization).
- Knowledge of q (e.g., by browsing verifier system files) without knowledge of dsv does not lead to a simple attack.

One might question the value of ensuring that disclosure of q does not lead to a compromise, when disclosure of dsv may lead to a compromise. The difference results from p values (hence q values) needing to be changed from time to time (to avert the risks of external disclosure), while devices and their corresponding dsv's can remain in existence for much longer times. Any of these values is much more susceptible to exposure at the time of changing (e.g., when password-change notifications are communicated) than while in long-term (protected) storage in verifier systems.

The above mechanism has different variations which are used in currently available non-cryptographic personal authentication devices.

Challenge-Response

Password-based schemes can be augmented by the challenge-response principle (which will also be employed in cryptographic authentication mechanisms described later). Challenge-response can greatly improve resistance to replay attacks, but usually at the expense of an increase in the complexity of the communication protocol.

Let us re-examine the protected password mechanism with replay protection (Figure 5-3). There are two significant problems with this mechanism. One is the need to maintain synchronization in order for both ends to know nrv values. The other is the difficulty of a verifier knowing if a nrv value is being repeated. The challenge-response approach overcomes these problems by having the verifier send the claimant a specific nrv value for a given authentication attempt in advance. The nrv value is known as a *challenge*. The set of protocol exchanges and the logic surrounding the *challenge* and *response* messages are shown in Figure 5-5.

The claimant end of the communication could be implemented in a general terminal, as indicated in Figure 5-5. Alternatively, it could be implemented in a personal authentication device. In that case, a device-specific value dsv could also be included in the function calculated, adding the benefits of the "something possessed" principle as in the personal one-time password generator. The resultant configuration is the same as in Figure 5-4, but with the *ts* value replaced by a challenge *nrv* value sent first from the verifier to the claimant. The device-holder enters both password *p'* and challenge *nrv* to the device, which then generates value *r'* to be sent to the verifier.

In mechanisms of this type, the ability to generate non-repeating values, which are the basis of replay detection, is entirely in the hands of the verifier. A very good replay-detection capability is therefore provided. However, the added protocol complexity means that this type of mechanism cannot be used in conjunction with conventional simple password protocols.

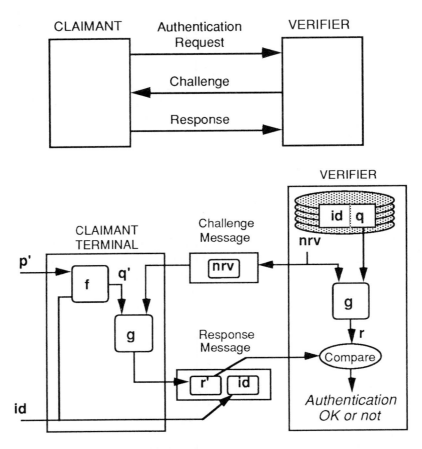

Figure 5-5: Challenge-Response Mechanism

Address-Based Mechanisms

Address-based mechanisms assume the authenticity of a claimant on the basis of the originating address of a call. Indications of calling address are available in most types of data network and are starting to become available on telephone networks in the form of Automatic Number Identification (ANI) features. Where such indications are not reliably available (such as certain telephone networks), the same basic effect can be achieved using an automatic call-back device. A verifier maintains a file of legitimate calling addresses for each principal. On an authentication attempt, the verifier will either check the calling address for legitimacy or clear the original call and call back to what is known to be a legitimate address.

This type of mechanism faces several potential problems. The biggest difficulty, in contemporary environments, is maintaining a continuing association of a principal (i.e., a person or even a piece of equipment) with a network address. Address changes are likely to occur so frequently that the change system will be overly expensive, unmanageable, and/or insecure. Network features such as call-forwarding or redirection create major problems with the call-back approach, opening various opportunities for attack.

Address-based mechanisms cannot be considered authentication mechanisms in their own right but may provide a useful secondary check in support of other mechanisms.

Mechanisms Using Personal Characteristics

When authenticating a person, there are many interesting technologies which may provide the basis for an authentication mechanism, including:

- fingerprint recognition;
- voice recognition;
- handwriting recognition;
- retinal scan; and
- hand geometry.

These technologies are beyond the scope of this book. In most respects, the results of applying one of these technologies in a network environment can be considered as applying a special password which, unlike conventional passwords, cannot be used by others. Use of these technologies has no significant impact upon network security protocols.

Personal Authentication Tokens

There are various types of physical tokens used to support the "something possessed" authentication principle, usually in conjunction with a password or PIN. The simplest tokens are memory-only tokens containing, for example, a subsidiary password used in addition to a user-memorized password. Such a token is virtually the electronic equivalent of a physical key. A special interface is generally needed to allow the contents of the token to be read.

More sophisticated tokens can support the one-time password or challenge-response mechanisms described above. These devices are typically self-powered and interface to the external world via:

- a keypad, through which the holder can enter sequences such as PINs and challenges; and
- a display, which outputs values such as one-time passwords or challenge responses which the holder re-enters into a network terminal as part of an authentication sequence.

Even more sophisticated devices have embedded processors and their own network communication capabilities (e.g., smart cards). Such devices typically employ cryptographic-based authentication methods, and are discussed in the following section.

5.4 Use of Cryptographic Techniques

Authentication mechanisms using cryptographic techniques are based on the principle of convincing a verifier that, because a claimant knows some secret key, that claimant is the principal claimed. Either symmetric or public-key techniques may be employed.

Using symmetric techniques, in the simplest approach, the principal and verifier share a symmetric key. The claimant either encrypts or seals some message using that key. If the verifier can successfully decrypt the message or verify that the seal is correct, the verifier can be assured that the message came from the principal. The contents of the encrypted or sealed message would typically include a non-repeating value, as protection against replay attacks. A challenge-response protocol may be used, in which case the verifier first sends the claimant a challenge message containing a non-repeating value to be included in the subsequent (encrypted or sealed) message back to the verifier.

Using public-key techniques, the approach is similar. The claimant signs some message using his private key. The verifier checks the signature, using the public key of the principal. If the signature checks correctly, the verifier can be assured the claimant is the principal. Again, the message may contain a non-repeating value as protection against replay attacks.

This type of mechanism is illustrated in Figure 5-6.

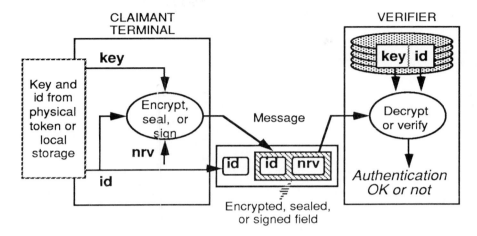

Figure 5-6: Simple Cryptographic-Based Authentication Mechanism

Role of On-line Servers

The symmetric cryptographic approach suggested above is not practical in a large network, because it would require every verifier (i.e., every host computer, server, etc.) to maintain a secret symmetric key with every principal who may access it. This key-explosion problem is averted by introducing a trusted on-line authentication server, with which every principal and every verifier shares a key. There are various ways to arrange the communications with such a server; the two most basic approaches are illustrated in Figure 5-7.

In approach (a) in Figure 5-7, the claimant encrypts or seals a message with his or her key as described above and sends this to the verifier. Because the verifier does not share the principal's key, the verifier cannot directly perform the verification. However, through a separate exchange with the authentication server, the verifier can obtain the verification. For the latter exchange to be secure, the verifier and the authentication server will need to use their shared key.

Approach (b) in Figure 5-7 differs in that the claimant first conducts an exchange with the authentication server in order to obtain a *ticket*, which it passes to the verifier. The communication between the claimant and authentication server is protected using their shared key. The ticket is constructed in such a way that it will be acceptable only to an entity knowing the key shared between verifier and authentication server (the Kerberos system, described in Section 5-6, provides an example).

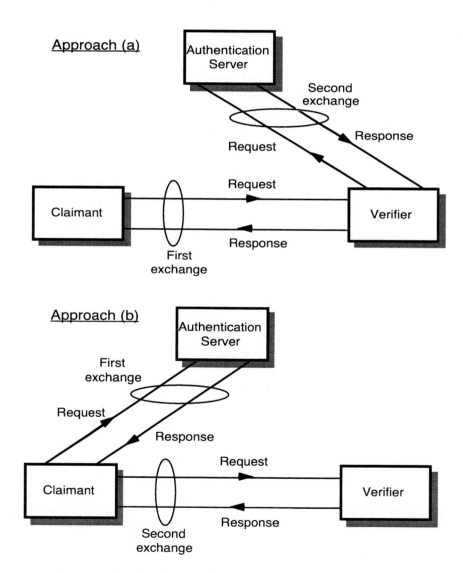

Figure 5-7: On-line Authentication Server Configurations

There are several variations on the actual exchanges that may occur in on-line server configurations, involving pre-exchange communication between claimant and server and/or post-exchange communication between verifier and server. Mutual authentication can also be provided. Needham and Schroeder [NEE1] produced one of the first analyses of this type of mechanism. They also pointed out how the approach could be extended to a configuration of multiple authentication servers, each supporting a part of the principal/verifier community.

Role of Off-line Servers

With public-key cryptosystems, the need for on-line authentication servers is obviated, because the characteristics of public-key systems naturally avert the key-explosion problem. However, there is still a need for verifiers to obtain certified public keys of principals, and certificate revocation lists (see Section 4.7). Usually, these certificates and revocation lists are also obtained originally from a server, although they can be cached and reused. Such a server is sometimes called an off-line authentication server, because it does not need to be an on-line participant in communication exchanges at authentication time. The functions of such a server can be realized through an untrusted directory service (this is followed up later in Chapter 14).

Off-line servers present several advantages over on-line servers, including:

- Response delays associated with accessing an on-line server at call establishment time can be averted (at least some of the time).
- The server requires much less communications capacity.
- Entities can continue to authenticate if the server is not available.
- Servers do not require trusted implementations.

Zero-Knowledge Techniques

Zero-knowledge techniques constitute a comparatively new cryptographic-based technology. They show great potential for future application in authentication but are still maturing. A zero-knowledge technique is a means by which possession of information can be verified without any part of that information being revealed, either to the verifier or to any third party. Full understanding of this subject requires a background in computational complexity theory and interactive proof systems, which is not assumed for readers of this book. Accordingly, tutorial coverage is not attempted here. For an introduction to the topic, readers are referred to [NEC1, QUI1]. For a more detailed overview of the mathematics, see [FEI1].

Several variations of zero-knowledge techniques applicable to network authentication have been proposed, e.g., [BET1, FIE1, FIA1, GUI1]. In general, these techniques involve having the verifier issue a number of challenges to the claimant. The claimant computes a response to each challenge, making use of secret information in the computation. By examining these responses (and possibly using a public key), the verifier is able to establish with a sufficiently high level of confidence that the claimant indeed possesses the secret information (although no part of the secret information is actually disclosed in the responses). The different techniques vary in terms of the number of challenge-response pairs required, and the complexity of the calculations required at both ends. These techniques are potentially cryptographically stronger than more conventional cryptographic techniques and may be less processing-intensive. However, many of these techniques require much larger data items to be transferred, and/or a more complex protocol. In particular, several protocol exchanges may be required to perform a single authentication.

The scheme proposed by Guillou and Quisquater [GUI1, GUI2] is particularly attractive as it requires only one challenge-response interaction. Use of such schemes can be expected to increase as more confidence in them and experience with them are gained.

Personal Authentication

Cryptographic techniques are not suitable for *direct* application in personal authentication (humans are not very good at remembering long random key vectors). However, password mechanisms and cryptographic-based mechanisms can be conveniently married when there is a mutually-trusted device close to the user. A common approach is for the person to authenticate himself to the device using a password, then the device authenticates itself to the ultimate verifier using a cryptographic technique. There are several other ways in which this marriage of mechanisms may work. Two important cases are password-derived keys and smart cards.

One of the simplest ways to link a password-associated user with a cryptographic system is to introduce a one-to-one mapping between an identity-password pair and a cryptosystem secret key. For example, [KOH1, RSA1] define procedures for generating a 56-bit DES key from an identity string and a password value. This is similar to protecting a password using a one-way function; however, the resultant value is specifically designed to be usable as a cryptosystem key. It enables a cryptographic-based authentication system to treat a person the same as it would treat an automated system with an embedded key. The transformation from identity/password to key at the claimant end must be performed securely, to prevent against disclosure of the unprotected password. This generally necessitates trusted terminal equipment.

A *smart card*, or *integrated circuit card* (IC-card), is a tiny processor and storage system realized in a VLSI microcircuit embedded in a plastic card the same size as a familiar plastic credit card. The card operates when inserted in an external terminal device designed to interface to it via six electrical contacts. Through these contacts, the terminal provides electrical power, and communicates with the card processor using a serial asynchronous character protocol. The basic physical, electrical, and communications aspects of the interface have been standardized by ISO/IEC.

In the early stages of smart card technology, the leading applications have been retail banking and telephone and broadcast communications access. However, the technology has a virtually unbounded range of future applications. Smart cards will almost certainly play a major role in the provision of network security services in the future. Given that a smart card is a tamper-proof, personalized device with a potential cryptographic processing capability, it can play an extremely important role in personal authentication. The card processor acts as a claimant, communicating with a verifier in either a nearby terminal device or a remote network-accessed system.

Early personal authentication schemes using smart cards employed either one-way functions or simple public-key cryptosystems. However, zero-knowledge techniques are receiving increasing consideration for use in such environments [GUI2].

One vulnerability of smart cards needs to be noted. Use of a smart card for authentication purposes depends upon the holder entering a PIN (a more common term than *password* in this context). This is needed as protection against card loss or theft. PIN entry relies upon use of a *trusted* terminal device to ensure that unprotected PINs are not disclosed to unauthorized persons. Smart card technology is advancing to the point where a PIN entry pad can be incorporated into the card itself; this will eliminate the vulnerability (at least for those of us with sufficiently good eyesight and dexterity to use such a facility).

ISO/IEC-standard smart cards are not the only type of cryptographic-based personal authentication device on the market, but they are particularly attractive because of the standardized interface. Another alternative interface (a *de facto* standard) which is emerging is the PCMCIA (Personal Computer Memory Card International Association) interface, which provides a convenient means for connecting a small personal cryptographic module to a personal computer (especially laptop computers).

5.5 Authentication Protocol Subtleties

The design of authentication mechanisms and protocols is a difficult task, because of the variety of attacks that need to be taken into account. There have been many instances where apparently sound authentication protocol designs have subsequently been shown to be flawed in the face of some conceivable type of attack [BIR1, BUR2, GAA1, MIT1, MOO1]. Some of the areas requiring special consideration are identified in the following subsections.

Replay and Interception Attacks

Active attacks, in which an intruder system is inserted in a network path in order to attack an authentication mechanism, include the following:

- *Replay on the same verifier*: An attacker replays an earlier authentication message from a legitimate principal to the same verifier. As suggested earlier, a way to counter this is to include a non-repeating value, e.g., sequence number, time-stamp, or random number, in authentication messages. Non-repeating values are discussed further in the next subsection.

- *Replay on a different verifier*: An attacker monitors a legitimate authentication message from principal p to verifier v_1, then (either immediately or later) replays that message to verifier v_2 so as to masquerade as p. This attack can potentially get around sequence number or time-stamp replay countering measures designed with one verifier in mind. However, this type of attack can generally be countered by ensuring that an identifier of the intended verifier is included in the (protected) message.

- *Reflection attack*: An attacker captures an authentication message from one entity, then (either immediately or later) replays that message or part thereof to the same entity, while representing it as having come from another entity. Such attacks can sometimes be designed against authentication schemes based on symmetric cryptography.

- *Interception-and-relay attacks*: An intruder system is inserted in the path between principal and verifier, and actively modifies messages such that it appears as a legitimate claimant to the verifier and a legitimate verifier to the principal. Analysis of such attacks is non-trivial, and the only sure way to avert them is to combine the authentication process with a key-establishment process (see *Preserving Authentication* below).

To be sure that an authentication protocol is resistant to attacks of the types described above, formal analysis would be necessary. Some formal analysis techniques have been proposed for this purpose (e.g., [BIR1, BUR2, GAA1, KEM1]). However, their practical value is yet to be shown; for example, how can a user be assured that the formal analysis was carried out correctly?

Use of Non-repeating Values

Non-repeating values are used in authentication messages to ensure that an attempt to replay an earlier successful authentication exchange will be detected. Potential sources of such values are:

(a) a sequence number maintained between principal and verifier;
(b) a time-stamp; and
(c) a random value sent previously from the verifier (e.g., a challenge).

With sequence numbers, a claimant and a verifier agree in advance on a policy for numbering messages in a particular way. The general approach is that a message with a particular number will be accepted only once (or only once within a specified time period). Messages received by a verifier are checked for acceptability within the agreed policy. An authentication attempt is rejected if the policy is violated. Use of sequence numbers requires a substantial management overhead. A verifier needs to maintain state information for every principal supported. More significantly, every principal needs to maintain synchronized state information with every verifier who might be used. While such arrangements may be acceptable in small closed environments, they are generally impractical in open-systems environments.

Time-stamps assume there is a common time reference which logically links a claimant and verifier, e.g., Coordinated Universal Time (GMT). A verifier will adopt an acceptance window of fixed size. On receipt of an authentication message, the verifier calculates the difference between the time-stamp in the message and the time of receipt. If this difference is within the window, the message is accepted. Uniqueness can be guaranteed by buffering copies of all messages received within the current window and rejecting any message repeats.

Use of time-stamps depends entirely upon the systems involved maintaining secure local clocks which are periodically synchronized with a reliable source of time. There are several potential problems with this type of approach:

- If a verifier system can be misled about the correct time, then old messages can be replayed very easily.
- If a legitimate principal system can be misled about the correct time, it can be induced to generate authentication requests which can be later replayed to a verifier with a sound time reference.
- If two parties' clocks drift sufficiently, they become unable to communicate, leading to an availability problem.

- In the many networks which employ time servers and time-synchroniz-
  ation protocols, the security of the authentication system becomes
  dependent upon the security of these servers/protocols.

Problems regarding use of time-stamps have been discussed in more detail in
[BEL1, BIR1, DIF1, GAA1].

Random values sent via challenges have a major strength in that they give
the verifier direct control over the variation of authentication messages. It is the
verifier's responsibility to ensure that the same challenge is not reused within
the time frame of concern. The values used do not require true statistical
randomness. The main requirement is that they be unpredictable and, with a
sufficiently high probability, non-repeating. This approach to providing non-
repeating values averts the management problems of sequence numbers and the
vulnerabilities of time-stamps, but it does have the disadvantage of requiring
additional protocol messages.

Mutual Authentication Protocols

Mutual authentication, in which both parties to a communication session need
to authenticate each other, is frequently an important requirement. In principle,
this can be achieved by combining two unilateral (single-party) authentication
protocol exchanges. However, such combinations need to be examined
carefully, as it is possible that a combination may be vulnerable to interception-
and-relay attacks for which the unilateral exchange was not vulnerable (see
[BIR1] for an example).

Also, it is possible to design mutual authentication exchanges in which
the number of protocol messages is significantly less than double the number of
messages for the corresponding unilateral exchange. For example, the
unilateral challenge-response protocol illustrated in Figure 5-5 required three
protocol messages. However, it is also possible to realize a mutual challenge-
response protocol in three messages as follows:

Message 1 (A-to-B):   Challenge$_{A-B}$
Message 2 (B-to-A):   Response$_{B-A}$ + Challenge$_{B-A}$
Message 3 (A-to-B):   Response$_{A-B}$

Hence, for both security and performance reasons, protocol exchanges
for mutual authentication are best designed specifically for that purpose and
subjected to their own vulnerability analysis.

Preserving Authentication

If active attacks are a real concern, then a major problem to face is how to ensure that authentication remains meaningful through subsequent information exchange, e.g., throughout the lifetime of a connection. A strong authentication exchange can authenticate a party involved in a communication session at one instant in time, but it provides no protection against an intruder inserting himself in the communications path immediately afterwards. Some protection can be provided by periodically re-authenticating, but a sufficiently intelligent active attack can be engineered to sidestep all such authentications. The only sure way to preserve authentication on a connection is to use a connection-integrity service simultaneously.

If keys for the connection-integrity service are to be established on-line, it proves important to combine the authentication and key exchange functions into one protocol.

Suppose, for example, we are going to use a two-way public-key-based authentication exchange, plus a Diffie-Hellman key derivation exchange to establish a key for connection integrity (and/or connection confidentiality) purposes. If these two exchanges are independent, regardless of which occurs first, there is a possibility of an intruder compromising the security of the connection. The intruder is able to switch-in, resulting in two keys, one between party *A* and the intruder and one between party *B* and the intruder. Figure 5-8 illustrates a possible attack scenario when the key exchange precedes the authentication exchange. (Moving the authentication exchange to precede the key exchange would make no difference.)

This problem has led to recognition of the need for *authenticated key exchange* protocols combining both functions [BAU1, DIF1, GUN1, OKA1].

5.6 Some Specific Mechanisms

Following are three examples of complete cryptographic-based authentication mechanisms built using the principles described above.

Kerberos

Kerberos was designed as part of Project Athena at the Massachusetts Institute of Technology (MIT) [MIL1, STE1]. The goal of this project was to build an educational computing network comprising high-performance workstations together with various types of network servers. Kerberos provides the means for authenticating workstation users (clients) to servers, and vice versa.

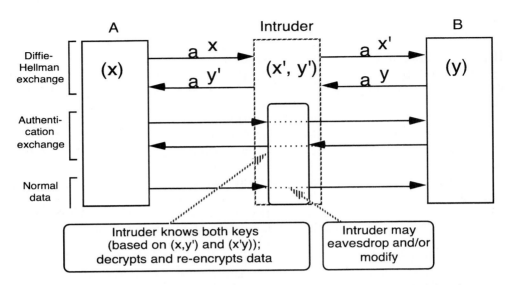

Figure 5-8: Attack on Unauthenticated Diffie-Hellman Key Derivation

Kerberos uses symmetric cryptography and on-line authentication servers, based on the proposals of Needham and Schroeder [NEE1] with modifications suggested by Denning and Sacco [DEN1]. The Version 5 Kerberos specification was developed within the Internet community [KOH1].

Kerberos employs the ticket approach, whereby the client conducts a communication exchange with an authentication server prior to the actual authentication exchange, which occurs when establishing a session with the target server (see Figure 5-9). The result of successful completion of both exchanges is that both client and target server obtain knowledge of a secret session key generated for them by the authentication server. This knowledge provides the basis for mutual authentication and possibly also for other protection services on their communication session.

There are actually three different types of exchange:

- *Authentication Service (AS) Exchange*: This is an initial exchange between a client and the Kerberos authentication server which knows the client's secret key. This exchange obtains for the client a ticket to be used to access some other (nominated) server. This exchange is typically used at the start of a login session, when the user's password is known to the client (the password is commonly used to obtain the client's secret key via a one-way function). The nominated server is usually a ticket-granting authentication server, from which other tickets can be obtained subsequently in the login session.

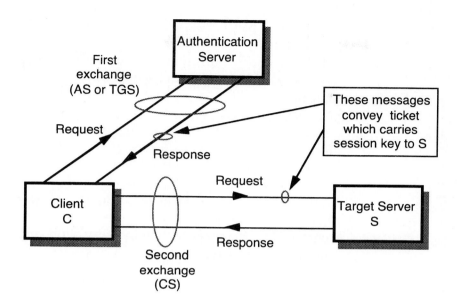

Figure 5-9: Kerberos Exchanges

- *Ticket-Granting Service (TGS) Exchange*: This is an exchange between a client and an authentication server, known as a ticket-granting server, which does not use the client's secret key (hence the client can erase all knowledge of this very sensitive key early in a login session). Instead, it uses a ticket for the ticket-granting server, obtained earlier in an AS exchange. This exchange obtains for the client a further ticket to be used to access any other (nominated) server. The TGS exchange is typically used within a login session, when a requirement to access any server arises.

- *Client/Server (CS) Authentication Exchange*: This is an exchange between a client and a target server which authenticates the client to the server and, optionally, the server to the client. It makes use of a ticket obtained earlier in either an AS or TGS exchange.

Below is a simplified description of the data items conveyed in the Kerberos exchanges. The following symbols are used:

C, S, G: identifiers of client, target server, and ticket-granting server respectively;

key_x: secret key of party x (known only to x and one Kerberos server);

key_{xy}:   a key generated by an authentication server, for use as a secret session key shared between parties x and y;

$E_x\{\}$, $E_{xy}\{\}$:   indicate encryption of a sequence of data values under key_x, key_{xy} respectively;

tkt_{xy}:   a ticket generated by an authentication server to allow client x to authenticate to server y; its contents, which can only be read by the authentication server and y, are:
$$tkt_{xy} = E_y\{x, key_{xy}, ltime_{xy}\}$$

$ltime_{xy}$:   lifetime details for a ticket tkt_{xy}, including start and expiry times; and

ts_{xy}:   a current time-stamp generated by party x to assist party y in detecting replayed messages.

Either the AS or TGS exchange serves to provide client C with knowledge of the secret session key, key_{CS}, plus a ticket which can be used to secretly convey knowledge of the same key_{CS} to server S. The items conveyed in the AS exchange are:

Request: C, S
Response: $E_C\{S, key_{CS}, ltime_{CS}, tkt_{CS}\}$

The items conveyed in the TGS exchange are:

Request: $S, tkt_{CG}, E_{CG}\{C, ts_{CG}\}$
Response: $E_{CG}\{S, key_{CS}, ltime_{CS}, tkt_{CS}\}$

The request item of the CS exchange serves to securely convey key_{CS} to S (so C and S will then share a secret key, which mutually authenticates them and possibly can provide other protection to their communication session). The request item also conveys a value known as an *authenticator*, which assures S of the timeliness of the request and provides protection against replay. The response is optional; if used, it serves to authenticate S to C, by demonstrating that S successfully decrypted the ticket and extracted ts_{CS} from the authenticator. The items exchanged in the CS exchange are:

Request: $tkt_{CS}, E_{CS}\{C, ts_{CS}\}$
Response: $E_{CS}\{ts_{CS}\}$

There are several additional options to the Kerberos protocols, which have been omitted from the above to facilitate understanding of the basic approach. For example, Kerberos includes procedures for use across multiple domains (*realms*) which employ independent authentication servers, possibly under the control of separate organizations. There are also comprehensive administrative protocol elements, which have not been described here.

The main benefits of Kerberos are that it provides a good level of protection, using relatively inexpensive technology. However, it has certain weaknesses (see [BEL1]). Disadvantages, in comparison with some other authentication schemes, are:

- the need for trusted (physically secured) on-line servers, with high availability;
- dependence on time-stamps for replay detection (which implies that synchronized and secure time clocks are required); and
- the fact that compromise of a key used in the authentication process (even at a much later time) will enable the compromise of all protected data conveyed in any session which used that key for authentication.

X.509 Authentication Exchanges

The OSI Directory standards, first published in 1988, include one part (ISO/IEC 9594-8 or ITU-T Recommendation X.509) addressing authentication. This standard is discussed in detail in Chapter 14. However, we here outline two authentication exchanges described in it. These serve as useful examples of public-key-based authentication mechanisms. As this standard is best known by its ITU designator, we identify the exchanges as the X.509 authentication exchanges.

To provide mutual authentication between parties A and B, there are options of either a two-way or three-way authentication exchange, as shown in Figure 5-10. In order to perform the authentication, A needs a certified copy of B's public key, and B needs a certified copy of A's public key. To check the certification, further certified public keys, relating to a certification authority chain, may also be needed.

The public key certificates are obtained via accesses to a directory service and/or direct communication of certificates between A and B along with the authentication exchange (the certificate distribution approach does not impact the contents of the basic authentication exchange).

In describing the contents of the authentication exchanges, the following symbols are used:

$E_x\{\}$: indicates encryption of a sequence of data values under the public key of party x;

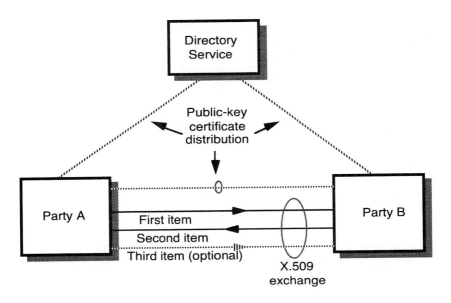

Figure 5-10: X.509 Authentication Exchanges

$S_x\{\}$:   indicates a sequence of data values, together with a
                signature over those values, using the private key of
                party x;

ts_{xy}:   a current time-stamp generated by party x to assist party
                y in detecting replayed messages (may contain both
                generation and expiry date/time for the message
                conveying it);

nrv_{xy}:   a non-repeating value sent by party x to assist party y in
                detecting replayed messages; and

key_{xy}:   a secret key, generated by x, to be used in protecting
                subsequent communications between x and y.

In the two-way exchange, the items conveyed are:

First item: $A, S_A\{ts_{AB}, nrv_{AB}, B, E_B\{key_{AB}\}\}$
Second item: $S_B\{ts_{BA}, nrv_{BA}, A, nrv_{AB}, E_A\{key_{BA}\}\}$

with the fields $E_B\{key_{AB}\}$ and $E_A\{key_{BA}\}$ being optional. On receipt of the
first item, B verifies A's signature, checks that the B identifier in the message is
correct, checks that the time-stamp is current, and (optionally, if an effective
non-repeating value procedure is in use) checks the non-repeating value as

protection against replay. On receipt of the second item, A performs the corresponding set of actions. Note that, for each message, the signature verification provides the basic authentication, the time-stamp and/or non-repeating value provide protection against replay on the same verifier, and inclusion of the receiver's identifier in the message provides protection against replay on a different verifier. The sending of key_{AB} and/or key_{BA}, in encrypted form, is optional. Their use is not specified, but typically one would be used to support symmetric-cryptographic-based confidentiality or integrity protection of data on a connection.

In the three-way exchange, the first two items conveyed are identical to those of the two-way exchange, except the time-stamps are not required. Subsequently, the following is conveyed from A to B:

Third item: $S_A\{B, \text{nrv}_{BA}\}$

With the three-way exchange, party A, on receipt of the second item, checks that the received nrv_{AB} is the same as that sent in the first item. Similarly, on receipt of the third item, party B checks that the received nrv_{BA} is the same as that sent on the second item (B also checks the signature on the third item). This extension to the two-way exchange provides the effect of a challenge-response replay protection scheme in both directions. The time-stamps are no longer needed for replay detection purposes.

In comparison with Kerberos, the X.509 exchanges have one major advantage — they do not require physically secured on-line servers, since a certificate includes a certification authority signature. Public-key certificates can be distributed off-line, using an untrusted directory service. The two-way X.509 exchange shares the Kerberos limitation of depending upon time-stamps, whereas the three-way X.509 exchange overcomes this limitation. Because of the method of symmetric-key distribution using public-key encryption, the X.509 exchanges retain the problem that compromise of a key used in authentication leads to compromise of all protected data conveyed in any session for which that authentication key was used.

Authenticated Diffie-Hellman Exchange

Diffie, van Oorschot, and Wiener [DIF1] developed a three-way authentication exchange which combines public-key-based mutual authentication with a Diffie-Hellman key derivation exchange. Following is a description of the protocol exchange for the case where the Diffie-Hellman derivation is carried out over the integers mod p. We can consider it as a variation of the X.509 three-way exchange, with different data items exchanged. New symbols introduced are:

a, p:	Diffie-Hellman parameters (see Section 4.6);
a^x:	Diffie-Hellman exponential, a^x mod p, where x is a secret value known only to party A;
a^y:	Diffie-Hellman exponential, a^y mod p, where y is a secret value known only to party B; and
$E_K\{\}$:	encryption under key $K = a^{xy}$ mod p, i.e., the key resulting from the Diffie-Hellman derivation.

Assuming the values of prime p and primitive element a are known in advance, the data items conveyed in the exchange are:

First item:	a^x
Second item:	$a^y, E_K\{S_B\{a^y, a^x\}\}$
Third item:	$E_K\{S_B\{a^x, a^y\}\}$

With these exchanges, the function S_x differs from that in the X.509 exchanges in that it does not need to convey the signed data items, only the signature appendix for those items. For the exchange to succeed, both parties need to successfully decrypt using key K and need to successfully verify the other party's signature. This scheme is simple and efficient and is resistant to the full range of replay and interception attacks.

The authenticated Diffie-Hellman exchange has an advantage over both the Kerberos and X.509 exchanges in that compromise of a signature key used in the authentication process will not compromise the secrecy of primary keys derived previously in conjunction with the authentication.

The authenticated Diffie-Hellman scheme also has an interesting variant in which the encryption process is replaced by a seal or signature process. For environments in which authentication and integrity are required, but confidentiality is not required, this can lead to a product which does not have encryption-decryption functions. Such a product may be more easily exportable than one containing encryption-decryption (as needed for Kerberos and X.509 schemes).

5.7 Data Origin Authentication

Data origin authentication provides assurance of the identity of the principal that was the source of a particular data item. It differs from entity authentication in that the principal need not necessarily be involved in current communication activities. The data item may have been relayed through many systems whose identities may or may not have been authenticated, and it may have been stored for substantial periods en route. Data origin authentication relates to integrity in that there must be assurance that the data item was not modified since it left its originator (otherwise that originator could no longer be considered the true source). However, data origin authentication does not necessarily protect against duplication, reordering, or loss of data items.

There are three basic approaches to providing data origin authentication:

- using encryption;
- using seals or digital signatures; and
- considering data origin authentication to be an extension of entity authentication.

Using encryption, a common approach is for an originator and a recipient to know, in advance, a value of a secret authenticator (a short random sequence of symbols generated and distributed securely by a trusted authority) and a value of a cryptographic key. To protect a data item in transit, the originator appends the authenticator to it, then encrypts the result. The recipient decrypts the received data to recover the original data item plus the authenticator which is checked for validity. This approach has been used extensively in military networks. It has the property that it provides confidentiality as well as data origin authentication. While this may sometimes be desirable, in unclassified applications it is frequently undesirable (e.g., products will be less easily exportable). It also presents substantial management problems, not only for keys but also for authenticators.

The approach of providing data origin authentication by applying a seal (MAC) or digital signature to a data item is very common. Whether or not a seal will give a sufficient level of confidence as to the identity of the originator depends upon the key management environment and on whether the authentication is for use only by the recipient. If it is necessary to be able to convince another party of the originator's identity, without any risk of the recipient having modified the data item, a seal may be inadequate and a digital signature may be required.

The third approach to data origin authentication is to treat it as an extension to entity authentication, in which a data item is linked with an authentication exchange by an integrity mechanism. For example, the data item or a digest of the data item (sometimes called a *digital fingerprint*) might be sealed within the authentication exchange. Alternatively, the data item might be conveyed in a connection in which connection integrity is linked to an authentication exchange. In [GUI2], Guillou et al. describe how to extend their zero-knowledge technique authentication scheme to also provide data origin authentication.

For further information on data origin authentication see [SIM1].

5.8 Protocol Requirements

Let us now consider the types of communications protocols needed for the transfer of information used to provide authentication services.

Authentication Exchanges

An authentication exchange is a sequence of data transfers in alternating directions between a claimant and a verifier, in order to assure the verifier of the claimant's identity (it may operate both ways in the case of mutual authentication). The number of data transfers varies with the authentication technique, e.g.:

- 1 for a simple exchange authenticating only one end;
- 2 for simple mutual authentication;
- 3 for a challenge-response mechanism; or
- n (possibly a variable number) for some zero-knowledge technique mechanisms.

An authentication exchange needs to be integrated into other protocols used at the same level. Entity authentication commonly relates to establishment of a connection, hence authentication exchanges commonly need to be integrated into connection establishment protocols. However, entity authentication may also occur within a connection, e.g., if a new user takes over at a terminal. Hence, provision sometimes needs to be made for embedding authentication exchanges within a connection protocol.

On-line Server Communications

Communication with an on-line authentication server typically involves a simple request message from client (either claimant or verifier) to server, followed by a response message from server to client. Such communications can be accomplished by the establishment of a short-duration connection between client and server. Alternatively, they might be accomplished by an exchange of two connectionless data items. Hence, specification of these communications involves specification of a complete (albeit procedurally simple) protocol.

Certificate Communications

With public-key techniques, the verifier needs to have a certificate for the public key of the claimant. The simplest way to achieve this is to have the claimant send a certificate, as part of the authentication exchange. However, this does not always satisfy the complete requirement. In the general case, where principal and verifier do not have a common certification authority, the verifier may require a chain of certificates in which authorities progressively authenticate the public keys of other authorities and eventually the public key of the principal. The claimant may or may not know a certification chain which the verifier will trust, hence may or may not be able to send the full chain of certificates needed. If the verifier does not have all certificates needed, these must be obtained from a directory server. This involves a directory access protocol, such as that defined in ISO/IEC 9594.

The verifier may need to check for revocations issued by the relevant certification authorities. Certificate revocation lists can also be distributed, in the form of certificates, via a directory server.

5.9 Architectural Placement

Entity Authentication

The appropriate architectural placement for entity authentication depends upon the type of entity being authenticated and the purpose of the authentication (e.g., for input to access control decisions or for supporting accountability). In terms of the architectural placement options described in Chapter 3, entity authentication exchanges may be placed at any of the following architectural levels:

- *Application level*: Entity authentication may be directly linked with an application-association, i.e., a party bound to the association is authenticated. This party might be the application protocol entity or it might be something above (e.g., a person responsible for initiating the application-association). Alternatively, entity authentication might be associated with an application-level relationship other than the application-association. For example, the OSI Distributed Transaction Processing application (ISO/IEC 10026) has the concept of a *dialogue*, which is an end-to-end relationship with a lifetime which does not map to an application-association (see Figure 5-11). Establishment or termination of a dialogue does not coincide with that of an application-association, and a dialogue may map to different application-associations at different times. Entity authentication may be used to authenticate a party to a dialogue. In general, the application level is the most appropriate level for locating entity authentication which supports identity-based access control or accountability goals.

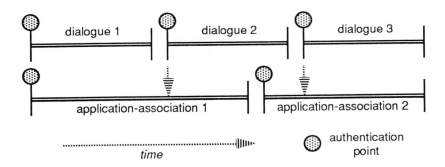

Figure 5-11: Entity Authentication at Application Level

- *End-system level*: At this level, entity authentication provides assurance to one end system that it is communicating with the correct system at the other end. This protects against security compromises in the intervening network, which may be untrusted. Without stipulating special constraints, entity authentication at this level is not suitable for supporting identity-based access control or accountability goals. However, it may be possible to establish constraints to make such support possible, e.g., by ensuring by other means that there is a secure binding between one (and only one) human user and an end system throughout the period that the entity authentication will apply. Entity authentication at the end-system level may play an important role in supporting rule-based access control, e.g., in ensuring that an end-system has an adequate security clearance before sending any sensitive data there.
- *Subnetwork level*: At this level, entity authentication provides assurance at one subnetwork attachment point that it is communicating with the correct subnetwork attachment point at the other end. This protects against security compromises in an untrusted intervening subnetwork. Entity authentication at the subnetwork level may play an important role in supporting rule-based access control, e.g., in ensuring that a network node has an adequate security clearance before sending any sensitive traffic there. Entity authentication at this level is not suitable for supporting identity-based access control or accountability goals.

While authentication exchanges need to be integrated into the basic protocol at the level at which the authentication service is provided, on-line server communications and certificates are not necessarily implemented at the same level. On-line server communications (which involve either a separate connection or an exchange of connectionless data units) would be more correctly placed at the application level, even when supporting entity authentication at end-system or subnetwork level. The same applies to certificate communications (except where certificates are conveyed as part of the authentication exchange). The directory access protocol (ISO/IEC 9594) provides for certificate retrieval.

Data Origin Authentication

Data origin authentication is significant in two different ways in a layered architecture. At the application level, data origin authentication is used to give assurance of the true source of a data item, regardless of the fact that that item may have traversed many different systems, networks, and/or storage facilities. The authenticated source of a data item may be any of:

- an application protocol entity;
- some part of a real end system, e.g., a specific application software process; or
- a person or piece of equipment which may or may not be in immediate communication with the end system (including the case of data forwarded through multiple application relays).

The granularity of protection may be at any level desired, ranging from a small field within a conveyed message to all the data conveyed on an application-association.

At the end-system and subnetwork levels, data origin authentication is used with connectionless modes of operation only, for authenticating the protocol entity that originated a particular connectionless data unit.

Summary

Authentication is the means of gaining assurance that people or things are who or what they claim to be. There are many different methods for providing authentication, some involving cryptography and some not.

Passwords, or personal identification numbers (PINs), are an authentication method on which most practical authentication systems depend. Password systems have vulnerabilities, the most serious being external disclosure and password guessing. These vulnerabilities can be countered by various administrative and procedural measures, including measures which require support in network equipment. Protected password mechanisms provide for protection against password disclosure through passive monitoring of password exchanges. A certain degree of protection against replay attacks can also be incorporated. One-time password mechanisms and challenge-response mechanisms provide progressively better protection against replay attacks.

Cryptographic-based authentication mechanisms may employ either symmetric or public-key techniques and involve encryption, sealing, or signing. In large networks, mechanisms using symmetric techniques depend upon trusted on-line authentication servers. Mechanisms using public-key techniques need off-line servers, which need not be trusted, for distributing public-key certificates and certificate revocation lists. Zero-knowledge techniques constitute an emerging technology in this area.

Authentication protocol design needs to take into account an array of possible attack scenarios, such as replay and interception attacks. Different approaches to sourcing non-repeating values for countering replay have advantages and disadvantages. While protocol exchanges for mutual authentication can be built from unilateral authentication exchanges, they are best designed specifically for the mutual authentication purpose, and subjected to their own vulnerability analysis. To preserve authentication throughout a connection, a connection-integrity service should be used in conjunction with an authentication service.

Three valuable examples of complete authentication system designs are the Kerberos system, the X.509 authentication exchanges, and the authenticated Diffie-Hellman exchange. Kerberos employs symmetric cryptographic techniques with on-line servers. The other other two examples employ public-key authentication techniques.

Communication protocol requirements for authentication include authentication exchanges (integrated with application communication protocols), on-line server communication exchanges, and/or certificate distribution communications.

Entity authentication may be associated with the application level, end-system level, or subnetwork level of a security protocol architecture. Data origin authentication may be associated with the application level or with connectionless modes of the end-system or subnetwork level.

Exercises

1. Identify seven password management practices that a user and/or his organization might adopt to reduce the vulnerabilities of password-based authentication systems. What features (if any) could be included in product designs in support of such practices?

2. Considering the two on-line server scenarios for symmetric cryptographic authentication systems shown in Figure 5-7, describe the contents of messages exchanged and the keys used to protect them. Ignore issues of protection against replay attack.

3.   Suppose parties *A* and *B*, who share a secret key, adopt a simple mechanism for authenticating to each other whereby the claimant sends to the verifier a message comprising a time-stamp sealed under the shared secret key. Ignoring risks of cryptanalysis and disclosure of the key, identify two possible types of attack.

4.   Suppose party *A* authenticates to multiple verifiers using a mechanism whereby he signs a time-stamp and the verifier checks the signature using *A*'s public key. Ignoring risks of cryptanalysis and private-key disclosure, identify two ways in which the possible types of attack differ from those in Question 3.

5.   List the comparative advantages and disadvantages of the following three types of non-repeating value used to counter replay attacks — random numbers, sequence numbers, time-stamps.

6.   Which of the following four architectural levels may be appropriate for placing (a) entity authentication and (b) data origin authentication: application level, end-system level, subnetwork level, direct-link level.

REFERENCES

[BAU1] F. Bauspiess and H.-J. Knobloch, "How to Keep Authenticity Alive in a Computer Network," in J.J. Quisquater, J. Vandewalle (Eds.), *Advances in Cryptology — EUROCRYPT '89 (Lecture Notes in Computer Science 434)*, Springer-Verlag, Berlin, 1990, pp. 38-46.

[BEL1] S.M. Bellovin and M. Merritt, "Limitations of the Kerberos Authentication System," *Computer Communication Review*, vol. 20, no. 5 (October 1990), ACM Press, New York, pp. 119-132.

[BET1] T. Beth, "A Fiat-Shamir-like Authentication Protocol for the El-Gamal-scheme," in C.G. Günther (Ed.), *Advances in Cryptology — EUROCRYPT '88 (Lecture Notes in Computer Science 330)*, Springer-Verlag, Berlin, 1989, pp. 77-84.

[BIR1] R. Bird, I. Gopal, A. Herzberg, P. Janson, S. Kutten, R. Molva, and M. Yung, "Systematic Design of Two-party Authentication Protocols," *Advances in Cryptology — CRYPTO '91 (Lecture Notes in Computer Science 576)*, Springer-Verlag, Berlin, 1992, pp. 44-61.

[BUR1] M.V.D. Burmester, Y. Desmedt, F. Piper, and M. Walker, "A General Zero-knowledge Scheme," in J.J. Quisquater, J. Vandewalle (Eds.), *Advances in Cryptology — EUROCRYPT '89 (Lecture Notes in Computer Science 434)*, Springer-Verlag, Berlin, 1990, pp. 122-33.

[BUR2] M. Burrows, M. Abadi, and R. Needham, "A Logic of Authentication," *ACM Transactions on Computer Systems*, vol. 8, no. 1 (February 1990), pp. 18-36.

[DEN1] D.E. Denning and G.M. Sacco, "Timestamps in Key Distribution Protocols," *Communications of the ACM*, vol. 24, no. 8 (August 1981), pp. 533-536.

[DIF1]   W. Diffie, P.C. van Oorschot, and M.J. Wiener, "Authentication and Authenticated Key Exchanges," *Designs, Codes and Cryptography*, vol. 2, no. 2 (June 1992), pp. 107-126.

[DOD1] U.S. Department of Defense, *Department of Defense Password Management Guideline*, CSC-STD-002-85, Department of Defense Computer Security Center, Fort Meade, MD, April 1985.

[FEI1]   J. Feigenbaum, "Overview of Interactive Proof Systems and Zero-Knowledge", in G.J. Simmons (Ed.), *Contemporary Cryptology: The Science of Information Integrity*, IEEE Press, New York, 1992, pp. 423-439.

[FIA1]   A. Fiat and A. Shamir, "How to Prove Yourself: Practical Solutions to Identification and Signature Problems," in A. Odlyzko (Ed.), *Advances in Cryptology — CRYPTO '86 (Lecture Notes in Computer Science 263)*, Springer-Verlag, Berlin, 1987, pp. 186-194.

[FIE1]   U. Fiege, A. Fiat, and A. Shamir, "Zero Knowledge Proofs of Identity," *Journal of Cryptology*, vol. 1, no. 2 (1988), pp. 77-94.

[GAA1] K. Gaarder and E. Snekkenes, "Applying a Formal Analysis Technique to the CCITT X.509 Strong Two-way Authentication Protocol," *Journal of Cryptology*, vol. 3, no. 2 (1991), pp. 81-98.

[GUI1]   L.C. Guillou and J.-J. Quisquater, "A Practical Zero-knowledge Protocol Fitted to Security Microprocessor Minimizing both Transmission and Memory," in C.G. Günther (Ed.), *Advances in Cryptology — EUROCRYPT '88 (Lecture Notes in Computer Science 330)*, Springer-Verlag, Berlin, 1989, pp. 123-128.

[GUI2]   L.C. Guillou, M. Ugon, and J.-J. Quisquater, "The Smart Card: A Standardized Security Device Dedicated to Public Cryptology," in G.J. Simmons (Ed.), *Contemporary Cryptology: The Science of Information Integrity*, IEEE Press, New York, 1992, pp. 561-613.

[GUN1] C.G. Günther, "An Identity-based Key Exchange Protocol," in J.-J. Quisquater, J. Vandewalle (Eds.), *Advances in Cryptology — EUROCRYPT '89 (Lecture Notes in Computer Science 434)*, Springer-Verlag, Berlin, 1990, pp. 29-37.

[KEM1] R.A. Kemmerer, "Analyzing Encryption Protocols Using Formal Verification Techniques," *IEEE Journal on Selected Areas in Communications*, vol. 7, no. 4 (May 1989), pp. 448-457.

[KOH1] J.T. Kohl and B.C. Neuman, Internet Activities Board, *The Kerberos Network Authentication Service (V5)*, Internet Draft, 1993. (RFC publication planned 1993; RFC number to be assigned.)

[LIN1]   P. Lin and E.S. Lee, "An Algorithm for the Generation of Pronounceable, Typeable Passwords," *Proceedings of the 1st Annual Canadian Computer Security Conference*, Ottawa, Ontario, 30 Jan-1 Feb 1989, pp. 165-176.

[LON1] T.A. Longstaff and E.E. Schultz, "Beyond Preliminary Analysis of the WANK and OILZ Worms: a Case Study of Malicious Code," *Computers & Security*, vol. 12, no. 1 (February 1993), pp. 61-77.

[MIL1] S.P. Miller, B.C. Neuman, J.I. Schiller, and J.H. Saltzer, "Kerberos Authentication and Authorization System," *Project Athena Technical Plan, Section E.2.1*, MIT Project Athena, Cambridge, MA, December 1987.

[MIT1] C. Mitchell, "Limitations of Challenge-response Entity Authentication," *Electronic Letters*, vol. 25, no. 17 (August 1989), pp. 1195-1196.

[MOO1] J.H. Moore, "Protocol Failures in Cryptosystems," *Proceedings of the IEEE*, vol. 76, no. 5 (May 1988), pp. 594-602.

[NEC1] J. Nechvatal, "Public Key Cryptography," in G.J. Simmons (Ed.), *Contemporary Cryptology: The Science of Information Integrity*, IEEE Press, New York, 1992, pp. 178-288.

[NEE1] R.M. Needham and M.D. Schroeder, "Using Encryption for Authentication in Large Networks of Computers," *Communications of the ACM*, vol. 21, no. 12 (December 1978), pp. 993-999.

[OKA1] E. Okamoto and K. Tanaka, "Key Distribution Based on Identification Information," *IEEE Journal on Selected Areas in Communications*, vol. 7, no. 4 (May 1989), pp. 481-485.

[QUI1] J.-J. Quisquater and L. Guillou, "How to Explain Zero-Knowledge Protocols to Your Children," in G. Brassard (Ed.), *Advances in Cryptology — CRYPTO '89 (Lecture Notes in Computer Science 435)*, Springer-Verlag, Berlin, 1990, pp. 628-631.

[RSA1] RSA Data Security, Inc., *Public-Key Cryptography Standards, PKCS#5: Password-Based Encryption Standard*, 1991.

[SEE1] D. Seeley, "Password Cracking: A Game of Wits," *Communications of the ACM*, vol. 32, no. 6 (June 1989), pp. 700-703.

[SIM1] G.J. Simmons, "A Survey of Information Authentication," in G.J. Simmons (Ed.), *Contemporary Cryptology: The Science of Information Integrity*, IEEE Press, New York, 1992, pp. 379-419.

[STE1] J.G. Steiner, B.C. Neuman, and J.I. Schiller, "Kerberos: An Authentication Service for Open Network Systems," *Proceedings of the Winter 1988 Usenix Conference*, February 1988, pp. 191-201.

[STO1] C. Stoll, *The Cuckoo's Egg*, Doubleday, New York, 1989.

Standards

FIPS PUB 112: U.S. Department of Commerce, *Password Usage*, Federal Information Processing Standards Publication 112, 1985.

ISO/IEC 9594: *Information Technology — Open Systems Interconnection — The Directory* (Also ITU-T X.500 series Recommendations).

ISO/IEC 10026: *Information Technology — Open Systems Interconnection — Distributed Transaction Processing* (Also ITU-T X.860 series Recommendations).

6   Access Control

Authorization is the granting of rights, by the owner or controller of a resource, for others to access that resource. *Access control* is a means of enforcing authorization.

These definitions can be interpreted broadly. The term *resource* embraces, for example, information resources, processing resources, communications resources, and physical resources. To *access* a resource can mean to obtain information from that resource, modify that resource, or cause that resource to perform some function.

The following terminology is used in this book, with respect to access control. A *target* is a resource subject to access control. An *authority* is the owner or controller of a target. A *user* is an accountable person who might conceivably gain access to a target. An *initiator* is a user, or a process acting on behalf of a user, which actively attempts to access a target.

There are two general approaches to preventing unauthorized users from accessing targets:

- *Access request filtering*: When an initiator attempts to access a target, a check is made that that initiator has been granted the right to access that target in the way requested.
- *Separation*: Unauthorized users are prevented from having any opportunity to try to access sensitive targets.

Both of these approaches relate to the subject of access control, and both are driven by the same policies.

Access request filtering involves *access control mechanisms*, which are the main subject of this chapter. Separation can involve any of a variety of countermeasures, including physical security, personnel security, hardware security, and operating system security. The *flow model* of security policy [DEN1, NAT1] is a formal model for providing confidentiality based on the separation approach; it is discussed further in Chapter 7. *Routing control*, which can be considered a form of *communications access control*, is a network mechanism to support separation.

This chapter addresses access control policies and mechanisms as they apply to network environments. The chapter is organized into sections which discuss:

(1) access control policies;

(2) the range of access control mechanisms available;

(3) an access control mechanism example, from the OSI File Transfer, Access, and Management (FTAM) application;

(4) a general model for distributing access control functions in a network environment;

(5) requirements for managing and distributing access control information in a network environment;

(6) communications access control and routing control; and

(7) protocol requirements and architectural placement issues.

6.1   Access Control Policies

Authorization is the granting of rights as to which users may access which targets for which purposes. Access control policies express authorizations at the system security policy level, i.e., they are directly enforced by system components.

Any access control policy can be modeled ultimately in terms of an *access matrix* [DEN1]. At any point in time, the policy can be expressed as a matrix with rows corresponding to users and columns corresponding to targets. Each matrix entry states the *access permissions* granted to the corresponding user, with respect to the corresponding target.[1] The matrix entry identifies the *actions* that the user may perform on the target.

Figure 6-1 provides an example, for the case of four users who may potentially try to access any of three stored information resources (targets). The possible actions are *read*, *modify*, and *manage* (the *manage* privilege might allow a user to perform management actions such as delete or change attributes).

Because of the size and sparseness of access matrices in a typical network, they are of little direct practical use, either in expressing access control policies or in implementing access control mechanisms. However, the access matrix is a valuable conceptual model for use in deriving or describing some important types of policies.

There are various types of access control policies. Different types result from differences in:

• The level at which the authorization decision is made. Some policies assume all decisions are controlled at the organizational level while others

---

[1] The term *rights*, or *privileges*, is sometimes used in place of *permissions*.

	Target x	Target y	Target z
User a	*read, modify, manage*		*read, modify, manage*
User b		*read, modify, manage*	
User $c1$	*read*	*read, modify*	
User $c2$	*read*	*read, modify*	

Figure 6-1: Access Matrix Example

support authority delegation, potentially to the extent where decisions are made by individuals responsible for specific targets.

- The ways in which users and/or targets can be grouped together for purposes of common handling.
- The extent to which policies can be stated in terms of general rules which can be automatically enforced by system components.

The concepts of mandatory and discretionary policies, derived from the classified sphere [DOD1, DOD2], mix the above factors to some extent. A mandatory policy is specified and enforced by the ultimate authority for a security domain. It is based on rules which can be automatically enforced. For such rule enforcement to be practical, it is necessary to use very broad groupings for users and targets. A discretionary policy provides particular users with access to information, then leaves it to those users to control further access to the information. With discretionary policies, there is much greater flexibility as to how users and targets may be grouped, ranging from explicit recognition of individual users and targets to the use of broad groupings.

The OSI Security Architecture (ISO/IEC 7498-2) does not use the mandatory/discretionary terminology, but instead distinguishes *identity-based* and *rule-based* policies. For all practical purposes, we can consider identity-based and discretionary policies to be equivalent, and rule-based and mandatory policies to be equivalent.

Below we describe some specific types of policy. Identity-based (discretionary) policies include *individual-based* policies and *group-based* policies. Rule-based (mandatory) policies include *multi-level* policies and *compartment-based* policies. We also discuss *role-based* policies which have characteristics of both identity-based and rule-based policies. In general, these policies can be combined, and can be refined through the use of additional controls such as value-dependent controls, multiple-user controls, and context-based controls.

Individual-Based Policies

An *individual-based policy* is expressed in terms of a list for each target stating which users may perform which actions on that target. This is equivalent to describing the access matrix column for a target. An example (based on Figure 6-1) would be the policy statement:

- For target *x*, user *a* is granted *read*, *modify*, and *manage* permissions, and users *c1* and *c2* are granted *read* permission.

An individual-based policy is one type of identity-based policy. Identity-based policy statements always depend upon an implicit or explicit *default policy*. In the example above, the assumed default is that all users are denied all permissions. This is the most common default policy. It supports what is known as the *principle of least privilege*, which requires that each user be granted the most restrictive set of permissions needed for the performance of authorized tasks. The application of this principle limits the damage that can result from accident, error, or unauthorized use.

Other default policies may be appropriate in some environments. For example, in a public bulletin-board environment, the default may be that all information is made publicly available. Also, as is discussed later, multiple policies may apply simultaneously to a target. The effective default can then be some other policy, which may have provided explicit access permission to some user(s). For this reason, identity-based policies commonly also have provision to explicitly *deny* permissions for identified users with respect to identified targets.

For example, the general rule in a corporation may be that employees are permitted *read* access to all proprietary technical information. However, exceptions might sometimes be necessary. For example, an employee subject to disciplinary action might not be permitted to access more sensitive targets. This can be achieved by keeping a simple default policy (*read* is granted), but placing identity-based denial restrictions on those sensitive targets.

Denial restrictions are also valuable for dealing with such situations as a stolen password or a lost or stolen personal authentication device. An appropriate denial restriction is simply added to the existing set of policy statements for all targets of concern. Clearly, denial restrictions should override any conflicting permission-granting statements.

Group-Based Policies

A *group-based policy* is another case of an identity-based policy, in which several users are granted the same permissions for one target. This arises, for example, when permissions are assigned to all the members of a team or all the employees of one department of an organization. Multiple users are grouped together and given a common identifier. This amounts to collapsing multiple rows of the access matrix into one. For example, in Figure 6-1, suppose users *c1* and *c2* can be considered to form a group. The access control policy for target *x* can then be expressed as a pair of statements:

- User group *c* comprises users *c1* and *c2*.
- For target *x*, user *a* is granted *read*, *modify*, and *manage* permissions, and user group *c* is granted *read* permission.

Note that the first of these statements can be reused for other targets, e.g., target *y*. Furthermore, the membership of the group can be changed without affecting the permission statements (e.g., the second statement above). These characteristics tend to make group-based policies easier and more efficient to express and to implement than individual-based policies.

Role-Based Policies

A *role-based policy* is another type of policy, which is particularly valuable in contemporary commercial environments. It can be considered a variation of a group-based policy — a *role* corresponds to a group which has major semantic significance in the formulation of an access control policy.

For example, in a banking environment, the user roles *Teller*, *Branch Manager*, *Customer*, *System Administrator*, and *Auditor* might be defined. An example of an access control policy statement might be:

- A *Teller* has permissions to modify customer account records with deposit and withdrawal transactions up to a specified dollar amount limit, and to query all account log entries.
- A *Branch Manager* has permissions to modify customer account records with deposit and withdrawal transactions without dollar amount limit, to query all account log entries, and to create and terminate accounts.
- A *Customer* has permission to query account log entries for his own account only.
- A *System Administrator* has permissions to query system log entries and to activate or deactivate the system, but not to read or modify customer account information.

- An *Auditor* has permission to read any data in the system, but to modify nothing.

This type of policy statement is very powerful for two reasons. First, it is couched in a way which is easily comprehensible to non-technical organizational policymakers. Second, it maps easily to an access matrix, or group-based policy statement, from which access control implementations can be derived.

It is also possible to consider a role-based policy as a type of rule-based or mandatory access control policy, which can be automatically enforced across a security domain (not unlike multi-level policies as described in the next subsection).

In group-based and role-based policies, it is generally possible for one individual user to be a member of more than one group or role. Restrictions may apply, e.g., in the above banking example, individuals may be forbidden from having both *Branch Manager* and *Auditor* roles.

See [FER1, LAW1, VIN1] for further discussion of role-based policies.

Multi-Level Policies

Multi-level policies are used extensively in government classified environments, but can also find application in unclassified environments. These policies are amenable to automated enforcement, i.e., as mandatory policies. They are most commonly used for protecting information from unauthorized disclosure, but they can also support integrity requirements.

A multi-level policy operates by assigning to each target a *classification* level, from a hierarchy of levels such as those shown in Figure 6-2. Each user is assigned a *clearance* level from the same hierarchy. The target's assignment reflects its sensitivity. The user's assignment reflects general trustworthiness based, for example, on an investigation of a person's background.

Figure 6-2: Typical Security Levels

The classical rules associated with this type of policy are described in the U.S. Department of Defense Trusted Computer Security Evaluation Criteria[2] [DOD1]. The underlying mathematical model is attributed to Bell and LaPadula [BEL1, PFL1]. This model defines a relationship, known as a *dominance relation*, between formal security levels of users and targets. Specific rules are then defined for granting read-only access and write-only access.

The rule for read-only access, known as the *Simple Security Condition*, is somewhat obvious. It stipulates that a user with a given clearance level can only read information with the same or a lower classification level. The rule for write-only access, known as the **-Property* (read "Star Property"), is less obvious. It stipulates that a user with a given clearance level can only write information to a target with the same or a higher classification level. The reason for this rule is to prevent a user from declassifying information without authorization, and to prevent against Trojan horse attacks. There is also a rule that when information is combined from several targets, the result is assigned the highest classification level.

A corresponding policy model addressing integrity conditions, as opposed to confidentiality conditions, was developed by Biba [BIB1, PFL1]. Use of this model can result in targets being assigned integrity classification levels as well as sensitivity classification levels.

Compartment-Based Policies

In a compartment-based policy, sets of targets are associated with a named security *compartment* or *category*, which isolates them from other targets. Users need to be given a distinct clearance for a compartment to be able to access targets in that compartment.

For example, within a corporation, distinct compartments might be defined for *Contracts* and *Personnel*. Clearance for one compartment does not necessarily imply clearance to the same level in another compartment.

Furthermore, accesses in a compartment may be subject to special rules. For example, within a particular compartment, two cleared users may need to present a combined request in order to be able to retrieve information.

Value-Dependent Controls

Discussion thus far has assumed that an identified target data item has fixed access control permissions, regardless of the data value stored therein. However, sometimes the sensitivity of a target can vary depending upon values currently stored. For example, information regarding contracts with a dollar value exceeding a certain threshold might be afforded greater protection than

---

[2] Commonly known as the *Orange Book*. See Chapter 16.

other contracts in the same corporate database. This constitutes a value-dependent control.

Multiple-User Controls

It is possible to devise access control policies which require more than one user to jointly present a request before access to a target will be granted. Examples are:

- requiring two specified individuals to agree;
- requiring individuals with two specified roles (e.g., a company officer and a board member) to agree; and
- requiring a specified number of members of a group (e.g., a majority) to agree.

Context-Based Controls

Context-based controls allow an access control policy to specify that access to a target will depend upon external factors such as:

(a) the time of day;
(b) the current location of the user;
(c) the communications path used between initiator and target; and/or
(d) the strength of the authentication method used in confirming the identity of the initiator (sometimes known as *authentication level*).

Such controls can augment identity-based or rule-based policies. Their purpose is to protect against possible weaknesses in other safeguards such as access control mechanisms, authentication mechanisms, or physical security measures.

For example, access to a particular target might be restricted to business hours only and to terminals located on corporate premises. This may eliminate risks of outside hacker attack. It combines context-based controls of types (a) and (b) above.

Controls of type (c) provide protection against penetrations which are considered more likely on a particular part of a network. For example, regardless of initiator, access to some types of information may be inhibited on calls traversing radio links, because of risks of eavesdropping.

Controls of type (d) take into account the different levels of certainty of knowing an initiator's true identity, depending on the type of authentication method used. For example, for accessing some targets, it may be deemed that authentication by password is adequate, but that for accessing more sensitive targets the initiator must be authenticated using a cryptographic-based authentication mechanism. This type of control is discussed further in [OSH1].

Target Granularity and Policy Interactions

In devising any access control policy, target granularity is an important issue. Consider, for example, a corporate personnel database. At one level, it is meaningful to consider the whole database as one target. This target can only be accessed by corporate personnel; it is not to be accessed from terminals off corporate premises; and all modifications must be made from within the corporate administrative branch. However, for some purposes, a much finer granularity may need to be recognized for the same database. Corporate policy might dictate that any employee is to have the right to read all database information pertaining to himself or herself but not that pertaining to other employees. Communication system administrators might be authorized to read and modify communication addresses for any employee but not have access to other fields. Reading and modification of salary information might be limited to officers in the salaries department.

Different levels of granularity of the same information structure may have logically distinct access control policies, and different access control mechanisms may be employed.

Different access control granularities often relate to *policy delegation*. The authority for a target at a coarse level of granularity delegates responsibility for component targets of finer granularity to other authorities. For example, a corporation delegates responsibility for parts of the corporate database to departments who, in turn, delegate parts to individual employees.

When more than one policy applies to a target (as a result of multiple granularities or other reasons), it is necessary to establish rules as to how these policies interact. Typical rules involve:

- stating policy precedence relationships, whereby the rules of one policy for granting and/or denying permissions will apply regardless of potential conflicts with another policy; and
- recognizing that denials under any of the policies will apply, regardless of conflicting permission granting in other policies.

Figure 6-3 illustrates how multiple policies might be combined to produce an access matrix column for a target. The illustrated example has no conflicts but suppose, for example, one of the following statements was added to *G. Smith*'s policy: *auditors* denied *read*, or *A. Suspect* (an outsider to the corporation) granted *read*. This would present a conflict which necessitates another rule, such as one stipulating that either corporate policy or *G. Smith*'s policy has precedence.

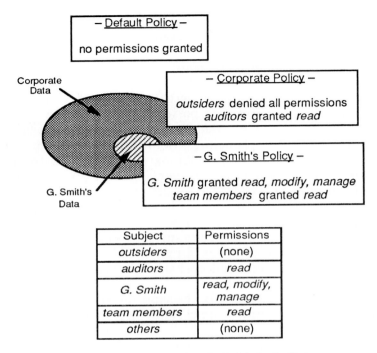

Figure 6-3: Example of Multiple Policies

6.2   Access Control Mechanisms

Having identified the policy options facing a security authority, let us now turn to access control mechanisms which may be used in enforcing such policies.

Access Control Lists

An access control list is an attribute of a target object, stating which users can invoke which actions on it.   Maintenance of the access control list and enforcement of the access control are essentially the responsibility of the system and environment immediately surrounding the target.

An access control list reflects the contents of the access matrix column for the object concerned. Hence, identity-based access control policies, including individual-based, group-based and role-based policies, can be realized in a straightforward way using access control lists. The basic access control list concept can be extended in various ways, such as by adding context-based controls for selected user entries. Figure 6-4 illustrates a possible access control list structure and some example entries.

Identity	Type	Permissions Granted	Permissions Denied	Time-of-day Restrictions	Location Restrictions
G. Smith	individual	read, modify, manage			
team members	group	read			
auditors	role	read	modify, manage		
Contractor XYZ Inc.	group	read, modify	manage	8:00-18:00 Mon-Fri	Only local terminals

Figure 6-4: Example Access Control List

Access control list mechanisms are best suited to situations where there are relatively few users (individuals, groups, or roles) needing to be distinguished, and where the population of such users tends to be stable. Management of access control lists can become a major problem if they are too large or change frequently. Unlike some other mechanisms, access control lists are suitable for wide ranges of target granularities, including very fine granularities. Another advantage is that they make it easy for a target owner or manager to revoke previously granted permissions.

Access control list mechanisms are used in the FTAM and Directory applications. The former use is described in Section 6.3; the latter in Chapter 14. For further information on access control lists, see [DEN1, DOD2, RAN1, SAL1].

Capabilities

Capabilities were introduced as a computer access control concept as long ago as 1966 [DEN2]. A capability is effectively a ticket, possessed by an initiator, which authorizes the holder to access a specified target in specified ways. Capabilities have the properties that they can be passed from one user to another, and that they cannot be altered or fabricated by anyone apart from the responsible authority.

Capabilities are generated in an *initiator's* environment, on the basis of a stored list of access permissions for a user. In terms of the access matrix, the generation of capabilities uses knowledge of the access matrix row for the user involved.

To help explain the difference between access control list and capability schemes, we can use an analogy. Consider a large corporation which needs to operate separate restricted areas on its premises for dealing with separate sensitive projects. There are two approaches to controlling employee access to such areas. In the capability-like approach, each employee is given a special badge indicating which restricted areas he is entitled to enter. The badges are designed to make counterfeiting difficult. When entering a restricted area, the employee presents the badge to an entrance guard who checks its authenticity. Badges might even bear numbers, and the guard might check a *hot list* for lost or stolen badges. However, there is no need to maintain lists, for each restricted area, of employees entitled to enter. In an approach like access control lists, employees wear simple identification badges and each entrance guard is supplied with a list of the employees entitled to enter that area. The guard checks the list and a participant's identification to decide whether or not to grant entry. With this approach, the authority responsible for each restricted area can maintain its own access list, and there is not necessarily *any* integrated list of all the restricted areas a particular employee may enter.

Capabilities find less applicability in network environments than in more closely-coupled systems [FAB1]. Networks often involve multiple security domains, and the security domain immediately surrounding a target usually demands a voice in access decisions regarding that target. However, capability mechanisms may be suitable for situations where there are relatively few targets, and where it is convenient for access control decisions to be made close to initiators. Implementation of a capability mechanism depends upon a secure means for transferring capabilities between systems. A disadvantage of capabilities is that it is not easy for a target owner or manager to revoke previously granted permissions.

Security Labels

In the most general terms, a security label is a set of security attribute information items bound to an "object" such as a communicated or stored data item, a physical resource, or a person. In the context of access control, a security label is attached to either a user, a target, an access request, or access control information in transfer.

The most common use of security labels as an access control mechanism is in supporting multi-level access control policies. In an initiator's environment, a label is attached to every access request, identifying the clearance level of the initiator. This label must be generated and attached by a trusted process and must be conveyed along with the access request, bound to it in a secure manner. Every target also has a label bound to it, identifying the classification level of that target. In processing an access request, the target environment compares the label on the request with that on the target, and applies policy rules (e.g., the Bell Lapadula rules) to decide whether to grant or deny access.

Labels are typically more complex than suggested above, containing additional attributes for use in access control decision making. Such attributes might include, for example, handling and distribution caveats, compartment indicators, timing constraints, and/or initiator identification information. Labels also contain security policy/authority identification and, possibly, reference identifiers for use in verification and/or audit.

The security policy/authority identification is particularly important, as the significance of all other fields depends upon the security policy. Labels generated in one security domain may or may not be significant in another domain. Consider, for example, labels of identical format generated by two different organizations with multi-level policies. Information classified as *confidential* in the first organization is not necessarily to be disclosed to persons with *confidential* clearance in the other organization. However, if the two organizations have a suitable security policy relationship (e.g., they are both members of one corporate family) some classification/clearance levels may be significant in both domains.

A label-based access control mechanism is used in the Message Handling Systems application; this use is discussed in Chapter 13. For further discussion of the use of security labels in unclassified networks, see [NAZ1].

Information Model Relating the Mechanisms

The above three types of mechanism — access control lists, capabilities, and security labels — were historically considered to be distinct approaches to implementing access control. However, it is being increasingly realized that modern network access control mechanisms often cannot be simply categorized as one of the three types. More commonly they mix characteristics of at least two types.

An interesting view, promoted by the European Computer Manufacturers Association [ECM1] and later recognized in ISO/IEC 10181-3, is that the three types of mechanism and their variations are points on a continuum of access control mechanisms, based on one overall information model. Access control decisions are based on access control information of various types including, in particular, *initiator-bound information* and *target-bound information*. Initiator-bound information is directly associated with an initiator, and its source is the initiator's domain. Target-bound information is directly associated with a target, and its source is the target's domain.

Figure 6-5 illustrates how the access control information used in access control list, security label, and capability mechanisms maps to initiator-bound and target-bound information. For access control lists, the only initiator-bound information required is knowledge of the initiator's identity, while there is a substantial amount of target-bound information describing the initiator's permissions. Conversely, for capabilities, substantial initiator-bound information is used in generating a capability, while the only target-bound information required is knowledge of the target's identity. Security label mechanisms fall between the other two, depending on more initiator-bound information than access control lists and more target-bound information than capabilities. Variations of the three basic mechanism types lead to other points on the scale.

    This information-distribution view of access control mechanisms will prove useful later when considering communications protocol requirements for access control mechanisms.

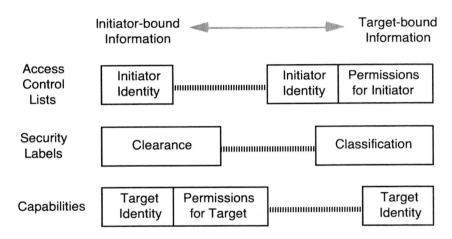

Figure 6-5: Range of Access Control Mechanisms

Password-Based Mechanisms

Password-based access control mechanisms are mentioned here more for completeness than because they are suitable for securing modern networks. A password is similar to a capability in that it constitutes a ticket to a target. Access to a particular target for a particular type of access is granted to anyone presenting the password for that target/access type combination. While this type of mechanism has been used extensively in mainframe computer operating systems, it has several serious problems. These problems were identified in the discussion of passwords in Chapter 5, which highlighted the difficulties in keeping passwords confidential, and the management problems and vulnerabilities when passwords are shared. While passwords are a valuable mechanism for authentication purposes, their use for access control purposes is not recommended.

6.3 Case Study: FTAM Access Control

The File Transfer, Access, and Management (FTAM) standards (ISO/IEC 8571) provide for the reading, writing, and management (e.g., creating or deleting) of files stored in a remote computer system. They include support for accessing components (e.g., records) of files. A stored file is accompanied by a set of stored *file attributes* of various types, as defined in the standards.

One file attribute is an access control list which governs who can access the file and in which ways. The access control list comprises a set of statements (called *elements* in the standard). Each statement has the following fields:

- *Identity*: An optional identity value which is to be matched against the identity of the user initiating the request. Matching may involve a simple textual comparison but could, dependent on local rules, be a more complex procedure. For example, the identity in the access control list could be a group identity, and the matching procedure could involve checking membership/non-membership of the initiating user in that group. Hence, individual-based, group-based, and role-based policies can all be supported.

- *Action-list*: A set of permissions granted. Permissions correspond to the defined actions on files (*read, insert, replace, extend, erase, read-attribute, change-attribute,* and *delete-file*).

- *Concurrency-access*: An optional set of additional permissions governing rights to set concurrency locks on files. For example, a user wanting to read a file can request either exclusive-read or shared-read access to the file. Some users may be permitted shared-read access but not exclusive-read access, e.g., to protect against denial-of-service situations. The value in this field is a bit-map specifying for each available concurrency lock (one for each of the defined file actions) the permissible values that the lock can assume in accesses governed by this statement. Possible values are *not-required, shared, exclusive,* and *no-access*.

- *Passwords*: A set of optional passwords, each corresponding to one of the defined file actions. The password, if present, must be supplied along with the access request in order to be granted access under this statement.

- *Location*: An optional identifier (application entity title) of the system from which the access request must originate. This provides a form of context-based control.

The FTAM access control list structure is generally in line with the access control list principles discussed in Section 6.2. Two points are worthy of note. First, the FTAM structure does not include explicit permission denials;

inclusion of these is recommended in any access control list. Second, note the inclusion of the *passwords* option, which is not recommended. However, use of this option is not mandatory so it can be easily avoided. Work is proceeding post-1992 to enhance FTAM's security features in various respects.

6.4 Network Access Control Function Distribution

Implementing access control in a network environment raises many problems not encountered in implementing access control in a single computer system. This results from the distribution of the components involved. In the general case, the initiator and target for any action reside in different systems, potentially in different security domains. Making and enforcing an access decision can involve functions in several further systems, possibly involving further security domains. The open systems Access Control Framework (ISO/IEC 10181-3) is a valuable publication which introduces an architectural basis for dealing with these distribution issues.

Figure 6-6 illustrates the basic logical components involved in making and enforcing an access control decision. The access control *decision function* (ADF) is a logical part of a network which makes access control decisions by applying access control policy rules to a requested action. The access control *enforcement function* (AEF) is a logical part of a network on the access path between an initiator and a target. This function enforces the decision made by the decision function.

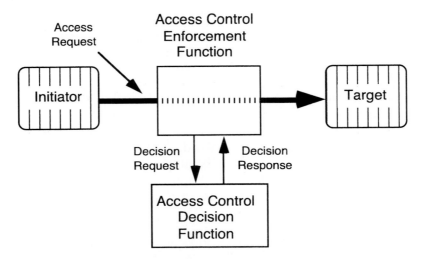

Figure 6-6: Basic Access Control Functional Components

The access control decision function uses information from the following sources:

- access request (which may include initiator-bound or target-bound information);
- retained information from earlier access requests, e.g., from the same initiator within the same communication session;
- applicable policy rules; and
- contextual information such as the time of day and the initiator's calling address.

In physical configuration terms, there are many ways to realize the decision functions and enforcement functions. The realization of each function may be spread across multiple physical systems, and both functions may or may not be realized in the same system(s).

Incoming, Outgoing, and Interposed Access Control

There is often good reason to locate an enforcement function in the same system as (or very close to) either the target or the initiator. Enforcing access at a target is known as *incoming access control*. This is very common where authority is delegated to a low level, such as individual user workstations. Enforcing access at an initiator is known as *outgoing access control*. This may be appropriate when protecting a network of simple systems which do not themselves have adequate access control facilities, or when seeking to avert unsuccessful outgoing communication attempts to minimize resource costs.

There are sometimes good reasons for locating an enforcement function (or part thereof) at some intermediate point in a network between initiator and target — this is known as *interposed access control*. It will commonly arise when an access request traverses a boundary of two large security domains, and one or both of the domain authorities wishes to filter out undesirable access requests.

In general, incoming, outgoing, and interposed access controls may be combined by considering the (logical) enforcement function to be realized via components in multiple systems.

Example Configurations

Figure 6-7 illustrates some possible mappings of functions to systems for incoming, outgoing, and combined incoming/outgoing scenarios.

Configurations (a) and (b) represent fully integrated incoming and outgoing scenarios, respectively. Configurations (c) and (d) represent incoming and outgoing scenarios, with remote decision functions. Configurations (e) and (f) represent two possible cases of combined incoming and outgoing access control.

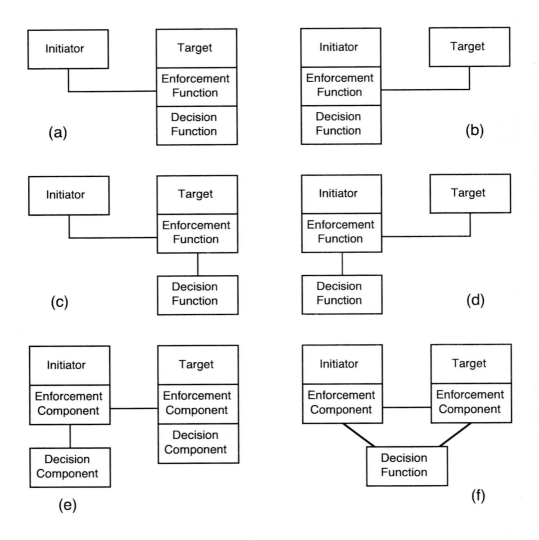

Figure 6-7: Incoming and Outgoing Access Control Examples

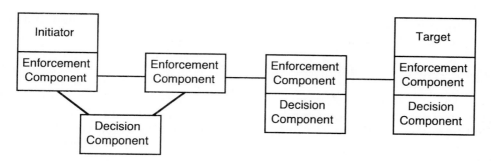

Figure 6-8: Example Configuration with Interposed Access Control

There is not necessarily a firm tie between the type of authentication mechanism used (e.g., access control list vs. capabilities) and the choice of access control configuration (e.g., incoming vs. outgoing). However, it is obvious that some combinations fit naturally together, and their use together will minimize communications requirements. The incoming scenarios [cases (a) and (c) in Figure 6-7] fit naturally with access control list mechanisms, and the outgoing scenarios [cases (b) and (d)] fit naturally with capability mechanisms.

If interposed access control is introduced, the range of configurations becomes boundless. Figure 6-8 illustrates a possible scenario, with two stages of interposed access control combining different configuration options.

Policy Mapping Through Cooperating Domains,

When providing access control over a path which involves multiple security domains, there will sometimes be a need to translate, or map, access control information which accompanies an access request at a domain boundary. This results from adjacent domains having different (albeit compatible) security policies. Examples include:

- Identifiers for individuals, groups, or roles need to be mapped to different identifiers in the next domain, e.g., individual *GSmith* in domain *X* may need to be recognized as individual *X.GSmith* in domain *Y*.
- Roles need to be mapped between domains, e.g., the role *security-administrator* in a private network attached to a public carrier network may map to the different role *subscriber-security-administrator* in the public carrier network.
- Individuals in one domain may need to be mapped to a role in the other domain, e.g., mapping all individuals on a private network to the role *subscriber-individual* on an attached public carrier network.

Such mappings will typically occur in conjunction with an enforcement function component at an interdomain boundary.

Access Control Forwarding

In distributed systems environments, it is often necessary for a user or system to request another system to perform some action on its behalf. Some examples are file servers, print servers, and distributed processing resources. Figure 6-9 illustrates typical interactions. Initiator *A* wants system *B* to access a target in system *X* on its behalf. To achieve this, *A* may need to *forward* some of its access rights to *B*.

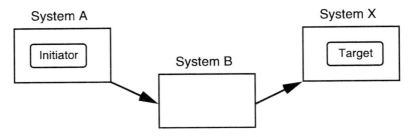

Figure 6-9: A Simple Case of Access Control Forwarding

Dependent on policy, there are various arrangements that may be necessary, such as:

(a) If *B* already has sufficient rights to access the target, then no special transfer of access control information is necessary.

(b) *A* might transfer to *B*, along with the access request, necessary access-granting information such as a capability or other certificate which grants access rights.

(c) *A* might request prior authorization from *X* before requesting *B* to carry out the action. *X* provides *A* with a signed data item (a token) which *A* passes on to *B*, and *B* on to *X* with the access request. *X* recognizes the token as originating from its original interaction with *A*.

The above scenario can be extended indefinitely through a chain of systems, to the extent that the system managing the target makes an access control decision based on a combination of information about the true initiator and about other systems through which rights have been forwarded.

Such arrangements need careful study, because it is possible they may allow an access which is not permitted directly. The general problem of discretionary access control also has to be emphasized. In forwarding *B* the rights to access the target, *A* no longer has control. If *B* is not trustworthy, or if *B*'s computer system could be subject to an information leakage problem (e.g., a Trojan horse), then the confidentiality or integrity of the target may be violated.

Access control forwarding may employ the concept of a *proxy token*. This is a statement of rights and privileges, together with a grantor name and a bearer name, conveyed between systems in an integrity-protected form.

6.5   Management of Access Control Information

Generation, Distribution, and Storage

The effectiveness of an access control mechanism depends entirely upon the accuracy and trustworthiness of the information used in making access control decisions. Great care must be taken to ensure that information describing access control policy can only be generated or revised by an appropriately authorized individual. Such information is therefore subject to *its own* access control policy and *its own* access control protection mechanism, at a level even more sensitive than that of the ultimately protected targets.

For example, given an access control list for target *x*, it is necessary to establish who can modify the access control list. This can be done by including in the list a different type of permission (sometimes known as a *control permission*) such as *modify-ACL*. It is recommended that control permissions always be recognized as logically distinct from target access permissions (e.g., *modify x*), because of the inherent extra sensitivity.

In a network environment, access control information needs to be communicated between systems, either in advance of or in conjunction with an access request, to be available for use in access control decision functions. All such communication needs to be protected by integrity and data origin authentication services. There is no general need to protect access control information by a confidentiality service, although in some environments this may be an additional requirement. To satisfy the integrity and data origin authentication requirement, access control information is often transferred in the form of an *access control certificate*, signed by some authority whom users of the information (i.e., decision functions) will trust.

A *privilege attribute certificate* (PAC) is a type of access control certificate used in distributed computing environments [ECM1]. When a user workstation first logs on to a network, it executes a transaction with a privilege attribute server to obtain a certificate containing privilege information for that user, such as authenticated name, role memberships, capabilities, and security labels. This certificate is subsequently presented to target host systems to which the user connects, where it is used as input to access control decision making.

While in storage or being processed, the integrity of access control information must also be protected. Hence, consideration always needs to be given to appropriate use of computer security and physical security counter-measures.

Revocation

Access control information may need to be revoked in such circumstances as:

- removal of a user from a security domain;
- removal of a target from a security domain;
- change in security attributes of a user or target, e.g., change of clearance or classification; or
- suspected compromise of sensitive information, e.g., a signing authority's private key.

Such revocation usually needs to be advised immediately, i.e., before the next access attempt which might use the information. Furthermore, revocation of a permission may require immediate halting of ongoing activities which depended upon that permission for their initiation. For example, if an initiator is currently performing a series of operations on a database, and it is determined that the access control certificate used earlier to grant access to the database may have had a forged signature, then the series of operations may need to be stopped immediately.

Unless carefully designed into an access control implementation, revocation may be extremely difficult. Suppose, in an environment using access control lists, a user is removed from a security domain (e.g., an employee leaves a corporation). It may be impossible to systematically apply the revocation, if there is no integrated knowledge of the entire set of access control lists which hold entries for that user.

Removal of a user or target requires special attention if there is any possibility of the user or target identifier being later reused by a new user or target. Suppose, for example, *G. Smith* leaves a corporation and, some time later, a new *G. Smith* joins the corporation. If there are still obsolete access control list entries for the original *G. Smith* in existence, the new *G. Smith* may unwittingly receive unintended access permissions.

6.6 Communications Access Control and Routing Control

The material in this chapter thus far has been applicable to access control to any type of resource, including stored information, processing resources, and communications resources. Let us now examine two important cases of access control which are intimately linked with network communications:

- *Connection access control*: Controlling whether or not two given systems are permitted to establish a connection with each other.
- *Network-data access control*: Controlling whether a particular data item is permitted to be sent on a given link to a given system. This can apply to both connection-oriented and connectionless modes of networking.

Connection access control may or may not employ protocol elements in the connection establishment protocol exchange. Depending on the circumstances of use, the access control decision may be made by either the system initiating the connection establishment request or by the system which receives such a request. Closed user groups in an X.25 network constitute a simple form of connection access control.

Network-data access control operates by conveying with each data element a security label, indicating such attributes as its classification level. Before a data item is forwarded on a link, its label is compared with a value indicating the security attributes of that link (and the system or environment at the other end of the link). If the comparison indicates an access control inconsistency (e.g., the clearance level of the destination system is inadequate) then the data item will be discarded in preference to sending it on the link.

Routing control is a mechanism which ensures that data items are routed over only those subnetworks, links, or relay systems which have appropriate security attributes. In the Network Layer, routing control uses connection access control and/or network-data access control. Routing control can also occur in the Application Layer, in the case of store-and-forward applications like electronic mail.

In architectural terms, routing control at the Network Layer is driven by specifying a *protection quality-of-service* either for all the traffic on a connection or for one connectionless data unit. A basic function of the Network Layer is to make routing decisions on the basis of various quality-of-service criteria, such as performance and cost. Protection requirements are simply another ingredient in making a routing decision. Protection quality-of-service can be specified in either of two ways:

- On the basis of a protection *level* for each security service. For example, a data item may require confidentiality protection at a level of 5 from a possible range of 1 to 10 (meaningful within some security policy).
- On the basis of a label-matching requirement.

In the Message Handling Systems application, which is a case of routing control at the Application Layer, the only approach used is label-matching.

6.7   Protocol Requirements and Architectural Placement

Communications protocol requirements for supporting access control services fall into three categories:

- protocols used for the management (including maintenance, distribution, and revocation) of access control information;
- protocol elements in layer protocols which directly support connection access control or network-data access control; and
- protocol elements used in association with access requests for targets residing in remote end systems.

Protocols for the management of access control information are naturally placed at the application level. There is currently no standard open-system protocol for this purpose. Standard ISO/IEC 10164-9 *Objects and Attributes for Access Control* addresses requirements for transferring access control information for the internal purposes of OSI systems management, and could conceivably be applied to the management of access control information for other purposes.

Connection access control and network-data access control can be located at the application level, end-system level, and/or subnetwork level. Connection access control may employ protocol elements within the connection establishment procedure of a network or transport protocol, or the association-establishment procedure of an Application Layer protocol. These protocol elements convey information as to the identities and security attributes of the entities at either end of the connection/association, possibly together with security attribute requirements for the connection/association. Integrity and data origin authentication may be provided by conveying this information in the form of an access control certificate. Protocol elements for connection access control purposes may be combined with protocol elements for other purposes such as authentication and key derivation.

Network-data access control involves attaching a security label to each data element at a suitable level of granularity, typically a protocol-data-unit. The label needs to be securely bound to the data unit, using an integrity service. The formats of labels and the semantics of their internal fields will vary greatly in different environments and with different security policies. Therefore, they cannot be broadly standardized. Generic labels can be defined, in which label fields are specified separately from the base protocol and their formats and semantics registered. The registration process assigns an identifier (e.g., an ASN.1 object identifier) which is conveyed in the encoded label in protocol, to permit parsing and interpretation of the field.

Standard protocol elements supporting connection access control and network-data access control are discussed in Chapter 11.

Protocol elements to support access requests for targets residing in remote systems are located at the application level. These protocol elements form part of Application Layer protocols designed to access targets of the appropriate type. For example, with the FTAM application, access control protocol elements associated with file access are defined as part of an FTAM-based application-context. Generic security protocol elements, which can be imported into multiple different Application Layer protocols, are discussed in Chapter 12.

Summary

Authorization is the granting of rights, by the owner or controller of a resource, for others to access that resource. Access control is a means of enforcing authorization. An access control mechanism is used to confirm that, when a user attempts to access a target resource, it has been granted the right to access that resource in the way requested. Alternatively, authorization can be enforced through an access prevention approach, which ensures that an unauthorized user never has an opportunity to try to access a resource.

There are various types of access control policies. An identity-based or discretionary policy states access rights for individual users or groups of users, and specific targets. A rule-based or mandatory policy is expressed in terms of rules applying to all users and all targets in a security domain. Identity-based policies include individual-based and group-based policies. Rule-based policies include multi-level and compartment-based policies. Role-based policies include characteristics of both identity-based and rule-based policies. A target resource may be simultaneously subject to multiple policies, in which case rules are needed to govern how such policies interact.

Access control mechanisms include access control lists, capabilities, and security labels. Network access control mechanisms may mix characteristics of at least two of the above. The FTAM application provides an example of the use of access control lists.

In a network configuration, access control can involve multiple functional components in different systems. These include access control enforcement functions which allow or block access requests, and access control decision functions which make the required decisions on the basis of information from various sources.

Access control information needs to be generated, distributed, and stored in a manner which assures its integrity. For distribution purposes, an access control certificate can provide the necessary protection. Provision also needs to be made for revocation of access control information.

The access prevention approach to access control may employ connection access control, that is, controlling whether or not a connection may be established between two systems, and/or network-data access control, that is, controlling whether or not a particular data item is permitted to be sent on a given link.

Access control may require protocol support at various architectural layers. Protocol elements for managing access control information and for controlling access to targets in remote end systems are located at the application level. Protocol elements for connection access control and network-data access control may be located at the application level, end-system level, and/or subnetwork level.

Exercises

1. How do access control services relate to achieving the basic security goals of confidentiality, integrity, availability, and legitimate use? Give an example of the application of access control for each goal.

2. Describe the similarities and differences between a role-based and a multi-level access control policy.

3. In each of the following environments, suggest arguments favoring the choice of an access control list mechanism or a capability mechanism?

   (a) A large, dynamic population of initiators will be accessing a small, stable population of targets.

   (b) A small, stable population of initiators will be accessing a large, dynamic population of targets.

4. What roles do digital signature mechanisms play in the provision of access control services?

5. What access control purposes (if any) will protocol elements in the following OSI layers serve:

   (a) Application Layer;
   (b) Presentation Layer;
   (c) Session Layer;
   (d) Transport Layer; and
   (e) Network Layer?

REFERENCES

[BEL1] D.E. Bell and L.J. LaPadula, *Secure Computer Systems: Unified Exposition and Multics Interpretation*, MTR-2997 Rev.1, MITRE Corp., Bedford, MA, March 1976.

[BIB1] K. Biba, *Integrity Considerations for Secure Computer Systems*, U.S. Air Force Electronic Systems Division, 1977.

[DEN1] D.E. Denning, *Cryptography and Data Security*, Addison-Wesley, Reading, MA, 1982.

[DEN2] J.B. Dennis and E.C. Van Horn, "Programming Semantics for Multiprogrammed Communications," *Communications of the ACM*, vol. 9, no. 3 (March 1966), pp. 143-155.

[DOD1] U.S. Department of Defense, *Department of Defense Trusted Computer System Evaluation Criteria*, DOD 5200.28-STD, National Computer Security Center, Fort Meade, MD, December 1985.

[DOD2] U.S. Department of Defense, *A Guide to Understanding Discretionary Access Control in Trusted Systems*, NCSC-TG-003 Version-1, National Computer Security Center, Fort Meade, MD, September 1987.

[ECM1] European Computer Manufacturers Association, *Security in Open Systems — A Security Framework*, Technical Report ECMA TR/46, July 1988.

[FAB1] R.S. Fabry, "Capability-Based Addressing," *Communications of the ACM*, vol. 17, no. 7 (July 1974), pp. 388-402.

[FER1] D. Ferraiolo and R. Kuhn, "Role-Based Access Controls," *Proceedings of the 15th National Computer Security Conference*, October 1992, Baltimore, MD, pp. 554-563.

[LAW1] L.G. Lawrence, "The Role of Roles," *Computers & Security*, vol. 12, no. 1 (February 1993), pp. 15-21.

[NAT1] National Research Council (U.S.), *Computers at Risk: Safe Computing in the Information Age*, National Academy Press, Washington, DC, 1990.

[NAZ1] N. Nazzario, "Security Labeling in Unclassified Networks," *Proceedings of the 13th National Computer Security Conference*, October 1990, Baltimore, MD, pp. 44-48.

[OSH1] G. O'Shea, "Controlling the Dependency of User Access Control Mechanisms on Correctness of User Authentication," *The Computer Journal*, vol. 31, no. 6 (1988), pp. 503-509.

[PFL1] C.P. Pfleeger, *Security in Computing*, Prentice Hall International, Inc., Englewood Cliffs, NJ, 1989.

[RAN1] M. Ransom, "Standardized Access Control for the OSI Directory," in *Handbook of Local Area Networks — 1992 Supplement*, Auerbach, New York, 1992.

[SAL1] J. Saltzer and M. Schroeder, "The Protection of Information in Computer Systems," *Proceedings of the IEEE*, vol. 63, no. 9 (September 1975).

[VIN1] S.T. Vinter, "Extended Discretionary Access Controls," *Proceedings of the 1988 Symposium on Security and Privacy*, Oakland, CA, IEEE Computer Society Press, 1988, pp. 39-49.

Standards

ISO/IEC 7498-2: *Information Technology — Open Systems Interconnection — Basic Reference Model — Part 2: Security Architecture* (Also ITU-T Recommendation X.800).
ISO/IEC 8571: *Information Technology — Open Systems Interconnection — File Transfer, Access and Management (FTAM)*.
ISO/IEC 10164-9: *Information Technology — Open Systems Interconnection — Systems Management — Objects and Attributes for Access Control* (Also ITU-T Recommendation X.741) (Draft).
ISO/IEC 10181-3: *Information Technology — Security Frameworks in Open Systems — Access Control Framework* (Also ITU-T Recommendation X.812) (Draft).

7   Confidentiality and Integrity

The goal of confidentiality is to protect against information being disclosed or revealed to anyone not authorized to have that information. The goal of data integrity is to protect against data being changed, deleted, or substituted without authorization. These goals are quite distinct. In many environments only one of these services is required; in other environments both are required. However, because the means of providing these two services can be closely related, it is convenient to address them both in this one chapter. The chapter is organized into sections discussing:

(1) the general means of providing confidentiality;
(2) specific types of confidentiality mechanisms;
(3) the general means of providing integrity;
(4) specific types of integrity mechanisms;
(5) the potential for combining confidentiality and integrity mechanisms;
(6) protocol requirements for confidentiality and integrity mechanisms;
(7) architectural placement options for confidentiality and integrity; and
(8) options for configuring physical equipment.

7.1   Provision of Confidentiality

As pointed out in Chapter 2, information can be stored and communicated in many different forms. Information can be disclosed through *information channels* of different types, including:

- interpreting a data item which represents some information;
- observing the existence or non-existence of a data item (regardless of its contents);
- observing the size of a data item; and
- observing dynamic variations in data item characteristics, e.g., contents, existence, or size.

Confidentiality services potentially need to protect against all such means of information disclosure.

Two Approaches to Confidentiality

There are two basic approaches to providing confidentiality:

- *Access control approach*: Prevent intruders from ever observing representations of the sensitive information.
- *Information-hiding approach*: Accept that an intruder may observe a representation of information, but make it infeasible for him to deduce information content from the representation.

The access control approach involves countermeasures such as:

- *access control mechanisms*, which filter requests from everyone seeking read access to an information resource;
- *flow control provisions*, which prevent the flow of information from one (sensitive) environment to another (less protected) environment;
- *physical security measures*, which protect against physical intrusion into the environment harboring sensitive information;
- *emanations security protection*, which prevents the release of electromagnetic field fluctuations from which sensitive information can be extracted;
- *information splitting techniques*, for example, communicating different components of a data item via multiple independent channels; and
- *protective transmission technologies*, such as spread-spectrum or frequency hopping techniques.

Of the above countermeasures, those which affect network protocols are access control mechanisms and flow control provisions. Access control mechanisms were covered in Chapter 6; flow controls are discussed further in the next subsection.

The information-hiding approach is needed when no reliable form of access control to information representations can be assumed, e.g., when information is transmitted by radio or other untrusted communications facilities. Encryption is the primary mechanism for information-hiding in data communications.

Information may move between different environments in which confidentiality is achieved in different ways. Figure 7-1 provides an example. An information item originates in an environment which is well protected using an access control approach, and in which information-hiding is unnecessary. It then moves into a different environment (e.g., a public network) which does not have reliable access control protection; confidentiality can still be preserved in this environment, using encryption (information-hiding). The item then moves into yet another environment which is well protected using an access control approach and in which information-hiding may be discontinued.

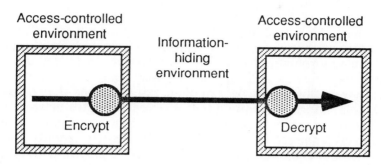

Figure 7-1: Confidentiality Preservation in Different Environments

Flow Controls

Flow controls are concerned with the right to disseminate information; they specify valid channels along which information may flow. A comprehensive lattice-based theoretical model for flow controls was developed by Denning [DEN1].

The primary purpose of flow controls is to allow multiple different protection environments to co-exist and share resources. Examples are different security levels when supporting a multi-level access control policy, or different compartments when supporting a compartment-based policy. A system which can reliably provide such support is known as a *multi-level secure* (MLS) system. The main concern is preventing information of a given classification level from flowing into an environment of a lower level, hence becoming accessible to users with an inadequate clearance. The basis of this concern is not that users at the higher level are untrusted, but that information may flow indirectly. Such indirect flows may result from a system weakness or from a user being duped by an attack such as a Trojan horse.

For example, when a user runs a utility program which processes his private information, is there any way that program can leak information to an unauthorized party , e.g., the creator of the utility program? (This is the Trojan horse concern.) A major feature of mandatory access control systems is that they are able to protect against such attacks, whereas discretionary access controls cannot.

One aspect of flow controls which bears on communications protocols is the provision of *secure channels*. These are communications channels which prevent leakage of information which may violate a security policy. In a network environment, the communications access control mechanisms described in Chapter 6 (especially routing control) are key elements in the provision of secure channels.

Consideration of flow controls also raises the interesting issue of *covert channels*. These are subtle information channels which are not intended for legitimate information transfer, but which may be used to leak information from a source in one environment to a recipient in another. For example, a running process (possibly part of a Trojan horse) may leak information to another environment via an observable pattern of accesses to some shared resource. As another example, information might be conveyed through a network via a time-pattern of call establishment attempts. There is no practical way to entirely eliminate covert channels, but steps can be taken to greatly restrict their bandwidth. Covert channels are not a significant concern in commercial and unclassified environments.

As flow controls are more a matter of secure computer system design than of network security techniques and protocols, they are not addressed in detail in this book. Nevertheless, network system designers need to be aware of the issues. For further reading, see [HAR1, LAM1].

Data Granularity

The open-systems standards recognize three different granularities at which data confidentiality can be applied:

- *Connection confidentiality*: All user data transmitted on a connection at some architectural layer is uniformly protected.
- *Connectionless confidentiality*: All user data in one connectionless data unit at some architectural layer is protected.
- *Selective field confidentiality*: One or more selected fields within a data unit (sent either on a connection or as a connectionless data unit) are protected.

Selective field confidentiality is required for various purposes. Sometimes, only a small piece of the total information communicated needs to be confidentiality protected, and protecting additional information along with it may be prohibitively expensive. In other cases, a protected field needs to be conveyed on to another system (e.g., via an application relay), and intermediate systems which process other parts of the same data unit do not know the decryption key. In fact, there are application protocols where different fields are protected under different keys known by different systems.

7.2 Confidentiality Mechanisms

Encryption

As explained in Chapter 4, encryption and decryption provide the means for converting a plaintext data block/stream to a ciphertext data block/stream and back again, on the basis of keys known at the points of encryption and decryption. This is the primary means of providing confidentiality through information-hiding.

Application of an encryption mechanism requires that several factors be agreed, including:

- *Cryptosystem type*: A choice needs to be made between symmetric and public-key cryptosystems. While public-key cryptosystems may have simpler key management requirements, they are more resource-intensive than symmetric cryptosystems of comparable strength. Hence, if bandwidth is a concern, i.e., in most bulk data protection scenarios, symmetric cryptosystems will usually be the more attractive.
- *Algorithm selection*: With either cryptosystem type, there are different algorithms from which to choose. Factors which may need to be considered include cryptographic strength, performance, implementation cost, recognition as a standard, and exportability.
- *Mode of operation*: With fixed-block-size algorithms like DES applied to data streams of arbitrary length it is necessary to choose a mode of operation.[1] This choice will depend upon such factors as resynchronization requirements and performance impact.
- *Padding requirements*: A data item to be encrypted will often not fit exactly into the block required by an encryption algorithm (e.g., 64 bits for DES). It therefore needs to be padded out to the required length by adding bits. Dependent on the algorithm, there may be arguments favoring different padding conventions.
- *Initialization requirements*: In providing confidentiality, there is a general requirement that encrypting one data item with the same key should not always generate the same result. Otherwise, observation of repeated patterns in the ciphertext stream can enable information to be gleaned, even if the key is unknown. For this reason, chaining and feedback cryptosystems use an initialization vector (IV) to start the process. The IV is different every time, and may or may not need to be kept secret.

---

[1] See Section 4.1 for technical details, and Section 11.1 for references to applicable standards.

- *Synchronization requirements*: The need for self-synchronization of a cryptosystem, in the event of a bit-transmission error, varies with the environment (e.g., it tends to be important in high-error-rate environments). This may govern the selection of algorithm or mode of operation.
- *Key management procedures*: Procedures need to be agreed for the various phases of key management, including key generation, key distribution, key destruction, and key revocation.

The above factors need to be agreed between all parties (usually two parties) to the confidentiality service. Some factors, such as cryptosystem type and key management procedures, will likely be fundamental to the application and its environment. They will be well understood in advance. However, other details may vary in different instances of use. Security protocols commonly provide for communicating an identifier of the encryption algorithm in use, plus parameter values applying to that algorithm. Algorithm parameters might include:

- indicators of mode of operation and/or padding convention;
- cryptosystem-specific parameters, e.g., modulus size for RSA; and/or
- initialization vector value.

Mode of operation and/or padding convention might be implied by the algorithm identifier; alternatively, they might need to be specified separately.

Data Padding

It was pointed out earlier that sensitive information may be disclosed if an eavesdropper can observe the *sizes* of data items transferred. For example, one might be able to deduce something from the observation that today's messages between the White House and the Pentagon are much longer than usual, even if one cannot decrypt them.

Data padding, used in conjunction with an encryption mechanism, protects against this type of disclosure. It involves padding out plaintext messages to a regular size prior to encryption.

Traffic Padding

Traffic flow confidentiality protects against sensitive information being disclosed by observing network traffic flows. For example, one might be able to deduce something by observing that the message traffic between the White House and the Pentagon today is much heavier than usual, without being able to interpret message content at all. Furthermore, additional information may be disclosed if an eavesdropper can determine that the additional traffic is between some particular White House office and some particular Pentagon department.

Traffic padding is a basic mechanism for providing traffic flow confidentiality. It involves generating spurious instances of communication, spurious data units, and/or spurious data within data units. This mechanism needs to be used in conjunction with encryption, because it is necessary to hide information distinguishing the real data from the "dummy" data.

Note, however, that traffic padding and resource sharing (as in a packet-switching network or a local area network) are inherently in conflict. Traffic padding on a route results in that route always operating to full capacity, which greatly curtails resource-sharing potential.

In a resource-sharing multi-hop network environment, traffic flow confidentiality becomes particularly difficult to achieve. In general, a communication instance, such as connection establishment or a connectionless data unit transfer, needs to convey an address which can be interpreted by intermediate relaying systems. Dependent upon trust relationships between all network components, different parts of this address information can be cryptographically protected to different extents. Hence, *address-hiding* becomes an important consideration in multi-point and multi-hop protocols.

Other Mechanisms

Other methods of providing confidentiality include routing control, data splitting, spread-spectrum techniques, and frequency hopping techniques.

Routing control in network protocols supports information flow controls. As described in Chapter 6, this is a form of access control which employs a security labeling mechanism in conjunction with trusted system components.

Data splitting can be realized in many different ways. For example, to transmit a file confidentially, one can separate the bit-sequence of the file into two separate files, one containing the sequence of odd-numbered bits and the other containing the sequence of even-numbered bits. These two files are then transferred independently, e.g., via different communications systems, via different routes, and/or at different times. This type of approach can very effectively counter many types of eavesdropping threats.

Split knowledge is a variant of data splitting, referring to the situation of highly sensitive data being in the hands of humans. It applies particularly to key management, such as when a master key needs to be manually delivered to a system. The key is split into two parts, with the responsibility for each part being assigned to a different person. Compromise of the key would require collusion of the two people, which is considered much less likely than a single person compromising it.

Technologies like spread-spectrum and frequency hopping find little application in commercial and unclassified environments — the interested reader is referred to [TOR1].

7.3   Provision of Data Integrity

A data integrity service protects data from corruption (modification, loss, re-play, reordering, or substitution), either by accident or by deliberate tampering. There are two basic approaches to providing data integrity:

- *Access control approach*: Prevent intruders from having an opportunity to tamper with data.
- *Corruption-detection approach*: Accept that data may be (accidentally or deliberately) corrupted, but ensure that such corruptions are detected and either corrected or advised to the recipient.

The access control approach for integrity is similar to that for confidentiality. If data can be contained within trusted environments, the risks of deliberate tampering can be eliminated, making data integrity comparatively easy to achieve. Note, however, that access control may not protect against accidental data corruption (e.g., one can have a secure, but noisy, channel).
Corruption-detection mechanisms are described in the following section.

Data Granularity

As with confidentiality, a data integrity service applies to a particular data granularity. Three important cases are:

- *Connection integrity*: All user data transmitted on a connection at some architectural layer is uniformly protected.
- *Connectionless integrity*: The user data in one connectionless data unit at some architectural layer is protected.
- *Selective field integrity*: One or more selected fields within a data unit (sent either on a connection or as a connectionless data unit) are protected.

An integrity service is required to protect against creation or modification of data at the applicable granularity. Note that, in the case of connection integrity, this necessitates protection against replay, reordering, or loss of individual data units sent *within* the connection.

Integrity services do not necessarily protect against replay, reordering, or loss of complete data units at the granularity involved. For example, connection integrity does not necessarily protect against replay of an entire connection, and connectionless integrity does not necessarily protect against replay, reordering, or loss of distinct connectionless data units. This further protection is sometimes required and can be achieved using a *sequence integrity* mechanism.

Recovery

There are two ways of responding to detected data corruption. The corruption may be reported to the recipient, who may abandon the activity in progress or take other special action. Alternatively, an attempt may be made to automatically recover from the corruption, by such means as causing the corrupted data to be retransmitted. The latter option requires an additional *recovery mechanism*.

In principle, automatic recovery could be applied to any detected corruption. However, the OSI Security Architecture only recognizes use of recovery as applying to corrupted data units within a connection, i.e., it recognizes the service *connection integrity with recovery*. Recovery of complete data units at the granularity of the service (i.e., entire connections, connectionless data units, and selective fields) is considered a problem for the layer above.

7.4 Data Integrity Mechanisms

Testwords

Banking systems have used a corruption-detection integrity mechanism known as *testwords* for many years. These systems were designed to protect financial transactions conveyed over unprotected telex/telegraph networks. They were based on bilateral agreements as to transaction fields to be protected (e.g., account name, date, and amount), a static interinstitutional key, and a card containing a sequence of random numbers. The sending institution input this information through an agreed algorithm to generate a string of characters (a *testword*) which was appended to a transaction. The receiving institution repeated the same process using the received transaction data, and was thereby able to verify the integrity of the transaction. A testword is an early-technology realization of a seal.

Seals or Signatures

Chapter 4 introduced the concepts of seals and signatures and described how they can be used to provide data integrity.[2] The most common sealing and signature techniques involve cryptographically generating a value which is conveyed as an *appendix* to a plaintext data item. When intended specifically for data integrity purposes, such an appendix is commonly called an *integrity check-value* (ICV).

Application of a seal or signature mechanism requires that several questions be resolved between the parties involved, e.g., common understandings are needed as to algorithm selection, padding requirements, and key management procedures. The bulk of the discussion in Section 7.2 on use of an encryption mechanism for confidentiality purposes applies equally to use of a seal or signature mechanism for data integrity purposes.

Encryption

Some encryption mechanisms can be used to provide data integrity, while simultaneously providing confidentiality. Provided a data item to be protected possesses some redundancy, transmitting it encrypted can have the effect of providing data integrity. This results from the infeasibility of an intruder modifying a piece of ciphertext, without knowing the encryption key, in a way that will yield a valid data value from the decryption transformation.

The redundancy can be achieved in various ways. In some cases, the data item may possess sufficient natural redundancy. Alternatively, redundancy can be obtained by appending to the data item, prior to encryption, a check-value called a *modification detection code* (MDC). Examples of an MDC are a digest of the data generated by a hash function, or a cyclic redundancy check. Unlike a seal or signature, an MDC does not need to be cryptographically generated.

Not all encryption mechanisms can be used this way. For example, a reversible public-key algorithm, used in encryption mode, cannot provide integrity this way. An intruder can be assumed to know the encryption key (the public key) and hence can generate and encrypt a false data item.

Sequence Integrity

Sequence integrity provides a means to detect replay, reordering, or loss of data items forming part of a sequence. It is assumed that the internal integrity of

---

[2] A seal or message authentication code (MAC) is a basic integrity mechanism. A signature can meet requirements beyond basic integrity, in particular, non-repudiation. See Chapter 11 for references to applicable standards.

each item is protected by one of the above mechanisms. Two alternative ways to provide sequence integrity are:

- attachment of an *integrity sequence number* (ISN) to a data item, prior to protecting by seal, signature, or encryption; and
- employing cryptographic chaining in the seal, signature, or encryption process, with the chain extending over the sequence of data items.

Typical procedures (at the sending end) for both of these alternatives are illustrated in Figure 7-2.

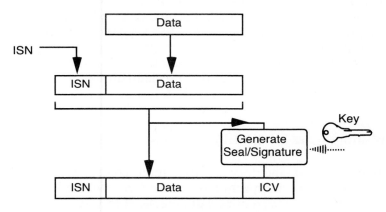

(a) Integrity Sequence Number Approach

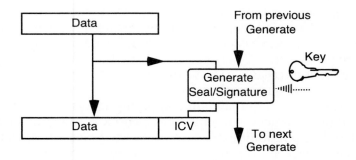

(b) Cryptographic Chaining Approach

Figure 7-2: Two Alternative Sequence Integrity Mechanisms

Replication

A measure of data integrity can be provided by replicating stored information in multiple storage areas or by communicating multiple copies of data via different paths. It is assumed that attackers cannot simultaneously compromise all copies, and that the genuine data can always be reconstructed from uncompromised copies.

Integrity Recovery

The mechanism required to support integrity recovery is simply a standard communications error recovery mechanism. The usual approach is to resynchronize back to a checkpoint before the detected corruption occurred and retransmit all data after that point. Any active cryptographic processes, whether for confidentiality or integrity purposes, will need to be simultaneously resynchronized back to the same checkpoint. Any failure to properly recover will be detected by the same integrity mechanism that detected the original failure.

7.5   Combining Confidentiality and Data Integrity

Confidentiality and data integrity are often required together. It was previously pointed out that some encryption mechanisms can be used to simultaneously provide both services. This can be valuable, as both services are obtained with minimal cryptographic complexity and minimal key management overhead.

However, when both services are required, it is generally preferable to use independent mechanisms for each. Even when the same cryptographic algorithm is used for both purposes (e.g., DES encryption plus DES-based seal), it is recommended that different keys be used for both purposes. Then if one mechanism (or key) is compromised, it does not automatically mean the other is compromised.

The question remains as to whether the data should be processed first by the encryption mechanism then by the integrity mechanism, or vice versa. There are significant arguments for applying integrity first [DAV1]. These relate to subtle weaknesses if an integrity check is calculated on an encrypted string. There are possibilities that the same encrypted string could be assigned a new meaning (e.g., through a key change or other parameter change following compromise of the encryption mechanism) which will not be detected by the integrity mechanism. Such weaknesses are averted if the integrity mechanism is applied before the encryption mechanism.

A significant benefit of taking an integrated approach to the provision of confidentiality and integrity is that the same key management procedures can be employed for both purposes (even though different keys may be used for each purpose).

7.6 Protocol Requirements

We now identify the areas in which provision of confidentiality and integrity impact communications protocol design. Specific issues of architectural layer placement, and the whole subject of key management, are deferred to the subsequent section.

Security Transformations

Confidentiality and data integrity place unique requirements upon layer protocols because of the need to *process* user data (communications protocol functions below Layer 6 usually transport user data transparently, having no concern with the values of such data). Encryption and decryption involve transforming user data at sending and receiving ends. Integrity mechanisms typically involve, at the sending end, processing user data to obtain an appendix to accompany the data during transfer. At the receiving end, all of the received data is processed to strip the appended value and generate an indication of integrity check success or failure. These procedures can be considered special cases of a concept known as a *security transformation*, which has the model shown in Figure 7-3.

The details of a particular security transformation could be specified as part of a communications protocol specification. However, there is a wide range of different security transformations that may be useful in various environments. Figure 7-4 provides some examples. Security protocols will have longer lives if they can be designed to operate with any security transform-

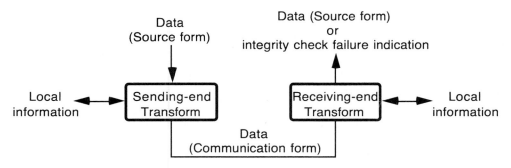

Figure 7-3: Security Transformation Model

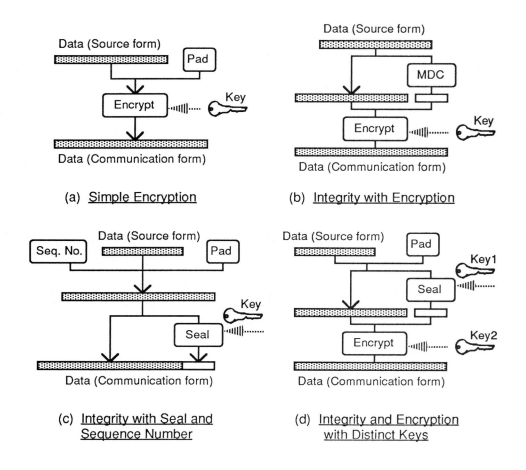

Figure 7-4: Example Security Transformations

ation. This implies separately specifying the security transformations and the basic protocol. This approach has been taken with several OSI security protocols, including the Network Layer Security Protocol, Transport Layer Security Protocol, and Generic Upper Layers Security standard (discussed in Chapters 11 and 12).

Protocol Control Information

Security protocols supporting confidentiality and/or integrity need to convey certain information in addition to the communication forms of user data. Such information includes an indication of the security transformation or its characteristics, e.g., algorithm identifiers, algorithm parameters, and/or key identifiers. This information can be conveyed either directly or indirectly in protocol control information (protocol headers).

The direct approach means the information is carried in explicit protocol fields; this has a weakness in that it cannot be protected at the same level as the transformation to which it relates. Hence, unless there is further confidentiality at a lower layer, this information cannot itself be confidentiality protected. In many scenarios this is not a concern, e.g., the strength of a confidentiality mechanism is recognized as depending fully upon key secrecy — algorithm and parameter secrecy are not required. In other scenarios, secrecy of such information is considered important.

In the indirect approach, transformation details such as algorithm identifiers, algorithm parameters, and key identifiers are agreed in advance and assigned an identifier (known variously as a security association identifier, security relationship identifier, or key package identifier). The protocol using the transformation need only communicate that identifier which, being nothing more than an arbitrary bit string, conveys no information to an eavesdropper. The mapping from the identifier to the transformation details is established separately, e.g., in a key management protocol which is itself confidentiality protected.

Security Labels

Access-control-based approaches to confidentiality and data integrity, and the provision of secure channels for flow control purposes, commonly necessitate the attachment of security labels to communicated data items. At any points where routing or delivery decisions are made, these labels may need to be checked and may influence such decisions.

7.7   Architectural Placement

Selective Field Confidentiality and Integrity

Selective field confidentiality or integrity implies that the service-user layer entity must understand the semantics of separate protocol fields, to the extent that it can request specific forms of protection for different fields. This can only occur at the Application Layer. (In the OSI stack, the Application Layer is then considered to use functions in the Presentation Layer to provide the requisite security transformations.)

Connection and Connectionless Confidentiality and Integrity

Confidentiality and/or integrity (either the connection or connectionless variant, as appropriate) can be applied at any of the four levels:

- application level;
- end-system level;
- subnetwork level; and
- direct-link level.[3]

The appropriate level will be governed by the perceived trust characteristics of the environment, as discussed in Chapter 3.

At the application level, the security service is considered to be provided by the Application Layer (in the OSI stack, Presentation Layer services will then be used to provide the security transformations). At the end-system level, alternative options are presented in the Transport and Network Layers. Subnetwork level services are associated with Network Layer protocols. Direct-link level services can be associated with either the Data Link or Physical Layer, depending upon the media technology.

The situation with LANs can be confusing, because the 1988 OSI Security Architecture standard did not take LAN technologies into account. LAN protection is logically a case of subnetwork level protection, and confidentiality and/or integrity protection may be warranted. However, LAN protocols are considered to map to the Data Link Layer. This issue is pursued further in Chapter 11.

Traffic Flow Confidentiality

Traffic flow confidentiality employs traffic padding and address-hiding. The only level at which *complete* traffic flow confidentiality can be provided is the direct-link level, because this is the only level where complete address-hiding can occur. At any higher level, traffic information would be revealed in the protocol headers of underlying layers. Even at the direct-link level, full address-hiding is possible only in pure point-to-point protocols. Multi-point protocols, for example, always convey some address information unprotected.

However, complete traffic flow confidentiality is a dubious requirement in unclassified environments. Effective traffic flow confidentiality can generally

---

[3] The OSI Security Architecture suggests that integrity is not appropriate at the Data Link or Physical Layer, but this argument is not generally sustainable. In fact, integrity is often obtained as a side effect of an encryption mechanism used primarily for confidentiality purposes.

be achieved through traffic padding (i.e., generation of "dummy" traffic). This may occur at any of the architectural levels — usually that at which connection or connectionless confidentiality is applied.

Integrity Recovery

Integrity recovery is an end-system level or application level function. The OSI Security Architecture states that integrity recovery (applying within a connection) can be provided at either the Transport Layer or the Application Layer. At the Transport Layer, standard transport protocol error recovery mechanisms, which deal with errors detected by either the Network or Transport Layer, are used.

Key Management

Key management is a critical part of the provision of confidentiality and integrity. While there are many aspects to key management, the aspect placing most demands on communications protocols is key distribution. Given that system *A* wishes to transfer to system *B* some confidentiality and/or integrity protected data, the two systems need first to establish required keys. (In the most common case, i.e., symmetric cryptosystems, this means establishing a common key.)

The systems potentially involved in key management communications are systems *A* and *B* and a key management center, as shown in Figure 7-5. There are two basic types of key distribution protocol exchange:

- *Direct exchange*: Data items are exchanged between systems *A* and *B*, for the purpose of establishing a key (or keys) for protecting data transferred subsequently between those systems.
- *Center exchange*: Data items are exchanged between either system *A* or system *B* and a key management center, as part of the key establishment process.

This general model can be assumed, regardless of the particular key management technique used. Some examples[4] are:

(a) *ANSI X9.17*: System *A* executes a center exchange to obtain a new primary key in a form whereby it is encrypted under a master key shared between the center and System *B*. System *A* then sends this encrypted key to system *B* in a direct exchange.

---

[4] See Section 4.6 for more details of these examples.

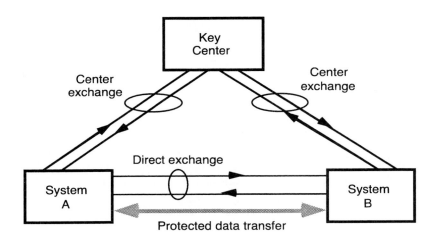

Figure 7-5: Key Management Communications

(b) *Symmetric-key establishment using reversible public-key system*: As a direct exchange, system *A* sends system *B* a new symmetric key encrypted under system *B*'s public key.

(c) *Diffie-Hellman key derivation*: In a direct exchange, systems *A* and *B* derive a secret symmetric key.

In cases (b) and (c), center exchanges are not necessarily required, but might be required in support of authentication, e.g., public-key certificate verification.

In terms of architectural placement, all of these protocol exchanges can be logically considered as Application Layer functions, possibly part of systems management. With center exchanges, the usual approach is to either establish a short-duration connection for the purpose of the exchange or to realize the exchange as a simple sequence of connectionless data transfers. In either case, the Application Layer exchange can be considered to map onto underlying protocols in the usual manner.

However, in the case of direct exchanges, the issue of mapping to lower-layer protocols can warrant special consideration. This applies particularly to direct exchanges for establishing keys for use in connection-oriented data protection at the Transport, Network, or Data Link Layer. Recognizing that the direct exchange is typically followed by protected data transfer between the same two systems, using the newly established key(s), two important protocol-mapping alternatives arise:

(a) The direct exchange, considered to be Application Layer protocol, is mapped onto underlying protocols in the usual manner. A problem with this approach is that it requires use of a connection separate from that used subsequently for protected data transfer.

(b) Provision is made for embedding the direct exchange in the data-protecting protocol (i.e., Transport, Network, or Data Link Layer protocol) at a point prior to transmission of protected data. The most obvious place for embedding the direct exchange is in conjunction with the connection establishment procedure at the layer concerned; all user data on that connection can then be protected using the newly established key(s). Provision might also be made for embedding the exchange at other points, e.g., to establish a new key on cryptoperiod expiry.

Alternative (a) is the most architecturally pure, but alternative (b) can present significant performance improvements and cost savings. Hence, both of these alternatives can be useful, and direct key management exchanges should ideally be specified in such a way that they can be used with either.

7.8 Physical Equipment Options

As confidentiality, and possibly integrity, can be placed at any of the architectural levels, there are several different physical equipment options. These include:

- For direct-link level protection, a transparently-insertable device known as a *link encryptor* is commonly used. Such devices may depend upon manually-inserted master keys or may be linked to a centralized key management system.
- For protection of a subnetwork, a subnetwork-dependent protection product can be used. Such products may be transparently insertable, and are available for common subnetwork types such as X.25 or LANs; integrated management systems may be available.
- For end-system level protection, support generally needs to be integrated into end-system Transport or Network Layer implementations. Attached cryptographic hardware modules may be employed.
- For application level protection, support generally needs to be integrated into application-specific software in end systems. Again, attached cryptographic hardware modules may be employed.
- Security management systems (providing key management and other functions such as security audit) may be supported by separate items of equipment.

The opportunities for both hardware and software products to support confidentiality and integrity are unbounded. Innovative product designs can be anticipated well into the future.

Summary

The goal of confidentiality is to protect against disclosure of information to anyone not authorized to know that information. The goal of data integrity is to protect against data being changed, deleted, or substituted without authorization. Either one or both of these services may be required in a given environment.

Confidentiality can be provided using either an access control approach, which prevents intruders from observing representations of sensitive information, or an information-hiding approach, which makes it infeasible for an intruder to deduce information content from an information representation. The access control approach employs an access control mechanism (see Chapter 6) or flow control provisions such as secure channels. The information-hiding approach employs confidentiality mechanisms such as encryption (to hide data values), data padding (to hide data item sizes), and traffic padding (to protect against information disclosure by observing network traffic patterns).

Data integrity can be provided using either an access control approach (as for confidentiality) or a corruption-detection approach. The latter may optionally include automatic recovery from corruptions. Integrity mechanisms include seals, signatures, and encryption for detecting corruption of a single data item, and sequence integrity mechanisms for detecting replay, reordering, or loss of data items in a sequence.

Protocol designs to support confidentiality and/or integrity can use the concept of security transformations. A security transformation, at a particular architectural layer, processes unprotected user data to generate a protected data item. Many different types of security transformation may be defined, using different combinations of basic building blocks, such as encryption, padding, signing, sealing, and sequence number insertion. Network security protocols can be designed to operate with any security transformation; the protocols and security transformations are specified separately. Security protocols may need to accommodate the communication of algorithm identifiers, algorithm parameters, key identifiers, and security labels.

Depending upon the particular type of confidentiality or integrity service required and upon other factors, confidentiality and/or integrity mechanisms may be located at any of the four possible architectural levels. Key management is generally considered an Application Layer function, but lower-layer security protocols may provide special fields for conveying key establishment information.

There are many different ways in which confidentiality and integrity mechanisms may be configured in physical equipment, with various hardware/software alternatives being available.

Exercises

1. What are the goals of confidentiality and integrity respectively? Does either one necessarily imply the other? Give examples to support your answer.

2. Suppose that a pair of systems have agreed to encrypt the contents of all electronic mail messages sent between them, and that the cryptographic algorithm to be used will be DES. What other factors need to be agreed in order for the two systems to interoperate?

3. Describe how traffic flow confidentiality can be provided in a layered architectural environment.

4. What role(s) can the following types of access control mechanisms play in the provision of confidentiality and integrity services: (a) access control list, and (b) security labels?

5. Two different approaches to providing sequence integrity are (a) integrity sequence numbers, and (b) cryptographic chaining. Describe these two approaches. Is either more widely applicable than the other?

6. Under what conditions will applying an encryption mechanism to a data item also have the effect of providing an integrity check on it? (Identify constraints on characteristics of the data item and/or on characteristics of the encryption mechanism.)

7. For each of the following functions, identify the architectural level(s) (application, end-system, subnetwork, and/or direct-link) at which it will most likely be encountered:

    (a) connection confidentiality;
    (b) traffic flow confidentiality;
    (c) selective field confidentiality;
    (d) integrity recovery; and
    (d) key management.

REFERENCES

[DAV1] D.W. Davies and W.L. Price, *Security for Computer Networks*, Second Edition, John Wiley and Sons, New York, 1989.

[DEN1] D.E. Denning, *Cryptography and Data Security*, Addison-Wesley, Reading, MA, 1982.

[HAR1] M.A. Harrison and W.L. Ruzzo, "Protection in Operating Systems," *Communications of the ACM*, vol. 19, no. 8 (August 1976), pp. 461-471.

[LAM1] B.W. Lampson, "A Note on the Confinement Problem," *Communications of the ACM*, vol. 16, no. 10 (October 1973), pp. 613-615.

[TOR1] D.J. Torrieri, *Principles of Secure Communication Systems*, Second Edition, Artech House, Inc., Norwood, MA, 1992.

Standards

ISO/IEC 7498-2: *Information Technology — Open Systems Interconnection — Basic Reference Model — Part 2: Security Architecture* (Also ITU-T Recommendation X.800).

ISO/IEC 10181-5: *Information Technology — Security Frameworks in Open Systems — Confidentiality Framework* (Also ITU-T Recommendation X.814) (Draft).

ISO/IEC 10181-6: *Information Technology — Security Frameworks in Open Systems — Integrity Framework* (Also ITU-T Recommendation X.815) (Draft).

8 Non-repudiation

Non-repudiation services provide a communications user with protection against another user later denying that some communications exchange took place. While these services do not prevent a user from repudiating another user's claim that something occurred, they ensure the availability of irrefutable evidence to support the speedy resolution of any such disagreement. In general, the evidence must prove convincing to a third party arbitrator.

In data networking environments, repudiation scenarios can be separated into two distinct cases (which lead to two distinct variants of non-repudiation service):

- *Repudiation of origin*: There is disagreement as to whether a particular party originated a particular data item (and/or disagreement as to the time this origination occurred).

- *Repudiation of delivery*: There is disagreement as to whether a particular data item was delivered to a particular party (and/or disagreement as to the time this delivery occurred).

This chapter describes the types of mechanism used to satisfy non-repudiation requirements. It is organized into sections addressing the following topics:

(1) phases involved in the non-repudiation process and roles assumed by various parties in these phases;
(2) mechanisms used to provide non-repudiation of origin;
(3) mechanisms used to provide non-repudiation of delivery;
(4) functions of trusted third parties; and
(5) communication protocol requirements for supporting non-repudiation.

8.1 Phases and Roles in the Non-repudiation Process

The sequence of events associated with non-repudiation involves up to five distinct phases of activity: service request, evidence generation, evidence transfer/storage, evidence verification, and dispute resolution.[1]   Different parties play different roles in these phases. For the purposes of this discussion, we shall use the term *critical action* to refer to the event or activity which is the target of the non-repudiation service; examples of critical actions are origination of a particular data item and delivery of a particular data item.

Service Request

It is essential that the planned use of a non-repudiation service be agreed prior to the critical action's occurrence. Suppose parties *A* and *B* are to participate in some communication event, and party *B* wants to obtain assurance that party *A* will not subsequently falsely deny what occurred. Provision of this service requires the cooperation of party *A*, who needs to participate in the generation of the required evidence.

This may require that party *B*, or some other concerned party, make an explicit advance request to party *A* that non-repudiation is to apply to the particular forthcoming event. Such explicit requests are not always necessary, as there may be a standing arrangement, or common policy, between the parties that non-repudiation will always apply to certain types of events.

As a paper transaction analogy, suppose the critical action is the commitment by party *A* to immediately pay a certain amount to party *B*, and the mechanism to be used is passing a check. The "non-repudiation" mechanism is a signature on the check. In general, it will not be necessary for party *B* to explicitly request party *A* to sign the check, as there is a well-established understanding that anyone writing a check is expected to sign it. However, in some circumstances party *B*, or party *B*'s lawyer, might explicitly request a particular *type* of non-repudiation from party *A*, e.g., a certified check.

The roles associated with this phase are a *service requestor* role and an *evidence generator* role. The service requestor is often one of the communicating parties directly involved in the critical action, but could alternatively be an arm's-length party, such as a security domain authority. In the check-passing analogy, the service requestor role is assumed by party *B* or party *B*'s lawyer.

Evidence Generation

Evidence generation occurs in conjunction with the critical action and is carried out by one party or a group of parties operating in concert, acting in an *evidence generator* role. The party who is considered a potential repudiator of the critical action needs to participate in the evidence generation. Trusted third parties may also participate

---

[1] The Non-repudiation Framework standard (ISO/IEC 10181-4) defines similar phases for the non-repudiation process, with minor differences in terminology.

Returning to the above analogy of payment by check, evidence generation involves producing the necessary check signature(s) and, if required, a bank certification.

Evidence Transfer/Storage

After the critical action has occurred and the evidence has been generated, the evidence has to be:

(a) transferred to the party or parties who may ultimately need to use it; and/or

(b) stored by a trusted third party for possible future reference, should that prove necessary.

In the case of payment by cheque, the evidence is transferred to the ultimate user in the form of the signature and (if required) bank certification on the check document. The bank may also store a record of the certification.

Evidence Verification

Evidence verification refers to the checking of the generated evidence by the party to whom it is transferred or entrusted for storage. This phase is a normal part of the sequence of events — it is not a consequence of a dispute arising. Its purpose is for all parties to gain confidence that the supplied evidence will indeed be adequate in the event a dispute does arise.

In the case of payment by check, this phase would involve the recipient checking that the document is signed by the appropriate party, correctly dated and, if necessary, properly certified by the bank. It could extend to performing a subjective signature check, if the recipient was familiar with the payer's signature.

This phase introduces a new role — that of *evidence verifier*. This role is assumed by a single party or multiple parties operating in concert. Such parties typically include the party requesting the non-repudiation service and/or trusted third parties.

Dispute Resolution

The final phase that might occur is a dispute resolution phase. This might occur in a quite different time frame to the preceding phases. It could conceivably be soon after those phases (e.g., within the same communication session) but would more likely be much later (possibly several years later).

If this phase occurs, it is necessary to retrieve the evidence, re-verify it, and resolve the disagreement. This may need to involve another role — an *arbitrator* role. This role is assumed by a third party, such as a court of law.

Network security standards do not standardize the way this phase is performed. However, they need to recognize that such a phase may occur and they need to prepare for it.

8.2 Non-repudiation of Origin

Non-repudiation of origin relates to potential disagreement as to whether a particular party originated a particular data item (and/or disagreement as to the time this origination occurred). One should not read too much meaning into the term "originate" in this context. It simply implies that the party was holding the data item at some time — it does not necessarily (but might in some circumstances) have connotations of ownership.

With this form of non-repudiation, the evidence generator role includes the originator and, in some cases, one or more trusted third parties. The service requestor role includes potential recipients of the data and/or parties representing the interests of such recipients. The evidence verifier role includes recipients of the data and/or trusted third parties.

The evidence needs to be able to irrefutably associate, or link together, various pieces of information, including at least:

- the identity of the originator; and
- the precise value of the data item;

and, in some cases, other information such as:

- the date and time at which "origination" occurred;
- the identity of the intended recipient(s); and
- the identities of any trusted third parties involved in evidence generation.

While this book is focusing on non-repudiation of origin in a data communications context, the service and most of the mechanisms which provide it are equally applicable to data item creation followed by storage in a database. In this case, a party who *retrieves* the data item replaces the *recipient* recognized in the communications context.

Some basic approaches to providing non-repudiation of origin are outlined in the following subsections.

Originator's Digital Signature

One mechanism for providing non-repudiation of origin is for the originator to digitally sign the data item and send the signature to the recipient(s). This is illustrated in Figure 8-1. The digital signature constitutes the primary evidence. The evidence verification phase involves a recipient verifying the digital signature. The digital signature is then stored by the recipient. In the event the originator later denies origination of the data item, a recipient can furnish the stored digital signature as irrefutable evidence to the contrary.

Assuming a public-key-based digital signature scheme, let us consider the role of trusted third parties. The checking and retaining of public-key certificates is an essential part of the process. If, in dispute resolution, a recipient were to produce evidence comprising a digital signature for which he believes he has the correct public key, this would not, in itself, be sufficient to convince a third party arbitrator. Corroboration of the validity of the public key will be needed from a trusted third party.

The verification process must use a public-key certificate from a recognized certification authority who is prepared to reaffirm the validity of the certificate and its contents at any time a dispute might arise. Hence, the responsibilities assumed by a certification authority who issues public-key certificates for non-repudiation purposes may be somewhat greater than the responsibilities of one who issues public-key certificates for basic authentication, confidentiality, or integrity purposes.

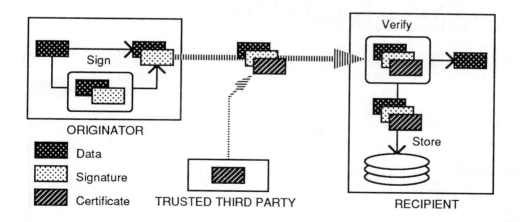

Figure 8-1: Originator's Digital Signature

The subject of key revocation also requires more careful attention in the non-repudiation case. If a public-key certificate is revoked (for such reasons as suspected compromise of the private key or on the initiative of the certification authority), then the precise time of revocation needs to be made known to all evidence verifiers. Evidence generated using the certified key prior to its revocation is valid evidence, but evidence generated after the revocation is not valid. In their verification processes, evidence verifiers need to stringently check for possible revocation of a key or certificate. Furthermore, non-repudiation may demand *real-time revocation*, which is more difficult to realize than the usual approach of periodically distributing revocation lists.

The possibility of a key being revoked subsequent to verification and storage of evidence is particularly problematical. The consequences of such an event will depend upon non-repudiation policy. It may be necessary for an originator to store copies of applicable certified revocation lists to support the originator's case in an arbitration situation.

Trusted Third Party Digital Signature on Data

An alternative mechanism employs a trusted third party's digital signature instead of the originator's own digital signature (see Figure 8-2). The trusted third party can be considered to be vouching for the originator. With this mechanism, the originator conveys the data item to a trusted third party, who generates a digital signature over a concatenation of the data item, the identity of the originator, and any other required information such as a time-stamp. This signature becomes evidence, and is sent to the recipient(s) for verification and storage.

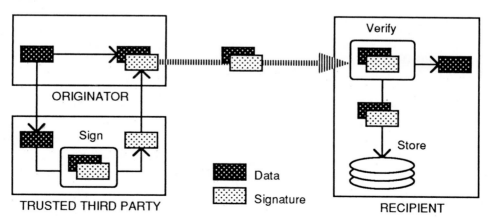

Figure 8-2: Trusted Third Party Digital Signature

The communication from originator to trusted third party requires integrity and data origin authentication protection, so that the trusted third party can be sure it is signing a legitimate value. The communication from trusted third party back to originator does not necessarily need integrity protection, as the originator has the opportunity to itself check the digital signature before sending it on to recipients.

This mechanism has some advantages over using the originator's digital signature. One advantage is that verification will generally involve fewer key pairs, hence reducing the requirements for certificate acquisition, checking, and storage. A relatively small number of signers can support a large community of originators/recipients, providing greater potential for verifiers to retain and reuse certified public keys. Another advantage is that, provided the signing trusted third party is recognized as maintaining a trusted time source, a time-stamp can be included in the signature, providing recipients with an assured time of origination.

Trusted Third Party Digital Signature on Digest

As a variant of the above scheme, the originator generates a digest or digital fingerprint of the data item by applying a hash function to it. The digest is sent to the trusted third party, who generates a digital signature over the digest, the identity of the originator, and any other required information such as a time-stamp. This digital signature becomes the evidence, which is returned to the originator, then forwarded to the recipient as in the preceding scheme.

There are advantages in using a digest of the data item instead of the data item itself in generating the signature. The digest approach reduces the volume of data needing to be sent to the trusted third party. It also enables the confidentiality of the original data to be preserved in communications between the originator and the trusted third party and within the trusted third party system (which then needs to be trusted for signature purposes but not necessarily for confidentiality purposes).

If there is any possibility of multiple different hash functions being used by the originator (and this is a reasonable assumption, given the volatility of sound hash function definitions), then it is important for the digest to always be accompanied by an unambiguous identifier of the particular hash function used. This identifier must also be included in the value signed by the trusted third party. If this is not done, there is an arguable case that an originator might originate two different data items which, under two different hash functions, generate the same digest. If this could occur, and there were no hash function identifier securely associated with the digest, then the signature would not provide irrefutable evidence of the data item generated in a particular case.

Trusted Third Party Token

Trusted third party token schemes are alternatives to the above trusted third party signature schemes, which use symmetric cryptographic techniques in place of public-key techniques. A token is similar to a signature except that, instead of being signed, it is sealed using a symmetric algorithm and a secret key known only by the trusted third party. The information included in the seal calculation involves the data item or a digest of the data item, the identity of the originator, and other required information such as a time-stamp. The procedure is illustrated in Figure 8-3. The token is generated for the originator by the trusted third party and sent to the recipient. The difference from the signature schemes is that the recipient cannot directly verify the token, but instead sends it back to the trusted third party for verification.

The communication exchanges between originator and trusted third party, and between recipient and trusted third party, both require integrity and data origin authentication protection.

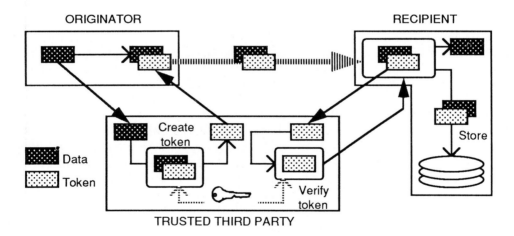

Figure 8-3: Trusted Third Party Token

In-line Trusted Third Party

Another type of mechanism involves the insertion of a trusted third party in the communication path between originator and recipient. There are different ways this trusted third party might operate. The simplest way is illustrated in Figure 8-4. The trusted third party simply captures and stores sufficient evidence to support resolution of future disputes regarding the origin of passing data. Such

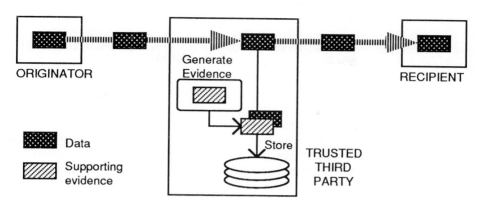

Figure 8-4: In-line Trusted Third Party — Evidence Stored

evidence would typically include a copy or digest of the data, the identity of the originator, and a time-stamp.

This type of mechanism has the advantage of not impacting the formats of the application protocol fields. However, it depends on the use of other security services. In particular, integrity and data origin authentication services must apply to the communications between originator and trusted third party, and between trusted third party and recipient.

Another variant of in-line trusted third party is shown in Figure 8-5. In this case, the trusted third party generates a digest as evidence and forwards it to recipients for verification and storage. It is similar to the trusted third party signature mechanism described earlier except that, in this case, integrity and data origin authentication services must apply to the communications between the originator and the trusted third party.

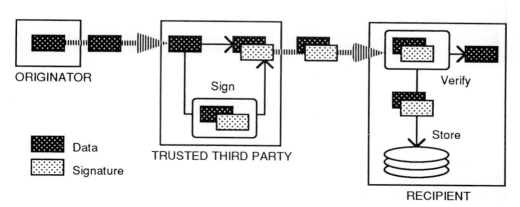

Figure 8-5: In-line Trusted Third Party — Evidence Forwarded

Mechanism Combinations

Any of the digital-signature-based mechanisms can be enhanced to involve multiple parties in the signing process. This may employ either multiple independent signatures or a multi-party signature, i.e., multiple parties contribute parts of the key to generate a signature. These schemes greatly improve resistance to attacks resulting from key compromise and reduce dependence on individual people.

Furthermore, any of the above mechanisms can be combined. For example, generated evidence can include an originator signature plus one or more trusted third party signatures, all generated in different systems.

Time-Stamping

In many applications, secure time-stamps need to be generated for data items, in addition to securely associating these data items with originators. Time-stamps are needed for such purposes as confirming filing times of electronic business documents. Furthermore, secure time-stamping can be a fundamental requirement of some non-repudiation mechanisms. For example, in a simple originator's digital signature mechanism, it is conceivable that an originator can cause his or her own past signatures to become invalid by deliberately publicizing the private key then instigating revocation. To protect against such attacks it may be necessary to have secure time-stamps associated with all signatures and with the revocation request.

A time-stamp is generated by a time-stamping service, which is a trusted third party recognized as providing a reliable time source. A time-stamp for a given data item can be obtained by having the time-stamping service append a time value to the data item or to a digest of the data item, then digitally sign the result. This signature is then handled as other non-repudiation evidence. The time-stamping function may be able to be combined with another non-repudiation signature function. For example, one trusted third party may attest to both an originator's identity and the correct time. Alternatively, a dedicated time-stamping service may be employed, in which case a further signature is added to the evidence.

For further discussion of time-stamping services and the potential for using a time-stamping which is less than fully trusted, see [HAB1].

8.3 Non-repudiation of Delivery

Non-repudiation of delivery relates to potential disagreement as to whether a particular party received a particular data item (and/or disagreement as to the time the delivery occurred). Note that this form of non-repudiation does not extend beyond delivery — it does not necessarily imply that the recipient read the data or acted upon it in any way. It is equivalent to signing for receipt of a certified letter, where the signature implies nothing about reading the contents.

With this form of non-repudiation, the evidence generator role includes the recipient and, in some cases, one or more trusted third parties. The service requestor role includes the originator of the data and/or parties representing the interests of the originator. The evidence verifier role includes the originator and/or trusted third parties.

The evidence needs to be able to irrefutably associate, or link together, various pieces of information, including at least:

- the identity of the recipient; and
- the precise value of the data item;

and, in some cases, other information such as:

- the date and time at which delivery occurs;
- the identity of the originator; and
- the identities of any trusted third parties involved in evidence generation.

Some approaches to providing non-repudiation of delivery are outlined in the following subsections.

Recipient Acknowledgment with Signature

One mechanism involves the recipient generating an acknowledgment message back to the originator, with this message containing a digital signature computed on:

- a copy or a digest of the contents of the original delivered data item; plus
- other required evidence, e.g., delivery time.

The signature must be generated by the recipient or a trusted third party who is vouching for the recipient. Figure 8-6 illustrates the operation of this mechanism for the case where the recipient's digital signature is used. The configuration using a trusted third party signature is left as an exercise to the reader.

In most respects, this mechanism is equivalent to applying non-repudiation of origin to an acknowledgment message which contains the necessary evidence (except that it is not necessary to actually send the copy of the original message or the digest back to the originator). The same qualifications regarding certificates and key revocation apply to this non-repudiation of

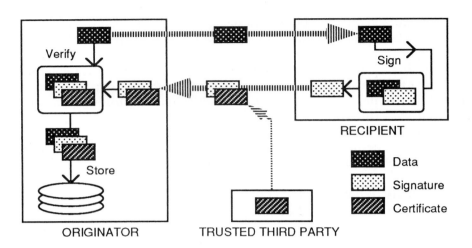

Figure 8-6: Non-repudiation of Delivery Using Recipient's Signature

delivery mechanism as to the non-repudiation of origin mechanisms discussed in Section 8.2.

Recipient Acknowledgment with Token

As a variation of the above scheme, a token generated by a trusted third party using symmetric cryptographic techniques can be used instead of the signature. As with the corresponding non-repudiation of origin scheme (see Figure 8-3), verification of the token (in this case, by the originator) requires it to be sent back to the trusted third party.

Trusted Delivery Agent

One problem that can arise with the above mechanism is that of the *reluctant recipient*. There is no protection against a recipient choosing not to acknowledge a particular delivered data item after having seen its contents.

Some protection can be provided by introducing a trusted third party known as a delivery agent. The delivery agent intervenes in the communication path between originator and recipient, in comparatively close proximity to the recipient. The originator sends the data item to the delivery agent, who acknowledges its receipt using a signature-based mechanism like that described above. Usually, the delivery agent will not generate the acknowledgment until the final delivery to the recipient has occurred. However, in some circumstances, the delivery agent may generate the acknowledgment prior to final delivery; in this case the delivery agent assumes responsibility for ensuring that the data item is delivered to the recipient.

The trusted delivery agent approach is akin to the use of a police officer to deliver certain legal documents (e.g., a summons) to a person.

Two-Stage Delivery

Two-stage delivery is specifically designed to counter the *reluctant recipient* problem. It may be used when sending a data item from originator to recipient or from trusted delivery agent to recipient; for description purposes we shall assume it is from originator to recipient. The originator first sends a *prepare-to-receive* message to the recipient. This message contains a digest of the data item, but not the data item in a form the recipient can interpret. The recipient responds with a *ready-to-receive* message, which contains a signed copy of the digest. After verifying the digital signature on the ready-to-receive message vis à vis the correct digital fingerprint, the originator sends the full data item. The recipient responds with a further signed acknowledgment, the same as for the basic recipient's signature mechanism shown in Figure 8-5.

The advantage of the two-stage delivery mechanism over the basic recipient's signature mechanism is that, in sending the *ready-to-receive* message, the recipient both confirms the current operational status of the communications path and commits to the eventual receipt of a data item with the agreed digest, even though the full data item value is unknown. Although it is possible that a communications failure immediately after the *prepare-to-receive* message can delay the delivery of the full data item, both originator and recipient are equally committed to the transfer of the data item. Without the preliminary exchange, the recipient could feign communications failures indefinitely, if reluctant to receive that particular data item.

If agreement on delivery time is important, this can also be assisted by the two-stage delivery procedure. The recipient includes in the signed *ready-to-receive* message its current time value. The originator can check that this value is reasonable and record it as evidence before sending the full data item.

Progressive Delivery Reports

Many distributed communications applications, such as electronic mail and EDI, involve forwarding of data items through multiple distinct administrative domains. In such applications there is a risk of loss of a data item en route, without being able to attribute the loss to any particular party or domain. Consequently, it may be agreed to apply non-repudiation of delivery at multiple points as a message traverses its path, e.g., at each point of entry into a different administrative domain. This gives a system in which responsibility for a message is securely associated with a particular administrative domain at any time. This approach is employed with the Message Handling System application described in Chapter 13.

8.4   Functions of Trusted Third Parties

Non-repudiation always depends upon the involvement of trusted third parties, because an arbitrator cannot be expected to make a decision on the basis of unsupported claims presented by two disputing parties.

There are several different functions that a trusted third party may perform. The term *notary* is often used in the security field to refer to some types of trusted third party, but there is little agreement as to which of the trusted third party functions a notary performs. Therefore, use of that term is avoided where possible in this book.

The trusted third party functions identified in this chapter are:

- *Key certification*: The trusted third party certifies that a particular public key corresponds to the private key known only to a particular party, by issuing a public-key certificate. The trusted third party must also take responsibility for revoking certificates in situations of compromise.
- *Identity certification*: The trusted third party vouches for the identity of a data item's originator, by signing the data item on behalf of the originator.
- *Time-stamping*: The trusted third party certifies that it has affixed a signature to a data item at a particular time.
- *Evidence storage*: The trusted third party undertakes to securely store evidence until such time as it might be required to resolve a dispute.
- *Delivery agent*: The trusted third party acts as an intermediary between an originator and recipient, guaranteeing to the originator that a particular data item has been or will be delivered to the recipient.
- *Arbitration*: The trusted third party acts as an independent arbiter in deciding the outcome of a dispute. This function differs from those identified above, in that it is not normally reflected in network protocols.

What type of organization takes on these trusted third party functions? The basic requirements are that the assignee of the function be both neutral and reliable, and that the assignee's role be accepted by all other parties involved. Recognition of this acceptance may be embodied in cooperative or contractual arrangements, or in regulations or laws. In some application environments, it may be appropriate for a government agency to assume trusted third party functions. In other environments, a private organization may assume the functions, typically in conjunction with other communications service functions. For example, a value-added network (VAN) operator may provide some trusted third party functions as part of its service offerings.

8.5 Protocol Requirements

The architectural placement of non-repudiation is straightforward. Because it depends upon application semantics and relates to particular fields in application protocols, non-repudiation is always at the application level.

The protocol elements potentially required include:

- *Service request*: A protocol element requesting application of non-repudiation to a particular data item. With non-repudiation of origin this will be in a protocol message preceding the origination of the data item to which the service is to apply. With non-repudiation of delivery, it may accompany the data item to which it is to apply, i.e., the originator requests that non-repudiation of delivery apply to a particular data item, as indicated by a request flag accompanying the data item.
- *Signatures and certificates*: Protected data items will often be signed and may be accompanied by certificates. This is no different from using signatures and certificates for other purposes, such as authentication or access control, although non-repudiation signatures may be more complex because of the prevalence of multiple party signatures.
- *Non-repudiation exchanges*: *n*-way protocol exchanges may sometimes be required to support non-repudiation, e.g., the two-stage delivery exchange. In protocol-mechanistic terms, these are little different from *n*-way authentication exchanges discussed in Chapter 5. Chapter 12 introduces the *security exchange* concept to model such *n*-way exchanges.

These protocol elements need to be built into application layer protocols. The best practical example is in the Message Handling Systems (MHS) protocol described in Chapter 13.

When designing non-repudiation systems, one aspect deserves special attention. Non-repudiation evidence will often need to be stored for a long period, possibly measured in years. Note also that non-repudiation evidence is computed on a data string, which *represents* certain information. Therefore, as well as establishing and preserving signed or sealed data items as evidence, it is necessary to establish and preserve a common view of the data representation scheme. This extends, for example, to agreeing upon, and preserving through the lifetime of evidence, the particular versions of ASN.1 notation and/or application program (e.g., spreadsheet or word processor) formats used. This issue is left with the reader to ponder.

Summary

Non-repudiation services provide a communications user with protection against another user later denying that some communications exchange took place. This protection is provided through the collection of irrefutable evidence to support the resolution of any such disagreement. Non-repudiation of origin protects against a party falsely denying that it originated a data item. Non-repudiation of delivery protects against a party falsely denying that it was delivered a data item.

There are up to five distinct phases in the non-repudiation process. The service request phase may be explicit or implicit, but must precede the critical action (origination or delivery) to which the service is to apply. The evidence generation phase occurs in conjunction with the critical action. In the evidence transfer/storage phase, the evidence is transferred to where it may ultimately be needed and/or is stored for future reference. In the evidence verification phase, the evidence is checked by the party to whom it is transferred or entrusted for storage. The final possible phase is dispute resolution, which may occur much later than the other phases.

Non-repudiation of origin can be provided through the originator's digital signature or through the digital signature of a trusted third party who vouches for the originator on the data item in question or on a digest of that data item. Alternatively, trusted third party tokens based on symmetric cryptography can be used. Non-repudiation can also be provided by an in-line trusted third party, which generates required evidence and either stores the evidence or forwards it on to recipients. When the time of origination is important, a time-stamp, signed by a trusted third party, must be included in the evidence. For added protection, multiple mechanisms can be used in combination.

Non-repudiation of delivery can be provided through a recipient's acknowledgment, containing a signature or token computed on the contents of the delivered data. The signature can be generated by the recipient or a trusted third party who is vouching for the recipient. Alternatively, a trusted delivery agent may be employed. To counter the problem of a recipient choosing not to acknowledge a particular delivered data item after having seen its contents, two-stage delivery can be employed. In applications in which messages are forwarded through multiple administrative domains, non-repudiation of delivery can be applied at multiple points on the message path.

The non-repudiation process involves trusted third parties performing various functions, including key certification, identity certification, time-stamping, evidence storage, delivery agent, and arbitration. Parties assuming these functions need to be neutral, reliable, and accepted by all parties involved.

In communications architectures, non-repudiation services are located at the application level.

Exercises

1. Why is it always necessary to involve trusted third parties in the provision of non-repudiation?

2. What are the advantages of using a trusted third party digital signature, as opposed to an originator's digital signature, in non-repudiation of origin? When using a trusted third party digital signature, what are the advantages of generating it on a digest of the data item rather than on the full plaintext data item?

3. Following the style of Figure 8-5, illustrate the process involved in non-repudiation of delivery using an acknowledgment from the recipient which employs a trusted third party signature.

4. Section 8.2 outlined a scheme for non-repudiation of delivery using a recipient acknowledgement and sealed token. Describe the full set of data exchanges involved in such a scheme and the types of protection which need to be applied to the various transfers.

REFERENCES

[HAB1] S. Haber and W.S. Stornetta, "How to Time-Stamp a Digital Document," *Journal of Cryptology*, vol. 3, no. 2 (1991), pp. 99-111.

Standards

ISO/IEC 10181-4: *Information Technology — Security Frameworks in Open Systems — Non-repudiation Framework* (Also ITU-T Recommendation X.813) (Draft).

PART II

STANDARD PROTOCOLS

AND TECHNIQUES

9 Security Architecture
and Frameworks

Developing standards to support security in a layered communications architecture is a complex task, as all parts of the architecture (e.g., all layer protocols and all applications) are potentially impacted. The challenge is not only to provide the necessary security functionality, but also to ensure that the standards lead to cost-effective implementations. There is tremendous potential for:

- functions being unnecessarily duplicated throughout the architecture;
- incompatible security features being used in different parts of the architecture; and
- diverse techniques being employed in different applications or layers, when fewer techniques would suffice and be more economical.

When the decision was made to add security to the OSI architecture, it was apparent that a coordinated approach was needed to develop a broad, coherent *family* of standards. This chapter introduces the resultant standards family and describes the central standards that tie the family together. While the standards described in this chapter were all developed as part of the OSI program, their applicability extends well beyond OSI protocol stacks.

Members of the security standards family can be categorized as follows:

(a) *Security architecture and framework standards*: Documents providing a reference base for building standards in the other categories.
(b) *Security techniques standards*: Specifications of broadly applicable techniques, such as authentication exchanges and digital signature mechanisms.
(c) *Layer security protocol standards*: Application-independent protocol specifications for various architectural layers, such as the Network and Transport Layers.
(d) *Application-specific security standards*: Parts of or extensions to application standards, such as electronic mail or directory standards.
(e) *Security management standards*: Specifications that support the management of security functions or that provide for the protection of network management communications.

This chapter addresses standards in the first category. The other categories are covered in Chapters 10 through 15.

This chapter comprises sections which discuss:

(1) the background behind the OSI Security Architecture standard and the terminology from that document which is now used throughout the standards family;

(2) the security services and mechanisms defined in the OSI Security Architecture and the conclusions drawn in that standard as to appropriate architectural placement of these services and mechanisms;

(3) the open systems Security Frameworks project, which is developing standards which expand upon OSI Security Architecture concepts on a topic-by-topic basis and which generalize those concepts to apply beyond OSI;

(4) the various parts of the Security Frameworks series;

(5) the utility of the architecture and framework standards now and in the future; and

(6) an introduction to the security techniques and protocols standards categories, which are covered in Chapters 10 through 15.

9.1   The OSI Security Architecture

Background

Work on the OSI Security Architecture commenced in 1982, when the content of the OSI Basic Reference Model had just stabilized. The development cycle was completed in 1988, with the publication of standard ISO 7498-2, a new part to be added to the OSI Reference Model. This project was carried out by ISO/IEC JTC1/SC21. In 1990, the ITU resolved to adopt the text of ISO 7498-2 as Recommendation X.800.

The OSI Security Architecture is not an implementable standard — it is a standard writer's standard. Hence, products cannot legitimately claim conformance to this standard, and the buyer should treat any such claim with scepticism.

This standard defines many important terms and concepts which are used throughout the entire range of open-system security standards. It also establishes some significant architectural principles. Some of the material has proven irrelevant and other material, designed to fill a pre-1988 tutorial gap, has outlived its usefulness. The material which is still significant falls into three areas:

- terminology;
- definition of security services and mechanisms; and
- placement of services in OSI layers.

These parts of the contents are described below.

Terminology

Clause 3 of the OSI Security Architecture provides the formal definitions of several terms used by standards throughout the open-system security field. While "better" definitions for many of these terms unquestionably exist (some in other standards), knowledge of the formal definitions can be useful. Significant definitions are as follows:[1]

> **access control:** The prevention of unauthorized use of a resource, including the prevention of use of a resource in an unauthorized manner.
>
> **access control list**: A list of entities, together with their access rights, which are authorized to have access to a resource.
>
> **authentication information**: Information used to establish the validity of a claimed identity.
>
> **authentication exchange**: A mechanism intended to ensure the identity of an entity by means of information exchange.
>
> **authorization**: The granting of rights, which includes the granting of access based on access rights.
>
> **capability**: A token used as an identifier for a resource such that possession of the token confers access rights for the resource.
>
> **ciphertext**: Data produced through the use of encipherment. The semantic content of the resulting data is not available.
>
> Note: Ciphertext may itself be input to encipherment such that super-enciphered output is produced.
>
> **cleartext:** Intelligible data, the semantic content of which is available.[2]
>
> **confidentiality**: The property that information is not made available or disclosed to unauthorized individuals, entities, or processes.
>
> **credentials**: Data that is transferred to establish the claimed identity of an entity.

---

[1] Source: ISO 7498-2-1988(E); reproduced with permission of ISO.

[2] The term *plaintext* is a more common alternative to *cleartext*.

cryptographic checkvalue: Information which is derived by performing a cryptographic transformation (see **cryptography**) on the data unit.

Note: The derivation of the checkvalue may be performed in one or more steps and is a result of a mathematical function of the key and a data unit. It is usually used to check the integrity of a data unit.

cryptography: The discipline which embodies principles, means, and methods for the transformation of data in order to hide its information content, prevent its undetected modification and/or prevent its unauthorized use.

Note: Cryptography determines the methods used in encipherment and decipherment. An attack on a cryptographic principle, means, or method is cryptanalysis.

data integrity: The property that data has not been altered or destroyed in an unauthorized manner.

data origin authentication: The corroboration that the source of data received is as claimed.

decipherment: The reversal of a corresponding reversible encipherment.

decryption: See **decipherment**.

denial of service: The prevention of authorized access to resources or the delaying of time-critical operations.

digital signature: Data appended to, or a cryptographic transformation (see **cryptography**) of, a data unit that allows a recipient of the data unit to prove the source and integrity of the data unit and protect against forgery, e.g. by the recipient.

encipherment: The cryptographic transformation of data (see **cryptography**) to produce ciphertext.

Note: Encipherment may be irreversible, in which case the corresponding decipherment process cannot feasibly be performed.

encryption: See **encipherment**.

identity-based security policy: A security policy based on the identities and/or attributes of users, a group of users, or entities acting on behalf of the users and the resources/objects being accessed.

notarization: The registration of data with a trusted third party that allows the latter assurance of its characteristics such as content, origin, time and delivery.

peer-entity authentication: The corroboration that a peer entity in an association is the one claimed.[3]

repudiation: Denial by one of the entities involved in a communication of having participated in all or part of the communication.

routing control: The application of rules during the process of routing so as to choose or avoid specific networks, links or relays.

rule-based security policy: A security policy based on global rules imposed for all users. These rules usually rely on a comparison of the sensitivity of the resources being accessed and the possession of corresponding attributes of users, a group of users, or entities acting on behalf of users.

security audit: An independent review and examination of system records and activities in order to test for adequacy of system controls, to ensure compliance with established policy and operational procedures, to detect breaches in security, and to recommend any indicated changes in control, policy and procedures.

security audit trail: Data collected and potentially used to facilitate a security audit.

security label: The marking bound to a resource (which may be a data unit) that names or designates the security attributes of that resource.

Note: The marking and/or binding may be explicit or implicit.

security policy: The set of criteria for the provision of security services (see also **identity-based** and **rule-based security policy**).

Note: A complete security policy will necessarily address many concerns which are outside the scope of OSI.

security service: A service, provided by a layer of communicating open systems, which ensures adequate security of the systems or of data transfers.

selective field protection: The protection of specific fields within a message which is to be transmitted.

traffic analysis: The inference of information from observation of traffic flows (presence, absence, amount, direction and frequency).

traffic flow confidentiality: A confidentiality service to protect against traffic ananysis.

---

[3] The term *peer entity* here is generally considered as meaning an OSI layer (n)-entity. Because there are many other types of objects that may need to be authenticated in an authentication exchange, the more general term *entity authentication* has been adopted in more recent standards. *Peer-entity authentication* can be considered a special case of *entity authentication*.

traffic padding: The generation of spurious instances of communication, spurious data units and/or spurious data within data units.

trusted functionality: That which is perceived to be correct with respect to some criteria, e.g., as established by a security policy.[4]

In general, these terms have been adopted throughout the follow-up body of work on open-system security. In retrospect, some terms (e.g., *credentials, peer-entity authentication, security policy*, and *security service*) were defined too narrowly; this is understandable, recognizing that the scope of this standard is limited to OSI. Broader interpretations have been adopted for some of these terms in other standards.

9.2 OSI Security Services and Mechanisms

Security Services

Security services were discussed in detail in Part I of this book. Table 9-1 lists the full set of security services, and their variations, specified in the OSI Security Architecture (references to relevant material in Part I are given).

Security Mechanisms

The OSI Security Architecture does not attempt to describe in any detail how the security services are to be provided. As guidance, it identifies a set of *security mechanisms* which may be used in implementing the services. The basic mechanisms are:

- encipherment;
- digital signature;
- access control;
- data integrity;
- authentication exchange;
- traffic padding;
- routing control; and
- notarization.

In addition, it identifies a set of *pervasive security mechanisms* which are not used specifically to provide any particular security service, but which may nevertheless be required. These are as follows:

---

[4] This cryptic definition refers to trusted hardware/software system components.

Security Service	Refer to Section (of this book)
Authentication Peer entity authentication Data origin authentication	2.3, 5 9.1 (Footnote 3) 5.9
Access Control	2.3, 6
Confidentiality Connection confidentiality Connectionless confidentiality Selective field confidentiality Traffic flow confidentiality	2.3, 7.1, 7.2
Integrity Connection integrity with recovery Connection integrity without recovery Selective field connection integrity Connectionless integrity Selective field connectionless integrity	2.3, 7.3, 7.4
Non-repudiation Non-repudiation with proof of origin Non-repudiation with proof of delivery	2.3, 8 8.2 8.3

Table 9-1: Security Services in the OSI Security Architecture

- trusted functionality (trusted hardware and/or software system components);
- security labels;
- event detection;
- security audit trail; and
- security recovery.

The standard provides the table reproduced as Table 9-2, indicating which mechanisms might be used in implementing which services. Production of this table was a contentious issue in completing this standard, because vendors did not want the standard to hamper opportunities for innovation in providing security services. Hence, the final text emphasizes that the information in this table is illustrative only and "is *not definitive*."

The discussion of security mechanisms in the OSI Security Architecture is superficial and certainly non-definitive. A much more complete analysis of the subject is provided in Part I of this book.

Mechanism Service	Encipherment	Digital Signature	Access Control	Data Integrity	Authentication Exchange	Traffic Padding	Routing Control	Notarization
Peer Entity Authentication	Y	Y	•	•	Y	•	•	•
Data Origin Authentication	Y	Y	•	•	•	•	•	•
Access Control Service	•	•	Y	•	•	•	•	•
Connection Confidentiality	Y	•	•	•	•	•	Y	•
Connectionless Confidentiality	Y	•	•	•	•	•	Y	•
Selective Field Confidentiality	Y	•	•	•	•	•	•	•
Traffic Flow Confidentiality	Y	•	•	•	•	Y	Y	•
Connection Integrity with Recovery	Y	•	•	Y	•	•	•	•
Connection Integrity without Recovery	Y	•	•	Y	•	•	•	•
Selective Field Connection Integrity	Y	•	•	Y	•	•	•	•
Connectionless Integrity	Y	Y	•	Y	•	•	•	•
Selective Field Connectionless Integrity	Y	Y	•	Y	•	•	•	•
Non-repudiation, Origin	•	Y	•	Y	•	•	•	Y
Non-repudiation, Delivery	•	Y	•	Y	•	•	•	Y

Legend: •   The mechanism is considered not to be appropriate.

Y   Yes: the mechanism is considered to be appropriate, either on its own or in combination with other mechanisms. Note: In some instances, the mechanism provides more than is necessary for the relevant service but could nevertheless be used.

Source: ISO 7498-2-1988(E); reproduced with permission of ISO.

Table 9-2: Illustration of Mechanisms to Implement Services

Placement of Services in OSI Layers

The most important contribution of the OSI Security Architecture is its conclusion as to appropriate layer placement of security services, which is shown in Table 9-3.

Service	Layer						
	1	2	3	4	5	6	7*
Peer Entity Authentication	•	•	Y	Y	•	•	Y
Data Origin Authentication	•	•	Y	Y	•	•	Y
Access Control Service	•	•	Y	Y	•	•	Y
Connection Confidentiality	Y	Y	Y	Y	•	Y	Y
Connectionless Confidentiality	•	Y	Y	Y	•	Y	Y
Selective Field Confidentiality	•	•	•	•	•	Y	Y
Traffic Flow Confidentiality	Y	•	Y	•	•	•	Y
Connection Integrity with Recovery	•	•	•	Y	•	•	Y
Connection Integrity without Recovery	•	•	Y	Y	•	•	Y
Selective Field Connection Integrity	•	•	•	•	•	•	Y
Connectionless Integrity	•	•	Y	Y	•	•	Y
Selective Field Connectionless Integrity	•	•	•	•	•	•	Y
Non-repudiation, Origin	•	•	•	•	•	•	Y
Non-repudiation, Delivery	•	•	•	•	•	•	Y

Legend: Y   Yes, service should be incorporated in the standards for the layer as a provider option.

•   Not provided.

*   It should be noted, with respect to layer 7, that the application process may, itself, provide security services.

Source: ISO 7498-2-1988(E); reproduced with permission of ISO.

Table 9-3: Relationship of Security Services and Layers

This table in the standard also carries the emphasized rider that it *"illustrates* the layers of the Reference Model in which particular security services can be provided." Several qualifying statements are included in the accompanying text to refine the picture presented in the table, and a little supporting explanation is given in Annex B.

The main conclusions can be summarized as follows:

- *Physical Layer*: Services provided are connection confidentiality and/or traffic flow confidentiality (there are no connectionless services at this layer).

- *Data Link Layer*: Services provided are connection confidentiality and connectionless confidentiality (it is considered that full traffic flow confidentiality cannot be provided above the Physical Layer).

- *Network Layer*: Authentication, access control, confidentiality (except selective field), and integrity (except selective field and recovery) can all be provided to some extent.

- *Transport Layer*: Authentication, access control, confidentiality (except selective field and traffic flow) and integrity (except selective field) can all be provided.

- *Session Layer*: No security services are provided at this layer.

- *Presentation Layer*: The fine print indicates that the Presentation Layer does not, by itself, provide any security services. However, "facilities" provided by the Presentation Layer may "support the provision of . . . security services by the Application Layer to the application-process". It is stipulated that such facilities "will" be provided in support of the basic data confidentiality services and "may also" be provided in support of authentication, integrity, and non-repudiation services.

- *Application Layer*: Provision of no service is precluded. Furthermore, this is the only layer at which selective field and non-repudiation services can be provided.

The above conclusions are fully in line with the four-level architectural model presented in Chapter 3. Apart from being more difficult to explain, the biggest weakness in the OSI Security Architecture analysis is the failure to clearly distinguish between subnetwork level protection and end-system level protection at the Network Layer. This is a natural consequence of the architectural richness of the Network Layer which too often becomes lost in the seven-layer view of OSI.

9.3   The Security Frameworks Project

Background

The Security Frameworks project was initiated before the ink was dry on the OSI Security Architecture in 1988. There were three main motivations:

- The realization that the OSI Security Architecture had reached the point where it *must* be published, even though many participants in the project would like to see additional work done on some of the subject matter. A follow-up project was needed to allow refinement of the material to proceed.

- Pressure from the Directory and Message Handling Systems projects, which forged ahead of the OSI Security Architecture work in crafting their own security solutions. It was desirable to fold those security solutions back into generic security standards.

- The growing realization that OSI was not, by itself, the whole answer to the open systems call. Areas such as database systems and operating systems needed to be accommodated in a consistent way, so security standards needed a perspective extending beyond OSI.

The goal of the Open Systems Security Frameworks project was to develop a multi-part standard with each part expanding upon one of the fundamental security topics identified in the OSI Security Architecture: *authentication, access control, confidentiality, integrity,* and *non-repudiation,* respectively. The topic of *security audit* was subsequently added.

This project was undertaken by ISO/IEC JTC1/SC21/WG1, the developers of the OSI Security Architecture. The Frameworks are largely an extension of the Architecture, but their declared scope is broader. They aim to address "security services in an Open Systems environment, where the term 'Open Systems' is taken to include areas such as Database, Distributed Applications, Open Distributed Processing, and OSI."[5]

The Frameworks' main contribution to the wider standardization process is a base of concepts and terminology for use in other standards. This allows other standards to interrelate better, and averts unnecessary duplication of concept development.

Like the OSI Security Architecture, the Frameworks are standards writers' standards — not implementors' standards.

---

[5] This statement is from the *Scope* clause of the various parts of the ISO/IEC 10181 Frameworks standard.

General Concepts

The Frameworks provide definitions of some general concepts which are important in providing security services, including:

- *Security policy*: A set of rules that constrain security-relevant activities of one or more sets of elements. A security policy defines what is meant by security within a security domain, the rules for achieving this security and the activities that are to be constrained. A security policy may also define which rules apply in relations with other security domains.
- *Security authority*: An entity responsible for the implementation of a security policy. The security authority may delegate the enforcement of of a security policy to other entities.
- *Security domain*: A set of elements, a security policy, a security authority and a set of security-relevant activities in which the elements are subject to the security policy, administered by the security authority, for the specified activities.
- *Secure interaction rules*: Common aspects of the rules necessary in order for interactions to take place between security domains.

Two other general concepts assist the development of security protocols:

- *Security certificate*: A set of security-relevant data which is protected by integrity and data origin authentication from an issuing security authority and includes an indication of a time period of validity. This is a general definition which embraces, as special cases, public-key certificates and access control certificates.
- *Security token*: A set of security-relevant data which is protected by integrity and data origin authentication from a source which is not considered a security authority. Again, this is a general definition. Special cases arise, for example, in message handling systems (see Chapter 13).

9.4   The Framework Parts

The parts of the Security Frameworks series (ISO/IEC 10181) are:

- Part 1: Frameworks Overview;
- Part 2: Authentication Framework;
- Part 3: Access Control Framework;
- Part 4: Non-repudiation Framework;

- Part 5: Confidentiality Framework;
- Part 6: Integrity Framework; and
- Part 7: Security Audit Framework.

Individual parts are discussed in the following subsections. The extent of discussion depends on the maturity level of the particular part.

Frameworks Overview

The purpose of the Overview is twofold. First, it serves as a general introduction to the multi-part standard. Second, it defines a set of terms and concepts which apply to more than one of the other parts. These include the general concepts described above, plus some other useful terms such as *seal*, *one-way function*, *private key*, *public key*, and *secret key*.[6]

Authentication Framework

The Authentication Framework led the progression of the Frameworks series. It provides some valuable terminology to describe authentication principles and architectures, and also provides a high-level classification scheme for different authentication exchange mechanisms.
Some useful terms defined in this standard are:

- *Principal*: An entity whose identity can be authenticated.
- *Claimant*: An entity that is or represents a principal for the purposes of authentication.
- *Verifier*: An entity that is or represents the entity requiring an authenticated identity.

The Authentication Framework models authentication configurations in terms of claimants, verifiers, and trusted third parties. There are different variants of a trusted third party — an *on-line trusted third party* corresponds to an ANSI X9.17 key distribution center or a Kerberos authentication server; an *off-line trusted third party* corresponds to a certification authority who signs certificates distributed through a directory service.
Various types of *authentication information* are also defined:

- *Exchange authentication information (exchange AI)*: Information exchanged between a claimant and a verifier during the process of authenticating a principal.

---

[6] The meanings of these terms are explained in Chapter 4.

- *Claim authentication information (claim AI)*: Information used by a claimant to generate exchange AI needed to authenticate a principal.
- *Verification authentication information (verification AI)*: Information used by a verifier to verify an identity claimed through exchange AI.

As an example to explain these terms, consider an authentication scheme whereby a claimant sends a message signed with his private key and the authentication is accomplished by the verifier checking the signature using the principal's public key. In this case, the signed message is exchange AI, the private key is claim AI, and the public key is verification AI.

Using the above terms, different authentication configurations can be identified, as illustrated in Figure 9-1.

Configuration (a) shows the basic model which applies in the absence of any trusted third party involvement. Configuration (b) is called *in-line authentication*. A principal is authenticated by an intermediary (trusted third party), who then vouches for the principal in a subsequent exchange.

Configuration (c) is the case of an on-line authentication server where either the claimant obtains a ticket for passing on to the verifier, or the verifier interacts with the server in performing the authentication (see Section 5.4 for further explanation). Configuration (d) is the case of an off-line server, such as a directory service distributing certified public keys.

The Authentication Framework also defines a set of phases of activity in an authentication process and uses these as the basis for defining a set of authentication *facilities*. The phases are:

- *Installation*: Claim AI and verification AI for a principal are defined.
- *Change-authentication-information*: A principal or an administrator causes claim and/or verification AI (e.g., a password) to change.
- *Distribution*: Verification AI (e.g., a public-key certificate) is distributed to an entity requiring it; this might occur before, in conjunction with, or immediately following the authentication claim.
- *Acquisition*: Information is obtained on-line by a claimant or verifier to support processing for a specific authentication attempt (e.g., obtaining a ticket from an on-line authentication server).
- *Transfer*: Exchange AI is communicated between claimant and verifier.
- *Verification*: At the verifier end, exchange AI and verification AI are processed to yield an authentication decision. This may involve further exchanges with a trusted third party.
- *Disable*: Authentication rights for a principal are temporarily suspended.
- *Re-enable*: Authentication rights for a suspended principal are reinstated.
- *Deinstallation*: A principal is permanently removed from an environment.

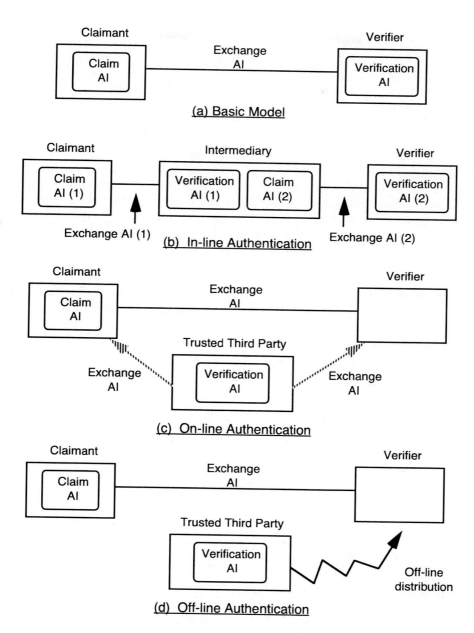

Figure 9-1: Authentication Configurations

Two different categories of facility are defined:

- *Management related facilities*: Facilities identified are *install*, *change-AI*, *distribute*, *disable*, *re-enable*, and *deinstall*. No indication is given of how such facilities might be implemented, hence the only value of this list is in providing common terminology for management activities that may be associated with authentication.

- *Operational-related facilities*: These facilities are *acquire* and *verify* (which map to phases described above), plus *generate* which a claimant uses to generate exchange AI for sending to a verifier (e.g., the generate facility might format and sign an authentication token). The information flows associated with these three facilities are illustrated in Figure 9-2. This set of facilities aims to model the activities that need to be implemented in immediate support of an authentication exchange. They could therefore serve as a high-level basis for defining an application program interface (API) to assist modular construction of authentication software. For example, a standard mechanism-independent interface could be defined for invoking a *generate* procedure in claimant systems, a *verify* procedure in verifier systems, and an *acquire* procedure in claimant and/or verifier systems. The same facility model can be applied to a mutual authentication exchange although, in this case, the generate and verify facilities become merged into a composite service at each end.

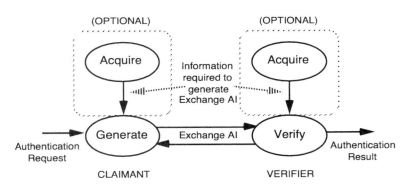

Figure 9-2: Information Flows in Operational-Related Facilities

Another contribution of the Authentication Framework is a classification scheme for authentication mechanisms, on the basis of their abilities to counter eavesdropping and replay attacks. This classification scheme is of limited practical value because of the use of a simplistic model which mixes different technologies (e.g., non-cryptographic, symmetric cryptographic, and public-key mechanisms) and mixes entity authentication and data origin authentication.

Access Control Framework

After the Authentication Framework, the Access Control Framework was the next fastest to progress. The most significant contributions of this framework are terminology and an architectural model for providing access control in network environments.

Some important terms defined in this framework (the same terms are used in Chapter 6 of this book) are:

- *Access control information (ACI)*: Any information used for access control purposes.
- *Access control decision function (ADF)*: A function that makes access control decisions by applying access control policy rules to an access request, to access control decision information (of initiators, targets, access requests, or that retained from prior decisions), and to the context in which the request is made.
- *Access control decision information (ADI)*: The portion (possibly all) of the ACI made available to the ADF in making a particular access control decision.
- *Access control enforcement function (AEF)*: A function that is part of the access path between an initiator and a target on each access and enforces the decision made by the ADF.
- *Contextual information*: Information about or derived from the context in which an access is made (e.g., time of day).
- *Initiator*: An entity (e.g., human user or computer-based entity) that attempts to access other entities.
- *Target*: An entity to which access may be attempted.

This standard also introduces the architectural model involving initiators, targets, access control enforcement functions, and access control decision functions (see Figure 6-6 in Chapter 6).

The standard also includes considerable material on access control policies and access control mechanisms, including access control list, capability, and label-based mechanisms. This material is generally tutorial in nature.[7]

---

[7] Of course, any attempt to write a tutorial by committee, using a consensus approach, is doomed to failure. Hence, the Security Frameworks cannot be recommended for tutorial purposes.

Other Frameworks

The other parts of the Frameworks series address Non-repudiation, Confidentiality, Integrity, and Audit, respectively. Development of these Framework parts has been very drawn-out, owing to minimal interest in their completion. At the time of publication of this book, the Non-repudiation Framework is too immature to warrant detailed discussion. The other three parts are particularly thin and provide little value to the reader.

9.5 Use of the Security Architecture and Framework Standards

The Security Architecture and Framework standards have two practical uses:

- as guides to the development of follow-up (e.g., *implementable*) open-system security standards; and
- as the source of material referenced by the follow-up standards.

The first use, especially for the OSI Security Architecture, has already been substantially realized. In particular, the material on layer placement of security services (e.g., Table 9-3) led to the focusing of subsequent security protocol standardization in two directions:

- *Lower layers*: Comprehensive security protocols have been defined in the Network and Transport Layers. LAN security protocols and subnetwork-technology-specific security features in the Data Link and Physical Layers have also been defined.
- *Upper layers*: General-purpose and application-specific security protocol components have been defined for the Application Layer, making some use of Presentation Layer functions.

The guidance role of the Security Architecture and Framework standards is declining with time, as the follow-up standards materialize. However, the reference-source role will guarantee them a long life, as official definitions of terms and concepts will always be needed by some standards users.

9.6 Introduction to the Techniques and Protocols Standards

The next four chapters of this book address standard security techniques and protocols. Figure 9-3 indicates the major standards considered and shows their relationship to the OSI architecture.

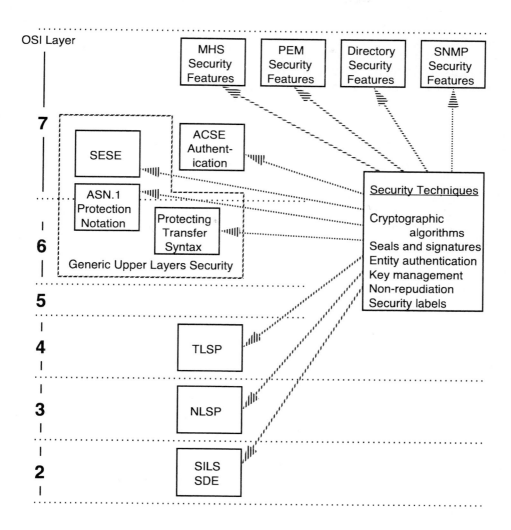

Figure 9-3: Major Security Techniques and Protocols Standards

The standards shown can be grouped as follows:

- *Security techniques*: These standards are not tied to any particular protocol layer or any particular application. They are addressed in Chapter 10.
- *Lower layers security protocols*: These standards include the Transport Layer Security Protocol (TLSP), Network Layer Security Protocol (NLSP), and Standard for Interoperable LAN/MAN Security (SILS) Secure Data Exchange (SDE) protocol. These standards are addressed in Chapter 11;
- *Upper layers security protocols*: These are Application Layer or Presentation Layer standards, which can support the provision of security in any application. They include the ACSE authentication option, and the collection of protocol construction tools (Security Exchange Service Element, ASN.1 Protection Notation, and Protecting Transfer Syntax) which constitute the Generic Upper Layers Security standard. These standards are addressed in Chapter 12.
- *Application-specific security standards*: These standards include the security features in Message Handling Systems (MHS) and Internet Privacy Enhanced Mail (PEM) (Chapter 13), the Directory application (Chapter 14), and the Simple Network Management Protocol (SNMP) (Chapter 15).

Summary

Incorporation of security into network standards impacts many standardization areas. Accordingly, the need for a coherent family of security-related standards has been recognized. Security architecture and framework standards constitute the cornerstone of this standards family. These standards provide a reference base for building standards in other categories, including lower layers and upper layers security protocols, application-specific security, and security management (these categories are addressed in Chapters 11 through 15).

The OSI Security Architecture standard defines some important terms, concepts, and architectural principles used by other standards. It defines security services for open-system communications and outlines the types of security mechanisms which may be used to provide these services. It also identifies appropriate layer placement options for these security services and mechanisms.

The Security Frameworks project is developing standards which expand upon the concepts in the OSI Security Architecture on a topic-by-topic basis and which generalize those concepts to apply beyond the OSI environment.

The Authentication Framework defines terms and concepts relating to authentication, together with a high-level classification scheme for different authentication exchange mechanisms. The Access Control Framework contributes terminology and an architectural model for providing access control in network environments. Other Framework parts addressing non-repudiation, confidentiality, integrity, and security audit are in development.

The Security Architecture and Frameworks are primarily standards developers' standards. Their utility, except for terminology reference purposes, is declining with time.

REFERENCES

Standards

ISO/IEC 7498-2: *Information Technology — Open Systems Interconnection — Basic Reference Model — Part 2: Security Architecture* (Also ITU-T Recommendation X.800).

ISO/IEC 10181-1: *Information Technology — Security Frameworks in Open Systems — Frameworks Overview* (Also ITU-T Recommendation X.810) (Draft).

ISO/IEC 10181-2: *Information Technology — Security Frameworks in Open Systems — Authentication Framework* (Also ITU-T Recommendation X.811) (Draft).

ISO/IEC 10181-3: *Information Technology — Security Frameworks in Open Systems — Access Control Framework* (Also ITU-T Recommendation X.812) (Draft).

ISO/IEC 10181-4: *Information Technology — Security Frameworks in Open Systems — Non-repudiation Framework* (Also ITU-T Recommendation X.813) (Draft).

ISO/IEC 10181-5: *Information Technology — Security Frameworks in Open Systems — Confidentiality Framework* (Also ITU-T Recommendation X.814) (Draft).

ISO/IEC 10181-6: *Information Technology — Security Frameworks in Open Systems — Integrity Framework* (Also ITU-T Recommendation X.815) (Draft).

ISO/IEC 10181-7: *Information Technology — Security Frameworks in Open Systems — Security Audit Framework* (Also ITU-T Recommendation X.816) (Draft).

10 Standard Security Techniques

Security techniques such as encryption, digital signatures, and authentication exchanges are the most fundamental building blocks of communications security. They are not peculiar to any interconnection architecture (e.g., OSI or TCP/IP), to any architectural layer, or to any application. They are not even peculiar to communications security — many are also applicable to fields such as operating system security and database security. Given this wide applicability, and the potentially high costs of implementing diverse security safeguards, tremendous benefit can be gained from standardizing such techniques.

The public standardization of security techniques has been led historically by the financial industry and by the U.S. federal government, with international standardization of general-purpose security techniques gaining momentum more recently. The need for security techniques standards was recognized in the United States in the early 1970s. This led to standards for the DES algorithm and supporting procedures being published by the U.S. federal government and by ANSI (e.g., FIPS PUB 46 and 74, and ANSI X3.92). These standards were established for the government and financial industry sectors, but clearly had wide applicability elsewhere.

In 1980, ISO TC97 (the forerunner of ISO/IEC JTC1) established a special working group on *Data Encryption* to move the U.S. DES-based work into the international arena. In 1984, subcommittee TC97/SC20 *Data Cryptographic Techniques* was spawned to continue this work and to develop other standards in the newly emerging area of public-key techniques. While there has since been considerable debate surrounding the public standardization of security techniques, this international committee work has continued. In 1990, the work was taken over by a new committee, JTC1/SC27 *Security Techniques*.

Independently, other relevant standardization has occurred. The ISO and ANSI committees on financial industry standards have continued to develop security techniques standards for the financial industry. A JTC1 subcommittee on *Identification Cards and Related Devices* has been developing standards for integrated-circuit cards (*smart cards*), with security techniques being prominent in its work. Other significant standards have resulted from the U.S. federal government and the Internet community.

This chapter addresses standard security techniques resulting from all of the above activities. It is organized into sections on different categories of techniques, as follows:

(1) cryptographic algorithms;
(2) seals and digital signatures;
(3) entity authentication;
(4) key management using symmetric techniques;
(5) key management using public-key techniques;
(6) security label standards;
(7) other standardization projects; and
(8) smart card standards.

10.1 Cryptographic Algorithms

Standardization of cryptographic algorithms is a controversial topic. Some level of standardization is clearly necessary if different equipment vendors are to construct security products which interwork. However, there are arguments against algorithm standardization. It is sometimes considered that keeping details of an algorithm secret will help preserve its effectiveness, by making cryptanalysis more difficult. Another argument is that standardization of an algorithm will increase its sphere of application, making it a more lucrative target for profit-motivated cryptanalysis. Further arguments result from the premise that cryptography and cryptanalysis are such powerful tools in the event of major threats to society (such as warfare, terrorism, and organized crime) that society needs to exercise close control over access to them.

ISO Policy on Standardization of Algorithms

In 1984–1985, a priority project of ISO TC97/SC20 was the international standardization of DES. In 1986, formal balloting procedures on the final text of DIS 8227 *Information Processing — Data Encipherment — Specification of Algorithm DEA 1* were completed. However, in a rare move, the ISO Council, on the basis of high-level national representations, decided not to publish the standard. Instead, a resolution was adopted that ISO would not standardize cryptographic algorithms.

Register of Algorithms

Following the decision not to standardize cryptographic algorithms, it was agreed that ISO/IEC should establish a service for registering cryptographic algorithms. Standard ISO/IEC 9979 was prepared, defining the procedures for such a registration service.

Registering a cryptographic algorithm means, primarily, assigning a unique identifier to it. This requires one organization — a *registration authority* — to assume responsibility for the registration process. The registration authority is charged with assigning identifiers to new register entries, and with maintaining and regularly publishing the register. The registration authority does not evaluate or make any judgment of the quality of protection provided by registered algorithms. ISO/IEC 9979 provides for three types of register entry:

- an entry which includes a complete description of the algorithm process;
- an entry for an algorithm defined in another ISO/IEC document or a national or liaison organization standard; and
- an entry not containing a description of the algorithm process.

A register entry includes:

- a formal entry name, which is an ASN.1 object identifier assigned by the registration authority;
- an algorithm name given by its owner;
- the intended range of applications, e.g., confidentiality, authentication, data integrity, digital signature, and hash function;
- cryptographic interface parameters, e.g., input size, output size, key length, and initialization vector size;
- name of sponsoring ISO/IEC national body or liaison organization;
- registration and modification dates;
- export license and patent restrictions (if any); and
- (optionally) description of algorithm, modes of operations, and other technical details.

The registration authority role was assigned to the National Computing Centre Ltd., Manchester, United Kingdom, and the registry commenced operation in 1992. Considering that the only technical function of the registration process is the assignment of a unique ASN.1 object identifier to an algorithm, and that virtually any organization can *itself* assign an object identifier (following the procedures of ISO/IEC 9834-1), the ISO/IEC 9979 registry is more an administrative convenience to prospective algorithm users than a technical necessity.

Independent of this international register, the North American OIW has provided a means of registering algorithms within its implementation agreements [NIS1]. It has established registrations (including assigning object identifiers) for the various modes of DES, plus certain common hash functions and digital signature algorithms.

Modes of Operation

The DES modes of operation were published as the U.S. federal government standard FIPS PUB 81 in 1981, and as ANSI X3.106 in 1983. In 1987, essentially the same specification was published as international standard ISO 8372. However, this standard is more generally applicable (not restricted to DES) — it specifies "modes of operation for a 64-bit block cipher algorithm."

In 1991, a more general version of the same standard was published — "modes of operation for an *n*-bit block cipher algorithm." This standard, ISO/IEC 10116, generalizes the definitions of the four DES modes of operation, to make them applicable to block ciphers of any block size.

10.2 Seals and Digital Signatures

Message Authentication Code

The term *message authentication code* (MAC) is used for the sealing technique defined originally in the U.S. national wholesale banking standard ANSI X9.9. This standard was developed as a basis for integrity protection of financial transaction messages between financial institutions or between a financial institution and a corporate or government customer. ANSI X9.9 addresses two issues:

- message formatting, i.e., determining the source bit string on which the sealing algorithm is to apply; and
- the particular sealing algorithm to use in computing the MAC value.

The message formatting issue arises because financial messages can be considered to be either binary or character data. With binary data, determination of the source bit string is trivial. However, with character data, the following options are provided:

- Integrity may apply to the entire message or to certain extracted message elements only. (This requires standard message element formats to be recognized.)
- The message may optionally be edited in accordance with stipulated rules prior to computation of the MAC value. This is done to eliminate

message variations due only to upper/lower case differences or formatting characters or control characters. (Such editing is necessary, for example, if network or terminal equipment might remove or modify certain characters.)

Characters are then encoded into octets, with the highest order bit set to zero and the remaining seven bits set in accordance with ANSI X3.4 (ASCII).

The ANSI X9.9 algorithm involves padding the source bit string with trailing zero bits as necessary to give a multiple of 64 bits, then applying DES in CBC (or 64-bit CFB) mode to generate a 64-bit value.[1] The *m*-bit MAC value is obtained from the left-most *m* bits of the 64-bit value.[2] (For further detail, see Section 4.3 of this book or [JUE1].)

A more detailed description of the same MAC algorithm was published in ANSI X9.19, intended for retail banking applications. The U.S. federal government also standardized the DES-based MAC algorithm in FIPS PUB 113, for use in government applications.

At the international level, ISO TC68 produced related standards ISO 8730 and ISO 8731. These are MAC standards, based on the ANSI X9.9 technique, but designed to permit other cryptographic algorithms than DES. ISO 8730 is algorithm-independent, while ISO 8731 has multiple parts, each part specific to one algorithm. ISO 8730 serves two main purposes:

- It specifies, in an algorithm-independent way, methods to be used for protecting the integrity of wholesale financial messages by means of a MAC. This reflects the message formatting material in ANSI X9.9.
- It specifies the method by which specific algorithms are to be approved for inclusion in ISO 8731.

Part 1 of ISO 8731 deals with the use of DES to calculate a MAC. The combination of ISO 8730 and ISO 8731-1 can therefore be considered equivalent to ANSI X9.9. Part 2 of ISO 8731 contains a special-purpose algorithm known as the Message Authenticator Algorithm. This algorithm was designed for high-speed MAC calculations in a computer which uses 32-bit arithmetic and is optimized for efficient implementation in software. For further details, see [DAV1].

For the retail banking sector, ISO TC68 produced standard ISO 9807. This standard is the international equivalent of ANSI X9.19 but, like ISO

---

[1] The MAC process can be strengthened by using two keys, K_1 and K_2. First, the CBC process is applied using K_1. The 64-bit result is then subjected to a DES decryption using K_2, followed by a DES encryption using K_1, to give the 64-bit output.

[2] *m* is most commonly 32, but a value of 48 or 64 is permitted.

8730, it provides for the use of algorithms other than DES (e.g., the Message Authenticator Algorithm).

All of the preceding MAC standards were targeted specifically at the financial industry. ISO/IEC JTC1 produced a general-purpose MAC standard ISO/IEC 9797. This uses the same basic approach as ANSI X9.9, i.e., application of a block cipher algorithm in CBC mode, but it avoids direct links with DES. It is defined in terms of any block cipher algorithm using n-bit data blocks and generating an m-bit MAC. It also introduces two alternative padding methods. The first method (which is the same as in ANSI X9.9) involves padding the source data with as few (possibly none) 0-bits as necessary to obtain a multiple of n bits. The second method involves first appending a single 1-bit, then appending as few (possibly none) 0-bits as necessary to obtain a multiple of n bits. The second method ensures that the original data length is conveyed correctly to the verifying end.

Digital Signature with Appendix

Generation of an appendix-based digital signature involves four main steps:

(a) Apply a hash function to a source data value to give a digest data value.
(b) Pad the digest to give a *signature block*, which has a bit string length suitable for the generate process.
(c) Mathematically process the signature block to give an appendix bit string.
(d) Build a composite string suitable for conveying, in a communications protocol, values of the appendix, source data value (if required), and algorithm information (if required).

In principle, these steps may be dealt with in one or more independent standards. Typically, step (a) is dealt with in a hash function standard and steps (b) and (c) are dealt with in a signature algorithm standard.

The Directory Authentication Framework (ISO/IEC 9594-8 or ITU-T Recommendation X.509) was the first standard attempting to address the full signature process. This standard defines a signature format for use in any network application. ASN.1 notation is used to specify a data item format which can include source data value, appendix, algorithm identifier, and algorithm parameters. Details of this format are provided in Section 12.6. The inclusion of the algorithm identifier (an ASN.1 object identifier) enables the format to be employed with any desired hash function/signature algorithm combination. The Directory Authentication Framework originally included a hash function definition for the *square mod n* hash function, but this was later removed after flaws in the hash function were identified. A signature algorithm definition was also included — this specifies the RSA algorithm, while permitting any desired padding convention to be employed.[3]

Self-contained hash function standards are being developed. The U.S. federal government Secure Hash Algorithm (SHA) has been published as FIPS PUB 180 and as Part 2 of ANSI X9.30. The DES-based hash function MDC2 is being published as Part 2 of ANSI X9.31. The MD2, MD4, and MD5 hash functions are Internet RFCs [KAL1, RIV1, RIV2]. ISO/IEC JTC1 is developing the multi-part standard ISO/IEC 10118 to cover a variety of hash functions, concentrating initially on block-cipher-based (e.g., DES-based) hash functions.

Self-contained signature algorithm standards are also being developed. The U.S. Digital Signature Algorithm (DSA) is being processed as a U.S. federal government (FIPS PUB) standard and as Part 1 of ANSI X9.30. An RSA signature algorithm is being published as Part 1 of the ANSI X9.31 standard. This specification includes a particular padding convention derived from ISO/IEC 9796 (see the following subsection).

Digital Signature with Message Recovery

The JTC1 standard ISO/IEC 9796, first published in 1991, defines a digital signature technique which can be used in either of two ways:

- As a method for signing very small messages. No hash function is involved, and the plaintext content of the signed value is recovered as part of the verification process (the signed value is effectively transferred in an encrypted form via the signature process).
- As a signature algorithm applied to a hashed digest of a larger message. This amounts to applying a sophisticated padding convention to the digest.

This technique depends upon the use of a reversible public-key cryptosystem, such as RSA. For further details, see Section 4.4.

10.3 Entity Authentication

The primary emerging international standard for entity authentication techniques is the multi-part standard ISO/IEC 9798. Part 1 is introductory, providing terminology definitions which are generally aligned with the open-systems Authentication Framework (see Section 9.4). Parts 2 and 3 address entity

---

[3] This constitutes a deficiency in this RSA signature algorithm definition. Various padding schemes are possible, and both parties need to know the scheme that is used.

authentication using symmetric techniques and public-key techniques, respectively. Entity authentication techniques are also addressed in Internet standards, in financial industry standards, and in the Directory Authentication Framework.

Techniques Using Symmetric Cryptography

One of the most prominent entity authentication techniques based on symmetric cryptography is the Kerberos system. Kerberos was designed originally as part of Project Athena at the Massachusetts Institute of Technology (MIT) [MIL1, STE1]. It quickly gained acceptance in academic environments, primarily for use with UNIX systems, and its acceptance has subsequently spread to other environments and other systems. Kerberos Version 5 was developed under the auspices of Internet [KOH1]. The underlying authentication method is described in Section 5.8 of this book. The Kerberos specification includes precise ASN.1 definitions of the messages communicated between the various systems involved in Kerberos exchanges.

In the arena of formal international standards, ISO/IEC 9798-2 defines a selection of entity authentication mechanisms which use symmetric cryptography. The defined mechanisms vary in terms of:

- whether unilateral or mutual authentication is provided;
- whether or not an on-line authentication server (trusted third party) is used; and
- which (if any) of the two authenticating systems communicate with the on-line authentication server.

The Kerberos scheme can be considered a special case of one of these mechanisms.

In the arena of financial industry standards, the U.S. banking standard ANSI X9.26 defines entity authentication techniques. It addresses three *types* of authentication:

- *Type 1*: The authentication of a user via *personal authenticating information* (a password).
- *Type 2*: The authentication of a user via a user-unique key.
- *Type 3*: The authentication of a node via a node-unique key.

Type 1 uses DES encryption for password protection. Types 2 and 3 are based upon proving knowledge of a secret DES key. The techniques for types 2 and 3 are virtually the same, except for different granularity of the DES key. With all types, provision is made for the incorporation of time-variant parameters as protection against replay. ANSI X9.26 also includes definitions of character-encoded messages for conveying authentication exchanges based on these techniques, and for conveying password change notifications and error notifications.

ISO 11131 is the international adaptation of ANSI X9.26, which removes the link to the DES algorithm.

Techniques Using Public-Key Cryptography

The first established standard defining public-key-based entity authentication was the Directory Authentication Framework (ITU X.509 or ISO/IEC 9594-8). This standard, which is described further in Section 14.3, defines three public-key-based authentication exchanges:

- a one-way exchange, providing unilateral authentication;
- a two-way exchange, providing mutual authentication; and
- a three-way exchange, providing mutual authentication, with replay detection capabilities that are superior to the two-way exchange.

For a technical analysis of the latter two exchanges, see Section 5.6.

ISO/IEC 9798-3 is a more recent standard dedicated to public-key entity authentication exchanges. It defines several authentication exchanges, some for unilateral and some for mutual authentication. They are very similar to the X.509 exchanges, with some small technical improvements.

10.4 Key Management Using Symmetric Techniques

As explained in Chapter 4, key management is a complex subject, and standardization beyond organizational or community boundaries is not easy to achieve. The subject can be conveniently separated into two parts — key management using symmetric techniques and key management using public-key techniques.

ANSI X9.17

Following the adoption of DES-based standards for confidentiality and integrity in the U.S. financial industry, the need for a supporting key management standard was apparent. This led to the development of the landmark standard ANSI X9.17 *Financial Institution Key Management (Wholesale)*, which was first published in 1985 [BAL1, GRE1].

ANSI X9.17 is a comprehensive standard, addressing the generation, exchange, use, storage, and destruction of DES keys. It provides a sound basis for electronic key management to support DES protection of messages between pairs of communicating financial institutions. It not only describes necessary key management techniques, but also provides a full key management protocol specification. The contents include:

- Protection requirements for a key management facility.
- A description of a key management architecture employing either two layers or three layers of keys. A key at one layer protects keys at the next lowest layer during distribution. The keys at the highest layer are manually distributed.
- A description of three key management environments (system configurations) — a point-to-point environment, a key distribution center environment, and a key translation center environment.[4]
- Techniques for encrypting keys, key pairs, and initialization vectors, under either a single key or a key pair (using the triple-DES approach).
- Definitions of the formats of a set of Cryptographic Service Messages, for use in communicating key information between systems.
- Specifications of the procedures associated with generating and processing Cryptographic Service Messages in each of the three key management environments identified above.

The latter two items constitute a complete key management protocol specification.

ANSI X9.17 was input to ISO TC68, and became the basis of the international standard ISO 8732 *Banking — Key Management (Wholesale)*. Another derivative of ANSI X9.17 is the U.S. federal government FIPS PUB 171, which defines a restricted set of ANSI X9.17 options for government use, with a view to reducing the costs of building ANSI X9.17 systems.

Multiple-Center Key Management

A major limitation of ANSI X9.17 is the impracticality of supporting a very large population of communicating systems. Every two terminal systems which might ever require to communicate securely with each other both need to have a master key relationship with some key center. As populations become large, this leads to one of the following situations:

---

[4] See Section 4.6 for further details.

(a) Terminal systems need to maintain master key relationships with a large number of key centers. (This is unacceptable for reasons of terminal cost and manual key distribution cost.)

(b) A small number of extremely large key centers is needed, each maintaining master key relationships with virtually all terminals. (This is unacceptable because separate organizations require the freedom to choose or operate their own key centers.)

To resolve this dilemma, ANSI X9.28 was developed. This standard extends ANSI X9.17 to support the distribution of keying material between terminal systems which do not share a common key center. Two or more key centers implementing this standard can together form a *multiple-center group*. Any subscriber to the multiple-center group can exchange keying material securely with any other subscriber to the same multiple-center group. The standard defines the necessary protocol for use in communications between different key centers in a multiple-center group.

Other Standards

ISO/IEC JTC1 is developing multi-part standard ISO/IEC 11770 addressing key management techniques, with emphasis on key establishment (or key distribution) techniques. Part 2 of this standard is concerned with mechanisms using symmetric techniques.

Standards for key management in retail banking environments have also been developed. These standards address the key management issues arising with such systems as banking terminals and point-of-sale terminals. ANSI X9.24 is a comprehensive standard for this area, but built upon the assumption that DES will be used throughout. ISO 11568 is a newer international equivalent, which is not linked to DES and which will, in due course, accommodate public-key cryptosystems as well as symmetric cryptosystems.

10.5 Key Management Using Public-Key Techniques

This section is concerned with key management techniques which employ public-key cryptosystems. Such techniques are of two distinct types, as the keys being managed can be either symmetric algorithm keys or public keys.

Directory Authentication Framework

The Directory Authentication Framework (ISO/IEC 9594-8 or ITU-T Recommendation X.509) gives substantial coverage to techniques for distributing public keys. It describes the basic functions of public-key certificates, certification authorities, certificate chains, and certificate revocation lists. It provides data structure definitions for certificates, certificate chains, and certificate revocation lists. In conjunction with other parts of the Directory standard, it provides the basis for a complete public-key management system built around the Directory application. (See Section 14.3 for more details.)

This standard also indicates how a symmetric cryptosystem key can be transferred in conjunction with a public-key-based authentication exchange, by encrypting the transferred key under the recipient's public key. However, no detailed specifications are given in support of this type of key distribution.

Financial Industry Standards

The first U.S. financial industry standard employing public-key cryptography is ANSI X9.30 on *Public Key Cryptography using Irreversible Algorithms for the Financial Services Industry*. It is concerned with digital signature techniques and key management techniques to support both digital signatures and the distribution of symmetric cryptosystem keys. Both the digital signature and key management techniques employ the DSA and SHA algorithms.

Parts 1 and 2 of X9.30 are the specifications of DSA and SHA, respectively, and are identical to the corresponding FIPS PUBS in all technical respects. Part 3, on *Certificate Management for DSA*, addresses the distribution of public keys. The material in this part is based on the Directory Authentication Framework, but is more comprehensive. It describes certificate management procedures at length. It includes data item definitions for public-key certificates, attribute certificates (which hold subsidiary information linked to a public-key certificate), certificate revocation lists, and multiply signed certificates. Part 4 of X9.30 addresses derivation of symmetric data keys.

The separate standard, ANSI X9.31 *Public Key Cryptography using Reversible Algorithms for the Financial Services Industry* addresses basically the same requirements as ANSI X9.30, but presents alternative techniques. In particular, it includes an RSA-based digital signature technique as an alternative to DSA. This standard was developed as a result of industry pressure for RSA (a popular *de facto* standard) to retain acceptability after the establishment of DSA as the federal government standard.

Independently of the ANSI work, ISO TC68 commenced development of standard ISO 11166 *Banking and Related Financial Services — Key Management by Means of Asymmetric Algorithms*. This European-driven development is focused on techniques for distributing symmetric cryptosystem keys. It is, in many respects, a public-key extension of ISO 8732. It defines a new set of Cryptographic Service Messages which use public-key rather that symmetric techniques to protect the communication of keying material. Protection can be based either on *key transport*, in which a key is sent RSA-encrypted from one party to another and *key exchange* which employs techniques like Diffie-Hellman key derivation.

Other Standards

Part 3 of the ISO/IEC JTC1 Key Management standard (ISO/IEC 11770) addresses key establishment (or key distribution) mechanisms using public-key techniques. The mechanisms are described at an application-independent level. This standard focuses upon techniques and does not specify full key management protocols.

10.6 Security Labels

In a network, security labels are used primarily for routing control purposes — a label attached to a datagram, a message, or a connection governs whether or not the associated data is permitted to be passed to or through a particular environment. The information carried in a security label depends upon the security policy in force. For example, a label may contain classification level (e.g., confidential, secret), category (e.g., staff-in-confidence), and/or other markings. Both the set of permitted values and the semantics of the values are policy-dependent and may differ greatly in such environments as government classified, government unclassified-but-sensitive, financial industry, and corporate/private networks. Therefore, it is not practical to fully standardize security labels.

However, labels authorized by different organizations must be unambiguously distinguishable from each other. Furthermore, it is desirable to keep label formats as similar as possible to minimize the costs of tailoring a product to recognize labels of different organizations. To these ends, the U.S. federal government and the Internet community have specified standard label structures for use in government open-system applications.

The first specification of this type was the Intenet Protocol Security Option (IPSO) [KEN1], designed for U.S. Department of Defense applications. It is used with both the Internet IP and the OSI Connectionless Network Protocol (ISO/IEC 8473), in accordance with the U.S. GOSIP specification. This label format was designed to support Department of Defense security policies and is not suitable for use in other environments. An extended form of IPSO, called Common IP Security Option (CIPSO), has since been developed. CIPSO is suitable for a range of government environments. This specification has, in turn, constituted a primary input into the work of NIST in their development of a federal government standard (FIPS PUB) for a security label format. The latest NIST proposal is very general, and suitable for both government and commercial use. It is also designed for use with security protocols at all architectural levels, including application-specific protocols (e.g., electronic mail protocols). An international standard security label format, possibly based on the NIST proposal, is likely in due course.

The proposed NIST standard security label format is illustrated in Figure 10-1. A label comprises a collection of one or more Registered Fields. Each Registered Field comprises a globally unique Tag Set Name (an ASN.1 object identifier), plus a set of security tags. A small set of permitted data types for security tags is defined in the proposed standard. The set of tags in a Registered Field and the semantics of the values conveyed in each tag field are implied by the Tag Set Name. NIST is planning to provide a registration service for Registered Fields.

The label format is specified in ASN.1 notation, with two distinct ways of mapping to protocol bit-strings being defined. When used in upper layers protocols, standard ASN.1 encoding rules may be employed. For use in lower layers protocols, a simpler bit-level mapping convention is defined in an appendix to the standard. This obviates the need to implement the full complexity of ASN.1 parsing in the processing of lower layer protocols.

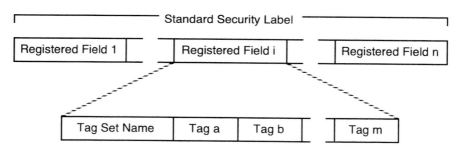

Figure 10-1: NIST Standard Security Label

10.7 Other Standardization Projects

Miscellaneous International Security Techniques Projects

In addition to standardization projects identified above, the ISO/IEC JTC1/SC27 subcommittee has projects in the following areas:

- *Guidelines for the management of information technology security*: A project to develop an ISO/IEC Technical Report addressing such areas as risk management, security life cycle management, and security awareness management. The Technical Report will provide guidance to security system analysts and administrators. The project does not aim to produce implementable standards.
- *Non-repudiation*: A project to develop a multi-part standard for non-repudiation techniques, using either symmetric or public-key cryptosystems.
- *Security information objects*: A project to develop standard procedures for specifying and registering widely applicable security-related data item definitions, such as certificates and security labels.

Miscellaneous Banking Security Projects

The following financial industry standards do not define security techniques in their own right, but describe the application of such techniques in the financial industry. They are included here to complete the reader's picture of the suite of banking security standards developed in the late 1980s and early 1990s.

ANSI X9.23 *Financial Institution Encryption of Wholesale Financial Messages* describes procedures for use of DES to protect the confidentiality of financial messages or of sensitive elements within messages. It also describes procedures to assist in achieving interoperability among different (character-oriented) transmission services. The international equivalent, ISO 10126, is a multi-part standard addressing confidentiality protection of a financial message or parts thereof. Part 1 describes general principles, and Part 2 describes the use of DES as the encryption algorithm.

ISO 9564 addresses protection of personal identification numbers (PINs) and includes a part on approved algorithms for PIN encryption.

10.8 Smart Card Standards

Smart cards were introduced in Section 5.3. Standards for the basic smart card interface, which uses six electrical contacts, were developed by ISO/IEC JTC1/SC17 and published as the ISO/IEC 7816 multi-part standard. Parts of this standard include Part 1 on physical characteristics, Part 2 on number and position of contacts, and Part 3 on electronic signals and exchange protocols. For further details, see [GUI1].

An alternative standard for a contactless smart card, which uses an inductively coupled interface, is ISO/IEC 10536.

ISO TC68 is developing standards supporting the use of smart cards in banking. Multi-part standard ISO 9992 is concerned with *Messages Exchanged with Integrated Circuit Cards*. It comprises several parts addressing such topics as concepts and structures, functions, messages (commands and responses), and common data elements. ISO 10202 is concerned with *Security Architecture of Banking Systems Using Integrated Circuit Cards*. It also has multiple parts, addressing such topics as card life cycle, transaction process, cryptographic key relationships, security application modules, use of algorithms, cardholder verification, and key management.

Summary

Security techniques, such as encryption and digital signatures, are applicable to all interconnection architectures, architectural layers, and applications. Tremendous benefit can be gained from standardizing such techniques. Historically, public standardization in this area has been led by the financial industry and by the U.S. federal government. International standardization has gained momentum only recently.

Standardization of cryptographic algorithms is a controversial topic. While DES is a U.S. standard, the move to standardize it internationally resulted in determination of an ISO policy not to standardize cryptographic algorithms. An international register for cryptographic algorithms has been established.

There are various formal standards on modes of operation of symmetric cryptographic algorithms, message authentication codes (MAC), digital signature algorithms, hash functions, entity authentication exchanges, and key management techniques which use symmetric or public-key cryptosystems. International standards are developed by ISO/IEC JTC1 (Information Technology) and ISO TC68 (Banking and Related Financial Services). In several cases, the international standards are based on U.S. standards from ANSI or the U.S. federal government. Table 10-1 summarizes the primary standards in these areas.

Some significant security technique specifications (e.g., the MD2, MD4, and MD5 hash functions and the Kerberos authentication scheme) have been published as Internet specifications.

In addition, standards have been established for security label formats, for application of security techniques in banking, and for smart cards. There are several ongoing projects on the standardization of information technology security techniques and guidelines for their use.

Topic	ISO/IEC JTC1 (Info.Technology)	ISO TC68 (Banking)	ANSI	U.S. Federal Government
Modes of operation	ISO/IEC 8372 ISO/IEC 10116		X3.106	FIPS PUB 81
MAC (general purpose)	ISO/IEC 9797	ISO 8730 ISO 8731	X9.9	FIPS PUB 113
MAC (retail banking)		ISO 9807	X9.19	
Digital signature algorithm	ISO/IEC 9594-8 ISO/IEC 9796		X9.30-1 (DSA) X9.31-1 (RSA)	FIPS PUB tba (DSA)
Hash function	ISO/IEC 10118		X9.30-2 (SHA) X9.31-2 (MDC2)	FIPS PUB 180 (SHA)
Entity authentication	ISO/IEC 9798 ISO/IEC 9594-8	ISO 11131	X9.26	
Key. Mgmt. (symmetric)	ISO/IEC 11770-2	ISO 8732 ISO 11568 (retail bkg.)	X9.17 X9.24 (retail bkg.)	FIPS PUB 171
Key. Mgmt. (symmetric multi-center)		ISO 11649	X9.28	
Key. Mgmt. (public key)	ISO/IEC 9594-8 ISO/IEC 11770-3	ISO 11166	X9.30-3	

Table 10-1: Principal Security Techniques Standards

REFERENCES

[BAL1] D.M. Balenson, "Automated Distribution of Cryptographic Keys Using the Financial Institution Key Management Standard," *IEEE Communications Magazine*, vol. 23, no. 9 (September 1985), pp. 41-46.

[DAV1] D.W. Davies and W.L. Price, *Security for Computer Networks*, Second Edition, John Wiley and Sons, New York, 1989.

[GRE1] M.B. Greenlee, "Requirements for Key Management Protocols in the Wholesale Financial Services Industry," *IEEE Communications Magazine*, vol. 23, no. 9 (September 1985), pp. 22-28.

[GUI1] L.C. Guillou, M. Ugon, and J.-J. Quisquater, "The Smart Card: A Standardized Security Device Dedicated to Public Cryptology," in G.J. Simmons (Ed.), *Contemporary Cryptology: The Science of Information Integrity*, IEEE Press, New York, 1992, pp. 561-613.

[JUE1] R.R. Jueneman, S.M. Matyas, and C.H. Meyer, "Message Authentication," *IEEE Communications Magazine*, vol. 23, no. 9 (September 1985), pp. 29-40.

[KAL1] B. Kaliski, *The MD2 Message-Digest Algorithm*, Request for Comments (RFC) 1319, Internet Activities Board, 1992.

[KEN1] S. Kent, *U.S. Department of Defense Security Options for the Internet Protocol*, Request for Comments (RFC) 1108, Internet Activities Board, 1991.

[KOH1] J.T. Kohl and B.C. Neuman, *The Kerberos Network Authentication Service (V5)*, Internet Draft, Internet Activities Board, 1993. (RFC publication planned 1993; RFC number to be assigned).

[MIL1] S.P. Miller, B.C. Neuman, J.I. Schiller and J.H. Saltzer, "Kerberos Authentication and Authorization System," *Project Athena Technical Plan*, Section E.2.1, MIT Project Athena, MIT, Cambridge, MA, 1987.

[NIS1] U.S. Department of Commerce, National Institute of Standards and Technology, *Stable Implementation Agreements for Open Systems Interconnection Protocols Version 6 Edition 1 December 1992*, NIST Special Publication 500-206, 1993.

[RIV1] R. Rivest, *The MD4 Message-Digest Algorithm*, Request for Comments (RFC) 1320, Internet Activities Board, 1992.

[RIV2] R. Rivest, *The MD5 Message-Digest Algorithm*, Request for Comments (RFC) 1321, Internet Activities Board, 1992.

[STE1] J.G. Steiner, B.C. Neuman, and J.I. Schiller, "Kerberos: An Authentication Service for Open Network Systems," *Proceedings of the Winter 1988 Usenix Conference*, February 1988, pp. 191-201.

Standards

ANSI X3.4: *American National Standard, Code for Information Interchange*, 1977.

ANSI X3.92: *American National Standard, Data Encryption Algorithm*, 1981.

ANSI X3.106: *American National Standard, Information Systems — Data Encryption Algorithm — Modes of Operation*, 1983.

ANSI X9.9: *American National Standard, Financial Institution Message Authentication (Wholesale)*, 1986.

ANSI X9.17: *American National Standard, Financial Institution Key Management (Wholesale)*, 1985.

ANSI X9.19: *American National Standard, Financial Institution Retail Message Authentication*, 1986.

ANSI X9.23: *American National Standard, Financial Institution Encryption of Wholesale Financial Messages*, 1988.

ANSI X9.24: *American National Standard, Financial Services Retail Key Management*, 1989.

ANSI X9.26: *American National Standard for Wholesale Financial Systems — Financial Institution Sign-On Authentication*, 1990.

ANSI X9.28: *American National Standard, Financial Institution Multiple Center Key Management (Wholesale)*, 1991.

ANSI X9.30: *American National Standard, Public-Key Cryptography Using Irreversible Algorithms for the Financial Services Industry*, 1993 (Draft).

ANSI X9.31: *American National Standard, Public-Key Cryptography Using Reversible Algorithms for the Financial Services Industry*, 1993 (Draft).

FIPS PUB 46: U.S. Department of Commerce, *Data Encryption Standard*, Federal Information Processing Standards Publication 46, 1977 (republished as FIPS PUB 46-1, 1988).

FIPS PUB 74: U.S. Department of Commerce, *Guidelines for Implementing and Using the NBS Data Encryption Standard*, Federal Information Processing Standards Publication 74, 1981.

FIPS PUB 81: U.S. Department of Commerce, *DES Modes of Operation*, Federal Information Processing Standards Publication 81, 1980.

FIPS PUB 113: U.S. Department of Commerce, *Computer Data Authentication*, Federal Information Processing Standards Publication 113, 1985.

FIPS PUB 171: U.S. Department of Commerce, *Key Management Using ANSI X9.17*, Federal Information Processing Standards Publication 171, 1992.

FIPS PUB 180: U.S. Department of Commerce, *Secure Hash Algorithm*, Federal Information Processing Standards Publication 180, 1993.

FIPS PUB (number to be assigned): U.S. Department of Commerce, *Digital Signature Standard*, Federal Information Processing Standards Publication, 1993 (Draft).

FIPS PUB (number to be assigned): U.S. Department of Commerce, *Standard Security Label for the Government Open Systems Interconnection Profile*, Federal Information Processing Standards Publication, 1993 (Draft).

ISO/IEC 7816: *Identification Cards — Integrated Circuit(s) Cards with Contacts*.

ISO/IEC 8372: *Information Technology — Modes of Operation for a 64-bit Block Cipher Algorithm*.

ISO 8730: *Banking — Requirements for Message Authentication (Wholesale)*.

ISO 8731-1: *Banking — Approved Algorithms for Message Authentication — Part 1: Data Encryption Algorithm (DEA)*.

ISO 8731-2: *Banking — Approved Algorithms for Message Authentication — Part 2: Message Authenticator Algorithm*.

ISO 8732: *Banking — Key Management (Wholesale)*.

ISO 9564: *Banking — Personal Identification Number Management and Security*.

ISO/IEC 9594-8: *Information Technology — Open Systems Interconnection — The Directory — Authentication Framework* (Also ITU-T Recommendation X.509).

ISO/IEC 9796: *Information Technology — Security Techniques — Digital Signature Scheme Giving Message Recovery*.

ISO/IEC 9797: *Information Technology — Security Techniques — Data Integrity Mechanism Using a Cryptographic Check Function Employing a Block Cipher Algorithm*.

ISO/IEC 9798-1: *Information Technology — Security Techniques — Entity Authentication Mechanisms — Part 1: General Model.*

ISO/IEC 9798-2: *Information Technology — Security Techniques — Entity Authentication Mechanisms — Part 2: Entity Authentication Using Symmetric Techniques.*

ISO/IEC 9798-3: *Information Technology — Security Techniques — Entity Authentication Mechanisms — Part 3: Entity Authentication Using Asymmetric Techniques.*

ISO 9807: *Banking and Related Financial Services — Requirements for Message Authentication (Retail).*

ISO/IEC 9979: *Data Cryptographic Techniques — Procedures for the Registration of Cryptographic Algorithms.*

ISO 9992: *Banking and Related Financial Services — Messages Exchanged with Integrated Circuit Cards.*

ISO/IEC 10116: *Information Technology — Security Techniques — Modes of Operation for an n-bit Block Cipher Algorithm.*

ISO/IEC 10118: *Information Technology — Security Techniques — Hash Functions for Digital Signatures and Authentication Mechanisms* (Draft).

ISO 10126: *Banking and Related Financial Services — Procedures for Message Encipherment (Wholesale).*

ISO 10202: *Financial Transaction Cards — Security Architectures of Financial Transaction Systems Using Integrated Circuit Cards* (Draft).

ISO 11131: *Banking and Related Financial Services — Sign-on Authentication.*

ISO 11166: *Banking and Related Financial Services — Key Management by Means of Asymmetric Algorithms* (Draft).

ISO 11568: *Banking and Related Financial Services — Key Management in Financial Transactions (Retail)* (Draft).

ISO/IEC 11770: *Information Technology — Security Techniques — Key Management* (Draft).

11   Lower Layers Security Protocols

Security protocols are communication protocols that directly contribute to the provision of security services. This chapter addresses security protocols mapping to OSI layers 1 through 4. In terms of the security architectural levels introduced in Chapter 3, these protocols support end-system level, subnetwork level, and direct-link level security services. Protocols supporting application level services are addressed in subsequent chapters.

Lower layers security solutions are not necessarily tied to particular underlying communications technologies. There are three standard lower layers security protocols with international recognition. All can operate over a range of underlying technologies.

The Transport Layer Security Protocol (TLSP) and Network Layer Security Protocol (NLSP) were developed by ISO/IEC JTC1/SC6, the international group responsible for the OSI layer 1 to 4 general protocol standards. These security protocols can be considered adjuncts to the OSI Transport Layer and Network Layer standards. The third security protocol is defined in the IEEE Standard for Interoperable LAN/MAN Security (SILS). SILS can be considered a security adjunct to the IEEE 802 series of LAN standards.

This chapter is organized into sections addressing:

(1) security services supported by lower layers security protocols;
(2) some security architectural concepts used by lower layers security protocols generally;
(3) the Transport Layer Security Protocol;
(4) the Network Layer Security Protocol;
(5) the IEEE Standard for Interoperable LAN/MAN Security; and
(6) other lower layer standards with security features, including standards for packet-switching protocols, connectionless network protocols, and the Physical Layer.

11.1 Security Services

Considering first the end-system and subnetwork levels, the security services supported depend on whether the protocol environment is connection-oriented or connectionless. In a connection-oriented (CO) environment, the following services can be supported:

- *Entity authentication*: Mutual authentication of the two systems at either end of a communication path. These may be end-systems or, at the subnetwork level only, either or both may be an interworking unit (e.g., a router).
- *Access control*: Association of a security label with a particular data item or with all data on a connection.
- *Connection confidentiality*: Confidentiality protection of all user data (and possibly some protocol header fields) on a connection.
- *Traffic flow confidentiality*: The generation of dummy traffic within a connection, such that an eavesdropper cannot determine whether meaningful or dummy traffic is flowing.
- *Connection integrity without recovery*: Detection of any modification of user data (and possibly protocol header fields) on a connection. Depending on configuration options, modifications to the sequence of data items on the connection may also be detected.
- *Connection integrity with recovery*: In the event of an integrity check, recovery is performed through retransmission of data. This recovery is transparent to layers above.

In a connectionless (CL) environment, the following services can be supported:

- *Data origin authentication*: Authentication of the system initiating a particular connectionless data unit. (This service is meaningful only when provided in conjunction with connectionless integrity.)
- *Access control*: Association of a security label with a particular connectionless data unit.
- *Connectionless confidentiality*: Confidentiality protection of the user data (and possibly some protocol header fields) in a connectionless data unit.
- *Traffic flow confidentiality*: The generation of dummy connectionless data units.
- *Connectionless integrity*: Detection of any modification of user data (and possibly protocol header fields) in a connectionless data unit in transit.

All of the above services can apply at either end-system or subnetwork level. The basic difference between these two levels is that the end-system level provides protection over all the network facilities interconnecting two end systems (regardless of subnetwork structures) whereas the subnetwork level provides protection over only one subnetwork or a group of adjacent subnetworks.

TLSP is an end-system level security protocol — the protocol implementation resides within the end-system equipment, not the network. NLSP can be either an end-system level or subnetwork level security protocol. With two exceptions, both TLSP and NLSP provide optional support for all services listed above. The exceptions are that connection integrity with recovery is supported only by TLSP, and traffic flow confidentiality is supported only by NLSP.[1] These two exceptions aside, there is clearly substantial functional overlap of TLSP and NLSP, and security architectects may be faced with deciding which to employ. (Provision of the same security service at both layers is not precluded, but would add little value and would result in unwarranted expense and performance degradation.) Criteria influencing this decision are discussed in Section 3.5.

Security Service	*TLSP (CO)*	*NLSP (CO)*	*TLSP (CL)*	*NLSP (CL)*	*SILS*
Entity authentication	Y	Y	•	•	•
Data origin authentication	•	•	Y	Y	Y
Access control (label)	Y	Y	Y	Y	•
Connection confidentiality	Y	Y	•	•	•
Connectionless confidentiality	•	•	Y	Y	Y
Traffic flow confidentiality	•	Y	•	Y	•
Connection integrity without recovery	Y	Y	•	•	•
Connection integrity with recovery	Y	•	•	•	•
Connectionless integrity	•	•	Y	Y	Y

Legend: Y = Yes, service supported; • = service not supported

Table 11-1: Security Services Provided by Lower Layers Protocols

---

[1] This assignment of security services to the Transport and Network Layers is fully consistent with the OSI Security Architecture recommendations.

The LAN security protocol defined in SILS is a subnetwork level security protocol. It protects traffic between pairs of stations connected to a LAN or to a bridged LAN configuration. It will not operate through a Network Layer router so cannot, in general, be considered an end-system level protocol. LAN protocols formally map to the Data Link and Physical layers but, from the security perspective, a LAN security protocol like SILS relates closely to connectionless Network Layer security protocols.[2]

Table 11-1 summarizes the security services supported by the TLSP, NLSP, and SILS protocols.

Direct-link level security refers to protection over a point-to-point link, and is fundamentally different from end-system level and subnetwork level security. Direct-link level security is restricted to providing the following security services:

- *Connection confidentiality*: Confidentiality protection of all user data (and, possibly, protocol header fields) on a link.
- *Connectionless confidentiality*: Confidentiality protection of individual frames on a link.
- *Traffic flow confidentiality*: The generation of dummy traffic on a link, such that an eavesdropper cannot determine whether meaningful or dummy traffic is flowing.

11.2 General Security Architectural Concepts

This section introduces some basic architectural concepts which are common to lower layers security protocols generally.

Security Associations

For secure communications to occur between two systems, they must both possess some pieces of shared or linked information, such as:

- the identity and/or address of the corresponding system;
- a common understanding as to which security services are to apply to which types of communicated data, and which security mechanisms are to be used; and

---

2 This view of LAN security is not fully reflected in the OSI Security Architecture, which was standardized before the architectural placement of LAN protocols was fully established.

- if a cryptographic technique is to be used, a common symmetric key or the respective members of an asymmetric key pair, for use with that cryptographic technique.

In general, such collections of information are not established for use with just a single data transmission. They are commonly used in providing the same type of protection to a sequence of distinct data transfers, for example:

- all data transfers on one connection;
- a sequence of related connectionless data transfers; or
- all data transfers between a pair of systems over a period of time (possibly involving transfers on multiple connections).

The concept of a *security association* is used to model the collections of related information maintained in two or more[3] systems for this purpose.

The information items maintained in a security association are known as *attributes* of that security association. Attributes fall into two categories. *Static attributes* maintain the same value throughout the security association. *Dynamic attributes* may change value — examples are an integrity sequence number which increments on each data transfer, or a cryptographic chaining value generated in the encryption of one data item and input to the encryption of the next.

A security association has a distinct lifetime. At establishment, the values of static attributes and the initial values of dynamic attributes are determined. Security association establishment may involve a communication protocol exchange between the two systems involved, or establishment may occur through some independent means, such as communications with a trusted security server. A security association establishment exchange may be built into the same security protocol that subsequently uses that security association (for protecting other traffic), or it may be supported in a protocol at another layer. Similarly, termination of a security association may or may not require a communication protocol exchange.

Any system may have multiple security associations active simultaneously. These can include multiple different security associations between the same pair of systems. This occurs when there are different types of traffic between the two systems, requiring different types of protection. For example, different security associations might be used for electronic mail traffic (requiring confidentiality protection only) than are used for business data transaction traffic (requiring integrity protection only). To avoid any confusion as to

---

[3] A security association usually involves only two systems, but can potentially involve more than two, e.g., in protecting a data item which is broadcast to multiple destinations. SILS permits multi-system security associations.

which security association is being used for a particular protected transmission, unambiguous security association identifiers need to be employed. A pair of systems sharing one security association may each use their own identifiers, both of which become attributes of the security association. From the perspective of either one of the systems, one identifier is the *local security association identifier* and the other is the *remote security association identifier*.

Agreed Set of Security Rules

An important characteristic of a security association is an agreement between the two systems as to which security mechanisms are to be used and which values are to apply to parameters of those mechanisms. To avoid having to negotiate or indicate many mechanism details with every security association establishment, the concept of an *agreed set of security rules* (ASSR) is introduced. An agreed set of security rules is a pre-defined package of security mechanism information, which is registered and assigned a unique identifier (an ASN.1 object identifier). The identifier is made known to all potential users. On security association establishment, only the ASSR identifier needs to be exchanged to establish agreement on a number of default security association attributes.

An agreed set of security rules is intended for reuse many times over. In general, its definition should not need to be kept secret. Hence, certain mechanism parameters are not appropriate for inclusion in an agreed set of security rules. For example, it may be appropriate for an agreed set of security rules to state that an encryption mechanism is to be used for confidentiality, and that a particular algorithm and mode of operation are to be used. However, it would not be appropriate for the agreed set of security rules to stipulate a key or initialization vector value; these need to be established by separate means for every security association.

Protection Quality-of-Service

An application signals its lower layers communications requirements using the concept of *quality-of-service*. This signaling occurs via a quality-of-service parameter which accompanies a connection-establishment request or connectionless data item passed from the upper layers to the lower layers across the Transport Layer service boundary.[4] The Transport Layer uses a similar quality-of-service parameter in a connection-establishment request or connection-less data item it passes to the Network Layer. If the Network Layer cannot

---

[4] Communications quality-of-service values are passed transparently through layers 5 and 6; hence they can be considered to be signals between an application and the Transport Layer.

provide an adequate quality-of-service, the Transport Layer should upgrade the provided quality-of-service to the requisite level by adding value in its own protocol. This is done by selecting the appropriate transport protocol class and options.

The quality-of-service parameter can convey a great deal of information covering, for example, such requirements as throughput, residual error rate, and connection failure probability. The component of quality-of-service relevant to security is called *protection quality-of-service*. It is used to indicate the security services that need to be invoked and, possibly, the strength of mechanism that needs to be used to support a security service.

TLSP and NLSP use a definition of protection quality-of-service which includes a component for each relevant security service. For each component, it is possible to specify an integer value which indicates a required *level* for that service. The range of integers available and the meanings of the particular values are not specified in a standard. They are implied by the particular agreed set of security rules for the security association in use. The use of integers implies an ordering relationship between the levels, with a higher level implying a "stronger" mechanism. This can sometimes, but not always, be a useful concept. For example, with the connection integrity service, an agreed set of security rules might specify that the mechanism to be used is a DES-based MAC. The rules might further specify that there are three levels of connection integrity: level 1 indicates a 32-bit MAC, level 2 a 48-bit MAC, and level 3 a 64-bit MAC. The foregoing is an example where levels of "strength" are meaningful. However, there are many mechanisms (e.g., access control mechanisms) where a range of "strengths" is not meaningful.

The level-based approach to protection quality-of-service can be supplemented by the passing of a security label between the layers (i.e., transport or network service boundary), as an indicator of required quality-of-service. The security labels used for this purpose may be the same sort of labels as are used to support access control (as discussed in Chapter 6), but would have additional semantic significance. For example, the label "unclassified-but-sensitive" might imply use of a commercial-grade confidentiality mechanism based on DES encryption, whereas the label "secret" implies use of a confidentiality mechanism with a higher-grade classified encryption algorithm.

At either Transport or Network Layer, the establishment of quality-of-service for a connection involves negotiation between the two peer entities, with the aim of best matching the quality-of-service requirements of the two service users with the capabilities of the two service providers. With protection quality-of-service, another element is introduced. Either peer entity may inject, at the service provider level, *administration protection quality-of-service constraints* (see Figure 11-1). These are minimum security requirements imposed by system administration in order to satisfy the local system security policy. For example, a user application may request a connection with no security protection at all but, depending upon circumstances, the local system administration at one or both peer entities may upgrade the required quality-of-service to make confidentiality protection of a certain level mandatory. The negotiation of protection quality-of-service can take place partly in security association establishment and partly in the regular exchange of quality-of-service parameters in the connection-establishment protocol.

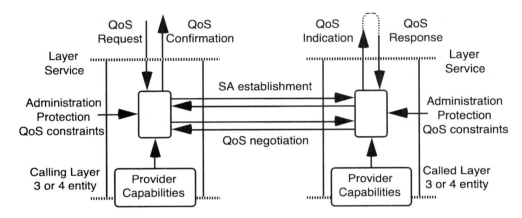

Figure 11-1: Protection Quality-of-Service (QoS) Determination

11.3 Transport Layer Security Protocol

Background

The basic Transport Layer standards are the ISO/IEC 8072 transport service definition, the ISO/IEC 8073 connection-oriented transport protocol specification (both first published in 1986), and the ISO/IEC 8602 connectionless transport protocol specification (first published in 1987). Readers of this section are assumed to have a basic knowledge of the material covered in these standards. The addition of security functionality to the Transport Layer was a more recent project. It matured in 1993, with the completion of the TLSP standard, ISO/IEC 10736.

The primary technical input to the development of TLSP was the specification *Security Protocol 4* (SP4), produced in the U.S. government-sponsored *Secure Data Network System* (SDNS) project. SDNS was initiated by the National Security Agency (NSA) to investigate methods of implementing security in a distributed computer network. U.S. government agencies, consultants, and equipment vendors participated in this project. The results include a set of specifications for security services, protocols, and mechanisms for protecting user data in networks based on the OSI model. Use of particular cryptographic algorithms is not specified. The publicly available documents include the specification of SP4 (published in [DIN1]), which was input by ANSI to the TLSP project. Consequently, TLSP is largely based on SP4, although other national contributions to the international project have resulted in modifications.

Architecture

TLSP is located fully within the Transport Layer. Except for the passing of protection quality-of-service parameters, the existence and operation of TLSP are fully transparent to both the upper layers and the underlying Network Layer.

TLSP is designed to supplement the regular Transport Layer protocols, rather than modify those protocols. In particular, it operates in conjunction with the TPDUs[5] and associated TPDU generation/processing procedures specified in ISO/IEC 8073 and ISO/IEC 8602, without any modification to formats and procedures. TLSP effectively adds another protocol sublayer. At the sending end, regular TPDUs are protected by being encapsulated within TLSP PDUs, prior to being passed to the Network Layer. At the receiving end the encapsulation is removed, to produce the regular TPDU, which is then subjected to normal protocol processing. Figure 11-2 illustrates this architectural arrangement.

In the connection-oriented case, the protection of all regular PDUs associated with one transport connection is governed by one security association, i.e., the same form of protection is applied to all PDUs. Note, however, that Transport Layer multiplexing may be located below TLSP. This enables different transport connections and/or different connectionless TPDUs to be afforded different types of protection, even though the PDUs may be multiplexed onto one network connection between the two end systems.

If Transport Layer concatenation procedures are used, they are located above TLSP. The concatenated PDUs must all be protected under the same security association. The concatenated sequence of TPDUs is processed by TLSP in the same manner as a single TPDU without concatenation.

Security Mechanisms

The encapsulation function of TLSP is a type of security transformation (see Section 7.6). It supports provision of several of the security services identified

---

[5] TPDU means Transport PDU (protocol-data-unit). We shall use the acronym TPDU for regular Transport Layer PDUs, i.e., as specified in ISO/IEC 8073 or ISO/IEC 8602. For PDUs forming part of TLSP, we shall use the term TLSP PDU.

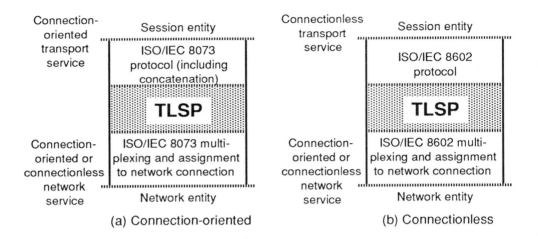

Figure 11-2: Architectural Placement of TLSP

in Section 11.1. Encapsulation can involve any required combination of the following security mechanisms (when multiple mechanisms are used, they are applied in the order as listed):

- *Security label*: A security label may be prefixed to the TPDU to support the provision of an access control service. No particular label format is specified in the standard — fields are provided to convey a unique *defining authority* identifier plus a label value in a format governed by the defining authority.
- *Direction indicator*: A flag field is prefixed, containing a bit indicating the direction of the TPDU transfer (with reference to a recognized initiator/responder relationship determined at security association establishment). This can counter reflection attacks.
- *Integrity check-value*: An integrity check-value (ICV) is computed and appended. If required by the ICV mechanism, padding octets are added to the data before the ICV computation. The ICV might use either of two techniques. If encryption will not be occurring subsequently, the ICV must involve a sealing or signing process. If encryption will be occurring, then a non-cryptographic modification detection code (MDC) is adequate. The ICV is the primary mechanism for providing connection integrity and connectionless integrity services.

- *Encryption padding*: If required by an encryption algorithm, or for the purposes of hiding lengths of protected PDUs, further padding octets may be incorporated into the data.
- *Encryption*: The resultant data, after applying any of the above mechanisms as required, is encrypted. This is the mechanism for providing connection confidentiality or connectionless confidentiality and for providing necessary protection to information generated by other security mechanisms. No particular algorithm is specified, although it is specified that encryption is to be performed in multiples of octets.

For the connection-oriented case, some security services are provided through the combined behavior of the TLSP encapsulation function and the normal procedures of the Transport Layer. Sequence integrity is achieved using the sequence numbers provided by class 2, 3, or 4 transport protocol, in conjunction with connection integrity. Separate sequence numbering systems are maintained for normal data and expedited data flows.[6] Integrity recovery is accomplished using the class 4 transport protocol recovery procedures, in conjunction with connection integrity. Note that if the class 0 or class 1 transport protocol is used, sequence integrity cannot be provided.

Entity authentication is effectively a two-stage process. The first stage is security association establishment which results in each transport entity knowing a key which it can use to convince the other entity of its identity. With security association establishment complete, the second stage is entity authentication on connection establishment. This is accomplished through each entity demonstrating knowledge of the applicable key by using that key for ICV generation or encryption in the encapsulation of the connect request TPDU. As protection against replay, the connect request and connect confirm TPDUs use connection reference values (in source reference and destination reference fields) which must be unique within the lifetime of the key. This is most easily achieved by having a sequential component in the connection references; a system increments this component for each new connection establishment attempted.

In the connectionless case, data origin authentication uses the same basic two-stage process. The requisite authentication for a connectionless TPDU is provided through demonstrating knowledge of an appropriate key by using that key in the encapsulation process.

As further protection against possible masquerade attacks, peer addresses in connection establishment or connectionless TPDUs are also required to be checked for consistency with the key used for authentication purposes.

---

[6] Note also that, if cryptographic chaining is used for integrity or encryption, distinct chains need to be maintained for normal and for expedited data.

Security Encapsulation

The TLSP Security Encapsulation PDU is used to convey an encapsulated regular TPDU or concatenated sequence of TPDUs. Figure 11-3 illustrates the process of generating the Security Encapsulation PDU when all the features are provided. Note that security labels, ICV processing, and encryption are all optional for any particular PDU, depending upon the requirements of the security association in use.

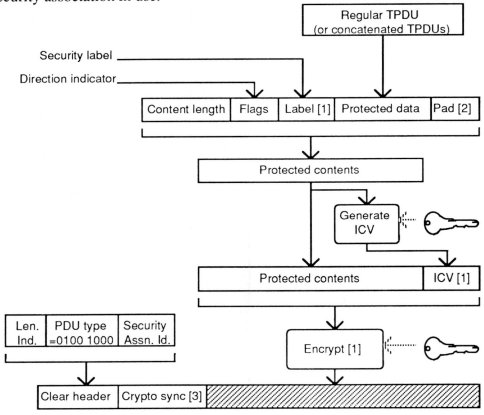

Notes:

[1]   Security label, ICV, and/or encryption may be omitted, subject to security association requirements.

[2]   Distinct pad fields may optionally be included for satisfying ICV-generation and encryption needs.

[3]   The *crypto sync* field is optional; it can carry algorithm-specific data.

Figure 11-3: Construction of TLSP Security Encapsulation PDU

Security Association Attributes

The concepts of security association and agreed set of security rules (ASSR) are important to TLSP. Security association attributes held by a TLSP entity include:

- *Security association identifiers*: Local identifier and remote identifier, each in the form of an octet string of a length determined by the ASSR. When a security association terminates, the corresponding identifiers are frozen for a period of time.
- *Initiator/responder indicator*: Indicates which TLSP entity takes the role of initiator and which the role of responder, in setting the direction indicator.
- *Peer TLSP entity address*: NSAP address of the peer entity. If the security association is tied to a particular transport connection, then the connection references must also be stored.
- *ASSR identifier*: An ASN.1 object identifier.
- *Protection quality-of-service*: A quality-of-service label plus an integer *level* value for each security service as identified in Section 11.1. The quality-of-service label format and the range of integer values for each service is defined by the ASSR.
- *Security mechanisms*: An indication of which of the following security mechanisms will be used — security labels, encryption, integrity check values, integrity sequence number procedure, and entity authentication (using an exchange of encapsulated connect request/response PDUs).
- *Label mechanism attributes*: The set of allowable security labels for the security association.
- *ICV mechanism attributes*: Algorithm (object identifier), block size (for determining necessary padding), key references, and key granularity (e.g., a separate key for each transport connection, or one key for all transport connections between an end-system pair).
- *Integrity sequence number attributes*: Last sequence numbers sent/received for normal and expedited data streams.
- *Encryption mechanism attributes*: Algorithm (object identifier), block size (for determining necessary padding), key references, and key granularity (as for ICV mechanism).

Security Association Protocol

In general, there are three different ways in which a security association may be established:

- through protocol exchanges at the same architectural layer that uses the security exchange;
- through Application Layer protocol exchanges, even though the security exchange will be used by a lower layer protocol; or
- through unspecified (possibly non-standard) means, which may or may not involve on-line data communications.

In order to accommodate the first of these options, TLSP includes an optional *security association protocol*.

The security association protocol defines PDU formats capable of supporting security association establishment, security association release, and rekeying (i.e., establishment of a new data key) within a live security association. Security association establishment is the most substantial of these activities, as it involves establishing values for all security association attributes, and also establishing initial data keys.

The TLSP standard does not stipulate particular techniques for key establishment or rekeying. It describes one suitable technique, based on an Authenticated Diffie-Hellman exchange (see Sections 4.6 and 5.6), but also provides for privately agreed techniques.

11.4 Network Layer Security Protocol

Background

The Network Layer is a complex layer, requiring many standards to specify transmission, routing, and interworking functions for the variety of network technologies available. The central standards are ISO/IEC 8348, which defines the network service, and ISO/IEC 8648, which describes the internal organization of the Network Layer. ISO/IEC 8880 provides an overview of Network Layer protocols. Readers of this section are assumed to have a basic understanding of the material covered in these standards.

NLSP (ISO/IEC 11577) is a more recent addition to the Network Layer family of standards. It was developed by the same committee that developed TLSP, with NLSP's progression through the standards process trailing that of TLSP by a few months. Consequently, TLSP and NLSP have much in common. The initial technical inputs to the development to NLSP were from three main sources. The United States contributed the specification of *Security Protocol 3* (SP3) developed in the SDNS project [DIN1]. This is a Network Layer security protocol for the connectionless mode only. The United States and Canada also presented a separate proposal addressing security over packet-switching networks. The United Kingdom contributed a proposal addressing both connection-oriented and connectionless modes of operation. The final form of NLSP resulted from effectively merging these three proposals.

Architecture

The Network Layer can be considered to comprise multiple sublayers, with different sublayers performing different roles, such as subnetwork access protocol (SNAcP) and subnetwork-dependent convergence protocol (SNDCP).[7] Above the highest sublayer is either a Transport Layer entity (in an end system) or a relay and routing function (in a relay system, such as a router). NLSP can be considered to be a sublayer, which might be positioned at any of several different places within the Network Layer, as indicated in Figure 11-4.

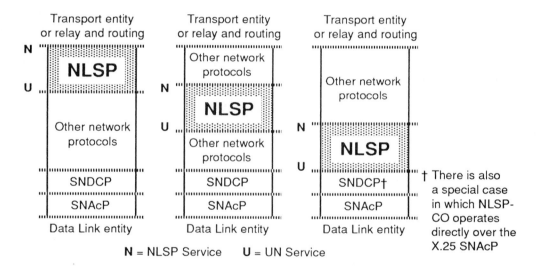

Figure 11-4: Architectural Placement of NLSP

NLSP is defined in terms of two service interfaces: the *NLSP service* is the interface presented to an entity or sublayer above; the *underlying network service* (UN service) is the service interface to a sublayer below. Each of these service interfaces is defined to look like the network service (as defined in ISO/IEC 8348). There are two basic variants of NLSP — *connection-oriented NLSP* (NLSP-CO), in which both the NLSP service and UN service are

---

[7] See Section 2.3 for a brief description, or see ISO/IEC 8648 for details.

connection-oriented, and *connectionless NLSP* (NLSP-CL), in which both services are connectionless.

The ability of NLSP to support either end-system level or subnetwork level security services results from its architectural flexibility (as seen in Figure 11-4). Let us consider some possible configurations.

Figure 11-5 presents some examples for connection-oriented NLSP, assuming X.25 as the underlying subnetwork technology. Example (a) shows NLSP providing end-system level security. NLSP is at the top of the Network Layer, such that the NLSP service equates to (a secure version of) the OSI network service. The underlying protocols, i.e., X.25, are oblivious to the fact that security is being provided above them.

Examples (b) and (c) show NLSP providing subnetwork level security. In (b), one subnetwork is trusted while the other is not. NLSP adds the necessary security over the untrusted subnetwork only. In this case, the NLSP service equates to (a secure version of) the OSI network service in the end system. However, in the relay system, it equates to the *network internal layer service* (NILS) defined in ISO/IEC 10028. In (c), a further untrusted subnetwork is shown, illustrating the use of NLSP in an environment which includes untrusted relay systems.

In the connectionless case, what is most interesting is the possible relationships between NLSP and the connectionless network protocol (CLNP) defined in ISO/IEC 8473. Three possible arrangements, all of which have practical applications, are:

- CLNP headers are transferred fully unencrypted.
- CLNP addresses are encrypted, but other parts of the headers are not encrypted.
- CLNP headers are fully encrypted.

Figure 11-6 gives some examples, from the sublayering perspective, of the connectionless case. In these examples, placement of NLSP below CLNP is an indication that CLNP protocol header information may be encapsulated by NLSP. (These illustrations do not map straightforwardly to an implementation structure, as the interactions between CLNP and NLSP can be quite complex.)

In example (a), NLSP can be placed either above or below CLNP. In example (b), which illustrates a trusted relay system, NLSP is placed below CLNP. CLNP information is then protected while it transits the untrusted subnetwork. Such protection includes hiding of trusted domain addresses. Example (c) shows the use of one CLNP sublayer for the trusted domain, with the trusted end system and relay system providing a mapping to another CLNP layer (below NLSP) for the untrusted domain. This protocol stack is particularly flexible and ideally suited for use in network environments involving both trusted and untrusted subnetworks.

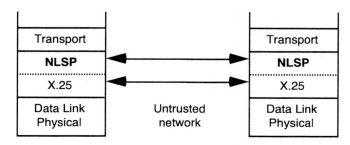

(a) NLSP at end-system level

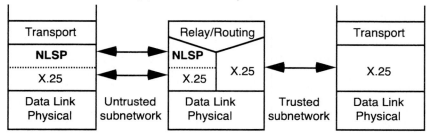

(b) NLSP with untrusted subnetwork

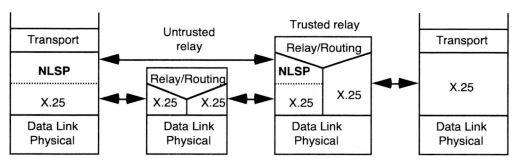

(c) NLSP with untrusted relay system

Figure 11-5: Configuration Examples — Connection-Oriented NLSP

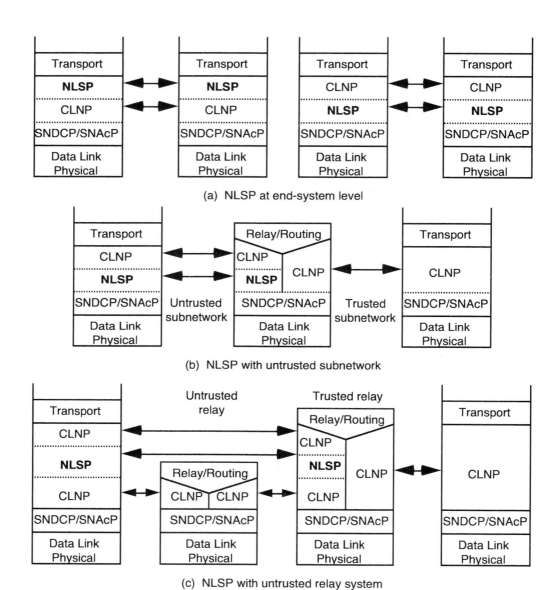

(a) NLSP at end-system level

(b) NLSP with untrusted subnetwork

(c) NLSP with untrusted relay system

Figure 11-6: Configuration Examples — Connectionless NLSP

Secure Data Transfer

The primary function of both connection-oriented and connectionless NLSP is to protect user data and sensitive parameters originating on request or response primitives issued at the NLSP service. This is done by applying a security encapsulation function to generate data values for corresponding request or response primitives issued at the UN service. The encapsulation function is reversed at the receiving end. This process relates closely to that used by TLSP in the generation and processing of the Security Encapsulation PDU (see Section 11.3).

In NLSP, provision is made for selecting different encapsulation functions for different environments. The basic encapsulation function defined in the standard is very similar to that defined in TLSP, with some additional features incorporated. The octet string to be protected comprises a string of fields which may include:

- An indicator of the type of primitive (e.g., unitdata, connect request, connect response, data, data acknowledge, expedited data, disconnect).
- User data requiring protection.
- Test data (e.g., for use to test cryptographic system operation, following connection establishment or new key establishment).
- Address parameters (on unitdata or connect primitives) requiring protection.
- Quality-of-service parameters requiring protection.
- Security label.

The protection process is the same as that for TLSP (see Figure 11-3) with provision made for two additional fields in the generated PDU:

- An integrity sequence number (ISN), to support sequence integrity. This was not required in TLSP because transport protocol sequence numbers could serve the same purpose.
- A traffic padding field, which is added because the Network Layer needs to support the traffic flow confidentiality service, but the Transport Layer does not.

A clear header is prefixed to the resulting protected octet string to give a NLSP secure data transfer PDU. The clear header contains the security association identifier.

As an alternative to the above basic encapsulation function, a *no-header encapsulation* process is also defined, for optional use with connection-oriented NLSP only. The no-header option can be used when:

(a) the only security mechanism applied is encryption; and

(b) the encryption/decryption processes do not change data lengths (e.g., DES encryption).

In this case, the secure data transfer PDU is replaced by an encrypted version of the data requiring protection. This option allows NLSP to be inserted transparently within the Network Layer, without affecting data characteristics of underlying services, e.g., packet sizes, data rates, and bandwidth. This can be of tremendous benefit, especially if security functions are being added to an existing service. However, because security labels, ICV, ISN, and padding cannot be used, the range of security services that can be supported is greatly reduced. Basic confidentiality and, in some circumstances,[8] integrity services can still be supported.

In general, NLSP operates by mapping NLSP service primitives to UN service primitives of the same type (connection establishment and release are special cases; they are discussed further in the next subsection). Fields not requiring protection are copied directly from one service primitive to the other. NLSP service fields requiring protection are processed by the encapsulation function, and the resultant secure data transfer PDU is mapped to a user data parameter of the UN service primitive. Segmentation may need to occur because of data expansion resulting from application of the encapsulation function.

Connection Establishment and Release

With connection-oriented NLSP, special procedures need to be introduced to handle connection establishment. The procedures depend upon whether or not security association establishment needs to occur in conjunction with connection establishment (as with TLSP, NLSP can support an internal security association protocol, but also permits security associations to be managed by other means).

Let us consider first the case which does not involve security association establishment, i.e., a suitable security association pre-exists. Even in this case, there is a need for a special NLSP protocol exchange at connection establishment to accomplish the following:

• Perform peer entity authentication.

• Establish particular encryption and/or integrity keys for use on the connection.

---

[8] Integrity can still be obtained if the user data has sufficient natural redundancy and if cryptographic chaining is employed.

- Establish starting integrity sequence numbers.

For conveying this information, a connection security control PDU is defined in NLSP. A two-way exchange of these PDUs occurs at connection establishment. The precise contents of the PDU may vary with the type of connection authentication mechanism specified for the particular security association. The standard describes one possible mechanism, which would have PDU fields as follows:

- Encrypted versions of two integrity sequence numbers (one for each traffic direction). Successful decryption of this field can simultaneously confirm starting integrity sequence numbers, demonstrate key knowledge (for authentication purposes), and provide protection against replay attacks on authentication.
- Security label.
- Key reference or key derivation information.

In the case where security association establishment is to occur in conjunction with connection establishment, the data exchanges may be much more complex. There may be a need for more than a two-way exchange for authentication and key derivation purposes, plus substantial attribute negotiation. For this purpose, a separate security association PDU is defined. Like TLSP, NLSP does not stipulate a particular security association establishment technique, but describes one suitable technique, based on an Authenticated Diffie-Hellman exchange.

Let us now consider how the protocol exchanges for NLSP connection establishment map onto the UN service. Ideally, they would map directly onto the UN connection establishment primitives. However, this is not always possible, because the required NLSP protocol exchanges add substantial overhead. Recognizing that user data fields of network protocols are commonly limited in length, there may not be room in the UN connection establishment PDUs for all the data that needs to be transferred. Furthermore, a multi-way protocol exchange may be needed to establish a security association. Therefore, two basic mapping alternatives are defined. If only a two-way exchange is necessary, and if all required data (including NLSP PDUs) can fit in the user data fields of the UN connect primitives, then NLSP connection establishment maps directly to UN connection establishment. Otherwise, the required data transfers map to UN data exchanges following UN connection establishment.

When the data transfers map to UN data exchanges, there is a possibility that the quality-of-service parameters and other service parameters (e.g., throughput, window size) eventually negotiated do not match the characteristics of the UN connection. In this situation, the UN connection is released and a new UN connection established with the (now known) required characteristics.

NLSP disconnect (i.e., release of an NLSP connection) may also present a mapping problem if user data on the disconnect needs to be protected by the encapsulating function and the resultant PDU cannot fit in the user data parameter of UN disconnect. In this situation, the NLSP PDU needs to map to a UN data exchange preceding UN disconnect.

The various possible mapping scenarios for NLSP make it a powerful (and complex) protocol.

11.5 IEEE LAN Security Protocol

Background

IEEE has historically led the development of LAN protocol standards, through its IEEE Project 802 committee. Several of the IEEE 802 standards have been fed into ANSI and ISO/IEC JTC1/SC6, and have formed the basis of the ANSI/IEEE 802 and ISO/IEC 8802 series of LAN standards. The principal IEEE 802 projects are as listed in Table 11.2.

IEEE Project	*Title*
802.1	Higher Layer Interface (HILI)
802.2	Logical Link Control (LLC)
802.3	CSMA/CD
802.4	Token Bus (TBUS)
802.5	Token Ring (TRING)
802.6	Metropolitan Area Networks (MAN)
802.7	Broadband Technical Advisory Group (BBTAG)
802.8	Fiber Optic Technical Advisory Group (FOTAG)
802.9	Integrated Voice and Data LAN (IVD)
802.10	LAN/MAN Security (SILS)
802.11	Wireless LAN (WLAN)

Table 11-2: IEEE 802 Projects

The IEEE 802.10 group was established in 1988, to develop standards to support vendor-independent security features in IEEE 802 LANs. The resultant project, known as the Standard for Interoperable LAN/MAN Security (SILS), has four parts:

- *The Model*: Describes the architectural framework for providing security in LANs and delineates the scope of the other three parts.
- *Secure Data Exchange* (SDE): Defines a security protocol to protect data in transfer between LAN stations.
- *Key Management*: Defines an upper layers key management protocol to support the key management requirements of SDE.
- *System/Security Management*: Describes network management support for the SDE protocol.

This chapter focuses on the SDE protocol, the first part of SILS to be formally published (in 1992).

Architecture

The IEEE 802 standards relate to the OSI Data Link and Physical Layers. The 802 architecture comprises its own logical layers. The Media Access Control[9] layer maps to OSI Layer 1 and part of Layer 2. Media Access Control depends upon the particular LAN medium (e.g., IEEE 802.3, 802.4, 802.5, 802.6). The Logical Link Control layer (IEEE 802) resides above the Media Access Control layer, within OSI Layer 2. IEEE 802.1 provides for LAN management and bridging, and also maps to OSI Layer 2.

The SILS SDE protocol is effectively inserted between the Logical Link Control and Media Access Control layers and is transparent to both. The various relationships are illustrated in Figure 11-7.

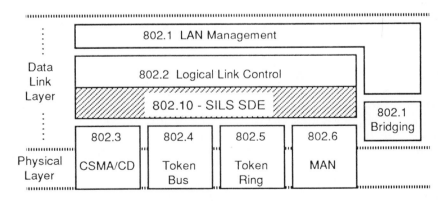

Figure 11-7: Architectural Placement of SILS SDE

---

[9] The acronym MAC is used for Media Access Control in the IEEE 802 standards, but will be not be used here to avoid confusion with Message Authentication Codes.

Implementation of the SDE protocol is optional, and not all stations on a LAN or MAN need support it. A station which supports SDE can communicate securely with any other station which supports SDE, or can communicate (without security protection) with stations which do not support SDE. The SDE protocol is transparent outside the Logical Link Control layer.

Secure Data Exchange Protocol

At the sending end, the SDE protocol involves applying security encapsulation to a Logical Link Control PDU to generate an SDE PDU which is passed to the Media Access Control layer. At the receiving end, the reverse process occurs, with encapsulation being removed. In service terms, the primitives occurring both above and below the SDE entity are UNITDATA request or indication primitives, consistent with the Media Access Control service definition ISO/IEC 10039.

The encapsulation process used to generate the SDE PDU is shown in Figure 11-8. It is similar to the encapsulation processes of TLSP or NLSP. In the SDE PDU, all fields except the data field are optional, and both the ICV generation and encryption processes are optional.

The primary security services supported are connectionless confidentiality and connectionless integrity. They are provided through the encryption and ICV processes, respectively. A limited form of data origin authentication is provided as a side effect of providing connectionless integrity and including a station identifier in the protected header. The source is authenticated on the basis of having demonstrated knowledge of the integrity key. However, SILS permits multi-party security associations; therefore, all data origin authentication assumptions need to be considered with care. SILS also suggests it provides access control, but this is simply a reference to the use of controlled key management procedures.

Security Associations and Key Management

The SILS protocol uses the security association concept in a way similar to TLSP and NLSP, but with some differences in attribute definitions. SILS also permits group (multi-party) security associations. No provision is made for managing security associations at the SDE level; it is assumed this will be done at the Application Layer.

In support of SDE, a key management protocol specification is being developed in the third part of the SILS project (Key Management). This specifies an Application Layer protocol which can support a range of key management techniques, such as ANSI X9.17 symmetric techniques plus public-key techniques. In addition to establishing keys, the protocol can establish values for other security association attributes as necessary. While such a protocol is required to support SDE, its applicability is not limited to LAN security — the same protocol can be used for key management in other lower layer protocols or application protocols.

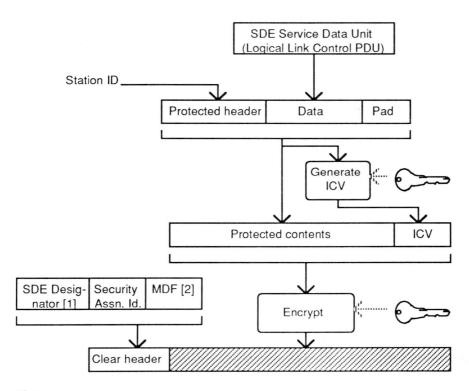

Notes:

   [1]   The SDE Designator contains a value which serves to differentiate a SDE PDU from any other PDU a Logical Link Control entity may process.

   [2]   The Management Defined Field (MDF) is an optional field which may contain mechanism-specific information, depending upon the particular security association.

Figure 11-8: Construction of SILS SDE PDU

11.6 Other Standards

Packet-Switching Protocols

The ITU X.25 specification has added a facility field, known as the *protection facility*, for conveying security-related information. This field can be used for conveying the NLSP connection security control PDU. This provides a means for mapping NLSP directly onto the X.25 packet layer (a SNAcP) without the need for an SNDCP sublayer, in accordance with ISO/IEC 8878. This makes the transparent provision of security over a X.25 network comparatively straightforward.

The other packet-switching protocol worthy of mention is ITU X.32, the Recommendation addressing access to a public X.25 network from the telephone network. This Recommendation is significant because of its specification of a public-key-based authentication exchange using the RSA algorithm. This authentication exchange is local to a particular network access point and has no networkwide significance. However, at some stage, standardized key management to support this feature will be required.

Connectionless Network Protocols

Both the Internet IP protocol and the OSI connectionless network protocol (CLNP) have provision for conveying a *security option* field along with every connectionless data unit (datagram). This field is used in supporting one security service — the routing control form of access control. A security label is carried in this field; a datagram bearing such a label should not be passed to an environment not authorized in accordance with that label.

For IP, the conventions for use of the security option (IPSO) field for U.S. Department of Defense applications are specified in [KEN1]; a non-Defense version is also being developed (known as *common IPSO* — CIPSO).

For CLNP, the U.S. GOSIP specification (FIPS PUB 146-1) defines a format which supports the use of IPSO labels and is being extended by NIST to support more general label formats (see Section 10.6 for more details).

Neither IP nor CLNP includes a security encapsulation capability but, as described in Section 11.4, NLSP can provide security encapsulation in conjunction with CLNP. The SDNS SP3 protocol included a mode of operation for encapsulating IP datagrams — this could be easily adapted to provide the basis of NLSP encapsulation of IP datagrams.

Physical Layer

Protection on point-to-point links (providing direct-link level security services) is generally realized in devices called *link encryptors*. Because there is not a strong requirement for intercommunication between devices of this type from different vendors, there are few formal standards in this area. In the United States, the federal government standard FIPS PUB 139 and the commercial standard ANSI X3.105 address this subject. These standards describe common procedures for the use of DES for encryption of traffic over synchronous or asynchronous serial lines. Data bits are encrypted using DES in the one-bit Cipher Feedback mode of operation. All bits are encrypted, except START and STOP bits during asynchronous operation and parity bits when an optional parity-restoration feature is used on traffic comprising seven-bit-plus-parity characters. With parity-restoration, only the seven data bits are encrypted, then a new parity bit is calculated on the encrypted result. The standards also define a procedure for transmitting an initialization vector on communications establishment.

An international adaptation of ANSI X3.105 is published as ISO/IEC 9160.

Summary

Lower layers security protocols relate to OSI layers 1 through 4. They support end-system level, subnetwork level, and direct-link level security services. The security services at the end-system and subnetwork levels include authentication, access control, confidentiality, and integrity services, with the particular variants of these services depending upon whether the environment is connection-oriented or connectionless. Direct-link level protocols support confidentiality only.

The concepts of security associations and protection quality-of-service are used throughout the lower layers. A security association models the collections of related attribute information maintained between systems for providing a consistent type of protection to a sequence of data transfers between those systems. A security association can be established through lower layer protocol exchanges (the same layer that uses the security exchange), through Application Layer protocol exchanges, or through non-standard means. Protection quality-of-service is used to signal protection requirements across layer boundaries, and to negotiate requirements between the two ends.

The Transport Layer Security Protocol (TLSP) is an end-system level security protocol which supplements the regular OSI transport protocols. It encapsulates a regular transport PDU, prior to assignment to a network connection. The encapsulation process optionally includes attaching a security label, padding, generating an integrity check-value, and encrypting. Optional protocol support is provided for establishing security associations.

The Network Layer Security Protocol (NLSP) can function at either end-system or subnetwork level. It is effectively a sublayer which can be positioned at any of several different places in the Network Layer. Depending on the positioning, NLSP is able to hide trusted subnetwork protocol information (especially addresses) while this information traverses an untrusted subnetwork. There are both connection-oriented and connectionless variants of NLSP, the first working in conjunction with such protocols as X.25 and the second working in conjunction with the Connectionless Network Protocol (CLNP). NLSP employs an encapsulation process very similar to that of TLSP. Optional protocol support is provided for establishing security associations.

The IEEE Standard for Interoperable LAN/MAN Security (SILS) defines a security protocol called Secure Data Exchange (SDE). This a subnetwork level security protocol for use on a LAN or a bridged LAN configuration. It resides in the IEEE 802 Logical Link Control layer, immediately above Media Access Control. It defines a security encapsulation process, which encapsulates a Logical Link Control PDU before passing to Media Access Control. The encapsulation process involves optional generation of an integrity check value and encryption.

Both the CLNP and Internet IP protocols provide for labels to support routing control, and common label formats have been defined for U.S. federal government purposes.

Exercises

1. What is the difference between the end-system and subnetwork security architectural levels? To which level(s) do the following security protocols relate: (a) TLSP; (b) NLSP; (c) SILS SDE?

2. List five security services that may be supported at the subnetwork level for each of: (a) connection-oriented environments; (b) connectionless environments.

3. (a) What is a security association and how is it used?
    (b) Describe the difference between static and dynamic security association attributes and give two examples of each.
    (c) How are security associations established?

4. In the TLSP security encapsulation process, what security mechanisms are used to support: (a) access control; (b) confidentiality; (c) integrity?

5. When connectionless NLSP is used in conjunction with the Connectionless Network Protocol (CLNP), which protocol operates above the other? Explain.

6. How does the SILS SDE protocol relate to the IEEE Logical Link Control and Media Access Control layers?

7. Consider a network configuration in which end system *A* communicates with end system *E*, via interconnected subnetworks as follows:

For each of the following scenarios, indicate which of the protocols TLSP, NLSP, and SILS SDE can, on its own, provide protection against attacks in the untrusted part of the configuration:

(a) Subnetwork *B* untrusted; subnetworks *C* and *D* trusted.
(b) Subnetwork *C* untrusted; subnetworks *B* and *D* trusted.
(c) Subnetworks *B* and *C* untrusted; subnetwork *D* trusted.
(d) Subnetworks *B*, *C*, and *D* untrusted.

REFERENCES

[DIN1] C. Dinkel (Ed.), *Secure Data Network System (SDNS) Network, Transport, and Message Security Protocols*, U.S. Department of Commerce, National Institute of Standards and Technology, Report NISTIR 90-4250, 1990.

[KEN1] S. Kent, *U.S. Department of Defense Security Options for the Internet Protocol*, Request for Comments (RFC) 1108, Internet Activities Board, 1991.

Standards

ANSI X3.105: *American National Standard, Information Systems — Data Link Encryption, 1983*.

ANSI X9.17: *American National Standard, Financial Institution Key Management (Wholesale)*, 1985.

FIPS PUB 139: *Interoperability and Security Requirements for Use of the Data Encryption Standard in the Physical Layer of Data Communication*, Federal Information Processing Standards Publication 139, 1983 (Originally designated Federal Standard 1026).

FIPS PUB 146-1: *Government Open Systems Interconnection Profile (GOSIP)*, Federal Information Processing Standards Publication 146-1, 1991.

IEEE Std 802.10-1992: *Interoperable LAN/MAN Security (SILS): Currently Contains Security Data Exchange (SDE) Clause 2*.

ISO/IEC 8072:   *Information Technology — Open Systems Interconnection — Connection Oriented Transport Service Definition* (Also ITU-T Recommendation X.214).

ISO/IEC 8073:   *Information Technology — Open Systems Interconnection — Connection Oriented Transport Protocol Specification* (Also ITU-T Recommendation X.224).

ISO/IEC 8208:   *Information Technology — Data Communications — X.25 Packet Level Protocol for Data Terminal Equipment.*

ISO/IEC 8348:   *Information Technology — Data Communications — Network Service Definition* (Also ITU-T Recommendation X.213).

ISO/IEC 8473:   *Information Technology — Data Communications — Protocol for Providing the Connectionless-Mode Network Service.*

ISO/IEC 8602:   *Information Technology — Open Systems Interconnection — Protocol for Providing the Connectionless-Mode Transport Service.*

ISO/IEC 8648:   *Information Technology — Data Communications — Internal Organization of the Network Layer.*

ISO/IEC 8802-2:   *Information Technology — Local Area Networks — Part 2: Logical Link Control* (Also ANSI/IEEE 802.2).

ISO/IEC 8802-3:   *Information Technology — Local Area Networks — Part 3: Carrier Sense Multiple Access with Collision Detection (CSMA/CD) Access Method and Physical Layer Specification* (Also ANSI/IEEE 802.3).

ISO/IEC 8802-4:   *Information Technology — Local Area Networks — Part 4: Token-Passing Bus Access Method and Physical Layer Specification* (Also ANSI/IEEE 802.4).

ISO/IEC 8802-5:   *Information Technology — Local Area Networks — Part 5: Token Ring Access Method and Physical Layer Specification* (Also ANSI/IEEE 802.5).

ISO/IEC 8802-6:   *Information Technology — Local Area Networks — Part 6: Distributed Queue Dual Bus Access Method and Physical Layer Specification* (Also IEEE 802.6) (Draft).

ISO/IEC 8878:   *Information Technology — Data Communications — Use of X.25 to Provide the OSI Connection-mode Network Service.*

ISO/IEC 8880:   *Information Technology — Data Communications — Protocol Combinations to Provide and Support the OSI Network Service.*

ISO/IEC 9160:   *Data Encipherment — Physical Layer Interoperability Requirements.*

ISO/IEC 10028:   *Information Technology — Telecommunications and Information Exchange Between Systems — Network Internal Layer Service* (Draft).

ISO/IEC 10039:   *Information Technology — Local Area Networks — Media Access Control Service Definition* (Draft).

ISO/IEC 10736:   *Information Technology — Telecommunications and Information Exchange Between Systems — Transport Layer Security Protocol* (Also ITU-T Recommendation X.824).

ISO/IEC 11577:   *Information Technology — Telecommunications and Information Exchange Between Systems — Network Layer Security Protocol* (Also ITU-T Recommendation X.823) (Draft).

ITU-T Recommendation X.25:   *Interface between data terminal equipment (DTE) and data circuit-terminating equipment (DCE) for terminals operating in the packet mode and connected to public networks by dedicated circuit* (ISO/IEC adaptation in ISO/IEC 8208).

ITU-T Recommendation X.32: *Interface between data terminal equipment (DTE) and data circuit-terminating equipment (DCE) for terminals operating in the packet mode and accessing a packet switched public data network through a public switched telephone network or an integrated services digital network or a circuit switched public data network.*

12 Upper Layers Security Protocols

The discussion of layer placement of security services in Chapter 3 identified the need for *application level security services*. Provision of these services is associated with *upper layers protocols*. Reasons for locating security services at this level include:

- satisfying security requirements which are inherently meaningful only to a particular application, e.g., access control to application-internal resources, or non-repudiation;
- protecting selected fields within application protocols, e.g., the PIN in a financial transaction;
- protecting information conveyed through multiple end systems in distributed applications, e.g., application level store-and-forward; and
- providing end-system level protection, without forcing an application to depend on a particular underlying protocol (e.g., the OSI transport or network protocol).

Application level security mechanisms need to be tailored to particular applications, and supporting security protocols need to be designed in conjunction with the application protocol. Hence, there can be no *universal* application level security protocol. However, much can be done to produce common security protocol building tools and security protocol components for use in incorporating security into many different applications. Such tools and components have the dual benefits of simplifying the task of the application protocol designer and of encouraging the use of the same security techniques in different applications. The latter factor facilitates reusability of security hardware and software modules in different applications, thereby reducing implementation costs.

The earliest open-system network applications to include substantial security provisions were the Message Handling Systems (MHS) and Directory applications. The MHS and Directory protocols were designed without the benefits of pre-existing security protocol tools and components. However, in the development of those protocols, the first common tools and components were produced. These were a set of reusable, security-related ASN.1 macro and data type definitions, included in the Directory Authentication Framework standard. They found use in both the MHS and Directory protocols.[1]

Subsequently, standardization activities were established in the Upper Layers Working Group of ISO/IEC JTC1/SC21 to develop a comprehensive set of security protocol tools and components for use in securing new applications. While this work was directed foremost at OSI applications, many of the resultant tools and components are suitable for any ASN.1-based application, including TCP/IP applications.

This chapter describes the international standardization work on common upper layers security protocol-building tools and protocol components. It is organized as follows:

(1) an introduction to OSI upper layers architectural concepts upon which some of the later material depends;

(2) an overview of the main concepts introduced in the OSI Upper Layers Security Model standard;

(3) a description of the protocol feature to support entity authentication in conjunction with application-association establishment;

(4) a description of the security exchange concept and supporting protocol-building tools from the Generic Upper Layers Security (GULS) standard[2];

(5) a description of the security transformation concept and supporting protocol-building tools, also from the GULS standard;

(6) a discussion of ASN.1 notational constructs for specifying selective field protection; and

(7) a brief discussion of how the various standards can be used in designing a secure application protocol.

12.1 OSI Upper Layers Architectural Overview

The OSI Application and Presentation Layers can, in many respects, be considered as an integrated set of functionality. However, to fully understand the provision of security in OSI upper layers, it is necessary to understand something of the internal structuring of the Application Layer and of the (sometimes subtle) relationship between Application and Presentation Layers.

---

[1] Chapters 13 and 14 describe the MHS and Directory security features in detail.

[2] As this book goes to print, the GULS standard is at the Draft International Standard stage of progression. Because details are still subject to change, discussion is kept to a general level.

Application Layer Structure

The Application Layer is the most complex of the OSI layers, with a rich internal structure designed to support modular protocol construction. The Application Layer Structure standard ISO/IEC 9545 defines the structuring concepts and terminology.

Let us consider first the model for communication between two OSI end systems via a single presentation-connection. From the Application Layer perspective, the presentation-connection equates to one application-association. The Application Layer structures at either end are typically as shown in Figure 12-1. Note that the structuring suggested here is primarily the structuring of pieces of protocol specification — not necessarily the structuring of implementation software (although, if an implementor chooses to derive software modules systematically from protocol specification modules, the same structure will be apparent).

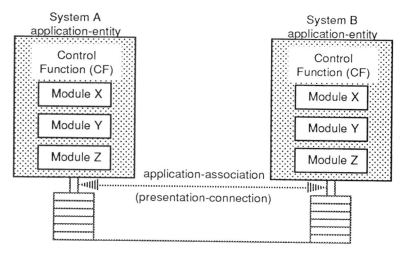

Figure 12-1: Simple Application Layer Structure

In this simple case, the specification of the Application Layer protocol involves a set of specification modules (X, Y, and Z), together with a control function (CF) specification which states how the modules operate together, how they provide a coherent service to the communications service user above, and how they interface to the presentation service below.

The modules are called either application-service-elements (ASEs) or application-service-objects (ASOs). The difference is that an ASE implies a self-contained module specification, whereas an ASO is itself a structure of specifications obtained by combining a control function and a group of lower-level modules (ASEs and/or ASOs).

An ASE specification defines a set of Application Layer PDUs and rules regarding their use. Control functions add further rules, constraining the ways PDUs from different ASEs must relate to each other and to the presentation service. The complete collection of application PDU formats and protocol rules applying to an application-association is called an application-context.

In this two-system, single-application-association case, one of the modules in each system is always the ASE known as the Association Control Service Element (ACSE). ACSE supports the establishment and termination of application-associations by defining application PDUs to be carried in conjunction with presentation-connection establishment and termination. The ACSE PDUs exchanged at application-association establishment convey addressing information, determine the application-context to be used, and provide for authentication of the two ends (the authentication aspect is discussed further in Section 12.3). ACSE is defined in ISO/IEC 8649 and 8650.

Figure 12-2 provides an example of the Application Layer structure for a Directory-accessing application. The application-context definition indicates three ASEs — ACSE, the Remote Operations Service Element (ROSE), and the Directory ASE.

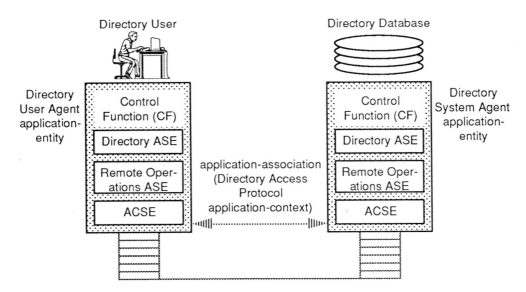

Figure 12-2: Simple Application Layer Structure Example

Beyond the single-application-association scenario, more complex structures can be built. The same recursive structuring approach is always used, whereby an ASO is built by combining a set of modules (ASEs and/or ASOs) together with a control function.

A structure like that in the Directory example above could itself be considered an ASO, used to build higher-level ASOs and ultimately the application-entity (which is, by definition, the *outermost* ASO). Multiple application-associations can be modeled, with the application-associations not necessarily existing at the same time. For example, in a store-and-forward messaging environment, one level of ASOs can deal with the passing of messages between transfer agents, while a higher level of ASOs deals with originator-recipient relationships.

In the more complex scenarios, a relationship between peer ASOs is called an ASO-context. An application-context is a special case of an ASO-context, which applies to the single-application-association scenario.

Operation of the Presentation Layer

The role of the Presentation Layer is to negotiate, generate, and interpret bit string representations for Application Layer information items for communication purposes. The representation format used during communication is called a *transfer syntax*. The transfer syntax may be different to the local representation of the same information in either or both of the end systems.

Interactions between the Application and Presentation Layers are described using two concepts:

- *Abstract syntax*: A specification of Application Layer information items in a form which is independent of the bit string encoding; essentially an abstract data type specification.

- *Presentation data value (pdv)*: The unit of information/data traversing the Application/Presentation Layer boundary. Such a unit is recognized by both layers as an abstract syntax item, and is processed by the Presentation Layer so that the abstract syntax item is mapped to/from a corresponding transfer syntax (bit string) item for communication purposes.

An abstract syntax may have more than one possible corresponding transfer syntax. For example, an abstract syntax for transferring financial transactions may define a presentation data value for a credit/debit request as a sequence of the following fields: account number (an integer), account name (a character string), credit/debit indicator (a Boolean value), and dollar amount (an integer). A variety of suitable transfer syntaxes might be defined, employing, for example, different character sets and/or different integer encodings.

In general, an abstract syntax is defined as part of an Application Layer protocol and assigned a unique ASN.1 object identifier. A transfer syntax can also be identified by an ASN.1 object identifier, which points to a specification of rules whereby a particular transfer syntax can be derived for a given abstract syntax.

OSI has two approaches for establishing the transfer syntax to be used for an abstract syntax in a particular instance of communication:

- *Presentation protocol*: The OSI presentation protocol provides for negotiating, on-line, a mapping between an abstract syntax and a transfer syntax.
- *Embedded presentation data value*: ASN.1 notation provides for embedding presentation data values within each other, with mixes of abstract syntaxes (and transfer syntaxes) being supported (this mechanism is not tied to the OSI presentation protocol, hence can be used with non-OSI protocol stacks if desired).

With the presentation protocol approach, the negotiated mapping between an abstract syntax and a transfer syntax is called a *presentation context*. A presentation context is assigned an integer identifier which is attached to a presentation data value to indicate the applicable abstract and transfer syntaxes to a destination system. Presentation contexts are established using presentation protocol exchanges, either when a presentation-connection is established or later on an established connection. These exchanges negotiate the required mappings, using the globally-recognized object identifiers for abstract syntaxes and transfer syntaxes.

A presentation protocol data PDU can convey multiple presentation data values, from the same or different abstract syntaxes. Each presentation data value must have a pre-established presentation context. The presentation context identifier accompanies each encoded bit string. This provides a means for concatenating presentation data values for transfer purposes (see Figure 12-3). Application-context rules govern when such concatenation is to occur.

The embedded presentation data value approach is also illustrated in Figure 12-3. This mechanism does not involve the presentation protocol directly. It employs the *embedded pdv* feature (formerly the *external* feature) of the ASN.1 notation. Essentially, an abstract syntax definition of a presentation data value identifies a gap in the specification, which is to be filled by the encoding of another presentation data value. From the security perspective, an important characteristic of this mechanism is that any security protection (e.g., encryption or digital signature) employed in the encoding of the outer structure is also applied to the encoding of the embedded presentation data value. Hence, this provides the basis of security enveloping techniques.

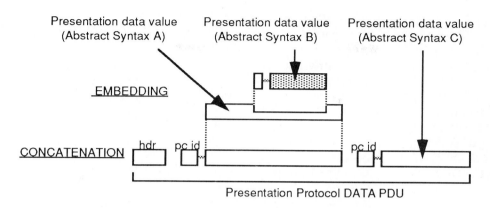

Figure 12-3: Embedding and Concatenation of Presentation Data Values

With embedded presentation data values, there are two methods of indicating the abstract syntax-transfer syntax pair — the *indirect method* and the *direct method*. The indirect method uses a presentation context established earlier by the presentation protocol; the presentation context identifier is attached to the embedded encoding. The direct method does not use a presentation context; the object identifiers of the abstract syntax and transfer syntax are attached to the embedded encoding. The direct method has the disadvantages of higher transmission overhead and of not permitting the recipient to participate in negotiating the transfer syntax used. However, it has an advantage in that the encodings and attached identifiers are suitable for forwarding through multiple end systems, as required in distributed applications (e.g., store-and-forward message transfer).

To relate back to the earlier discussion of Application Layer structure, an abstract syntax definition forms part of an ASE definition. One abstract syntax typically corresponds to the set of application PDUs generated by one ASE. However, this is not a rigid convention. In the example in Figure 12-2, there are two abstract syntaxes: one for ACSE PDUs and one for ROSE PDUs. The ROSE PDUs contain fields which are filled in by values defined in the Directory ASE. The Directory-access application-context specifies how the various PDUs interrelate.

Role of ASN.1 Notation

ASN.1 notation (defined in ISO/IEC 8824) provides a standard means for specifying an abstract syntax. The accompanying encoding rules standard

(ISO/IEC 8825) provides a set of convenient, systematic ways for deriving transfer syntaxes for abstract syntaxes defined using ASN.1.

In principle, OSI applications do not *have* to use ASN.1 notation. Nothing precludes an application protocol developer from using any notation of choice for specifying an abstract syntax and transfer syntaxes to support it. However, ASN.1 has many features which contribute substantially to the goal of modular protocol construction. It has therefore received widespread acceptance.

While ASN.1 was developed as part of OSI, it is also used extensively for non-OSI protocols, including some Internet protocols and some of the newer banking protocols.

Tutorial notes on ASN.1 are provided in Appendix B.

Relaying of Presentation Data Values

The Presentation Layer was originally characterized as a point-to-point layer, i.e., it could operate only between a pair of end systems which have an application-association between them. Indeed, this architectural constraint must apply if the presentation context negotiation capabilities of the presentation protocol are to be employed. However, this constraint is not tolerable for scenarios like secure store-and-forward messaging, where intermediate application-relay systems do not possess the necessary information (e.g., keys) to fully decode and re-encode all of the data.

Accordingly it is now recognized that *representations* of presentation data values may, under appropriate circumstances, be preserved in application-relay systems and forwarded on to another system later. Clearly, presentation context negotiation cannot operate in this situation. However, the direct method of presentation data value embedding can. Other methods of *announcing* (as opposed to *negotiating*) a presentation context are also being developed.

12.2 Upper Layers Security Model

The OSI Upper Layers Security Model (ISO/IEC 10745) provides the modeling basis for general upper layers security protocol-building tools and protocol components.

The main contribution of this standard is to introduce the following concepts:

- *system security functions* and *security communications functions*, which help in structuring standards and implementations;

- *security exchanges* and *security transformations*, which support the design of general security protocol-building tools and protocol components; and
- *security associations*, which model the sharing of security state and attribute information between systems.

Security Functions

The functions which realize network security can be categorized as follows:

- *System security functions*: Security-related processing, such as encryption/decryption, digital signature generation/verification, or authentication token generation/verification.
- *Security communication functions*: Communication functions which support the transfer of security-related information between systems.

This distinction is significant in two respects. First, it delineates two different types of standards. System security functions are specified in security mechanism or security technique standards, which are usually designed to be general-purpose in nature, not linked to any particular communication protocol or layer, and possibly useful for purposes other than communications security. Security communication functions, on the other hand, are part of particular communications protocol specifications (e.g., upper layers OSI), but are not rigidly linked to particular security mechanisms or techniques.

The other significance of the distinction is that it models the separation between security functionality and communications functionality in an implementation. A collection of system security functions will typically be implemented as a secure module, e.g., as a trusted software subsystem or a tamperproof hardware module, potentially applicable in a variety of communications or other environments. Hence, the boundary between system security functions and security communication functions provides a valuable starting point for the definition of standardized implementation interfaces, e.g., a security application program interface (API).

The ACSE authentication feature described in Section 12.3 provides an illustration of the system security function and security communication function concepts.

Security Exchanges and Security Transformations

The Upper Layers Security Model paves the way for the development of security protocol-building tools and protocol components by introducing two important concepts: security exchanges and security transformations. These concepts reflect two different types of behavior potentially required of a security protocol.

The first is the generation/processing of protocol data items communicated between a pair of systems in direct support of a security mechanism. Examples are the communication of authentication tokens (for entity authentication purposes), key derivation exchanges (in support of a confidentiality or integrity service), or communication of an access control certificate. The precise information items transferred are mechanism-dependent, but the protocol construction approach can be mechanism-independent. The security exchange concept is introduced to model this type of behavior.

The second type of behavior relates to the transformation of unprotected user data, in order to protect it during communication. Such a transformation may involve, for example, encryption/decryption or appending/checking of a digital signature. This behavior relates more to the processing of data from another part of the application than it does to the generation of security-specific protocol. The security transformation concept is introduced to model this type of behavior.

Figure 12-4 illustrates how the security exchange and security transformation concepts relate to the architectural concepts of system security functions and security communication functions. Both types of function are involved in both cases. With a security exchange, system security functions are the sources and sinks of the information transferred by the protocol. With a security transformation, the system security functions are not the sources or sinks of the information, but they perform the data transformation processes, e.g., encryption/decryption.

These concepts are used heavily in the Generic Upper Layers Security standard which defines general-purpose security protocol construction tools (ISO/IEC 11586). Tools associated with security exchanges and security transformations are discussed in Sections 12.4 and 12.5, respectively.

Security Associations

The security association concept used in the lower layers was described in Chapter 12. The same concept is also used in the upper layers. A security association is a relationship, between two or more systems, with attributes which model shared rules and state information (e.g., entity identifiers, selected algorithms, keys, and parameters) maintained between two systems. A security association supports the provision of a consistent type of protection to a sequence of data transfers.

A security association may apply to systems which intercommunicate directly via an application-association. Alternatively, it may apply to less direct communications relationships (mapping to other types of ASO-associations).

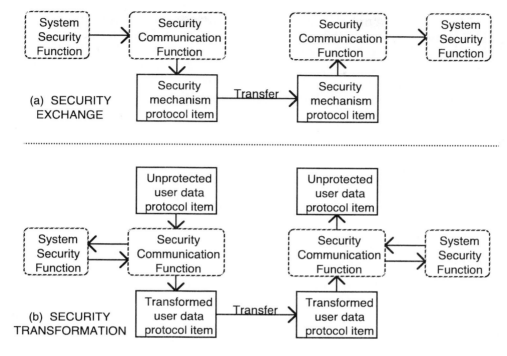

Figure 12-4: Security Exchanges and Security Transformations

For example, a security association may apply between systems which intercommunicate via Application Layer relay systems (e.g., a security association between the end systems of a store-and-forward messaging path).

Security associations are discussed further in Section 12.5.

12.3 Authentication at Association Establishment

The Association Control Service Element (ACSE), defined in ISO/IEC 8649 and 8650, is an ASE which supports the establishment and termination of application-associations. It defines application PDUs to be carried in conjunction with presentation-connection establishment and termination.

The association establishment procedure (the A-ASSOCIATE request and response) can optionally include a one-way or two-way exchange of authentication information. This procedure is intended primarily for mutually authenticating the application-entities at the two ends of an application-association. However, the standard does not restrict its use to that purpose, and the exchange can include any required security-related information, e.g., for establishing security attributes, deriving keys, or exchanging access control information. This exchange of security information can be viewed as a special case of the general *security exchange* concept, although this ACSE feature pre-dates the Upper Layers Security Model which introduced that general concept.

The association establishment PDU in each direction includes the fields:

- *Authentication-mechanism name*:   An object identifier, denoting a particular authentication mechanism which has been specified and registered by some organization.
- *Authentication-value*: A value of some ASN.1 type; the particular type is governed by the authentication mechanism specification as identified by the authentication-mechanism name field.

The ACSE authentication feature provides a good example of the distinction between system security functions and security communication functions, as introduced in the Upper Layers Security Model. The generation and processing of the authentication value is performed by a system security function.   However, the incorporation of the authentication value and the corresponding authentication mechanism name into a protocol-data-unit at the sending end, and the parsing and extraction of those fields at the receiving end are performed by a security communication function. The security communication function is part of the ACSE ASE (i.e., an integral part of the OSI stack), but the system security function is external to the OSI stack.

The ACSE standards do not directly specify particular authentication mechanisms. They provide what is sometimes called a *bucket protocol*, i.e., they define the buckets but leave it to someone else to specify what is carried in the buckets.

The definition of particular mechanisms has been taken up by the OSE Implementors' Workshop (OIW). One very useful mechanism was obtained by simply referencing the entity authentication exchange used in the Directory protocol. This can support unilateral or mutual authentication using any of: passwords, transformed passwords, or public-key signed tokens (see Section 14.6 for details). OIW mechanisms are assigned object identifiers in the OIW agreements [NIS1].

12.4 Security Exchanges

The security exchange concept also works in conjunction with a *bucket protocol* approach. It provides a way for security mechanisms to be designed independently of communications protocols and for communications protocol components in support of these mechanisms to be generated automatically.

This is pursued in the Generic Upper Layers Security standard (ISO/IEC 11586), which provides a means for specifying security exchanges and an ASE for conveying them.

A security exchange models a related sequence of security-related information transfers between a pair of systems. Let us identify the two systems as *A* and *B*. A security exchange involves transfer of an initial information item from *A* to *B*, optionally followed by a series of information item transfers between the two systems until one such transfer carries a flag indicating the exchange is considered complete. Usually, a security exchange involves a sequence of data items transferred in alternating directions, but this is not a firm constraint.

Figure 12-5 shows some examples of security exchanges. Example (a) is a three-way authentication exchange corresponding, for example, to either the X.509 three-way exchange or authenticated Diffie-Hellman exchange described in Section 5.6. Example (b) is a simple one-way transfer of an access control certificate. The certificate may optionally be associated with a particular access request (e.g., a management command or database access request) by virtue of being concatenated with that request for transmission purposes. Example (c) is a more complex case, in which an access request is securely bound together with an access certificate, using presentation data value embedding. Discussion of this example will be deferred until after security transformations have been introduced.

While a security exchange is in progress, other information transfers may occur and other security exchanges may be in progress on the same application-association. However, application-context rules will often constrain such overlapping activities. For example, other communications may be prohibited while an authentication exchange is occurring.

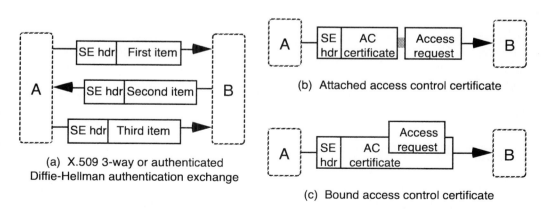

(a) X.509 3-way or authenticated Diffie-Hellman authentication exchange

(b) Attached access control certificate

(c) Bound access control certificate

Figure 12-5: Example Security Exchanges

Defining a Security Exchange

A security exchange specification is produced by a security mechanism designer. Ideally, such a specification should be usable by different applications and different communications environments (e.g., OSI, Internet, and proprietary architectures).

A security exchange specification includes:

(a) a statement of the data types of the information items transferred in the exchange;

(b) a statement of ordering constraints as to which items may be transferred in which direction at which stages of the exchange;

(c) a statement of error conditions which may arise, and the data types of error indications sent to the other end in the event of an error being detected;

(d) an assignment of a globally unique identifier for this type of security exchange, for signalling its use in protocol; and

(e) a statement of the purpose of the security exchange, and the meaning of the possible outcomes (the *semantics* of the security exchange).

Considering points (a), (c), and (d), specification tools can be provided which will permit automatic generation of the communications protocol to support the security exchange. The modular protocol construction features of ASN.1 are well suited to this purpose. To complete the specification, aspects (b) and (e) also need to be specified, but these are less amenable to the application of standardized tools.

A security exchange specification uses the *information object specification* notation, introduced into the 1993 ASN.1 standard (ISO/IEC 8824-2) as a replacement for the earlier *macro* notation. The Generic Upper Layers Security standard defines an information object class for security exchanges; this is effectively a set of table column headings for the information items associated with any security exchange. A particular security exchange is defined subsequently (by a user of the standard) by filling in the values for one row of this table. One of these values is the unique ASN.1 object identifier for that security exchange.

The Security Exchange Service Element (SESE)

The SESE is part of ISO/IEC 11586. Its primary purpose is to define the general form of an abstract syntax for use in transferring the protocol items needed for any security exchange. It includes PDUs to convey SE-item transfers, and error indications.

The precise abstract syntax definition is completed by combining this general definition with the definitions of the set of specific security exchanges to be supported in a particular protocol. This combining process can be automated if the specific security exchanges are defined using the standard information object class definition described above.

Use of the SESE in an Application-Context

The SESE generates PDUs which can be combined with PDUs from other ASEs as required. An application-context specification states how such combinations can occur, and how the SESE PDUs are mapped onto other services (i.e., either conveyed directly by the presentation service or embedded in PDUs of other ASEs).

For example, an application-context may use the SESE to support a two-way authentication exchange, and may specify that the two transfers of this exchange are to be embedded in the A-ASSOCIATE request and response PDUs (defined as part of ACSE) which are used in establishing an application-association. As a more complex example, a three- or four-way authentication exchange might be used in conjunction with establishing an application-association. In this case, the application-context may specify that the first two transfers of the exchange are to be embedded in the A-ASSOCIATE request and response PDUs, and the subsequent transfers are to be mapped directly to the presentation service. Furthermore, the application-context rules may specify that, until the authentication exchange is successfully completed, no other information transfers may occur.

Note that, for the purpose of conveying a one-way or two-way information exchange at association establishment time, either the ACSE authentication option or the SESE could be used. However, the SESE is more general, in not limiting an exchange to one-way or two-way and in not restricting the exchange to occurring at association establishment time.

12.5 Security Transformations

Security transformations address a different requirement than security exchanges, but the modular definition approach taken is similar.

As discussed in Section 7.6, there can be many different types of security transformation, supporting different variants and combinations of padding, encryption, signatures, integrity check-values, and integrity sequence numbers. The Generic Upper Layers Security standard permits security transformations to be specified and registered by anyone, with the requisite communications protocol components to support them being generated automatically.

A security transformation is part of the process of generating a bit string representation of an information item in an *encoding system* and recovering the information from the bit string in a *decoding system*. Typically, the encoding system is the sending system in a communication activity, and the decoding system is the receiving system. However, security transformations are not tied to communications, being designed for protecting stored information as well as communicated information.

In Presentation Layer terminology, the bit string representation is called a transfer syntax. When a security transformation is involved, the transfer syntax is denoted a *protecting transfer syntax*.

A security transformation has an *encoding process*, used in a sending system, and a *decoding process*, used in a receiving system. The complete processes of generating and interpreting a protecting transfer syntax representation for one data item are illustrated in Figure 12-6.

The item to be protected (the *unprotected item*) may be a value from an ASN.1-defined abstract syntax, or it may be specified by other means, e.g., it may be simply an arbitrary bit string. Step (a) only applies when the unprotected item is an ASN.1 value. This step involves generating a bit string encoding using a standard (non-protecting) encoding process, such as one of the sets of ASN.1 encoding rules in ISO/IEC 8825. The encoding rules used for this step are denoted *initial encoding rules*. Step (f) is the corresponding decoding process, which uses the same rules. Step (f) is only needed if one of the outputs required is a recovered copy of the unprotected item. This is typically needed with an encryption transformation, but not necessarily with other types of transformation. For example, with a digital signature transformation, the only output might be an indication of success/failure of the signature verification process; the unprotected item is not necessarily recovered.

Steps (b) and (e) are the encoding and decoding processes, respectively, of the security transformation in use. Step (b) operates on a bit string to generate an ASN.1 value called the *transformed item*. The process applied is specified as part of the transformation — it is typically encryption, signature generation, or integrity-check generation. Step (e) is the complementary process applied to the transformed item at the decoding end — typically decryption, signature verification, or integrity checking.

Steps (c) and (d) involve encoding/decoding the transformed item to/from a bit string for communication purposes. This may be done as part of the encoding/decoding of an encompassing ASN.1 construct, one case being a protecting transfer syntax construct that attaches supporting information such as a transformation identifier and parameter values. This is discussed further in the subsection *The Generic Protecting Transfer Syntax*.

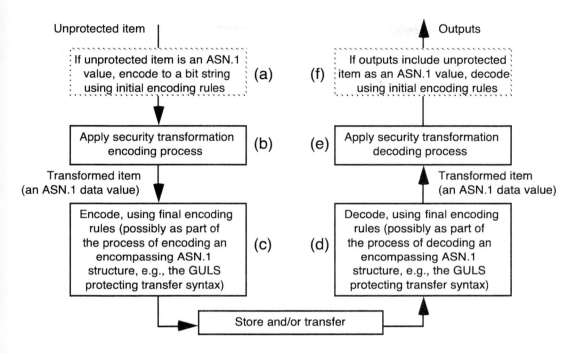

Figure 12-6: Protected Storage or Transfer of a Data Item

Role of Security Associations

It is common to apply the same type of security transformation repeatedly to a sequence of presentation data values sent from one system to another, with the same type of protection being applied to each. These presentation data values are not necessarily sent immediately adjacent in time — they may be interspersed among other presentation data values. However, they represent a logical sequence, and it may be necessary to retain attribute values (e.g., a key) and dynamic state information (e.g., an integrity sequence number or cryptographic chaining value) throughout the sequence. Such a sequence of protected presentation data values is modeled in terms of a security association.

Different types of security association include:

- *Externally established security association*: The security association is established by some external process (e.g., a separate Application Layer protocol exchange[3]) and is assigned an identifier which can subsequently be attached to presentation data values.

- *Explicit (single-item) security association*: The security association is limited to a single, independent embedded presentation data value, without establishing a negotiated presentation context. Information required to describe the encoding/decoding process (e.g., identification of the transformation used) is explicitly conveyed along with the encoded presentation data value.

- *Explicit (presentation-context) security association*:   The security association maps one-to-one to a negotiated presentation context. Information required to describe the encoding/decoding process is explicitly conveyed with the first encoded presentation data value in the presentation context.

Transformation Parameters

When using a security transformation, various parameter values may need to be known by the encoding and decoding functions in the different systems. Provision needs to be made in the transfer syntax protocol to communicate this information. There are two types of parameters — *static parameters* and *dynamic parameters*.

Static parameters are established before, or in conjunction with, the first transmission of a presentation data value within a security association. The values of these parameters remain constant for all subsequent presentation data values in that security association. Examples are algorithm identifiers, and system identities.

Dynamic parameters may change while the security transformation is in use in a security association. An example is a key identifier, which may change on expiration of a crypto-period.

It may be acceptable for some parameters to be transferred unprotected, but other parameters may require confidentiality and/or integrity protection during transfer.

The Generic Protecting Transfer Syntax

The GULS standard provides a framework specification which, when combined with specification details of a particular security transformation, generates the complete specification of a protecting transfer syntax to support that security transformation.

---

[3] Such a protocol is a subject for follow-up standardization.

A protecting transfer syntax provides a standard means for representing, for communication purposes, the following information items:

(a) the transformed item which results from applying the encoding process of a security transformation to a bit-string representation of an unprotected information item;

(b) protected static and dynamic parameters of a security transformation [however, because these parameters are protected by some means internal to the security transformation, they are hidden within the output of (a) and not visible in the transfer syntax structure];

(c) unprotected static and dynamic parameters of a security transformation (the transfer syntax structure makes explicit provision for conveying these); and

(d) information which references or establishes a security association, e.g., an identifier of an externally established security association or an explicit indication of required attribute values (including an indication of the security transformation to apply).

Figure 12-7 illustrates the operations potentially involved in generating a protecting transfer syntax representation at an encoding system (the corresponding operations at a decoding system follow naturally).

The protecting transfer syntax defines the format of the bit string carried in presentation protocol. There are different variants of this format, depending on the type of security association and whether or not presentation-contexts are used. Because all presentation data values in a presentation context are protected under the same security association, only the first value has to identify the security association (for the externally-defined case) or the security transformation (for the explicit case), and only the first value has to convey static parameter values. Subsequent presentation data values need only provide for conveying dynamic parameter changes. For an explicit (single-item) security association, the fields conveyed are the same as for the first presentation data value in a protecting presentation context.

Defining a Security Transformation

The process of defining a security transformation is very similar to that of defining a security exchange. The specification is produced by a security mechanism designer and, ideally, should be usable by different applications and different communications/storage environments (e.g., OSI and non-OSI environments).

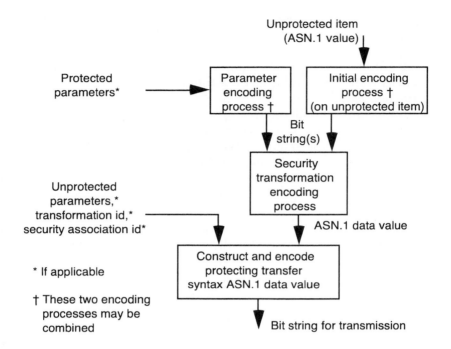

Figure 12-7: Protecting Transfer Syntax Construction in Sending System

A security transformation specification includes:

(a) a description of the encoding process and decoding process associated with the security transformation;

(b) a list of locally-sourced inputs required by encoding and decoding processes;

(c) an indication of the data type of the transformed item output from the encoding process (input to the decoding process);

(d) indications of the data types and semantics of any static and/or dynamic parameters needing to be conveyed (including both protected and unprotected parameters);

(e) an assignment of a globally unique identifier for this type of transformation, for use for signalling purposes in a protecting transfer syntax; and

(f) a description of any error conditions that may arise in the decoding process.

For points (c), (d), and (e), ASN.1 specification tools are provided. As with security exchange specifications, the ASN.1 information object specification notation is used.

The Need for Single-Valued Encoding Rules

Use of certain ASN.1 encoding rules to generate a bit string to which protection is to be applied can potentially cause a problem with sealing or signing transformations. Some ASN.1 encoding rules, notably the original Basic Encoding Rules (BER), do not always generate the same bit string for any given ASN.1 (abstract syntax) value. Different encodings can result because of various optional choices which can be made by the encoder, such as:

- choice of definite length form or indefinite length form of encoding;
- choice of constructed form or primitive form of encoding for a string type;
- choice of ordering of components of a *set* type; and
- choice of including or omitting redundant high-order zero bits in an integer encoding.

Hence, abstract syntax data value v can generate any of the bit string representations r_1, r_2, r_3, ... Furthermore, because encodings sometimes pass through relay systems which may decode and re-encode fields, the ultimate recipient may receive a representation different from that originally sent.

Without sealing or signing, this presents no problem because the decoder, applying the standard decoding rules, will always recover the correct v from any of these representations.

The problem arises if the representation of v is to be used in generating a seal or signature. Suppose, for example, v is a message sent from system A to system B, and that a field, s, which is a seal or signature computed on a representation of v, is also sent from A to B. If system A uses some arbitrary representation, r_i to generate s, it is infeasible for system B to check the seal or signature because it would not know which r_i to use in regenerating s. Even if v accompanies s in the same transfer, it is possible that the representation of v may be decoded and re-encoded en route, in which case the received representation may be different to the r_i used in generating s.

To avert this problem, it is necessary to use encoding rules which generate a unique representation r for every abstract syntax value v. For this purpose, the single-valued ASN.1 encoding rules defined in ISO/IEC 8825-3 were developed. This standard defines two different sets of encoding rules — the *Distinguished Encoding Rules* (DER) and the *Canonical Encoding Rules*

(CER); each is obtained by applying a different set of restrictions to the options in the Basic Encoding Rules.[4]

Secure Binding of Protocol Fields

There are many situations in which it is necessary to securely bind two pieces of protocol data together. Examples are binding an access control certificate or token to an access request, and binding a security label to a user data item. Furthermore, the data items involved may be from different ASEs, hence from different abstract syntaxes. This can be achieved using security transformations in conjunction with embedding of presentation data values (as discussed in Section 12.1).

Consider one presentation data value (*B*) embedded in another presentation data value (*A*), as shown in Figure 12-8.

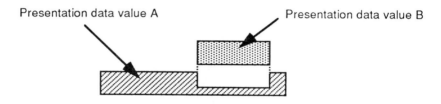

Figure 12-8: Embedded Presentation Data Value

The entire encoding is processed by any security transformation applied to presentation data value *A*. Hence, if this transformation includes a sealing or signing process, the entire contents of both presentation data values *A* and *B* are securely bound together.

For example, suppose presentation data value *B* is a PDU which constitutes an access request, e.g., a database retrieval or network management command. Presentation data value *A* may contain an access control certificate. The two are bound together with a sealing transformation. Security exchanges and the SESE can also play a role here. It is possible to define a one-way security exchange for a *bound access control certificate*, which generates presentation data value *A*. Then, dependent upon application-context rules, any desired PDU from any ASE can have an access control certificate attached to it through appropriate combining of that ASE and the SESE.

---

⁴ The Distinguished Encoding Rules are derived from the original Directory Authentication Framework. The Canonical Encoding Rules, introduced in 1993, contain some improvements.

12.6 Selective Field Protection

An application protocol developer needs to be able to specify that certain protocol fields are to be protected in certain ways, e.g., by confidentiality, integrity, and/or data origin authentication services. This needs to be done as part of an abstract syntax specification. The ASN.1 standard has no built-in support for specifying security requirements, but it has basic tools which enable standard security notation to be developed.

The two significant standardization activities which have developed such notation are the Directory Authentication Framework (used in the Message Handling Systems and Directory standards) and the more recent Generic Upper Layers Security standard.

The Directory Authentication Framework Notation

The Directory Authentication Framework (ISO/IEC 9594-8), which includes substantial general-purpose security material, is the subject of Section 14.3. Only the material concerned with selective field security notation is addressed here.

The most significant notational constructs in the Directory Authentication Framework are the ENCRYPTED, SIGNED, and SIGNATURE constructs. The original (1988) version of the standard defined these constructs using the (now-obsolete) ASN.1 macro notation. Later revisions define equivalent constructs, plus a new HASHED construct, using the new ASN.1 parameterized type notation.[5]

The ENCRYPTED construct is used to indicate that a value of some other ASN.1 type is to be protected by encryption. For example, an abstract syntax might need to specify that a particular field in a PDU is to convey an encrypted version of a password. If the unprotected password can be represented by a value of type PrintableString, then the field for conveying the protected password can be specified as being of type ENCRYPTED {PrintableString}.

The ENCRYPTED parameterized type definition and an illustration of the implied processing are shown in Figure 12-9. With this construct, the parameter of the parameterized type is the ASN.1 type of the value to be protected. The construct does not assist in indicating the encryption process to be used nor in conveying associated parameter information. An abstract syntax specification which uses this construct must provide such details separately.

---

[5] A parameterized type is a partial definition of an ASN.1 type contained in one specification module (in this case, a module defined in ISO/IEC 9594-8). It generates a precise ASN.1 type definition when referenced from another ASN.1 module (in this case, an application's abstract syntax definition) and supplied the value(s) of one or more parameters which are themselves ASN.1 values, types, objects, classes, value sets, or object sets.

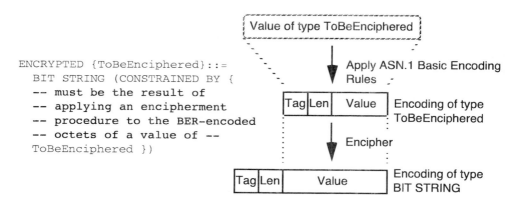

```
ENCRYPTED {ToBeEnciphered}::=
    BIT STRING (CONSTRAINED BY {
    -- must be the result of
    -- applying an encipherment
    -- procedure to the BER-encoded
    -- octets of a value of --
    ToBeEnciphered })
```

Figure 12-9: The ENCRYPTED *Construct*

The HASHED construct is used to indicate that a value of some other ASN.1 type is to be processed by a hash function, typically as part of the generation of a digital signature appendix. It is used by the SIGNATURE and SIGNED construct definitions. The ASN.1 parameterized type definition and the implied processing are shown in Figure 12-10. The HASHED construct is very similar to the ENCRYPTED construct, except that it employs single-valued encoding rules and generates an octet string rather than a bit string.

The SIGNATURE construct is used to generate a digital signature appendix for a value of some ASN.1 type. The encoding generated includes an encrypted hashed version of the value to be protected, plus an identifier of the digital signature algorithm. The definition of this construct employs the definitions of the ENCRYPTED and HASHED constructs. The ASN.1 parameterized type definition and the implied processing are shown in Figure 12-11. The definition of the algorithm identifier is not spelled out fully here — it comprises a sequence of an object identifier for the digital signature algorithm (implying both a particular hash function and a particular encryption process) and an optional set of parameters required by that algorithm.

The SIGNED construct is used to generate a digitally signed encoding of a value of some ASN.1 type. It is similar to the SIGNATURE construct, except that it includes a plaintext representation of the value to be protected, together with the digital signature appendix. The ASN.1 parameterized type definition and the implied processing are shown in Figure 12-12.

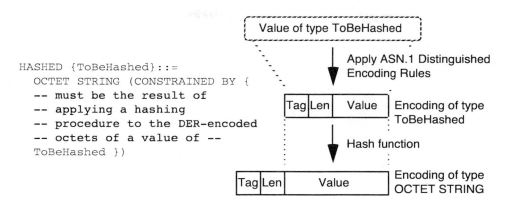

```
HASHED {ToBeHashed}::=
  OCTET STRING (CONSTRAINED BY {
  -- must be the result of
  -- applying a hashing
  -- procedure to the DER-encoded
  -- octets of a value of --
  ToBeHashed })
```

Figure 12-10: The HASHED *Construct*

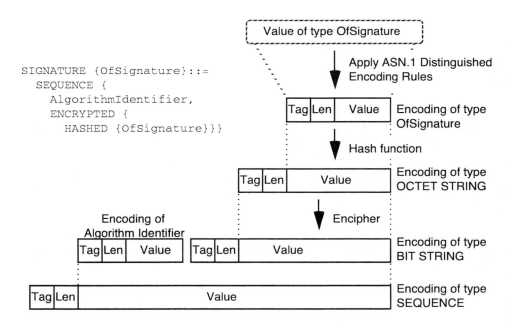

```
SIGNATURE {OfSignature}::=
  SEQUENCE {
    AlgorithmIdentifier,
    ENCRYPTED {
      HASHED {OfSignature}}}
```

Figure 12-11: The SIGNATURE *Construct*

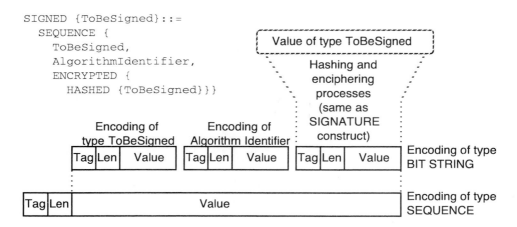

Figure 12-12: The SIGNED *Construct*

As an example of the use of SIGNED, an abstract syntax might need to specify that a particular field in a PDU is to convey the text of a message to which a non-repudiation service, based on a digital signature, is to be applied. If the unprotected message can be represented by a value of type Message, then the field for conveying the protected password can be specified as being of type SIGNED {Message}.

From the cryptographic viewpoint, one potential weakness in the SIGNATURE and SIGNED constructs should be noted. This weakness applies if the construct is employed in an environment where different signature algorithms are available for selection. While the algorithm identifier is always conveyed with the signature, its value is not protected by the signing process. It may be possible to attack such a digital signature by replacing the message plaintext with a different plaintext and by replacing the algorithm identifier with the identifier of a different algorithm which generates the same encrypted hashed value. To counter such attacks, the algorithm identifier needs to be included in the value which is signed. (Given its inclusion in that value, adding it again in the SIGNATURE or SIGNED construct constitutes redundant overhead.)

The Generic Upper Layers Security Notation

The ENCRYPTED, SIGNATURE, and SIGNED constructs proved adequate for the original Message Handling System and Directory applications. However, they have several deficiencies as a basis for selective field protection specification in applications generally. One deficiency is the tying of the various constructs to particular types of security transformation, e.g., SIGNATURE and SIGNED being tied to a hash-encrypt digital signature technique. More complex security transformations (as discussed in Section 7.6) are not accommodated. Other deficiencies are the inability to transparently convey parameters, and the unwieldy encoding/decoding processes which include various redundancies.

In conjunction with the general security transformation concept, the Generic Upper Layers Security standard introduced a new notation for specifying selective fields, capable of exploiting the full generality of security transformations and the associated specification tools. This notation employs parameterized types but, unlike the Directory types, they are not tied to specific transformations.

The Generic Upper Layers Security standard introduces a parameterized type called PROTECTED which has two parameters — a base (or unprotected) type and a protection indicator, for example:

```
PROTECTED { PrintableString, confidentiality }
```

The first parameter indicates that the value to be protected is a value of type PrintableString, e.g., a password. The second parameter identifies a separate piece of specification, called a *protection mapping*, which declares which transformation should be used to protect the field concerned. This provides great flexibility in being able to select different transformations for different application environments. For example, in one environment, confidentiality may map to DES encryption. In another environment, the underlying layers may be sufficiently trusted that no upper layer security transformation is needed at all. In yet another environment, multiple transformations may be available. The choice between them can be a run-time decision of the local system, based on local security policy.

The PROTECTED parameterized type is defined in such a way that it can generate an appropriate encoding for any of these situations. It can also be used in place of the Directory ENCRYPTED, SIGNED, and SIGNATURE constructs, generating bit-identical encodings for the following equivalent notations:

```
PROTECTED {BaseType, encrypted} and ENCRYPTED {BaseType}
PROTECTED {BaseType, signed} and SIGNED {BaseType}
PROTECTED {BaseType, signature} and SIGNATURE {BaseType}
```

This encoding-compatibility facilitates migration from the Directory notation to the PROTECTED notation.

The PROTECTED notation also has a variation which enables a qualifying parameter, e.g., an algorithm identifier, to be conveyed to the transformation from the calling abstract syntax:

```
PROTECTED-Q {BaseType, protectionMapping, qualifier}
```

The Generic Upper Layers Security standard includes some definitions of some generally-useful security transformations and protection mappings, to enable the notation to be used immediately. Other transformations may be defined and registered by other organizations as required, and new protection mappings can be developed by any user of the PROTECTED notation.

Compound Usage of Selective Field Notation

Separate applications of the selective field notations outlined above can be combined as required and can be nested within each other if necessary. As an example, consider a protocol with a PDU to convey an unencrypted value of type NonConfidentialString plus an encrypted representation of a value of type ConfidentialString, with the whole PDU protected under a sealing transformation for integrity purposes. Using the basic PROTECTED notation, this PDU can be defined as the following ASN.1 type:

```
PDU ::= PROTECTED {
    SEQUENCE
    {
        NonConfidentialString,
        PROTECTED { ConfidentialString, confidentiality }
    },
    sealed }
```

This example depends upon separate protection mappings which define what transformations are implied by the indicators confidentiality and sealed.

The above example could be extended to include, as another component of the SEQUENCE construct, the encryption key used by confidentiality, with that key encrypted under another key (e.g., the recipient's public key) using yet another transformation.

12.7   Building a Specific Application Protocol

The goal of the Generic Upper Layers Security standard is to provide security protocol-construction tools for use in building specific application protocols. It needs to be used in conjunction with other standards. Figure 12-13 illustrates the process a protocol designer might follow to incorporate security elements into a specific application protocol. The roles of various types of standards are indicated.

Note that this is the intended process to be followed after all the standards are complete. (The Message Handling Systems and Directory protocols discussed in the next two chapters were developed prior to the completion of the generic standards.)

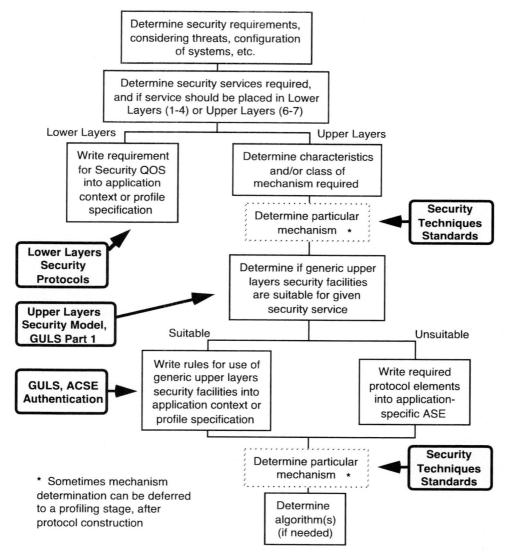

Figure 12-13: Incorporating Security into an OSI Application

Summary

Application level security is associated with upper layers protocols. The design of application level security features needs to be carried out in conjunction with the basic application protocol design and is partly application-specific. However, common security protocol building tools and security protocol components can greatly facilitate this task and cut implementation costs.

The Upper Layers Security Model establishes some valuable concepts to assist in providing application level security. The distinction between system security functions and security communication functions provides a basis for separating security functionality and communications functionality, both in standards specifications and in implementations. Security exchanges and security transformations provide a basis for common security protocol-building tools and protocol components. Security associations model security-related attributes and state information shared between systems for the purpose of protecting a sequence of data transfers.

The OSI ACSE authentication option provides a common means for conveying a two-way authentication exchange or other security information exchange in conjunction with establishing an application-association. Particular exchanges are specified and registered separately from the formal standard.

The security exchange concept models the communication of information at the Application Layer as part of the operation of a security mechanism. A security exchange corresponds to an *n*-way exchange of security-related data between a pair of systems (the ACSE authentication option is a simple case). The Generic Upper Layers Security standard specifies notational tools whereby anyone can define a security exchange and register its definition. For OSI application protocols, the security exchange service element (SESE) provides a way to automatically generate the protocol for conveying any set of defined security exchanges.

Security transformations model the security-related processing involved in generating a bit string representation of an Application Layer information item prior to sending and in recovering the information from the bit string representation upon receipt. Security transformations typically involve encryption, sealing, and/or signing processes. The Generic Upper Layers Security standard specifies notational tools whereby anyone can define a security transformation and register its definition. This standard also gives a definition of a generic protecting transfer syntax, which can be tailored by linking with specific security transformation definitions to give a protecting transfer syntax specification for use by the Presentation Layer.

Two standards provide ASN.1 constructs to assist application protocol designers in specifying that certain protocol fields are to be protected in certain ways. The Directory Authentication Framework defines constructs which invoke specific encryption, hash function, or digital signature transformations.

The newer Generic Upper Layers Security standard defines more general constructs which are able to invoke any registered transformation.

Exercises

1. Describe the difference between system security functions and security communication functions and give an example of each.

2. The exchange of security information supported by the ACSE authentication option can be viewed as a special case of the general security exchange concept. Identify two limitations of the ACSE authentication exchange model which were eliminated in the general security exchange model as used by the SESE.

3. What information needs to be specified in (a) a security exchange definition; (b) a security transformation definition?

4. With which of the following types of security transformations is it essential to use single-valued encoding rules in generating the unprotected encoding:

   (a) encryption;
   (b) seal;
   (c) appended integrity sequence number followed by encryption; and
   (d) digital signature followed by encryption?

REFERENCES

[NIS1] U.S. Department of Commerce, National Institute of Standards and Technology, *Stable Implementation Agreements for Open Systems Interconnection Protocols Version 6 Edition 1 December 1992*, NIST Special Publication 500-206, 1993 (or latest revision thereof).

Standards

ISO/IEC 8649: *Information Technology — Open Systems Interconnection — Service Definition for Association Control* (Also ITU-T Recommendation X.217).
ISO/IEC 8650: *Information Technology — Open Systems Interconnection — Protocol Specification for the Association Control Service Element* (Also ITU-T Recommendation X.227).

ISO/IEC 8822: *Information Technology — Open Systems Interconnection — Connection Oriented Presentation Service Definition* (Also ITU-T Recommendation X.216).

ISO/IEC 8823: *Information Technology — Open Systems Interconnection — Connection Oriented Presentation Protocol Specification* (Also ITU-T Recommendation X.226).

ISO/IEC 8824-1: *Information Technology — Open Systems Interconnection — Abstract Syntax Notation One (ASN.1): Specification of Basic Notation* (Also ITU-T Recommendation X.680).

ISO/IEC 8824-2: *Information Technology — Open Systems Interconnection — Abstract Syntax Notation One (ASN.1): Information Object Specification* (Also ITU-T Recommendation X.681).

ISO/IEC 8824-3: *Information Technology — Open Systems Interconnection — Abstract Syntax Notation One (ASN.1): Constraint Specification* (Also ITU-T Recommendation X.682).

ISO/IEC 8824-4: *Information Technology — Open Systems Interconnection — Abstract Syntax Notation One (ASN.1): Parameterization of ASN.1 Specifications* (Also ITU-T Recommendation X.683).

ISO/IEC 8825-1: *Information Technology — Open Systems Interconnection — Specification of ASN.1 Encoding Rules: Basic Encoding Rules (BER)* (Also ITU-T Recommendation X.690).

ISO/IEC 8825-3: *Information Technology — Open Systems Interconnection — Specification of ASN.1 Encoding Rules: Distinguished Canonical Encoding Rules* (Also ITU-T Recommendation X.692).

ISO/IEC 9545: *Information Technology — Open Systems Interconnection — Application Layer Structure* (Also ITU-T Recommendation X.207).

ISO/IEC 9594-8: *Information Technology — Open Systems Interconnection — The Directory: Authentication Framework* (Also ITU-T Recommendation X.509).

ISO/IEC 10745: *Information Technology — Open Systems Interconnection — Upper Layers Security Model* (Also ITU-T Recommendation X.803).

ISO/IEC 11586-1: *Information Technology — Open Systems Interconnection — Generic Upper Layers Security: Overview, Models and Notation* (Also ITU-T Recommendation X.830) (Draft).

ISO/IEC 11586-2: *Information Technology — Open Systems Interconnection — Generic Upper Layers Security: Security Exchange Service Element Service Definition* (Also ITU-T Recommendation X.831) (Draft).

ISO/IEC 11586-3: *Information Technology — Open Systems Interconnection — Generic Upper Layers Security: Security Exchange Service Element Protocol Specification* (Also ITU-T Recommendation X.832) (Draft).

ISO/IEC 11586-4: *Information Technology — Open Systems Interconnection — Generic Upper Layers Security: Protecting Transfer Syntax Specification* (Also ITU-T Recommendation X.833) (Draft).

13   Electronic Mail and EDI Security

There are two standard electronic mail (e-mail) architectures used for providing e-mail services directly to users and for interconnecting proprietary e-mail systems. The first architecture is defined in the Message Handling Systems (MHS) international standards, commonly known by their ITU designator *X.400*. The second is the Internet mail architecture.

MHS is a network application for e-mail and other store-and-forward message transfer purposes, including electronic business data interchange (EDI) and voice messaging. The security features of the MHS application are worthy of detailed study for two reasons. First, the security services provided are very comprehensive and demonstrate the use of a wide range of underlying security techniques. Second, the MHS security features were established as far back as 1988, making them a model used in securing other open-system applications. The bulk of this chapter is therefore devoted to MHS security. The full range of MHS security services is described, together with the methods for providing them, the options left for agreement among implementors, and the internationally agreed profiles to aid in option selection.

The Internet mail protocols are different from MHS, but are based on the same underlying architectural model. Use of Internet mail and the set of features supported, have been expanding steadily since the beginnings of Internet. However, security did not have a significant place on the Internet mail agenda until the late 1980s, when development of the Privacy Enhanced Mail (PEM) option commenced. PEM became operational in 1993. This chapter includes a general description of PEM.

The chapter is organized into sections addressing:

(1) basic MHS terminology, concepts, and models;
(2) threats in the MHS environment and the MHS security services used to counter them;
(3) MHS protocol elements used for security purposes;
(4) the provision of basic end-to-end MHS security services;
(5) the provision of other MHS security services;
(6) security techniques used in MHS;
(7) MHS security profiles developed in regional workshops;

(8) special provisions for protecting the exchange of EDI transactions, both in the MHS standards and in the ANSI X12 EDI standards;

(9) Internet Privacy Enhanced Mail (PEM); and

(10) the SDNS Message Security Protocol, which is an MHS adaptation for U.S. military and classified applications.

13.1 MHS (X.400) Overview

Background

The first version of the MHS standards was developed by the ITU (CCITT) in the 1981–1984 period. MHS (1984) was a ground-breaking OSI application standard, but had virtually no security provisions. During the 1985–1988 period, the ITU and ISO/IEC worked together on substantial modifications and enhancements to MHS [MAN1]. One major enhancement was the addition of the *secure messaging* features. MHS (1988) was published as both a revised version of the ITU X.400 Recommendations, and as the multi-part international standard ISO/IEC 10021.

In 1990, MHS was further extended to support the transfer of electronic business data interchange (EDI) transactions over the MHS backbone [GEN1, HIL1]. These extensions included additional security features required by EDI applications. In 1992, the MHS standards were again revised, but there were no significant changes to the security features.

Following is a brief overview of basic aspects of MHS which need to be understood before addressing MHS security in detail. For a complete tutorial on MHS, see [DIC1, PLA1].

Functional Model

Figure 13.1 illustrates the MHS environment. Messages originate from and are ultimately received by *users*, which may be people or automatic processes. A given message has one *originator* and one or more *recipient* users. The MHS environment has two logical levels. In the outer level are *user agents* (UAs), each supporting one user. A user agent performs such functions as preparing and submitting messages for its user, and receiving and preprocessing messages for its user.

The inner level is called the *message transfer system* (MTS), which is a store-and-forward backbone comprising a set of interconnected components called *message transfer agents* (MTAs). A message is submitted at one MTA (the *originating MTA*), then forwarded along any path of MTAs to a *delivering MTA* which delivers it out of the MTS. In order to deliver a message to multiple recipients, the message contents may be copied and sent on multiple paths at various points in traversing the MTS.

Delivery of a message may occur in either of two ways. A recipient UA may be directly connected to a delivering MTA, in which case messsages for the corresponding user are delivered directly to the UA. With the other type of delivery, a further component type, called a *message store* (MS), is introduced into the outer layer of the MHS environment. A message store acts on behalf of a UA, to receive and store messages until they are later *retrieved* by the UA. The message store configuration was introduced to accommodate UAs which are not regularly connected to the MTS, e.g., a UA based on a personal computer which dials up occasionally to send or receive mail. The MS can also submit messages for a UA but, in this case, the MS is simply a transparent relaying agent. From the perspective of the MTS, there is no observable difference between a UA and an MS. The term *MTS-user* embraces both UA and MS.

The MHS environment has one other component not shown in Figure 13-1. This is an *access unit* (AU), which constitutes a gateway to a different message transfer technology such as facsimile, telex, teletex, or physical delivery (i.e., the postal service). Depending on technology type, an AU may be able to submit and/or deliver messages. From the MTS perspective, an AU is another case of an MTS-user.

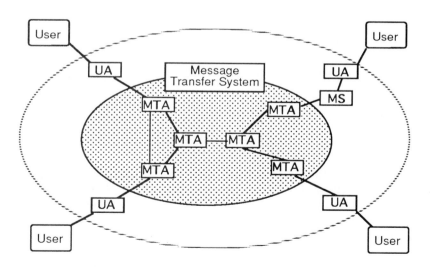

Figure 13-1: MHS Functional Model

MHS Protocols — Physical Configurations

The MHS standards specify a set of protocols which the functional components may use to intercommunicate. The protocols, as illustrated in Figure 13-2, are:

- *MTS transfer protocol* (P1): A protocol used for communication between two MTAs.
- *MTS access protocol* (P3): A protocol used for communication between an MTS-user (UA or MS) and an originating MTA or delivering MTA.
- *MS access protocol* (P7): A protocol used for communication between a UA and its corresponding MS.

These are three distinct Application Layer protocols, which operate in conjunction with layer 1 to 6 protocols to form a full OSI stack.

It is not essential that all communication between functional components employ these protocols. Multiple components may be co-located in the same physical system, in which case they may interface by non-standard means. Two common forms of co-location are systems which contain:

- MTA functionality, plus the MS functionality for one or more users; or
- MTA functionality, plus the UA functionality for one or more users.

The latter configuration may take various forms, such as a multi-user computer system, a LAN mail server, or a mail gateway system. In a mail gateway system, the "UA" will typically translate messages to and from a proprietary mail system format, instead of giving direct access to a user. Some physical configuration examples are shown in Figure 13-3.

Message Structure

A message has two main components:

- *Content*: The data the originator wishes to communicate to the recipient(s). The value of the content is generally of no concern to the MTS.
- *Envelope*: Data used by the MTS in the submission, transfer, and delivery processes (e.g., source and destination addresses, special function requests, progress information). Envelope definitions form part of the P1, P3, and P7 protocol specifications. To support messages with multiple recipients, there are two categories of envelope field — *per-message fields* (applicable to all recipients) and *per-recipient fields* (may take different values for different recipients).

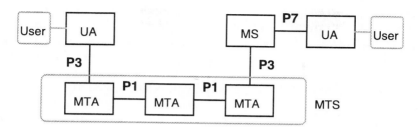

Figure 13-2: MHS Protocols

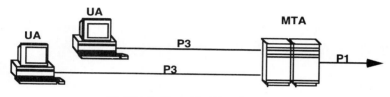

(a) Directly Connected User Agents

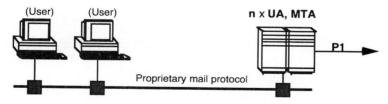

(b) Dial-up User Agents to MHS Service Provider

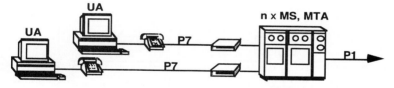

(c) Proprietary LAN Mail Server with MHS Gateway

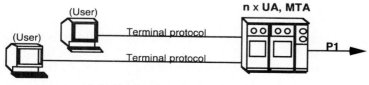

(d) Multi-user Mainframe/Minicomputer

Figure 13-3: Example MHS Physical Configurations

The form of the content needs to be standardized, as well as that of the envelopes. This is done in separate *content type* specifications, for use in different application environments. Content types defined in the MHS standards include an *interpersonal messaging* content type, an *EDI messaging* content type and a *voice messaging* content type. Other content types may be defined in future standards, or defined privately and registered.

The above three content types all structure message contents in the same basic way, as shown in Figure 13-4. The contents comprise a *heading* and a *body*. The heading has several fields, which are defined in the content type definition. The body comprises a set of one or more *body parts*. These are distinct parts of the message content, each having an identified body part type, e.g., text, voice encoding, facsimile encoding, or EDI transaction. This enables multi-media messages to be conveniently supported. The different content types vary with respect to heading field definitions, restrictions on body part type usage, procedural rules, and the use of notifications (discussed in the next subsection).

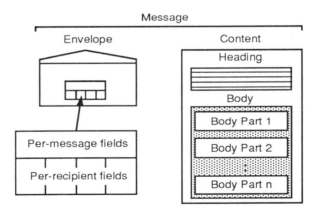

Figure 13-4: Message Structure

Notifications

Notifications are indications sent back to the originator of a message, following-up message submission. There are two categories of notification:

* *Delivery reports* and *non-delivery reports*: These notifications, generated within the MTS, advise of successful delivery or of a condition occurring that makes delivery impossible. Delivery reports are optional, at the originator's request, and are generated by delivering MTAs. Non-

delivery reports are generated automatically, on any non-delivery condition, at any MTA on the message path. The procedures and protocol elements associated with delivery and non-delivery reports are specified in the P1, P3, and P7 definitions.

*   *Content-level notifications*: These are follow-up messages, generated by a recipient MTS-user and sent back to the message originator using the standard MTS service. Details of these notifications depend upon the content type. For example, the interpersonal messaging content type defines *receipt notifications* and *non-receipt notifications*.

Probes

A probe is a content-less message sent by an originator for the purpose of determining deliverability of a subsequent real message. A probe is not delivered, but all applicable delivery and/or non-delivery reports are generated by the MTS. Probes are little used in practice in MHS, nevertheless security services are defined for them.

Names and Addessses

The MHS environment is designed for interconnecting users on a global scale, using equipment operated by a variety of organizations including public telecommunications carriers, governments, private corporations, and individuals. A highly flexible system is required for uniquely identifying users.

Users are identified by originator/recipient (O/R) names. An O/R name can be either a directory name (described in Chapter 14) or an *O/R address*. Routing and delivery within the MTS employ O/R addresses; if necessary, an MTA can obtain an O/R address from a directory name by a directory look-up.

There are several different forms of O/R address. The most common is the mnemonic form, which comprises a sequence of components that traverse a name hierarchy, starting from country at the highest level, followed by management domain, organization, organizational units, then the various components of a personal name.

Distribution lists are an optional MHS feature whereby an originator can address a message to a named list of recipients instead of individually specified recipients. The distribution list is expanded into a list of recipients at some point in the MTS. A distribution list has its own O/R address for use by originators.

Conversions

Conversions are an optional MHS feature whereby one or more body parts in a message may be delivered in a different encoding format to that used at message submission. For example, a text body part could be converted to a Group 3 facsimile body part for delivery to a terminal that only supports facsimile output. This feature constitutes an architectural anomaly as it requires the MTS to perform processing on message content.

Navigating the MHS Standards

The MHS standards are a large and complex set of specifications. The material pertaining to the provision of security is spread throughout the set and, except to the MHS specialist, is hard to find and to link together. Table 13-1 indicates where the main security-related material is located. This table is valid for the 1988, 1990 (EDI extensions), and 1992 versions of the ITU recommendations, and the aligned ISO/IEC standards published subsequently.

13.2 MHS Security Services

Threats

The MHS secure messaging facilities are designed to counter the following threats:

- *Masquerade (MTS-user)*: Impersonation of one UA or MS by another in order to gain unauthorized access to MTS facilities, to falsely claim to originate a message, or to falsely acknowledge receipt.
- *Masquerade (MTA)*: Impersonation of an MTA to a UA, MS, or other MTA.
- *Message sequencing*: Replay or reordering of messages.
- *Modification of information*: Modification or destruction of messages.
- *Repudiation*: denial of origin (by an originator), denial of submission (by an originating MTA), or denial of delivery (by a recipient UA or MS).
- *Information leakage*: Loss of confidentiality, loss of anonymity, or traffic analysis.
- *Security-label-related threats*: Misrouting, incompatible labeling policies.

The MHS secure messaging features comprise 19 *elements of service.* To introduce these services, they will be considered in five groupings, based on some important commonalities: basic end-to-end services, message path services, MTS corroborative services, non-repudiation services, and security management services.

Part of Standard	Security-Relevant Contents
ISO/IEC 10021-1 (ITU-T X.400 and F.400) — System and Service Overview	Clause 15: Brief overview of threats and security services. Annexes: Glossary of terms; brief definitions of all MHS elements of service.
ISO/IEC 10021-2 (ITU-T X.402) — Overall Architecture	Clause 10: Security model; descriptions of security services and security elements Annexes: Identification of threats and security services countering these threats; table listing protocol arguments used in providing security services.
ISO/IEC 10021-4 (ITU-T X.411) — MTS: Abstract Service Definition and Procedures	Clause 8: MTS abstract service definition; contains descriptions of all P3 remote operations, including security arguments and results (many of these carried forward into P1 and P7). Clause 9: MTS abstract syntax definition; detailed ASN.1 specification for all fields defined in clause 8. Clause 12: MTA abstract service definition; description of P1 remote operations (largely by reference to clause 8). Clause 13: MTA abstract syntax definition; detailed ASN.1 specification for all fields defined in clause 12 (many definitions imported from clause 9).
ISO/IEC 10021-5 (ITU-T X.413) — MS: Abstract Service Definition	Clauses 7 and 8: Description of P7 remote operations (almost all security-related definitions are by reference to ISO/IEC 10021-4 clause 8).
ISO/IEC 10021-8 (ITU-T F.435) — EDI Messaging Service	Clause 10: Brief overview of the EDI security services. Annex: General discussion of the EDI security features and the threats countered.
ISO/IEC 10021-9 (ITU-T X.435) — EDI Messaging System	Clauses 8 and 9: Definitions of EDI message and notification fields. Clause 17: Description of UA procedures. Annex: Discussion of the EDI enhancements to the ISO/IEC 10021-2 security model.

Table 13-1: Security-Relevant Material in the MHS Standards

Basic End-to-End Services

The basic end-to-end services provide originators and recipients with data origin authentication, confidentiality, and integrity protection of their messages, without having to trust the underlying MTS. They involve security relationships between originator and recipient MTS-user components (see Figure 13-5). Message envelope fields convey data to support the provision of these services, but this is the only role played by the MTS. The services are:

- *Message origin authentication (end-to-end)*[1]: Provides a recipient with assurance that a message came from the claimed originator.
- *Proof of delivery*: Provides the originator of a message with assurance that the message was delivered to an intended recipient without modification during transfer.
- *Content confidentiality*: Protects message contents against disclosure between originator and recipient.
- *Content integrity*: Protects message contents against modification between originator and recipient.
- *Message sequence integrity*: Protects against reordering, replay, or deletion of sequential messages between an originator and a recipient.

The use of any of these services is at the discretion of the originator on a per-message and (except for content confidentiality) per-recipient basis.

Two of these services — message origin authentication (end-to-end) and content integrity — are particularly closely related, to the extent that there is little point in providing one without the other. In combination, they effectively provide data origin authentication to a recipient.

Message Path Services

This group of services contributes to secure communications along a complete message path, potentially placing requirements on functional components of all types (UA, MS, and MTA). The services are:

- *Peer-entity authentication*: Provides any functional component with assurance of the identity of another component when an application-association is established between them.

---

[1] The MHS standards recognize only one message origin authentication service, but there are two different approaches to its realization, each of which has different service characteristics. In this book, an attempt is made to clarify this situation by recognizing two services — message origin authentication (end-to-end) and message origin authentication (MTS), respectively.

- *Message security labeling*: Provides for attaching a security label to a message, and for associating security labels with functional components. This service supports security policies restricting the parts of the MHS environment that may handle messages bearing security labels.
- *Security context*: Provides for establishing the set of security labels permitted on messages passing between a pair of functional components.

The security relationships involved are illustrated in Figure 13-6. Peer-entity authentication is required to protect against masquerade of UAs, MSs, or MTAs. Message security labeling and the security context service are used to support mandatory or rule-based access control policies (see Section 6.1).

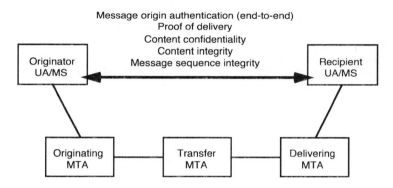

Figure 13-5: Basic End-to-End Services

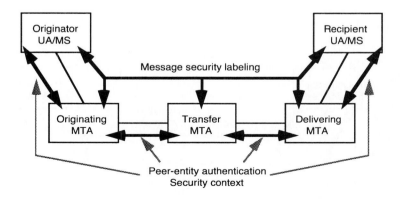

Figure 13-6: Message Path Services

MTS Corroborative Services

The following four services, which involve both the MTS and the originating MTS-user, provide corroboration to one or more components as to the authenticity of an MHS protocol message from another component.

- *Message origin authentication (MTS)*: Provides MTAs with assurance that a message came from the claimed originator. This is similar to the message origin authentication (end-to-end) service, except that it is used by different components and for different purposes. One important use is in conjunction with message security labeling, when MTAs along the route of a message need to check an attached label in making a routing or delivery decision. The message origin authentication (MTS) service is necessary to check the source and integrity of the attached label.
- *Probe origin authentication*: Provides MTAs with assurance that a probe came from the claimed originator. Recalling that a probe is a content-less message that is never delivered, this service closely relates to the message origin authentication (MTS) service.
- *Report origin authentication*: Provides an originator and/or transited MTAs with assurance that a (delivery or non-delivery) report comes from the claimed MTA.
- *Proof of submission*: Provides the originator of a message with assurance that the message has been accepted by the originating MTA for transfer to the requested recipient(s). This service is most useful when the originator UA or MS belongs to an organization separate from that of the originating MTA, e.g., a private UA connecting to a public MHS network provider.

The security relationships are illustrated in Figure 13-7.

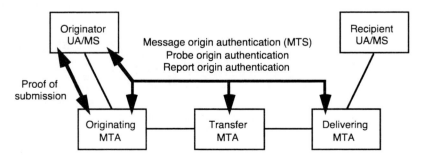

Figure 13-7: MTS Corroborative Services

Non-repudiation Services

The non-repudiation services are:

- *Non-repudiation of origin*: Provides a recipient with irrefutable proof of the origin of a message, its content, and its associated message security label.
- *Non-repudiation of delivery*: Provides the originator of a message with irrefutable proof that the message was delivered to an intended recipient without modification during transfer.
- *Non-repudiation of submission*: Provides the originator of a message with irrefutable proof that the message has been accepted by the originating MTA for transfer to the requested recipient(s).

Each of these services is a variant of another service described previously — message origin authentication (end-to-end), proof of delivery, and proof of submission, respectively. The distinction is that the non-repudiation services have stronger proof requirements. For example, the proof of submission service needs only to convince the originator that submission occurred successfully. The non-repudiation of submission service needs to provide the originator with evidence which can be used to convince a third party arbitrator that the submission occurred successfully, i.e., that the originating MTA assumed responsibility for the message.

Security Management Services

The MHS protocols provide support for three security management services:

- *Change credentials*: Enables one functional component to change the credentials (password or certified public key) regarding that component held by another component. It can be applied in either direction between a UA and an MTA (possibly via an intervening MS) or from a UA to an MS.[2]
- *Register*: Enables a UA to indicate to its closest MTA the set of security labels permissible for that UA. Such registration typically occurs in conjunction with the registration of other (non-security) information, such as supported content types.
- *MS-register*: Enables a UA to indicate to its associated MS the set of security labels permissible for that UA.

---

[2] This service would also be useful between a pair of adjacent MTAs, but no protocol support is provided in the standards.

Unsupported Services

The MHS security model identifies three further security services as potentially required, but provides no protocol support for these services:

- *Connection confidentiality* and *connection integrity*: Protection of all communications between a pair of communicating components.
- *Message flow confidentiality*: Protection against leakage of information through observing message flows.

The connection confidentiality and integrity services can be provided in lower layers, e.g., using the Transport Layer Security Protocol or Network Layer Security Protocol.

The MHS standards mention briefly how a limited form of message flow confidentiality can be provided through the use of a *double-enveloping technique*. This technique uses a specially defined content type[3] which conveys, as message contents, the full *envelope plus content* of another message. Through the use of content confidentiality at the outer level, the entire inner message, including its envelope information, can be confidentiality protected. This technique could be used to protect details of all messages between two points in the MTS, e.g., as messages traverse an MTS domain which is less trusted than the surrounding domains. While this is a viable concept, the standards do not expand upon details of its implementation.

Interactions Between Security Services and Other Services

Not all combinations of security services and other MHS optional services are practical. In particular, there can be problems when using security services in conjunction with conversions or with distribution lists. Provision of end-to-end confidentiality and integrity services depends upon the data representations transferred, hence it is not practical to have an intermediate system convert encoding formats. With distribution lists, the originator generally does not know the complete set of recipients, hence may be unable to maintain all necessary security relationships. The standards do not spell out the implications of all such interactions, but point out the possible need for security policies to specify restrictions upon such combinations of services.

---

[3] The *inner envelope* content type is defined in ISO/IEC 10021-4 (ITU-T X.411), and an object identifier is assigned to it in Annex A of that standard.

13.3 MHS Security Protocol Elements

Protocol support for the above security services is provided in the MHS protocols P1, P3, and P7. In this section, we identify the protocol elements involved. In subsequent sections, the security services are addressed in turn, and the specific use of these protocol elements is described.

The MHS protocols are constructed using the remote operations client-server model (see Section 3.2). The security protocol fields are either in arguments of operations invoked by the client or in results returned from the server. Several fields are in the protocol envelopes for messages, probes, and reports, respectively. (These envelopes are arguments of submission, transfer, and delivery operations.) There are other fields in the arguments of the bind (association establishment) and administration operations, and a few fields in operation results.

Figure 13-8 illustrates the protocol exchanges for successful message submission, transfer, delivery, and delivery-report for a message to a single recipient. For each operation, it is assumed that an application association has already been established between the pair of systems involved. (The diagram shows the message and report traversing only two MTAs, but it extends straightforwardly to the case of multiple MTAs.)

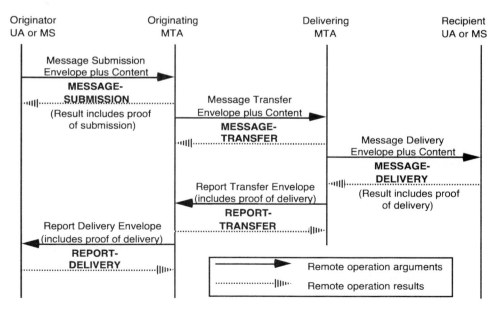

Figure 13-8: Successful Message Submission, Transfer, Delivery, and Report

Message Envelope Fields

There are three different types of message envelope — transfer envelope in P1, and submission and delivery envelopes in P3 and P7. Unless noted otherwise, the security fields can be assumed to be the same in all of them.

An envelope (see Figure 13-9) has per-message fields, which apply to all recipients, and per-recipient fields, which may take different values for each recipient.[4] The per-message fields related to security are:

- *Originator-certificate*: A certificate containing the originator's public key. This key may be used in verifying signatures in the message-origin-authentication check, message-token, or content-integrity-check field. Other supporting certificates, forming a certificate chain, may also be included. The certificate format is imported from the X.509 Directory standard (see Section 14.3).
- *Content-confidentiality-algorithm-identifier*: Identifier for the algorithm used to encrypt message content for the content confidentiality service.
- *Message-origin-authentication-check*: A field containing a digital signature algorithm identifier plus a digital signature appendix computed, using that algorithm, on the following parts of the message:
  (a)   the digital signature algorithm identifier;
  (b)   the message content as transmitted (i.e., the ciphertext form if content confidentiality is used);
  (c)   the content-identifier (an envelope field identifying the content type); and
  (d)   the message-security-label.
- *Message-security label*: A security label supplied by the originator for this message.
- *Proof-of-submission-request*: An indicator as to whether or not the proof of submission service is requested by the originator (this field exists only in the message submission envelope).

The per-recipient message envelope fields are:

- *Message-token*: A complex structure for conveying signed and optionally confidentiality-protected data from the originator to a recipient. It is described in detail below.

---

[4] This distinction is not made in a delivery envelope, because there is only one recipient at this stage.

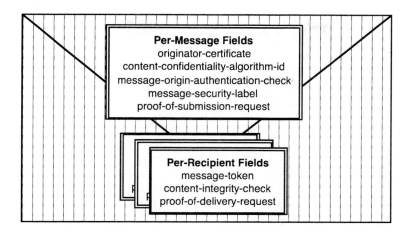

Figure 13-9: Message Envelope Security Fields

- *Content-integrity-check*: A field containing an integrity algorithm identifier plus an integrity check-value computed, using that algorithm, on the following parts of the message:

(a) the integrity algorithm identifier; and

(b) the message content, in unencrypted form.

- *Proof-of-delivery-request*: An indicator as to whether or not the proof of delivery service is requested by the originator.

Tokens

The message token is a structure designed for conveying various items of signed data, some of which may also be confidentiality-protected, from the originator to a recipient. In some parts of the MHS standards, the terms *Message Argument Integrity security element* and *Message Argument Confidentiality security element* are used when referring to the message token. The MHS standards recognize that there may be different ways of providing the requisite protection. In the 1988 and 1992 versions of the standard, one such way is specified, called the *asymmetric token*. Other alternative token structures may be added in later revisions.[5]

---

[5] The asymmetric token was originally intended for use specifically with asymmetric (public-key) cryptosystems. However, the 1992 MHS revision clarified that the same token structure could be used with symmetric sealing and encipherment algorithms, although some non-repudiation properties may then be lacking.

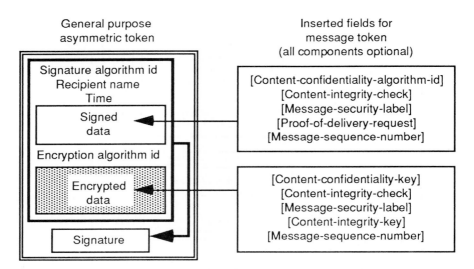

Figure 13-10: General-Purpose Asymmetric Token and Message Token

The asymmetric token has the following basic structure (see Figure 13-10). It comprises a sequence of data items, which is signed using an appendix-type of digital signature algorithm. The data items are:

- digital signature algorithm identifier;
- recipient name;
- time of token generation;
- a *signed-data* field (optional);
- encryption algorithm identifier (optional); and
- an *encrypted-data* field (optional).[6]

At this level, the token is designed to be general purpose, with the contents of the signed-data and encrypted-data fields being left unspecified.

The message token conveyed in message envelopes is considered a particular application of this general token. For the message token, the signed-data field contains a set of any of the following elements:

- content-confidentiality-algorithm-identifier, content-integrity-check, message-security-label, and proof-of-delivery-request fields as above; and

_____

6 As noted elsewhere in this book, the signing of encrypted data may lead to problems, and this represents a potential weakness in this token structure. [MIT1] expands upon this issue.

- a *message-sequence-number* that identifies the position of the message in a sequence of messages between the same originator and recipient.

The encrypted-data field contains any of:

- a *content-confidentiality-key* used in encrypting the message content (for use in conjunction with the symmetric algorithm identified by content-confidentiality-algorithm-identifier);
- a *content-integrity-key* used in generating the content-integrity-check (for use in conjunction with the symmetric algorithm identified by content-integrity-algorithm-identifier); and
- content-integrity-check, message-security-label, and message-sequence-number as defined above.

Note that various protocol options are introduced in the above. For certain protocol fields there are options as to whether the field is conveyed in (a) the basic envelope, (b) the signed-data part of the message token, or (c) the encrypted-data part of the message token. The fields content-confidentiality-algorithm-identifier, and proof-of-delivery-request can be conveyed in either (a) or (b). The field message-sequence-number can be conveyed in either (b) or (c). The fields content-integrity-check and message-security-label can be conveyed in any of (a), (b), or (c). In no case is it intended that multiple values of the field be conveyed in different ways. Resolution of these different options is addressed later in this chapter.

Probe Envelope Fields

The security fields in probe envelopes are a subset of those in message envelopes. Specifically, they are the *originator-certificate*, *message-security-label,* and *probe-origin-authentication-check* (equivalent to message-origin-authentication-check) fields.

Security Protocol Fields Associated with Reports

In most respects, reports can be considered as (content-less) envelopes sent back to an originator. There are two types of report envelope — transfer envelope (in P1) and delivery envelope (in P3 and P7). Security fields in both are the same. Furthermore, the generation of a *delivery* report is based on fields returned from the recipient UA or MS in the result of the P3 delivery operation.

The following security fields are common to the result of a message delivery and to the report envelopes:

- *Recipient-certificate*: A certificate containing the recipient's public key. This key may be used in verifying the signature in the proof-of-delivery field. Other supporting certificates, forming a certificate chain, may also be included.
- *Proof-of-delivery*: A field containing a digital signature algorithm identifier plus a digital signature appendix computed by the recipient, using that algorithm, on the following information pertaining to the delivered message:
  (a) the digital signature algorithm identifier;
  (b) the delivery time;
  (c) the actual recipient name;
  (d) originally intended recipient name;
  (e) the message content as delivered (i.e., the ciphertext form if content confidentiality is used);
  (f) the content-identifier (content type); and
  (g) the message-security-label.

The following security fields in report envelopes are generated by the report-generating MTA:

- *Message-security-label*: A security label associated with the message.
- *Reporting-MTA-certificate*: A certificate containing a public key for the MTA generating the report. This key may be used in verifying the signature in the report-origin-authentication-check field. Other supporting certificates, forming a certificate chain, may also be included.
- *Report-origin-authentication-check*: A field containing a digital signature algorithm identifier plus a digital signature appendix computed by the report-generating MTA, using that algorithm, on the following information pertaining to the referenced message:
  (a) the digital signature algorithm identifier;
  (b) the content-identifier (content type); and
  (c) the message-security-label;
  plus all relevant values of the following (per-recipient) arguments:
  (d) the actual recipient name;
  (e) originally intended recipient name;
  (f) the message delivery time (delivery report only);
  (g) the type of MTS user (delivery report only);
  (h) recipient-certificate (delivery report only);
  (i) proof-of-delivery (delivery report only);

    (j)   non-delivery-reason-code (non-delivery report only); and

    (k)   non-delivery-diagnostic-code (non-delivery report only).

Submission Result Fields

Two security-related fields may be conveyed in the result returned from an originating MTA to a submitting UA or MS as part of the *submission* operation:

- *Originating-MTA-certificate*: A certificate containing a public key for the originating MTA. This key may be used in verifying the signature in the proof-of-submission field. Other supporting certificates, forming a certificate chain, may also be included.
- *Proof-of-submission*: A field containing a digital signature algorithm identifier plus a digital signature appendix computed by the originating MTA, using that algorithm, on the following information pertaining to the submitted message:

    (a)   the digital signature algorithm identifier;

    (b)   all submission arguments (including envelope and contents);

    (c)   a message-submission identifier; and

    (d)   message-submission-time.

Bind Operation Fields

A *bind* is the remote operation dealing with association establishment between any pair of communicating MHS components. A bind operation maps onto the association-establishment procedure of ACSE, with the bind arguments being carried in A-ASSOCIATE request and the bind result being carried in A-ASSOCIATE response.

    The security-related fields in bind arguments are:

- *Initiator-credentials*: Either a *password* or an *initiator-bind-token* and, optionally, an *initiator-certificate*. The initiator-bind-token is another variant of the general-purpose token structure discussed above under *Tokens*. If the asymmetric token structure is used, the signed-data comprises a random-number, and the encrypted-data, which is optional, may convey key derivation information. This field is part of an authentication exchange (see Section 13.6).
- *Security-context*: One or more *security-labels* acceptable for messages conveyed on this association.

The security-related field in a bind result is:

- *Responder-credentials*: Same form as initiator-credentials above.

Administration Operation Fields

The MTS and MS access protocols (P3 and P7) have two remote operations, *register* and *change-credentials*, for conveying administration information between a UA and an MTA (if an MS is present in the path between UA and MTA, these protocol exchanges are relayed transparently). The register operation is from UA to MTA only. Its arguments include the following security-related field:

- *User-security-labels*: A set of security labels valid for the user.

The change-credentials operation may be invoked in either direction between UA and MTA. Its arguments are:

- *Old-credentials*: Either a password or public-key certificate of the requestor.
- *New-credentials*: Same form as old-credentials.

The MS access protocol (P7) also has the register-MS remote operation for conveying administration information from a UA to an MS. Its arguments include the following security-related fields:

- *Old-credentials* and *new-credentials*: Of similar form, and used for similar purpose as in the above change-credentials operation.
- *User-security-labels*: Of similar form, and used for similar purpose as in the above register operation.

13.4 Provision of the MHS Basic End-to-End Security Services

Message Origin Authentication (End-to-End) and Content Integrity

There are two approaches to providing proof of message origin and content integrity to a message recipient. The truly end-to-end approach is described here. An alternative approach, associated with the message origin authentication (MTS) service, is described in Section 13.5.

Message origin authentication (end-to-end) and content integrity employ the content-integrity-check message envelope field. Being a per-recipient field, this permits distinct security relationships to be supported between the originator and individual recipients. Content confidentiality can be provided simultaneously if required.

For each recipient requiring these services, an appendix-based sealing or signing algorithm is selected and a sealing/signing key identified (e.g., a pre-established shared symmetric key, the originator's private key, or a new randoml generated symmetric key which will accompany the message in the message token). The value for the content-integrity-check field is then determined by applying the algorithm to a concatenation of the algorithm identifier and the (unencrypted) message content. The content-integrity-check is then conveyed in either: (a) an unprotected per-recipient field, (b) the signed-data part of the message token, or (c) the encrypted-data part of the message token. Option (a) may be adequate if the key used establishes authentication, if security labels are not used, and if non-repudiation is not required. Otherwise, option (b) or (c) is necessary — these provide for binding a security label with the content-integrity-check and for using a separate key (the message token signature key) for establishing authentication. The encrypted option [option (c)] is recommended if content confidentiality is also required. If a public-key cryptosystem is used, either to generate the content-integrity-check or to sign the message token, the originator may also include a public-key certificate in the message envelope to assist the recipient in signature verification.

A message recipient using these services verifies the message token signature (if applicable) and verifies the content-integrity-check vis-à-vis the actual message content received. If all checks are correct, then the recipient can have confidence that the message is from the claimed originator and was not modified en route.

Proof of Delivery

Proof of delivery is requested by the originator, for one or more recipients, by setting the proof-of-delivery-request indicator in the message envelope. A recipient UA or MS receiving such a request computes a proof-of-delivery value, and returns it to the delivering MTA in the results of the delivery operation. This value is relayed by the MTS back to the originator in a delivery report.

The proof-of-delivery value is computed as follows. A sealing or signing algorithm is selected and a sealing/signing key identified (e.g., a pre-established shared symmetric key or the recipient's private key). The value for the proof-of-delivery field is then determined by applying the algorithm to a concatenation of the requisite set of items (see *Security Protocol Fields Associated with Reports* in Section 13.3).

One item included in the computation is the full message content. Regardless of whether the content is encrypted or not, the proof-of-delivery computation uses the form of the contents as delivered (i.e., possibly an encrypted form). For non-repudiation purposes, it would be better to always use the unencrypted form. However, this may not be possible, because the proof-of-delivery must be calculated by the MTS-user that takes delivery from the MTS. This MTS-user may be an MS, whereas the confidentiality key may be known only by the UA (which may not be on-line at the time). The ramifications of this are discussed further later.

If a public-key cryptosystem is used to generate the proof-of-delivery value, the recipient MTS-user may include a public-key certificate along with that value to assist the originator in signature verification.

The message originator obtains proof of delivery on receipt of a delivery report from the MTS. The originator UA verifies the proof-of-delivery value from this report in accordance with the procedures of the identified algorithm. In this verification, the originator UA will use the content of the message originally sent. Therefore, if the check is correct, then the originator can have confidence that the correct recipient's MTS-user system has received the submitted message, and that this message was not modified en route.

This proof of delivery service has some limitations which should be noted. First, if no delivery report is received by the originator, then the originator has no certainty as to what happened to the message — he has neither proof of delivery nor proof of non-delivery. Second, proof of delivery means no more than that the message was delivered to an MTS-user component. That component might be an MS; there is no proof that the message reached a UA, and certainly no proof that the *real user* has seen the message.

Content Confidentiality

To provide content confidentiality, the originator encrypts the message content using a selected encryption algorithm and an appropriate key. The encryption algorithm is indicated to recipients via the content-confidentiality-algorithm-identifier field in the message envelope. In the special case of a single-recipient message, the key could be a pre-established shared symmetric key or the recipient's public key. However, in the general multi-recipient case, the only practical option is a new randomly generated symmetric key, which accompanies the message in the encrypted-data part of the message token for every recipient. The secrecy of this key depends upon a set of distinct security relationships between the originator and each recipient. A key used for encryption of a token encrypted-data field can be either a pre-established shared symmetric key or the recipient's public key.

Message Sequence Integrity

Message sequence integrity depends upon an originator-recipient pair maintaining a system of sequence numbers for messages between them. The

MHS standards provide no support for maintaining this system; all they provide is the means for conveying such a sequence number along with each message for each recipient. The sequence number is conveyed in the message token, in which it can be bound to the content-integrity-check (and thence the message content). If required, the message-sequence-number can be confidentiality-protected in the encrypted-data field of the token.

13.5 Provision of Other MHS Security Services

This section describes how the message path services, MTS corroborative services, non-repudiation services, and security management services are provided.

Peer-Entity Authentication

Peer-entity authentication is provided at the time of establishing an application-association between two MHS functional components. Mutual authentication is achieved using a two-way authentication exchange conveyed in the initiator-credentials and responder-credentials fields of the bind argument and result, respectively. The authentication exchange can be either an exchange of simple passwords or the X.509 two-way cryptographic-based exchange described in Section 5.6. Subject to the strengths and vulnerabilities of these authentication mechanisms (as discussed in Chapter 5), the exchange will give each component a measure of confidence as to the true identity of the system with which it is communicating.

Message Security Labeling

Message security labeling supports certain access control policies (such as multi-level or compartment-based policies) which are shared by originators and recipients. Certain transit systems, i.e., routing MTAs and delivering MTAs, may also need to be parties to the same policy. An originating UA attaches a security label to a submitted message; dependent upon local security policy, this might be at the originator's discretion or, more likely, would be performed automatically by the originator's environment.

The message-security-label is conveyed in either: (a) a per-message envelope field, (b) the signed-data part of the message token, or (c) the encrypted-data part of the message token. Option (a) is used in conjunction with the message-origin-authentication-check field, which provides a digital signature binding the message-security-label to the message content and other information, and which can be verified by any MHS component using the certified public-key of the originator [see later subsection on *Message Origin*

Authentication (MTS)]. Options (b) and (c) are useful only in the restricted case of labels being significant on an end-to-end basis and not being required by MTAs en route. Option (c) would be chosen over option (b) if confidentiality of labels were considered a requirement.

With option (a), MTAs transferring or delivering a message should examine the label on every message and decide if the next system to which the message should logically be forwarded is authorized for messages with that label. This decision takes into account a security context, which is a set of labels that two connected systems recognize as being legitimate for messages passing between them.

The format for MHS security labels is described in Section 13.6.

Security Context

The security context service provides the means for the MHS component initiating an application-association with another component to indicate the set of security labels permitted on messages passing between those components. The set of applicable labels is conveyed in the security-context field of the bind argument.

This security service is of limited utility. In many environments using label-based access control, the set of applicable security labels is likely to be managed through procedures subject to much stronger controls.

Message Origin Authentication (MTS)

The message origin authentication (MTS) service is provided using the message-origin-authentication-check per-message field in the message envelope. The originator uses an appendix-based digital signature algorithm and his private key to compute a digital signature on the following data items: the digital signature algorithm identifier, the message content as transmitted, the content-identifier (which identifies content type), and the message-security-label (if present as a per-message field). Note that, if the message content is encrypted as a result of the content confidentiality service, the encrypted form of the content is used in computing the signature. The signature appendix is conveyed in the message-origin-authentication-check field. The originator's public-key certificate may be included in the envelope to assist other components in signature verification.

MTAs along the message route, and recipient MTS-users, may verify the signature as required. This enables them to check the integrity of and binding between the protected data items and to obtain corroboration that the data items are from the claimed originator.

Probe Origin Authentication

The probe origin authentication service is provided in a way similar to the message origin authentication (MTS) service, but using the probe-origin-authentication-check field in place of the message-origin-authentication-check field.

Report Origin Authentication

The report origin authentication service is provided using the report-origin-authentication-check field in the report envelope. The report-generating MTA uses an appendix-based digital signature algorithm and its private key to compute a digital signature on a concatenation of the requisite set of items (see *Security Protocol Fields Associated with Reports* in Section 13.3). The signature appendix is conveyed in the report-origin-authentication-check field. The report-generating MTA's public-key certificate may be included in the report to assist other components in signature verification.

MTAs along the report route, and the originator MTS-user, may verify the signature as required. This enables them to check the integrity of and the binding between the protected data items and to obtain corroboration that the data items are from the claimed MTA.

Proof of Submission

Proof of submission is requested by the originator by setting the proof-of-submission-request indicator in the message submission envelope. An originating MTA receiving such a request computes a proof-of-submission value, and returns it to the originator UA or MS in the results of the submission operation.

The proof-of-submission value is computed as follows. A sealing or signing algorithm is selected and a sealing/signing key identified (e.g., a pre-established shared symmetric key, a key established during association establishment, or the originating MTA's private key). The value for the proof-of-submission field is then determined by applying the algorithm to a concatenation of the requisite set of items (see *Submission Result Fields* in Section 13.3).

If a public-key cryptosystem is used to generate the proof-of-submission value, the originating MTA may include a public-key certificate along with that value to assist the originator in signature verification.

The message originator obtains proof of submission on receipt of the submission result. The originator verifies the proof-of-submission value in accordance with the procedures of the identified algorithm. In this verification, the originator will use the content of the message sent. Therefore, if the check is correct, the originator can have confidence that the originating MTA has assumed responsibility for the submitted message, and that this message was not modified in transmission to that MTA.

Non-repudiation Services

There are three non-repudiation services: non-repudiation of origin, non-repudiation of delivery, and non-repudiation of submission. There are no MHS protocol elements specifically to support these services. The MHS standards take the view that these services can be provided in either of two ways:

(a) through the provision of the message origin authentication, proof of delivery, and proof of submission services, respectively, under conditions such that the signatures used can be considered irrefutable, or

(b) through the involvement of a notary (trusted third party) to whom all protocol exchanges are copied.

The standards do not expand upon how option (b) might be pursued.

The main requirement in the first option is that the signing algorithm be a public-key-based digital signature algorithm. A sealing process, which may be adequate for a "proof" service, is not adequate for a non-repudiation service, for the reasons given in Chapters 4 and 8.

Another issue arises when content confidentiality is to be applied to the same message. With message origin authentication (MTS) and proof of delivery, the signature is calculated on the encrypted message content. This is not generally considered acceptable for a non-repudiation service, as all that can be inferred later is that the signer was in possession of the ciphertext known to the verifier. It cannot be inferred that both parties were extracting the same meaning from that ciphertext. With message origin authentication (end-to-end), this problem does not arise, as the signature is computed on the plaintext content.

Encryption is not a problem with non-repudiation of submission, because there is no implication that the originating MTA can interpret the message. This service simply provides irrefutable proof that the message was accepted for forwarding by the originating MTA.

Security Management Services

The remote operations involved in providing the security management services are illustrated in Figure 13-11.

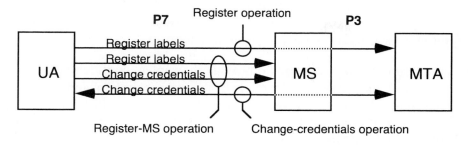

Figure 13-11: Provision of the Security Management Services

Provision of the change credentials service depends upon whether it is being invoked between a UA and MTA or between a UA and MS. Between UA and MTA it employs the change-credentials remote operation in the P3 or P7 protocol. This operation may be invoked by either the UA or MTA; if there is an MS in the path, it relays the protocol exchanges transparently. Two fields must be supplied as arguments — old-credentials and new-credentials. The value in each is either a password (if passwords are used for peer-entity authentication) or a public-key certificate plus supporting certificates to form a certificate chain (if the X.509 cryptographic-based exchange is used for peer-entity authentication). The purpose of supplying old-credentials is to provide some corroboration as to the genuineness of the request. It is intended primarily for the password case and is of little value in the public-key certificate case.

Change credentials can also be issued from a UA to an MS. This case employs the old-credentials and new-credentials arguments of the register-MS remote operation in the P7 protocol. The fields are used in the same way as the UA-MTA case described above.

The Register and MS-Register services allow a UA to advise an MTA and MS, respectively, of the set of security labels permissible for that UA. The UA-MTS case is provided using the user-security-labels argument of the register remote operation in the P3 or P7 protocol (if there is an MS in the path, it relays this field transparently). The UA-MS case is provided using the user-security-labels argument of the register-MS remote operation in the P7 protocol.

13.6 Security Techniques Used by MHS

For the benefit of the reader more interested in security techniques than in protocol details, this section presents the security technique perspective on MHS.

Encryption

Encryption is used directly for the following purposes:

(a) encrypting message content, to provide the content confidentiality service;

(b) encrypting the encrypted-data field of the message token; and

(c) encrypting the encrypted-data field of the bind token, if this field is to be used to convey keys intended for other purposes (such as connection confidentiality or integrity).

In no case is a particular encryption algorithm stipulated by the standard. Each encrypted field is (optionally) accompanied by an ASN.1 object identifier indicating the algorithm used, plus any necessary parameters for that algorithm.

For encrypting message content, in the general multiple-recipient case, a symmetric encryption algorithm is the most logical choice. A new randomly generated key is used, and this key is conveyed to each recipient in the encrypted-data field of the message token.

For encrypting the encrypted-data field of the message token or bind token, either a symmetric algorithm (using a pre-established shared key) or a public-key algorithm (using the decrypting party's public key) may be used. Key management support is provided for the public-key option by way of public-key certificates conveyed with the message. For the symmetric option, an additional key management protocol is needed.

Seals and Signatures

Seals or signatures are used in generating:

(a) content-integrity-check;

(b) message token;

(c) proof-of-delivery;

(d) proof-of-submission; and

(e) bind token.

Signatures are always used in generating:

(f) message-origin-authentication-check;

(g) probe-origin-authentication-check; and

(h) report-origin-authentication-check.

In no case is a particular sealing or signing algorithm stipulated by the standard. Each sealed/signed field is (optionally) accompanied by an ASN.1 object identifier indicating the algorithm used, plus any necessary parameters for that algorithm.

The choice between sealing and signing was explored in [FOR1]. In general, for items (a) through (e), either a sealing algorithm or a signing algorithm (using the sender's private key) may be used. Key management support is provided for the signing option by way of public-key certificates conveyed with the message. For content-integrity-check using a sealing algorithm, a new randomly generated key may be used, and this key conveyed in the encrypted-data field of the message token. Otherwise, with the sealing option, a pre-established shared key must be used and an additional key management protocol is needed.

The sealing/signing choice is not available when non-repudiation is to be provided using the field concerned. For non-repudiation of origin using content-integrity-check, an irrefutable signature must be used either for generating the content-integrity-check or for the message token which conveys the content-integrity-check. For non-repudiation of delivery and non-repudiation of submission, an irrefutable signature must be used for generating proof-of-delivery or proof-of-submission respectively.

There are sufficient cases demanding the use of digital signatures that public-key cryptography is generally considered an *essential* MHS security ingredient.

Authentication Exchanges

Mutual entity authentication between any pair of communicating MHS systems employs a two-way authentication exchange. This authentication exchange can be either an exchange of simple passwords or the X.509 two-way cryptographic-based exchange described in Section 5.6.

Security Labels

Provision is made for attaching a security label to any message, probe, or report, making it a *labeled item*. The term *security context* is used to denote the set of security labels recognized as legitimate for labeled items moving between a given pair of systems. A system must check a labeled item's label against the applicable security context before passing that item to another system.

A fixed security label format is defined in the MHS standards, but the associated semantics are very loosely defined. The format comprises the following set of *security-attributes*:

- *Security-policy-identifier*: An ASN.1 object identifier which identifies a security policy and, consequently, the precise semantics applying to other security-attributes.
- *Security-classification*: An integer value intended to indicate a level within a hierarchical classification scheme; values are defined for unmarked, unclassified, restricted, confidential, secret, and top-secret.
- *Privacy-mark*: A printable string (the standard suggests its use is for such purposes as indicating "IN CONFIDENCE," but this is entirely security-policy-dependent).
- *Security-categories*: This field may convey any ASN.1 type along with an identifier which implies that type and its interpretation (the standard suggests its use is for such purposes as indicating classification caveats, but this is entirely security-policy-dependent).

13.7 MHS Security Profiles

The MHS standards leave a wide range of options open to the implementor. Interworking implementations can be achieved only if agreement is reached outside the international standardization process on selection of these options. Security-related options include:

- selection of the security services (see Section 13.2) to be provided;
- choice of either content-integrity-check or message-origin-authentication-check for message origin authentication and content integrity;
- choice of either simple (password) or strong (cryptographic) peer-entity authentication;
- choice of conveying various per-recipient fields in either of three ways (see discussion under *Tokens* in Section 13.3);
- nomination of procedures for managing sequence numbers for message sequence integrity purposes;
- nomination of key management procedures for encryption, sealing, and/or signature techniques;
- algorithm selection for encryption, sealing, and/or digital signature; and
- establishment of security policy identifiers and associated security label conventions.

The North American OIW and European EWOS workshops agreed on a set of MHS security profiles which reduce the option combinations significantly [NIS1]. There are six basic profiles. Each profile makes the implementation of certain security services mandatory (in some cases with restrictions), while implementation of other security services is optional. Furthermore, some of the profiles require that certain security services *always be used*. The OIW/EWOS profiles can be conveniently expressed in terms of the service groupings used in Section 13.2. The individual profiles and mandatory services for each are:

- *Class S0*: The set of basic end-to-end services, with the exception of content confidentiality.
- *Class S0A*: Same as class S0, with content confidentiality added.
- *Class S1*: Class S0 services, plus the sets of message path services and security management services. Furthermore, in this class, message origin authentication (end-to-end) and the message path services must always be used.
- *Class S1A*: Same as class S1, with content confidentiality added.
- *Class S2*: Class S1 services, plus the sets of MTS collaborative services and non-repudiation services. Furthermore, in this class, message/ probe/report origin authentication must always be used.
- *Class S2A*: Same as class S2, with content confidentiality added.

The rationale behind these profile specifications is as follows. First, there are three basic *levels* of profile, with two variants in each level resulting from inclusion/exclusion of content confidentiality. The primary reason for this is the exportability problem that may arise with products which implement content confidentiality. For certain environments, profiles which mandate inclusion of content confidentiality may be unacceptable, while a range of profiles with different authentication/integrity/non-repudiation capabilities is required (S0, S1, S2). In other environments, content confidentiality is a firm requirement, while the same authentication/integrity/non-repudiation alternatives are also required (S0A, S1A, S2A).

The S0/S0A level was identified because it represents the best protection that can be achieved by implementing security features only in MTS-user equipment. The higher levels all require features in MTAs and are generally much more expensive to implement and deploy.

The S1/S1A level of functionality is, most importantly, the lowest level which supports security labels. Security labels are the only means to associate, with a message, an indication of its security handling requirements. This is done using the security-policy-identifier field of the label. The OIW/EWOS agreements include security-policy-identifier assignments for S1, S1A, S2, and S2A respectively. These can be used to indicate security requirements of a message, in the absence of organization-defined security policy identifiers (which are not precluded by the profiles). The strong peer-entity authentication in S1/S1A is a natural service to provide in conjunction with labels. The decision to include the security management services at this level is arbitrary.

The S2/S2A level is the highest level and includes all service options. This is the only level requiring public-key signatures.

Further details of the six profiles are given in Table 13-2. This table refers to component-to-component interfaces as indicated in Figure 13-12.

Profile	Mandatory Security Services	Interfaces (Refer to Fig. 13-12.)
Class S0	Message Origin Authentication (end-to-end)[1]	1
	Proof of Delivery	1, 8
	Content Integrity	1
Class S0A	*Class S0 plus ...*	
	Content Confidentiality	1
Class S1	*Class S0 plus ...*	
	Message Origin Authentication (end-to-end)[1,2]	1
	Content Integrity[2]	1
	Peer-Entity Authentication[2,3]	2, 3, 4, 5, 6, 7, 9
	Security Context[2]	2, 3, 4, 5, 6, 7, 9
	Message Security Labeling[2]	1, 2, 3, 4, 5, 6, 7, 8, 9
	Change Credentials	2, 4, 5, 7
	Register	2, 4
	MS-Register	2
Class S1A	*Class S1 plus ...*	
	Content Confidentiality	1
Class S2	*Class S1 plus ...*	
	Message Origin Authentication (MTS)[2,4]	1, 2, 4
	Probe Origin Authentication[2]	2, 4
	Report Origin Authentication[2]	5, 6, 7
	Proof of Submission	8
	Non-repudiation of Origin[5]	1, 4
	Non-repudiation of Submission	7
	Non-repudiation of Delivery[5]	1, 8
Class S2A	*Class S2 plus ...*	
	Content Confidentiality	1

Notes:

1. May be provided using content-integrity-check.
2. Service must always be used.
3. Strong (cryptographic-based) authentication exchange required.
4. Must use message origin authentication check.
5. In general, non-repudiation services must use an irrefutable signature.

Table 13-2: Basic MHS Security Profiles

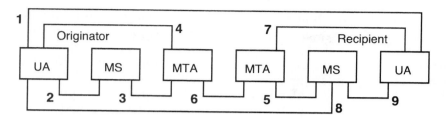

Figure 13-12: Interface Indicators for Profile Specifications

13.8 EDI Security

Electronic business data interchange (EDI) refers to the electronic exchange of business transactions such as purchase orders, invoices, and payment advices within large communities of corporate and/or government entities [SOK1]. EDI can employ various communications technologies, including dedicated links, dial-up links, packet-switching, and frame relay services. MHS is one suitable communications technology for EDI and has the advantage of being able to offer very comprehensive security provisions.

In 1990, ITU-T Recommendations F.435 and X.435 were published, extending the MHS standards to support the transfer of EDI interchanges over the MHS backbone. These extensions did not change the basic MHS protocols (P1, P3, and P7) but defined a new content type, known as P_{edi} or P35, for use in conjunction with those protocols.[7]

As an application, EDI is considered to have more stringent security requirements than interpersonal messaging. Protection against fraudulent or accidental modification of business transactions, and against repudiation, are *essential* to ensure that an EDI system has at least as strong safeguards as the paper-based system it replaces. Security is therefore a major element in the EDI extensions to MHS.

The EDI Content Type

The EDI content type defines two types of messages — *EDI messages* (EDIMs) and *EDI notifications* (EDINs). These are sent between *EDI*

---

[7] The content types for interpersonal messaging (P2 and P22) are not discussed in this book because they have virtually no security features. Up to the 1992 revision, the only security "feature" in the interpersonal messaging content types is an *Encrypted* body part type. This was intended to carry enciphered data, but no details are provided as to how algorithms, keys, and parameters might be communicated. There is therefore no internationally agreed way to use this "feature" in practice.

messaging users, which are generally computer-based EDI applications (not people, as in inter-personal messaging). An EDI message conveys an EDI interchange, encoded in any recognized EDI format such as ISO 9735 (EDIFACT), ANSI X12 or UNTDI (United Nations Trade Data Interchange) formats. This EDI interchange is always in the first (or primary) body part of the EDI message. There may be additional body parts conveying information associated with the EDI interchange, such as explanatory text, drawings, or voice annotations.

An EDI notification is a follow-up message sent by a recipient UA or MS back to the UA that originated an EDI message. EDI notifications are only sent if requested by the originating UA. Their significance depends upon the concept of *EDIM responsibility* — acceptance of EDIM responsibility means that the EDI message has been successfully passed by a recipient UA to its EDI messaging user. There are three types of EDI notification:

- *Positive notification* (PN): A UA has accepted EDIM responsibility.
- *Negative notification* (NN): A UA has refused to accept EDIM reponsibility because it cannot successfully pass the EDI message to its EDI messaging user and cannot successfully forward the EDI message elsewhere.
- *Forwarding notification* (FN): On the basis of (possibly automatic) EDI messaging user instructions, EDIM responsibility has not been accepted, but the EDI message has been forwarded to another recipient. The forwarding message comprises the complete original EDI message and, optionally, its original envelope, packed into a *forwarded EDIM* body part.[8]

Forwarding and the EDIM responsibility concept are important in the EDI environment, because multiple accountable organizations may be involved in handling a message. These may include commercial EDI service providers, as well as end-user organizations and regular MHS service providers. EDI service providers typically act as concentrating points for end-user messages, while providing additional optional services such as batching, logging, and format conversion. The EDIM responsibility concept can support demarcations between the various participants for legal purposes. Adequate security provisions are clearly needed in support of this concept.

---

[8] There is also a different type of forwarding in which some body parts may be removed before forwarding the rest of the message to a different recipient. However, in this case, EDIM responsibility is accepted at the point the body parts were removed. In all security respects, the forwarded message in this case is an entirely new message.

Security Services

The MHS security services described in Section 13.2 can be used to protect EDI messages. However, several additional security services may be needed for EDI. The EDI MHS standards specify how some of these services can be provided, using a combination of the protocol elements in Section 13.3, some security fields in the EDI content type, and certain procedures. These services, all of which are end-to-end services, are:

- *Proof of EDI notification*: Provides the recipient of an EDI notification (i.e., the originator of an EDI message) with proof of the origin of that EDI notification.
- *Non-repudiation of EDI notification*: A stronger version of proof of EDI notification in which the proof must be irrefutable; this proof can protect against any attempt by the originator of an EDI notification to falsely deny sending it.
- *Proof of content received*: Provides the originator of an EDI message with proof that the message content received by a recipient was the same as the message content sent by the originator.
- *Non-repudiation of content received*: A stronger version of proof of content received in which the proof must be irrefutable; this proof can protect against any attempt by the recipient to falsely deny receiving the content.
- *Non-repudiation of content originated*: Provides the recipient of an EDI message with irrefutable proof that the message content received was the same as the message content sent by the originator; this proof can protect against any attempt by the originator to falsely deny sending that content.

In addition to these end-to-end services, the EDI environment may require further services which impact MTS and MS behavior. The 1990 EDI MHS standards indicate that provision of these services is a local issue.[9] These services are:

- *Proof of retrieval*: Provides an MS administrator with proof that a particular message has been retrieved from the MS by the UA.
- *Non-repudiation of retrieval*: A stronger version of proof of retrieval in which the proof must be irrefutable.
- *Proof of transfer*: Provides an MTA or management domain with proof that a message has been transferred to another MTA within another management domain.

---

[9] These services are the subject of post-1992 extensions to the MHS protocols.

- *Non-repudiation of transfer*: A stronger version of proof of transfer in which the proof must be irrefutable.

Security Fields in EDI Messages and Notifications

Both EDI messages and EDI notifications have security-related fields within the transferred content. In an EDI message they are in the heading part of the content — significant fields are the *EDI Notification Requests Field* (a per-recipient field) and the *EDI Application Security Elements Field* (a per-message field). The EDI Notification Requests Field is used by the originator to indicate requirements for follow-up EDI notifications from a recipient. This field has subfields as follows:

- *EDI-notification-requests*: Three Boolean elements indicating which of the following types of EDI notification are requested (if applicable): positive notification, negative notification, forwarding notification.
- *EDI-notification-security*: Two Boolean elements indicating requirements for (a) proof of EDI notification, and (b) non-repudiation of EDI notification, respectively, on any EDI notification generated by that recipient following-up this EDI message.
- *EDI-reception-security*: Two Boolean elements indicating requirements for (a) proof of content received, and (b) non-repudiation of content received, respectively. If either element is set, the EDI message recipient will need to follow special procedures in generating any EDI notification following-up this EDI message.

The EDI Application Security Elements Field is for use by EDI applications in exchanging security information of end-to-end significance.[10]   This field is not used in providing the standard security services described above. It has optional subfields as follows:

- *EDI-application-security-element*: A bit string.
- *EDI-encrypted-primary-body-part*: A Boolean element.
- *EDI-application-security-extensions*: Provision for adding further subfields in later revisions of the standard.

It is left to profile writers or specific user communities to adopt agreements on exactly how these subfields are used.

---

[10] This usage of the term "end-to-end" implies security relationships which typically extend beyond the MHS environment, e.g., security relationships between cooperating application software processes in business information processing systems.

In an EDI notification, security-related information is conveyed in a Security Elements field, which has optional subfields as follows:

- *Original-content*: A copy of the full content of the EDI message which this EDI notification is following-up.
- *Original-content-integrity-check*: A copy of the content-integrity-check field from the message delivery envelope of the EDI message which this EDI notification is following-up.
- *EDI Application Security Elements*: Same as the EDI Application Security Elements Field field in an EDI message.
- *security-extensions*: Provision for adding further subfields in later revisions of the standard.

Provision of the Additional End-to-End Services

Provision of the proof or non-repudiation of EDI notification service involves two steps:

(a) The originator indicates to a recipient its requirements for either service, by setting the applicable element in the EDI-notification-security field in an EDI message.

(b) The recipient of an EDI message with either EDI-notification-security element set includes either a content-integrity-check or message-origin-authentication-check when submitting any follow-up EDI notification (the decision as to which envelope field to use depends on security policy). If the non-repudiation case, an irrefutable signature must be used.

Similarly, provision of the proof or non-repudiation of content received service involves two steps:

(a) The originator indicates to a recipient its requirements for either service by setting the applicable element in the EDI-reception-security field in an EDI message.

(b) The recipient of an EDI message with either EDI-reception-security element set generates an appropriate value (see below) for the Security Elements field in any follow-up EDI notification. Furthermore, a content-integrity-check or message-origin-authentication-check must be included when submitting that EDI notification (the decision as to which envelope field to use depends on security policy). In the non-repudiation case, an irrefutable signature must be used.

The value for the Security Elements field is determined as follows. If the content-integrity-check argument was present in the delivery envelope of the

EDI message, it is checked then copied into the original-content-integrity-check field of the EDI notification. Otherwise, the entire content of the EDI message is copied into the original-content field of the EDI notification.

The non-repudiation of content originated service is provided by the originator including either a content-integrity-check or message-origin-authentication-check when submitting an EDI message. (The decision as to which envelope field to use depends on security policy.) An irrefutable signature must be used.

Security Within an EDI Interchange — ANSI X12

The security features described above apply to a complete *EDI interchange*. This is a unit of data, the format of which is specified in another (e.g., ANSI X12 or EDIFACT) standard. These interchange formats are complex structures which may support their own security features internally.

The ANSI X12 interchange format standards have led the way in incorporating security features. An ANSI X12 interchange is a doubly nested structure, built out of a sequence of data *segments*, as shown in Figure 13-13. An interchange comprises one or more *functional groups*, each representing a collection of related business forms. A functional group comprises one or more *transaction sets*, each representing one business form.

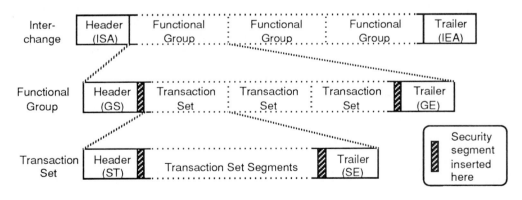

Figure 13-13: ANSI X12 Interchange Structure

Standard ANSI X12.58 specifies how security can be provided at either or both of the functional group and transaction set granularities. The security services provided are data origin authentication, confidentiality, and/or integrity. The supporting security techniques are (DES-based) encryption and/or message authentication code (MAC), imported from ANSI X9.9 and

X9.23. ANSI X12.58 defines security segments to be inserted in functional groups and/or transaction sets, as indicated in Figure 13-13. These segments convey such data as key identifiers, initialization vectors, and message authentication codes (MACs). ANSI X12.58 is also being extended to include *assurance segments*, which contain such elements as time-stamps and digital signatures.

The companion standard ANSI X12.42 defines a Cryptographic Service Message transaction set, designed to support transfer of keys between EDI systems. It is based on ANSI X9.17. It effectively provides a standard means for conveying X9.17 cryptographic service messages in ANSI X12 syntax.

13.9 Internet Privacy Enhanced Mail

Background

Electronic mail is a major application in the Internet environment, having evolved steadily since the Internet's beginnings. The Internet mail protocols are different to the MHS protocols, but share the same underlying architectural model (essentially as shown in Figure 13-1).

The major Internet mail protocol specifications are:

- *Simple Mail Transfer Protocol* (SMTP): This protocol defines the procedures for relaying files between message transfer agents, and the corresponding message envelope and error report formats. SMTP is functionally comparable to the MHS P1 protocol. It is defined in RFC 821 [POS1].
- *Standard for the Format of ARPA Internet Text Messages* (RFC 822): This standard [CRO1] specifies the message format, especially the set of header fields which precede the message body. RFC 822 is functionally comparable to the MHS interpersonal messaging content type specification.
- *Multipurpose Internet Mail Extensions* (MIME): A specification for structuring a message body, which includes support for multi-media messages. MIME is defined in RFC 1341 [BOR1].

A specification for interworking between the MHS and Internet mail environments has also been developed [KIL1], opening the way towards a ubiquitous global electronic mail environment in which both MHS and Internet may take their places.

For full tutorial coverage of the Internet mail protocols, including SMTP, RFC 822, and MIME, see [ROS1].

Historically, security has not been an important issue with Internet electronic mail. This is fully understandable, given the overall Internet philosphy of building up a vast electronically interconnected community in which information and ideas are exchanged freely. However, the more recent decision to make Internet a sound base for commercial applications has raised the priority of security on the Internet agenda. Privacy Enhanced Mail (PEM) is the result.

Work on PEM commenced in the late 1980s and led to the publication in 1993 of a four-part series of proposed draft Internet standards [BAL1, KAL1, KEN1, LIN1].

PEM is not compatible with MHS secure messaging, in that the two sets of end-to-end security features cannot interwork. However, PEM provides functions equivalent to a subset of the MHS secure messaging functions. Furthermore, it employs similar security techniques and a compatible public-key certification infrastructure.

Security Services

PEM was designed to be entirely an end-to-end facility, capable of being implemented through upgrading of those UAs which require the added security functionality. PEM also needed to be suitable for use through existing mail gateways (not designed with PEM in mind). Hence, PEM security services relate primarily to the basic end-to-end security services for MHS, as described in Section 13.2.

The security services that can be provided are:

- *Message origin authentication*: Provides a recipient with assurance that a message came from the claimed originator.
- *Content confidentiality*: Protects message contents against disclosure between originator and recipient.
- *Content integrity*: Protects message contents against modification between originator and recipient.
- *Non-repudiation of origin*: Provides a recipient with irrefutable proof of the origin of a message and its content.

The services provided for a given message depend upon the protected message type chosen by the originator. The three types of protected message available are:

- *ENCRYPTED*: Provides the services of message origin authentication, content confidentiality, and content integrity; non-repudiation of origin may also be provided if public-key based authentication is used. Both originator and recipient UAs must be PEM-capable.

- *MIC-ONLY*[11]: Provides the same security services as ENCRYPTED, except that content confidentiality is not provided. Both originator and recipient UAs must be PEM-capable.
- *MIC-CLEAR*: Provides the same security services as MIC-ONLY. This message type differs from MIC-ONLY in that this message type conveys a message in such a way that non-PEM-capable UAs are able to read the message contents (although only PEM-capable UAs can verify the message origin and integrity).

Security Techniques

PEM recognizes two alternative approaches to network-wide authentication and key management — a symmetric alternative and a public-key alternative. The symmetric alternative assumes that every communicating originator-recipient pair shares a symmetric key, e.g., through manual distribution or through an ANSI X9.17 infrastructure. The public-key alternative assumes the existence of a public-key certification infrastructure.

When content confidentiality is provided, a symmetric cryptosystem is used to encrypt message contents.[12] A random key, called a data encrypting key (DEK), is generated for every message. The DEK is sent in a PEM header field encrypted under another key, called an Interchange Key (IK). With the symmetric authentication alternative, the shared symmetric key provides the IK. With the public-key authentication alternative, DEK protection requires that a reversible cryptosystem such as RSA be used. The IK for encrypting a DEK is the public key of the recipient; a separate encrypted DEK must be included in the message for each recipient.

Message origin authentication and content integrity involve the use of a header field accompanying a message called a *message integrity check* (MIC). In principle, a MIC can be either:

- (a) an MDC or message digest, calculated from the message contents without using a key; or
- (b) a seal, calculated from the message contents using a symmetric cryptosystem key known to both originator and recipient.

---

[11] The acronym MIC stands for message integrity check.

[12] In the initial PEM specifications, the only algorithm specified is DES in CBC mode, but other options can (and will) be added.

Only approach (a) is supported by specific algorithm options in the initial PEM specifications. Two alternative algorithms are identified — the MD2 and MD5 hash functions [KAL2, RIV1].

With approach (a), the MIC needs to be protected against substitution by an active attacker. The way this is done depends upon whether the underlying authentication is symmetric or public-key based. With the symmetric approach, the MIC is encrypted under the shared symmetric key for transmission. With the public-key approach, the MIC is signed (either a reversible or irreversible algorithm may be employed) using the originator's private key. Only the signature appendix is transmitted (i.e., the plaintext MIC is not sent). If content confidentiality is in force, the signed-MIC-appendix is also encrypted under the same DEK as used to encrypt message contents — if this was not done, an eavesdropper looking for known messages could recognize a known message purely on the basis of a signed-MIC-appendix.

Message Representation

Internet mail is built upon an underlying text-string transport system, rather than a transparent binary transport system, as with MHS. This makes it necessary for PEM to incorporate some special processing steps beyond the usual cryptographic transformations.

At the originator, message processing generally involves four steps:

- *Step 1 (Local Form):*   A message to be protected is assembled in the source system's native character set, using standard line-delimiting conventions for that system.

- *Step 2 (Canonical Form):* The message is converted to a universal canonical form, which involves representing text with the ASCII character set, with a CR-LF character sequence used for line delimiting. The representation rules are derived from the SMTP specification.

- *Step 3 (Cryptographic Processing):* The canonical form is input to the applicable MIC algorithm to generate a MIC. If content confidentiality is being provided, the canonical form is also input to the encryption algorithm to generate a ciphertext bit string.

    Note: The output of step 3 can be considered to be the final message content in bit string format — if content confidentiality applies, it is the ciphertext bit string; otherwise it is the bit string representation of the canonical form of the message content.

- *Step 4 (Printable Encoding):*   This step generates a representation of the output bit string from step 3 that can pass unambiguously through any character-mapping (e.g., ACSII-to-EBCDIC) or format conversion (e.g., line-delimiter mapping) process, as might occur at a mail gateway or in a recipient's local environment. This printable encoding employs a 64-character alphabet, which is considered common to all systems (the 52 upper and lower case alphabetics, the 10 numerics, and the "+" and "/" characters). This enables six bits of the input bit string to be represented as one character. PEM specifies a precise algorithm for generating four output characters for each group of 24 input bits.

In the case of MIC-CLEAR mesages, step 4 is omitted. This means that a non-PEM-capable UA can read the message contents (but not verify the message origin and integrity). A PEM-capable UA can verify the message origin and integrity only in an environment where the MTS does not modify messages in transit, or where any such modifications can be determined and inverted before the MIC validation processing. A MIC verification failure on a MIC-CLEAR message will often not be caused by a security-significant event, but by an unexpected MTS translation. This may influence the type of error indication a system should give a user on such a verification failure.

PEM Message Format

The PEM message format defined in RFC 1421 involves an encapsulation structure, whereby PEM messages are enclosed within MTS messages for transfer purposes. The encapsulation process can be recursive. A problem with this message format is that it is not compatible with MIME, which was developed in parallel. This is being addressed subsequently, and is likely to result in an alternative to or revision of the RFC 1421 encapsulation process.

Putting the encapsulation process aside, we can look at the PEM protocol elements, which are in the form of header fields at the start of an encapsulated PEM message. Some fields are on a per-message basis and some, a per-recipient basis.

The per-message fields include:

- *Proc-Type*: Identifies the type of PEM processing to apply, in terms of a version number and one of the specifiers ENCRYPTED, MIC-ONLY, MIC-CLEAR, or CRL (see *Certification Structure* below).
- *Content-Domain*: Describes the type of content carried in the PEM message's encapsulated text; the only value defined initially is *RFC822*.
- *DEK-Info*: Identifies the content encryption algorithm, mode of operation, and any other required parameters such as initialization vector.
- *Originator-ID-Asymmetric*: Identifies the message originator and the originator's IK (key-pair). This field is used only with the public-key based key management approach, and only when the Originator-Certificate field is not present.

- *Originator-ID-Symmetric*: Identifies the message originator and a symmetric IK. This field is used only with the symmetric key management approach.
- *Originator-Certificate*: Transfers a certificate containing the originator's public key. This field is used only with the public-key-based key management approach.
- *MIC-Info*: Identifies the algorithm for MIC calculation, the algorithm for signing the MIC, and the MIC value signed with the originator's private key. In an ENCRYPTED message, the signed MIC is also symmetrically encrypted using the same DEK, algorithm, mode, and parameters as used to encrypt the encapsulated text. This field is used only with the public-key-based key management approach.
- *Issuer-Certificate*: Contains a certificate for a certification authority's public key, necessary for validating a certificate chain. There may be an arbitrary number of such fields.

The per-recipient fields include:

- *Recipient-ID-Asymmetric*: Identifies a message recipient and the recipient's IK (key-pair). This field is used only with the public-key-based key management approach.
- *Recipient-ID-Symmetric*: Identifies a message recipient and a symmetric IK. This field is used only with the symmetric key management approach.
- *Key-Info* (symmetric key management case): Conveys an encrypted DEK, an encrypted MIC, an IK-use indicator (identifying algorithm and mode in which the identified IK was used for DEK and MIC encryption for a particular recipient), and a MIC algorithm indicator. The DEK and MIC are symmetrically encrypted under the IK identified by a preceding Recipient-ID-Symmetric field and/or prior Originator-ID-Symmetric field.
- *Key-Info* (public-key-based key management case): Conveys a DEK which is encrypted with the recipient's public key, and an IK-use indicator which identifies the algorithm and mode for DEK encryption.

All header fields have appropriate representation rules which allow them to pass unambiguously through text recoding or reformatting processes.

Certification Infrastructure

While the PEM protocol can operate in conjunction with either a symmetric or public-key-based authentication and key management infrastructure, the latter approach is strongly recommended in the PEM specifications. Part II of these specifications provides the basis for a public-key certification infrastructure to support PEM on a potentially global scale. Certificate formats are consistent with the ITU X.509 format. The infrastructure is discussed in Section 4.7.

The PEM format includes provision for CRL messages. These are Internet mail messages for use in distributing certificate revocation lists.

13.10 The SDNS Message Security Protocol

The U.S. Government SDNS program was introduced in Chapter 11. One protocol defined in the SDNS program is the Message Security Protocol (MSP) [DIN1]. This is a protocol for providing secure message transfer over an otherwise-unsecured MHS network. Development of MSP commenced before (and independently of) the publication of the MHS (1988) secure messaging features. Consequently, MSP and MHS (1988) are largely alternative solutions to the same security problems.

MSP is a privately defined and registered content type, which encapsulates a complete message content of some other MHS content type, such as interpersonal messaging. MSP provides its own set of security services. These services include message confidentiality, integrity, data origin authentication, access control, non-repudiation of origin, and request/return of a signed receipt of the received message.

The MSP message content carries the original message content (encrypted if message confidentiality is requested) plus various security parameters required by recipients to decrypt and/or validate the message upon receipt. Also included are parameters which specify the algorithms used for encryption, sealing, and signing.

While MSP provides no security functions beyond those in MHS (1988), there are arguments that the MSP approach to message handling security provides for better separation of trusted and "less-trusted" system components. Also, the access control fields are better tailored to meet the requirements of classified environments.

Summary

The two standard electronic mail (e-mail) architectures are the Message Handling Systems (MHS) architecture and the Internet mail architecture.

The MHS (X.400) standards include very comprehensive security facilities. There are 19 basic MHS security services, which can be considered in five groupings. The basic end-to-end services provide message originators and recipients with data origin authentication, confidentiality, and integrity protection of messages, without having to trust the underlying MTS. The message path services contribute to secure communications throughout the MHS environment, placing requirements on functional components of all types (UA, MS, and MTA). The MTS corroborative services involve both the MTS and the originating MTS-user and provide corroboration to one or more components as to the authenticity of an MHS protocol message from another component. The non-repudiation services are variants of the MTS corroborative services, with the additional requirement that proofs be irrefutable. The security management services provide for changing credentials and registering details of supported security labels between communicating components.

Protocol support for these security services is provided in the MHS P1, P3, and P7 protocols. Various security fields are included in the protocol envelopes for messages, probes, and reports; in the bind operation arguments; and in a few operation results. The envelope fields include per-message fields and per-recipient fields. An important per-recipient field is the message token which is general structure for conveying signed and (optionally) encrypted data from the originator to a recipient. The ways of providing all the MHS security services, using the above protocol fields, are described in detail in the body of this chapter.

Security techniques used by MHS include encryption, sealing/signing, authentication exchanges, and security labels. For many functions, either symmetric or public-key cryptography could be used, but for some functions public-key cryptography is essential.

The MHS standards leave many options open to the implementor. A set of security profiles developed by the OIW and EWOS workshops reduces the option combinations significantly, while still being able to satisfy a variety of user requirements.

Transfer of EDI transactions over the MHS backbone employs a special MHS content type. This content type specification includes support for some additional security services beyond those addressed by the general MHS secure messaging facilities. Provision of these services employs special fields in the EDI content header and special procedures descibed in the standard. Security functions can also be provided within the EDI content, using features defined in EDI format standards. In particular, the ANSI X12 standards include provisions for data origin authentication, confidentiality, and/or integrity protection of transaction components, plus transfer of key management messages.

The Internet Privacy Enhanced Mail (PEM) option adds, to the Internet mail architecture, a subset of the security functions defined for MHS. PEM is entirely end-to-end, supporting the services of message origin authentication, content confidentiality, content integrity, and non-repudiation of origin. There are two alternative approaches to network-wide authentication and key management — a symmetric alternative and a public-key alternative. To support the public-key alternative, a comprehensive certification infrastructure has been established. When content confidentiality is provided, a symmetric cryptosystem is employed, with a random key generated for every message and sent encrypted with the message. Because Internet mail is built upon an underlying text-string transport system, rather than a transparent binary transport system, PEM needs to incorporate some special processing steps beyond the usual cryptographic transformations. These steps are necessary to ensure that messages can be decrypted and validated after passing through systems that recode or adjust text formatting.

The U.S. Government SDNS program developed the Message Security Protocol (MSP) which can provide secure message transfer over an otherwise-unsecured MHS network. MSP is a privately defined and registered MHS content type, which encapsulates a complete message content. MSP provides its own set of security services.

Exercises

1. In MHS, identify which of the following security services require crypto-graphic functions in MTAs, as opposed to only in MTS-user equipment:

    (a)   content confidentiality;
    (b)   proof of submission;
    (c)   proof of delivery;
    (d)   non-repudiation of origin;
    (e)   message sequence integrity; and
    (f)   report origin authentication.

2. Describe how message security labels can be used to support secure routing in MHS, consistent with a multi-level access control policy. Assume an MHS environment in which components have a variety of clearance levels (including no clearance). In sending a classified message from user agent A to user agent B, what systems would need to be trusted to at least the same level as the message?

3. Describe the relative advantages and disadvantages of the MHS content-integrity-check and message-origin-authentication-check approaches to providing content integrity and origin authentication to a recipient.

4. List the sequence of protocol exchanges involved in providing the MHS proof-of-delivery service. When a message is sent with its content encrypted, is proof of delivery applied to the unencrypted or encrypted content? Why?

5. Non-repudiation based on a digital signature requires that the signature be calculated on unencrypted data. If content confidentiality is applied to an MHS message, what are the implications on simultaneously providing the following services: (a) non-repudiation of origin, (b) non-repudiation of delivery, (c) non-repudiation of submission?

6. For each of the following MHS security services, identify any advantages favoring the use of either (i) symmetric cryptographic techniques, or (ii) public-key techniques:

   (a) content confidentiality;
   (b) proof-of-submission;
   (c) message-origin-authentication (MTS); and
   (d) non-repudiation of delivery.

7. Briefly describe the main characteristics of the OIW/EWOS MHS security profiles S0, S0A, S1, S1A, S2, and S2A.

8. In an Internet PEM message, in each of the two cases below, list the header fields required and describe their contents in general terms:

   (a) an ENCRYPTED message sent to a single recipient, assuming the symmetric key management approach; and
   (b) a MIC-ONLY message sent to two recipients, assuming the public-key-based key management approach for all parties.

REFERENCES

[BAL1] D. Balenson, *Privacy Enhancement for Internet Electronic Mail, Part III: Algorithms, Modes, and Identifiers*, Request for Comments (RFC) 1423, Internet Activities Board, 1993.

[BOR1] N.S. Borenstein and N. Freed, *Multipurpose Internet Mail Extensions*, Request for Comments (RFC) 1341, Internet Activities Board, 1992.

[CRO1] D.H. Crocker, *Standard for the Format of ARPA Internet Text Messages*, Request for Comments (RFC) 822, Internet Activities Board, 1982.

[DIC1] G. Dickson and A. Lloyd, *Open Systems Interconnection*, Prentice Hall, Englewood Cliffs, NJ, 1991.

[DIN1] C. Dinkel (Ed.), *Secure Data Network System (SDNS) Network, Transport, and Message Security Protocols*, U.S. Department of Commerce, National Institute of Standards and Technology, Report NISTIR 90-4250, 1990.

[FOR1] W. Ford and B. O'Higgins, "Public-Key Cryptography and Open Systems Interconnection," *IEEE Communications Magazine*, vol. 30, no. 7 (July 1992), pp. 30-35.

[GEN1] G. Genilloud, "X.400 MHS: First Steps Towards an EDI Communication Standard," *ACM Computer Communication Review*, vol. 20, no. 2 (April 1990), pp. 72-86.

[HIL1] R. Hill, *EDI and X.400 Using P_{edi}: The Guide for Implementors and Users*, Technology Appraisals, Isleworth, U.K., 1991.

[KAL1] B. Kaliski, *Privacy Enhancement for Internet Electronic Mail, Part IV: Key Certification and Related Services*, Request for Comments (RFC) 1424, Internet Activities Board, 1993.

[KAL2] B. Kaliski, *The MD2 Message-Digest Algorithm*, Request for Comments (RFC) 1319, Internet Activities Board, 1992.

[KEN1] S. Kent, *Privacy Enhancement for Internet Electronic Mail, Part II: Certificate-Based Key Management*, Request for Comments (RFC) 1422, Internet Activities Board, 1993.

[KIL1] S.E. Kille, *Mapping Between X.400 (1988) and RFC 822*, Request for Comments (RFC) 1327, Internet Activities Board, 1992.

[LIN1] J. Linn, *Privacy Enhancement for Internet Electronic Mail, Part I: Message Encryption and Authentication Procedures*, Request for Comments (RFC) 1421, Internet Activities Board, 1993.

[MAN1] C.-U. Manros, *The X.400 Blue Book Companion*, Technology Appraisals, Isleworth, U.K., 1989.

[MIT1] C. Mitchell, M. Walker, and D. Rush, "CCITT/ISO Standards for Secure Message Handling," *IEEE Journal on Selected Areas in Communications*, vol. 7, no. 4 (May 1989), pp. 517-524.

[NIS1] U.S. Department of Commerce, National Institute of Standards and Technology, *Stable Implementation Agreements for Open Systems Interconnection Protocols Version 6 Edition 1 December 1992*, NIST Special Publication 500-206, 1993.

[PLA1] B. Plattner, C. Lanz, H. Lubick, M. Müller, and T. Walter, *X.400 Message Handling Standards, Interworking, Applications*, Addison-Wesley, Reading, MA, 1991.

[POS1] J.B. Postel, *Simple Mail Transfer Protocol*, Request for Comments (RFC) 821, Internet Activities Board, 1982.

[RIV1] R. Rivest, *The MD5 Message-Digest Algorithm*, Request for Comments (RFC) 1321, Internet Activities Board, 1992.

[ROS1] M.T. Rose, *The Internet Message: Closing the Book with Electronic Mail*, Prentice Hall, Englewood Cliffs, NJ, 1993.

[SOK1] P.K. Sokol, *EDI: The Competitive Edge*, Intext Publications, McGraw-Hill Book Company, New York, 1988.

Standards

ANSI X12.42: *Draft Standard for Trial Use for Managing Electronic Data Interchange: Cryptographic Service Message Transaction Set (815)*, 1990.

ANSI X12.58: *Draft Standard for Trial Use for Managing Electronic Data Interchange: Security Structures*, 1990.

ISO 7372: *The United Nations Trade Data Elements Directory.*

ISO 9735: *Electronic Data Interchange for Administration, Commerce and Transport (EDIFACT) — Application Level Syntax Rules.*

ISO/IEC 10021-1: *Information Technology — Message Handling Systems — Part 1: System and Service Overview* (Also ITU-T Recommendations F.400 and X.400).

ISO/IEC 10021-2: *Information Technology — Message Handling Systems — Part 2: Overall Architecture* (Also ITU-T Recommendation X.402).

ISO/IEC 10021-4: *Information Technology — Message Handling Systems — Part 4: Message Transfer System: Abstract Service Definition and Procedures* (Also ITU-T Recommendation X.411).

ISO/IEC 10021-5: *Information Technology — Message Handling Systems — Part 5: Message Store: Abstract Service Definition* (Also ITU-T Recommendation X.413).

ISO/IEC 10021-6: *Information Technology — Message Handling Systems — Part 6: Protocol Specifications* (Also ITU-T Recommendation X.419).

ISO/IEC 10021-7: *Information Technology — Message Handling Systems — Part 7: Interpersonal Messaging System* (Also ITU-T Recommendation X.420).

ISO/IEC 10021-8: *Information Technology — Message Handling Systems — Part 8: EDI Messaging Service* (Also ITU-T Recommendation F.435).

ISO/IEC 10021-9: *Information Technology — Message Handling Systems — Part 9: EDI Messaging System* (Also ITU-T Recommendation X.435).

14 **Directory Systems Security**

The Directory standards, commonly known by their ITU designator *X.500*, provide the basis for constructing a multi-purpose distributed directory service by interconnecting computer systems on a potentially global scale. The Directory may act as a source of information for people, for communications network components, or for other automated systems. For computer network users, for example, a look-up of a person's name may be able to return such information as telephone number, data network address, and MHS O/R address, plus details of the application-contexts, profiles, and MHS content types that person's equipment supports. A broad range of services can be supported, ranging from simple name-to-address look-up to browsing or attribute-keyed searching. Information in the Directory may be owned by a wide variety of organizations and/or individuals.

In the context of network security, the Directory is significant in two ways:

- Requirements for confidentiality and integrity of Directory information, (which vary widely with different information owners) place strong demands on network security services.
- Services provided by the Directory can assist in the provision of security services to other applications.

The original Directory standards were developed in a joint project between the ITU (CCITT) and ISO/IEC JTC1/SC21 in the 1985–1988 period. They were published by the ITU in 1988 as the X.500 series of recommendations, and subsequently as the ISO/IEC 9594 multi-part standard. In 1993, the standards were enhanced in several areas [BOE1]. One enhancement was the addition of access control services [RAN1].

Environments in which the Directory standards are now being used include large corporations (for support of corporate personnel directories), public telecommunications carriers (for providing commercial directory services), and global networked communities (for such purposes as electronic mail address look-up).

This chapter describes the security features in the Directory standards for protecting the Directory environment, plus the contribution of these standards towards protecting other environments. The chapter is organized as follows:

(1) a brief overview of basic Directory terminology, concepts, and models;

(2) a description of security requirements pertaining to these standards;

(3) a discussion of the contents of the Directory Authentication Framework (X.509), including authentication exchanges, certificate formats, certificate management procedures, and general purpose ASN.1 constructs;

(4) a description of the access control list mechanism used to protect Directory information;

(5) a description of how Directory access control list scopes may vary and how multiple lists may work together to satisfy policy requirements and administrative flexibility goals; and

(6) a summary of the security elements in the Directory protocols.

14.1 Directory (X.500) Overview

Following is a brief overview of some basic Directory terminology, concepts, and models which the reader needs to understand. For complete tutorials, see any of [DIC1, ROS1].

The Directory Information Base

The collection of information held in the entire logical Directory is known as the Directory Information Base. Storage of this information may be distributed across many physical systems.

The Directory Information Base comprises a set of *entries*. An entry is associated with one *object*, e.g., a person, an organization, or a piece of equipment. For each object there is one *object entry*, which is the primary collection of information on that object and is said to *represent* the object. An object may also have one or more *alias entries*, which provide alternative names for the object and which act as pointers to the object entry. An entry consists of *attributes,* each with a type and one or more values. Attributes fall into two categories — *user attributes* and *operational attributes*. User attributes are placed in the Directory primarily for use by some sub-population of the end user community. Operational attributes are placed in the Directory primarily to facilitate administration of the Directory service and may or may not be visible to end users. The types of attributes contained in any entry are governed by the *class* of object which the entry represents. Some standard attribute types and object classes are defined in the standards. Organizations using the Directory may define their own private attribute types and object classes if required.

Every entry has a globally unambiguous name, known as its *distinguished name* (DN). To facilitate naming, the entries of the Directory Information Base are organized in a tree structure. The tree, known as the *Directory Information Tree* (DIT), has a conceptual root and unlimited further vertices. Each vertex (except the root) corresponds to a Directory entry. The distinguished name of an entry comprises the distinguished name of its superior entry in the tree, together with a *relative distinguished name* (RDN) which distinguishes this node from other subordinates of the same superior node. (The tree root has a null distinguished name.)

A relative distinguished name for an entry is a statement regarding values of one or more attributes of that entry. More precisely, it is a set of attribute value-assertions, each of which is true, concerning distinguished values (i.e., attribute values intended to provide uniqueness) of the entry. Commonly, a relative distinguished name is simply a statement of one attribute value, e.g., *Common Name = G. Smith*. Figure 14-1 illustrates the above concepts, and Figure 14-2 provides an example.

The term *directory name* is often used to unambiguously identify real-world objects. In the present standards, directory name is equivalent to distinguished name. However, other alternative name forms for *directory name* may be developed in the future.

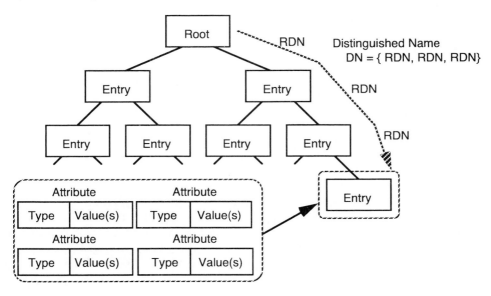

Figure 14-1: Directory Information Tree

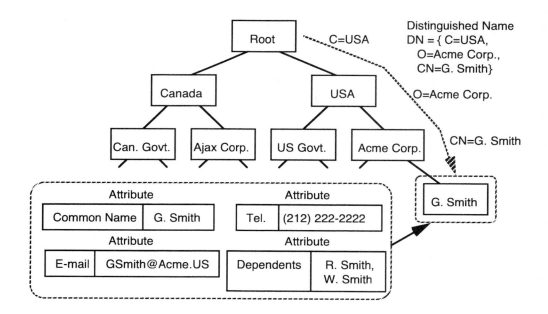

Figure 14-2: Directory Information Tree Example

Functional Model

Figure 14-3 illustrates the Directory environment. A Directory user is represented by a system called a *Directory User Agent* (DUA), which issues requests to and receives responses from the Directory. Communication within the Directory involves *Directory Service Agents* (DSAs). A DSA provides access to the Directory Information Base for DUAs or other DSAs. When presented with a request, a DSA may be able to directly service that request using information in locally attached databases. Alternatively, it may pass the request on to another DSA for processing (*chaining*), or it may advise the requestor to itself contact another DSA with its request (*referral*). A DSA may pass a request on to multiple DSAs simultaneously if desired (*parallel chaining*). A DUA is not necessarily associated with a particular DSA and may make its own decisions as to which DSA to use for a given request.

It is possible for entries to be replicated in multiple DSAs. The standards specify procedures for managing a form of replication known as *shadowing*.

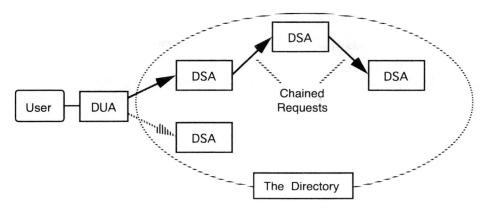

Figure 14-3: Directory Functional Model

Directory Services

The basic services provided to a user of the Directory fall into two categories —
interrogation services and *modification* services.
     The interrogation service requests are:

*   *Read*: A request aimed at a particular entry, which causes the values of
    specifically requested attributes or all attributes to be returned.
*   *Compare*: A request aimed at a particular attribute of a particular entry,
    which causes the Directory to check whether a value supplied by the
    requestor matches a value of that attribute.
*   *List*: A request for the Directory to return the distinguished name of each
    immediate subordinate of a particular entry in the DIT.
*   *Search*: A request for the Directory to return information from all of the
    entries within a certain portion of the DIT which satisfy some *filter*. The
    information returned comprises the values of specifically requested
    attributes or all attributes. A filter comprises a set of *matching rules* to
    apply to the values of specified attributes.
*   *Abandon*: A request informing the Directory that an earlier interrogation
    is no longer of interest, hence processing of it can cease.

     The modification service requests are:

*   *Add entry*: A request to add a new leaf entry (either an object entry or an
    alias entry) to the DIT.
*   *Remove entry*: A request to remove a leaf entry from the DIT.

- *Modify entry*: A request to execute a sequence of changes to an entry. Changes can include addition, removal, or replacement of attributes or attribute values. Each such request is indivisible — if any change causes an error, the entire request is rejected and the entry is left unchanged.
- *Modify distinguished name*: A request to modify the relative distinguished name of an entry by nominating different distinguished attribute values. This may have the effect of moving an entry and all its subordinates to another area of the DIT.

Service requests may be qualified by service controls which allow the user to limit use of Directory resources such as time and size of returned results.

Directory Administrative Model

The components of the Directory environment are owned and administered by a boundless collection of organizations. Structure is provided by recognizing the existence of *domains*. A *Directory Management Domain* denotes a set of DSAs (and, possibly, DUAs) managed by one organization (the *Domain Management Organization*). The directory information (i.e., part of the DIT) held in a Directory Management Domain is known as a *DIT Domain*. An *Administrative Authority* is an agent of the Domain Management Organization responsible for some aspect of Directory administration, such as naming administration, subschema administration, or security administration. The only aspect addressed in this book is security administration. An Administrative Authority concerned specifically with the security aspect is also known as a *Security Authority*. The above concepts are pertinent to later discussion of access control.

Directory Protocols

The Directory standards define the following Application Layer protocols, all of which employ the remote operations model (see Section 3.2):

- *Directory Access Protocol (DAP)*: A protocol between a DUA and a DSA, supporting requests to interrogate or modify directory information.
- *Directory System Protocol (DSP)*: A protocol between two DSAs to support the chaining of interrogation and modification requests.
- *Directory Information Shadowing Protocol (DISP)*: A protocol between two DSAs which have established shadowing agreements, to support the exchange of replication information.
- *Directory Operational Binding Protocol (DOP)*: A protocol for exchanging administrative information between two DSAs to administer operational bindings between them.

Navigating the Directory Standards

The coverage of security topics, especially access control, in the Directory standards is not easy to follow. However, the overview provided in this chapter should be adequate preparation for a reader to extract further details from the standards. Table 14-1 identifies where the main security-relevant material is located in the standards. This table is valid for the 1993 edition of the ITU recommendations and aligned ISO/IEC standards.

Part of Standard	*Security-Relevant Contents*
ISO/IEC 9594-2 (ITU-T X.501) — The Directory: Models	Clause 10: Directory Administrative Model. Clause 15: Security model introduction. Clause 16: Basic and Simplified Access Control schemes. Annexes: Basic Access Control in ASN.1, overview of Basic Access Control permissions, detailed example of Basic Access Control.
ISO/IEC 9594-3 (ITU-T X.511) — The Directory: Abstract Service Definition	Clauses 7-12: Description of the remote operations comprising the Directory access protocol, including arguments, results, and errors. Annexes: DAP abstract service in ASN.1, operational semantics for Basic Access Control.
ISO/IEC 9594-4 (ITU-T X.518) — The Directory: Procedures for Distributed Operation	Clauses 9-13: Description of the remote operations comprising the Directory system protocol, including arguments, results, and errors. Annexes: DSP abstract service in ASN.1, distributed use of authentication.
ISO/IEC 9594-8 (ITU-T X.509) — The Directory: Authentication Framework	Clause 6: Simple authentication procedures. Clauses 7-8: Certificate usage and definitions. Clause 9: Digital signatures; general ASN.1 macros. Clause 10: Strong authentication exchanges. Clause 11: Management of certificates. Annexes: Compendium of ASN.1 definitions, miscellaneous tutorial segments, reference definition of ASN.1 object identifiers (e.g., for RSA).

Table 14-1: Security-Relevant Material in the Directory Standards

14.2 Security Requirements

Directory Information Protection

As a network application, the Directory has its own security requirements. The most fundamental requirements are for confidentiality and integrity of information held in the Directory. The owner of any information may wish to limit its disclosure to a certain population of users; the owner will also wish to restrict who can modify information. The Directory is, by its very nature, open to attempted access by anyone. Hence, the primary security service for achieving confidentiality and integrity is *access control*. The provision of this type of access control depends, in turn, upon reliable knowledge of the identities of requesting users. *Entity authentication* is therefore an equally important service.

Protection of information in transfer is also a requirement. *Data origin authentication* and *integrity* may be important, especially for modification requests and, in some applications, the results of interrogation requests. Provision is therefore made to (optionally) sign the arguments and/or results of the remote operations. Confidentiality of communicated information may also be important. However, in the initial editions of the Directory standards, communications confidentiality is left to lower-layer security services.

Public-Key Certificate Distribution

In Chapter 4, the potential role of directory services in distributing public-key certificates was established. Any party which uses a public key to encrypt data or to verify an authentication token or digital signature needs to ensure it has a legitimate public key. This can be accomplished by distributing public keys in the form of certificates signed by mutually trusted certification authorities. Sometimes, communication of such certificates can be built into the using protocol, e.g., a digital signature can have the necessary verification public-key certificate attached. However, there are several circumstances in which a public-key user needs to be able to obtain public-key certificates on demand. These include obtaining a public key to encrypt confidential data destined to a new communication partner, obtaining public keys to satisfy trust requirements within a certification chain, and obtaining certificate revocation information. A ubiquitous directory service provides the ideal means for satisfying such requirements on a large (potentially global) scale.

Provision of such a facility depends upon supporting standards, in particular, standards for the syntax and semantics of public-key certificates. Standards are also needed to specify the use of these certficates for authentication, digital signature, and encryption purposes.

14.3 The Directory Authentication Framework (X.509)

When the Directory standards were first published in 1988, there were virtually no standards for public-key techniques. Such standards were important for the Directory for two reasons. The first was that, given the potentially global scope of the Directory environment, the only viable, strong (i.e., cryptographically based) authentication system was a public-key-based system. The second reason was that such standards were necessary to exploit the potential application of the Directory as a distributor of public-key certificates. Prospective users of a public-key distribution service were becoming apparent in at least two areas — MHS (the 1988 revisions of the MHS standards added public-key requirements) and the user community of the Directory itself.

It was concluded that the Directory standards should themselves incorporate the material needed to satisfy Directory authentication requirements. They should also include material needed for other applications (e.g., MHS) to employ public-key cryptography for authentication and/or digital signature purposes, using the Directory for public-key certificate distribution. One part of the Directory standards, the *Directory Authentication Framework* (ISO/IEC 9594-8 or ITU-T X.509), was dedicated to this purpose. Only minor changes were made to this standard in 1993.

Simple Authentication Exchange

For authenticating systems within the Directory environment, two alternative authentication methods are defined: *simple authentication* which employs passwords or protected passwords (see Section 5.2) and *strong authentication* which employs public-key cryptographic techniques (see Section 5.4).

The simple authentication method involves sending a user's distinguished name plus a data value which can be any of:

(a) an unprotected password;
(b) the result of applying a one-way function to the distinguished name, a password, a time-stamp (optional), and a random number[1] (optional); or
(c) the result of applying a further one-way function to the output of (b) and another time-stamp (optional) and another random number (optional).

Unprotected copies of any of the random number and/or time-stamp values may optionally be sent as well.

---

[1] The term "random number" used in the standard can be misleading, as the mere insertion of a random number in this field does not effectively counter replay attacks. A better term would be "non-repeating value." See Section 5.5 for an explanation of the issues.

This model is illustrated in Figure 14-4. It is capable of accommodating any of the protected password methods (using either one or two one-way functions) described in Section 5.2.

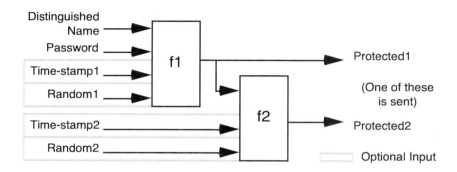

Figure 14-4: Simple Authentication Model

Strong Authentication Exchanges

Three variants of strong (public-key-based) authentication exchange are defined:

- *One-way authentication exchange*: Unilateral authentication is achieved by sending a distinguished name plus an authentication token signed with the sending party's private key.
- *Two-way authentication exchange*: Mutual authentication is achieved by executing the one-way exchange in both directions.
- *Three-way authentication exchange*: The two-way mutual authentication exchange is extended with a further transfer which effectively results in a challenge-response mechanism being used in both directions. This eliminates a reliance upon time-stamps for replay protection which exists in the one-way and two-way exchanges.

The authentication tokens exchanged also provide for conveying a secret key, encrypted using the receiver's public key, for possible use in (unspecified) confidentiality and/or integrity mechanisms.

These exchanges are described in detail in Section 5.6.

Note that the three-way exchange, which is the strongest option, cannot be used by either the Directory protocols or the MHS protocols. These protocols provide for only a two-way exchange.

Public-Key Certificates

The Directory Authentication Framework provides a detailed definition of a public-key certificate. Such a certificate binds a public key to some person or thing (called the subject), under the signature of an issuing certification authority. The certificate can be stored as a standard attribute in the subject's Directory entry and retrieved as necessary by any Directory user, by way of the Directory protocols. The 1993 ASN.1 definition is reproduced in Figure 14-5. The purposes of the various fields are:

- *Version*: Indicator of the particular certificate format, allowing for future revisions. Version 1 is as defined in the 1988 standards; version 2 the 1993 standards, etc.
- *Serial number*: Unique identifier for this certificate, assigned by the issuing certification authority.
- *Signature*: Algorithm identifier of the signature algorithm.
- *Issuer*: Directory name of the issuing certification authority.
- *Validity*: Start and expiration date/times for certificate.
- *Subject*: Directory name of the subject.
- *Subject public-key information*: An algorithm identifier plus a public-key value for the subject.
- *Issuer unique identifier*: An optional bit string field providing additional identification information on the issuing certification authority (permitted only in version 2 and later).
- *Subject unique identifier*: An optional bit string field providing additional subject identification information (permitted only in version 2 and later).

Note that the fields described as an *algorithm identifier* contain both an ASN.1 object identifier, assigned when the algorithm is registered, plus an optional set of algorithm-dependent parameters. The parameter sets for different algorithms can have different ASN.1 types — the type is declared when the algorithm is registered and is subsequently implied by the ASN.1 object identifier. This definition of algorithm identifier is used extensively throughout the Directory, MHS, and Generic Upper Layers Security standards.

The precise usage of the unique identifier fields is not mandated in the standards. Their inclusion was motivated by the fact that, while a directory name unambiguously identifies one entity, it is possible for an entity to stop using a particular name and for that same name to be subsequently assigned to another entity. If the directory name were the only identification information in a certificate, this could open a major security loophole. Directory administrators and certification authorities should use the unique identifier fields to avert

such problems.   The same unique identifiers are used in access control lists
(discussed in Section 14.4).

```
Certificate ::= SIGNED { SEQUENCE {
    version                         [0] Version DEFAULT v1,
    serialNumber                    CertificateSerialNumber,
    signature                       AlgorithmIdentifier,
    issuer                          Name,
    validity                        Validity,
    subject                         Name,
    subjectPublicKeyInfo            SubjectPublicKeyInfo,
    issuerUniqueIdentifier          [1] IMPLICIT UniqueIdentifier OPTIONAL,
                                    -- if present, version must be v2
    subjectUniqueIdentifier         [2] IMPLICIT UniqueIdentifier OPTIONAL
                                    -- if present, version must be v2 --}}


Version ::= INTEGER {v1 (0), v2 (1)}


CertificateSerialNumber ::= INTEGER


Validity ::=
    SEQUENCE {
            notBefore       UTCTime,
            notAfter        UTCTime}


SubjectPublicKeyInfo ::=
    SEQUENCE {
            algorithm       AlgorithmIdentifier,
            subjectKey      BIT STRING }


AlgorithmIdentifier ::=
    SEQUENCE {
            algorithm       ALGORITHM.&id({SupportedAlgorithms}),
            parameters      ALGORITHM.&Type({SupportedAlgorithms}
                            {@algorithm}) OPTIONAL }
-- Definition of the following information object set is deferred, perhaps
-- to standardized profiles or to protocol implementation conformance
-- statements.  The set is required to specify a table constraint on the
-- parameters component of AlgorithmIdentifier.
-- SupportedAlgorithms        ALGORITHM ::= {...|...}
```

Figure 14-5: Certificate Format in ASN.1

General-Purpose ASN.1 Constructs

As explained in Section 4.6, it is not practical in wide-scale environments like global Directory or MHS to rely on a single certification authority. In general, a public-key user will need to obtain and check a series of certificates corresponding to a chain of trusted certification authorities between itself and the public-key owner. From the perspective of any certification authority X, there are two types of certificate it might contribute — a *forward* certificate is generated by another certification authority and certifies X's public key; a *reverse* certificate is generated by X and certifies another certification authority's public key.

The Directory Authentication Framework recognizes the need to store and communicate certificate chains or parts thereof, and defines supporting ASN.1 constructs (see Figure 14-6). In particular, the constructs *Certificates* and *CertificationPath* provide for conveying a public-key certificate plus, optionally, certificates of certification authorities, to form a chain.[2] The standard does not mandate how certification authority structures are configured, nor exactly which additional certificates should be conveyed in the ASN.1 constructs.

```
Certificates ::= SEQUENCE {
          certificate           Certificate,
          certificationPath     ForwardCertificationPath OPTIONAL }

ForwardCertificationPath ::= SEQUENCE OF CrossCertificates

CrossCertificates ::=      SET OF Certificate
-----------------------------------------------------------------
CertificationPath ::= SEQUENCE {
          userCertificate       Certificate,
          theCACertificates     SEQUENCE OF CertificatePair OPTIONAL }

CertificatePair ::= SEQUENCE {
          forward        [0]    Certificate OPTIONAL,
          reverse        [1]    Certificate OPTIONAL
                    -- at least one of the pair shall be present -- }
```

Figure 14-6: Two ASN.1 Constructs for Certificate Chain

The Directory Authentication Framework also defines the ASN.1 parameterized types *ENCRYPTED*, *HASHED*, *SIGNATURE*, and *SIGNED*,

---

[2] The constructs *Certificates* and *CertificationPath* are functionally equivalent. One is imported into the Directory protocol and the other into the MHS protocol.

which support encryption and digital signatures in protocols. These are described in Section 12.6.

Certificate Management

The Directory Authentication Framework stipulates certain certificate management procedures:

- A certification authority must be satisfied with the identity of a subject before issuing a certificate for it, and must not issue certificates for two subjects with the same name.
- Certificates must have an expiry date, and a certification authority must ensure timely availability of replacement certificates to supersede expiring certificates. Overlap in the validity periods of successive certificates is permitted to facilitate changeover.
- Provision must be made for revocation of certificates, in such circumstances as compromise of a subject's private key, termination of recognition of a subject by a certification authority, or compromise of a certification authority. A certification authority must maintain a certified time-stamped list of the certificates it issued which have been revoked, and a certified time-stamped list of revoked certificates of all certification authorities known to that certification authority.

A format for a certificate revocation list is specified (using ASN.1) in the Directory Authentication Framework. Such a list can be stored in the Directory as an attribute of a certification authority entry and retrieved as necessary by any Directory user, by way of the Directory protocols.

Cryptographic Algorithms

While the Directory Authentication Framework does not mandate the use of any particular digital signature algorithm, it does require the use of an appendix-based digital signature computed on a hashed version of the data to be signed. Furthermore, the standard is written in a way which assumes the use of a reversible public-key cryptosystem, with each user having one key pair which can be used for both signature and encryption purposes. A description of the RSA algorithm (the only well-recognized public algorithm satisfying these assumptions) is included in an informative annex to the standard. Furthermore, an object identifier is assigned to RSA, establishing a formal registration for it.

The 1988 edition of the standard also had an annex describing the *square mod n* hash function, and an object identifier was assigned to this function in combination with RSA. However, flaws in this hash function were subsequently identified,[3] and it was removed prior to publication of the 1993 edition of the standard.

A slight loosening in the interpretation of the standard removes the binding to RSA; irreversible hash-appendix signature schemes such as ElGamal or DSS can be used without impacting the protocol. Profiling groups, including the OIW, have registered various algorithms, including El Gamal and the MD2, MD4, and MD5 hash functions [NIS1].

Deficiencies

Following the original 1988 publication of the Directory Authentication Framework, several perceived deficiencies were brought to light in formal defect reports on the standard and in the public literature [IAN1, MUL1]. Most of the agreed flaws were corrected prior to the 1993 revision of the standard; these included removal of a loophole in the original three-way authentication exchange and removal of the *square mod n* hash function.

Other perceived deficiencies are simply practical limitations. For example, some concerns were expressed regarding compromised or untrustworthy certification authorities issuing false certificates. The answer is that the user of a certificate chain cannot blindly use that chain to validate a public key. It is necessary to individually assess the trust one can place in each certification authority in a chain, and such assessment procedures are not amenable to standardization.

Certain improvements to the standard are warranted, and can be anticipated in future revisions. Support for multiple algorithms and/or multiple keys for different purposes is one likely area of improvement. Indicators may be added to indicate the intended usage of a key. Further fields may be added to revocation lists to better support non-repudiation requirements. These changes will necessitate extensions to the certificate format but no major changes to the basic protocol procedures.

14.4 Directory Access Control Lists

Given the breadths of the populations of information owners and potential accessors, there is a critical need for access control to information stored in the Directory. In the 1988 standards, access control was not standardized. This did not mean access control was non-existent. It was considered a local matter, depending on the features designed into a DSA implementation and the policy decisions of the DSA owner/operator. In the 1993 revision, standardized

---

[3] These flaws were documented in an unpublished note by D. Coppersmith of the IBM Research Division, Yorktown Heights, in 1989.

access control features were added, with the goals of giving equipment buyers and users consistent behavioral expectations and of providing standard means for communicating access control information between systems from different vendors.

The standards recognize that a variety of different *access control schemes* are potentially required by different administrations. Two such schemes, called the *Basic Access Control* scheme and the *Simplified Access Control* scheme, were defined initially. Other alternatives may be defined privately or in future standards. The Simplified scheme is a subset of the Basic scheme; the differences will be pointed out in Section 14.5.

The access control list mechanism which underlies the Basic and Simplified schemes is described below.

Access Control Statements

Because of the structural complexity of the Directory information base, Directory access control lists involve more than simply attaching a list of identities, permissions, and qualifiers to an object. Identification of the "object" being protected is non-trivial, in terms of both: (a) specifying the parts of a Directory entry to be protected, and (b) applying common access controls to multiple entries.

Directory access control information can be viewed as a collection of *access control statements*, each of which describes the parts of an entry it protects, together with identities, permissions, and qualifiers.[4] It is separately established which entry or entries the access control statement governs (the latter subject is deferred to Section 14.5).

The components of an access control statement are:

- *Protected items*: A specification of the parts of a Directory entry protected under this statement.
- *User classes*: A specification of the Directory users, i.e., initiators, covered by this statement.
- *Permissions*: A list of permissions granted and permissions denied;
- *Precedence*: A value indicating the extent to which this statement should prevail over conflicting statements applying to the same target(s) and initiator(s).
- *Authentication level*: An indicator of the strength of the authentication process which must be used to support decisions made based on this statement.

---

[4] The information in an access control statement corresponds to the information represented by the ASN.1 construct *ACIItem* defined in the standards.

There are two ways of structuring an access control statement, depending on whether it is most convenient to group multiple permissions with one *protected items* specification or with one *user classes* specification. Both alternatives capture the same information; the difference lies entirely in organizational convenience and efficiency of representation

More detailed descriptions of the various components follow.

Protected Items

Within a Directory entry, access control granularity may need to be at either the entry level or the attribute level. For example, hiding the existence of an entry or allowing an entry to be moved to a new point in the DIT is at the entry level. However, given permission to access an entry, there may be a need for further attribute level controls. For example, in a private individual's entry, access to the home telephone number may be restricted while the business telephone number is made publicly available. A value-dependent policy might also be appropriate for an attribute. For example, different corporate administrators may be authorized to update telephone numbers for personnel at different corporate sites, as implied by the telephone number prefix.

A Directory access control statement has a *protected items* component to indicate the parts of an entry protected under that statement. The granularities discussed above are all accommodated, together with other options, such as the ability to allow knowledge of an attribute *type* in an entry to be disclosed but not the *value* of that attribute.

A protected items specification is a set of one or more subspecifications. A subspecification is either the *entry level* subspecification (which governs overall access to an entry but does not necessarily govern access to attribute information), or an *attribute level* subspecification. Attribute level sub-specifications are selected from the following:

- *All-user-attribute-types*: All user attribute type information associated with the entry, but not values of the attributes.
- *All-user-attribute-types-and-values*: All user attribute information associated with the entry.
- *Attribute type*: Attribute type information associated with specific attribute(s), but not values of the attribute(s).
- *All-attribute-values*: All information associated with specific attribute(s);
- *Attribute-value*: A set of specific values of specific attribute(s).
- *Self-value*: (applies to an attribute which indicates a user name) an attribute value, to which access is allowed only if the user requesting access is the same as the user named in the attribute.

Multiple subspecifications in an access control statement are additive. This is convenient, especially for combining an entry level subspecification and an attribute level subspecification, both of which are often needed to gain access to attribute information. For example, to retrieve the telephone number for G. Smith, a user must have entry level access to G. Smith's entry plus attribute level access (e.g., the *all-attribute-values* subspecification) to values of the telephone number attribute.

User Classes

The *user classes* component of an access control statement specifies the Directory users, i.e., initiators, covered by that statement. This component is a set of one or more subspecifications selected from the following:

- *All-users*: All users in the entire Directory environment.
- *This-entry*: Only the user with the same distinguished name (plus, optionally, unique identifier) as the target entry.
- *Name*: A list of users, each identified by its distinguished name (plus, optionally, unique identifier).
- *User-group*: A list of named groups of users.
- *Subtree*: The set of users whose distinguished names fall within the definition of one or more identified DIT subtrees.

A group is a list of unique names held in an entry having the object class *group-of-unique-names*[5]. Each member name is that of a Directory user; it cannot be another group name. In general, the group definition needs to be known locally to the DSA evaluating the applicable access control condition. A DSA is not required to perform a remote operation to determine if a user is a member of a remotely defined group.

A subtree is specified by giving the distinguished name of a *base* entry to be considered the subtree's root. Furthermore, the downward extent of the subtree may be limited by means of a *chop* specification. Such a specification may identify specific nodes at which the subtree terminates, or simple limits on minimum and/or maximum number of levels.

---

[5] A group entry could alternatively be of object class *group-of-names*, as defined in the 1988 standards, but this is not recommended. As discussed in Section 14.3, unique identifiers were added in the 1993 revision. The *group-of-unique-names* object class is equivalent to the *group-of-names* object class with (optional) unique identifiers added.

Permissions

Permission indications in an access control statement specify either explicit granting or explicit denial of authorization to perform some action on the applicable protected item(s). The meanings of permissions depend on whether entry level or attribute level access control is being applied. Furthermore, certain permissions may be meaningful only in the context of certain Directory request operations.

The permissions that may be used at entry level are:

- *Read*: Permits read access to an entry for a Directory request that explicitly gives the entry name (read or compare operation).
- *Browse*: Permits read access to an entry for a Directory request that does not explicitly give the entry name (list or search operation).
- *Add*: Permits creation of an entry in the DIT, subject to access controls on all attributes and attribute values placed in the new entry.
- *Remove*: Permits an entry to be removed from the DIT, regardless of access controls on attributes or attribute values.
- *Modify*: Permits the information in an entry to be modified, subject to attribute and value permissions also being granted.
- *Rename*: Permits a modify-DN operation to change the relative distinguished name of an entry. Name changes implying new superior nodes would also be subject to import/export controls.
- *Disclose-on-error*: Permits the name of an entry to be disclosed in an error or empty result. This relates to requirements to keep knowledge of the existence of certain entries secret.
- *Export*: Permits a modify-DN operation to relocate an entry and its subordinates (if any) to a new location in the DIT, subject to the granting of requisite import permissions at the destination.
- *Import*: Permits a modify-DN operation to relocate entries and their subordinates (if any) at this location in the DIT.
- *Return-DN*: Permits the distinguished name of the entry to be returned in an operation result.

The permissions that may be used at the attribute level are:

- *Read*: Permits attribute type and/or value information to be returned in a read or search operation.
- *Compare*: Permits attribute type and/or value information to be returned in a compare operation.

- *Filter-match*: Permits attribute type and/or value information to be used in evaluation of a filter in a search operation.
- *Add*: Permits adding an attribute and value(s) to an entry, or adding values to an existing attribute.
- *Remove*: Permits a modify operation to remove an attribute (complete with all values) from an entry, or remove an attribute value (other than the last value) from an attribute.
- *Disclose-on-error*: Permits the presence of an attribute and/or an attribute value to be disclosed in an error indication.

Precedence

Precedence values are used to govern the order in which distinct access control statements are applied, when more statements than one apply to an entry. Precedence values are integers in the range 0 to 255, with higher values prevailing over lower values, when all other factors in the entries are equal. The standards do not stipulate how these values should be assigned, leaving this to local security policy.

Authentication Level

The authentication level in an access control statement indicates the strength of the authentication process which must be used to support decisions made on the basis of this statement. This reflects the existence of different options for authenticating Directory users, such as the simple (password-based) option and the strong (cryptographic-based) option. For some access control decisions, such as permission to read publicly available information, no authentication may be needed. For other decisions, such as permission to read private user attributes, simple authentication may be considered appropriate. For other decisions, such as permission to modify security administration information, strong authentication may be deemed essential. Three standard *basic* authentication levels — *none*, *simple*, and *strong* — are defined. Other measures can be defined outside the standard.

In chaining scenarios, access control decisions are not always made by the DSA which directly authenticates a requesting user. Authentication information, such as a password or signed authentication token presented at DUA-DSA association establishment, are not conveyed with a chained request. This may present some complications to the evaluation of authentication levels.

The 1992 standards provide for conveying, with a chained request, an indicator of the type of authentication performed by the originating DSA. This permits a DSA, which is required to make an access control decision on a chained request, to assume an authentication level higher than *none*. Such an assumption depends upon the DSA's willingness to trust the originating DSA and all intervening DSAs with respect to handling of this indicator. To cope with this trust requirement, a DSA needs to maintain a database of other DSAs it trusts. The OIW implementor agreements [NIS1] describe how this can be done.

Policy may also require all requests between DSAs to be signed. This enables a chained request to traverse a chain of trust. Each DSA is responsible for verifying the signature of the previous DSA in the chain, removing the signature of the previous DSA, then signing the arguments with its own signature before passing the request on to the next DSA.

As an alternative approach to trusting an authentication level indicator, a DSA may respond to a chained request by returning a referral to itself. This will be conveyed back to the requesting DUA, which can then resubmit the original request directly to the final target DSA. On the resubmission, the DSA can directly authenticate the user without having to trust other DSAs.

Decision Procedure

When faced with making an access control decision, there may be multiple access control statements that potentially apply. The decision procedure is as follows:

1. Replace any statement that both grants and denies permissions by two statements — one specifying only grants and one specifying only denials.
2. Discard grant statements that do not include the initiator's identity in the user classes component. Also discard grant statements that specify an authentication level higher than that associated with the initiator.
3. Retain denial statements that include the initiator's identity in the user classes component or that specify an authentication level higher than that associated with the initiator; discard all other denial statements. (The second condition is needed because the requestor may not have adequately proved non-membership in the user class for which the denial is specified.)
4. Discard all statements that do not include the protected item in the protected items component.
5. Discard all statements that do not include the requested permission in the permissions component.
6. Discard all statements having a precedence value less than the highest remaining precedence.
7. If more than one statement remains, choose the statements with the most specific user class. The order (from most specific to least specific) is: (a) name or this-entry, (b) user-group, (c) subtree, (d) all-users.

8.   If more than one statement remains, choose the statements with the most specific protected item. If the protected item is an attribute and there are statements that specify the attribute type explicitly, discard all other statements. If the protected item is an attribute value and there are statements that specify that value explicitly, discard all other statements.

9.   Grant access if and only if one or more statements remain and all grant access. Otherwise deny access.

Example

As an example of a set of access control statements for a Directory entry, consider the entry for *G. Smith* in the example DIT segment in Figure 14-2. Suppose the entry is primarily administered by the individual's employer *Acme Corp*. Members of a group of corporate administrative staff have authority to maintain the entry, and may also access it in any way they wish. Their permissions are identified in the first two of the four access control statements illustrated in Figure 14-7.

Protected Items	User Classes	Permissions	Authentication Level
entry	user-group (*Acme administration*)	grant-read, grant-browse, grant-add, grant-remove, grant-modify, grant-rename, grant-disclose-on-error, grant-return-DN	strong
all-user-attribute-types-and-values	user-group (*Acme administration*)	grant-read, grant-add, grant-remove, grant-compare, grant-disclose-on-error, grant-filter-match	strong
entry, all-attribute-values (*Common Name, Tel., E-mail*)	all-users	grant-read	none
entry, all-attribute-values (*E-mail, Dependents*)	this-entry	grant-modify	simple

Figure 14-7: Example Access Control Statements

Furthermore, some of the attributes (*Common Name*, *Tel.*, and *E-mail*) are intended for reading by the public, provided the requestor knows how to find the entry (the entry is not made available for browsing on the basis of *Tel.* or *E-mail*). The permissions for this purpose are in the third access control statement. In addition, the individual with whom the entry is associated (*G. Smith*) is authorized to change the values of the *E-mail* and *Dependents* attributes at will, but may not otherwise modify the entry. The permissions for this purpose are in the fourth access control statement. Note the use of different authentication levels in the different access control statements.

14.5 Scope of Access Control Statements

The preceding example illustrates some important characteristics of Directory access control. First, note that administration of a Directory entry may be assigned primarily to an organization which administers many entries, rather than to the party with whom the entry is associated. Second, note that the set of access control statements in Figure 14-7 is not expressly tied to the individual *G. Smith*. The identical set of statements could be used by *Acme Corp.* for the Directory entries of all corporate employees. These observations point to the benefits of recognizing areas of the DIT in which common access control statements are employed. Such areas, which must be subtrees of the DIT, are known as *administrative areas*.

For full administrative flexibility, there are two kinds of access control statements which may apply to an entry:

- *Entry-ACI*: An access control statement tailored to a specific entry, and stored as an operational attribute (the *entry-ACI* attribute) of that entry.
- *Prescriptive-ACI*: An access control statement associated with an *administrative entry* in the DIT and applying to entries in the administrative area (i.e., subtree) which has that administrative entry as root.

There are two types of administrative area pertaining to access control — Access Control Specific Areas and Access Control Inner Areas.

Access Control Specific Areas

The Directory Administrative Model partitions the DIT into subtrees termed *autonomous administrative areas*, each of which is fully within one DIT-Domain, i.e., under the management control of one organization. Within an autonomous administrative area, responsibility for access control administration may be further partitioned into non-overlapping subareas known as *Access*

Control Specific Areas. A new Access Control Specific Area may commence at any level in the autonomous administrative area subtree.

As a practical illustration, the information base of a large multi-national corporation will typically constitute a DIT-Domain. The information of different national subsidiary corporations might be separated into distinct autonomous administrative areas (these can be disjoint subtrees, e.g., have roots in different national directory structures). Within one autonomous administrative area, multiple Access Control Specific Areas may be recognized, corresponding, for example, to separate regional offices, corporate operating units, or corporate administrative functions (such as personnel and inventory). Each area has its own Security Authority who is authorized to administer all aspects of access control within that area.

An Access Control Specific Area represents a solid boundary for consideration of access control statements. An entry within a given Access Control Specific Area is not subject to any controls specified outside that area. The subtree root of an Access Control Specific Area is called the *administrative entry* for that area. Associated with an administrative entry are *subentries*, which hold administrative information. The prescriptive-ACI statements for an Access Control Specific Area are held in such subentries.

Figure 14-8 shows a partitioning of an autonomous administrative area into four Access Control Specific Areas. In this example, an entry in area 2 is subject to prescriptive-ACI in subentries of entry *B*, but not in those of entries *A*, *C*, or *D*.

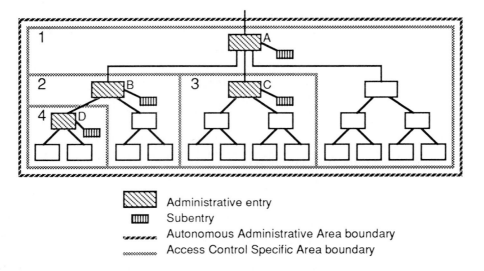

▨	Administrative entry
▥	Subentry
～～	Autonomous Administrative Area boundary
∞∞∞	Access Control Specific Area boundary

Figure 14-8: Example Partitioning into Access Control Specific Areas

Access Control Inner Areas

An Access Control Specific Area may be further partitioned into *Access Control Inner Areas*.

To continue the illustration of the multi-national corporation, let us look inside one of the Access Control Specific Areas, say that associated with personnel of a national subsidiary corporation. The central personnel department may wish to retain control over who can create, rename, or remove any entry. However, it may delegate access control authority for the maintainence of entry contents to corporate divisions. In turn, the corporate divisions may further delegate limited access control authority to specific departments. Such partial delegations are modeled as Access Control Inner Areas.

An Access Control Inner Area has many similarities with an Access Control Specific Area. It has an administrative entry, with subentries which hold prescriptive-ACI statements which apply to entries within the area. However, there is a very important difference between the two types of areas. An entry in an Access Control Inner Area is subject to access controls specified for that area and is also subject to access controls specified for the encompassing area, extending to the encompassing Access Control Specific Area boundary. Access Control Inner Areas may be nested. Hence, when making an access control decision for an entry in an Access Control Inner Area, it may be necessary to take into account multiple prescriptive-ACI statements in subentries of multiple administrative entries.

Figure 14-9 shows a partitioning involving both Access Control Specific Areas and Access Control Inner Areas. In this example, an entry in area 4 is subject to prescriptive-ACI in subentries of entries *A, C,* and *D*.

Directory Access Control Domains

There remains one further stage in refining the set of access control statements that apply to a particular entry. The area concepts described above serve to bound the scope of prescriptive-ACI statements in subentries of administrative entries. However, a particular prescriptive-ACI statement does not necessarily apply to *all* entries in the scoped area.

Every subentry contains one or more access control statements, together with a subtree specification identifying a *Directory Access Control Domain* (DACD). The subentry specification identifies precisely those entries within the administrative area to which the access control statements apply. The Directory Access Control Domain may span the full administrative area. Alternatively, as a result of subtree refinement specifications, it may be limited to only part of the administrative area.

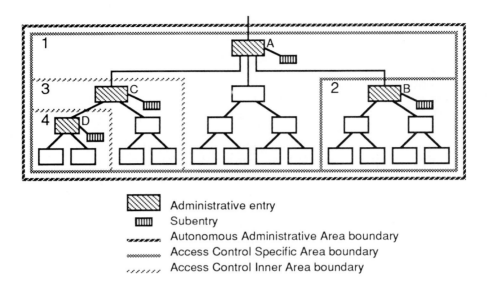

                    Administrative entry
                    Subentry
                    Autonomous Administrative Area boundary
                    Access Control Specific Area boundary
                    Access Control Inner Area boundary

Figure 14-9: Example Partitioning Including Access Control Inner Areas

Within an administrative area, there may be multiple Directory Access Control Domains which may arbitrarily overlap. Hence, any entry in the administrative area may be subject to the access control statements in multiple subentries.

Figure 14-10 illustrates a possible set of Directory Access Control Domains, DACD1 and DACD2. Note the entry in the intersection of the two domains. This entry is subject to access control statements in both subentries.

Basic and Simplified Access Control Schemes

In summary, under the Basic Access Control scheme, the set of access control statements applying to any entry comprises[6]:

(a) Entry-ACI statements held in an operational attribute of the target entry.

(b) Applicable prescriptive-ACI statements associated with the entry's Access Control Specific Area. These statements are held in subentries of the administrative entry of the area and applicability depends upon the subtree specification in the particular subentry.

---

[6] Subentry-ACI statements may also need to be taken into account. These are access control statements placed in an administrative entry to define controls on accessing the subentries of that administrative entry.

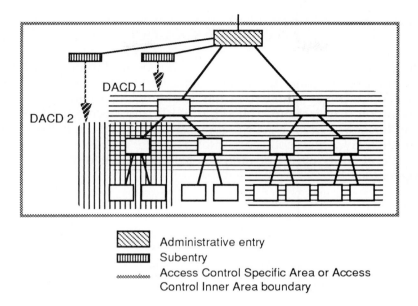

DACD 1

DACD 2

▨ Administrative entry

▥ Subentry

〰 Access Control Specific Area or Access
Control Inner Area boundary

Figure 14-10: Example Directory Access Control Domains

(c) Applicable prescriptive-ACI statements associated with the Access Control Inner Areas in which the entry lies. These statements are held in subentries of the administrative entry of the area and applicability depends upon the subtree specification in the particular subentry.

When there is more than one statement in this set, the decision procedure given in Section 14.4 is followed in making the decision to grant or deny requested access.

The Simplified Access Control scheme is the subset of the Basic Control Scheme which employs only item (b) of the above, i.e., neither entry-ACI nor the Access Control Inner Area concept is supported.

14.6 Directory Protocol Security Elements

Entity Authentication

Entity authentication can occur at the time of establishing an application association between a DUA and a DSA (with the Directory Access Protocol) or between a pair of DSAs (with the other protocols). A two-way exchange, which provides mutual authentication, is conveyed in the credentials fields in the argument and result, respectively, of the bind operation. This argument and result are in turn conveyed in the ACSE A-ASSOCIATE request and response PDUs, respectively.

The ASN.1 for the credentials fields is reproduced in Figure 14-11. This ASN.1 is suitable for importation into other application protocols where an X.509-based, two-way authentication exchange is required. The OIW Implementation Agreements [NIS1] provide the necessary linkages for conveying this ASN.1 in the ACSE authentication fields, in conjunction with any application layer protocol (see Section 12.3).

Unilateral entity authentication can also be obtained through the use of signed operations.

```
Credentials ::= CHOICE {
    simple                  [0]     SimpleCredentials,
    strong                  [1]     StrongCredentials,
    externalProcedure       [2]     EXTERNAL }

SimpleCredentials ::= SEQUENCE {
    name                    [0]     DistinguishedName,
    validity                [1]     SET {
            time1                   [0]     UTCTime OPTIONAL,
            time2                   [1]     UTCTime OPTIONAL,
            random1                 [2]     BIT STRING OPTIONAL,
            random2                 [3]     BIT STRING OPTIONAL } OPTIONAL,
    password                [2]     CHOICE {
            unprotected     OCTET STRING,
            protected       SIGNATURE { OCTET STRING }} OPTIONAL }

StrongCredentials ::= SET {
    certification-path      [0]     CertificationPath OPTIONAL,
    bind-token              [1]     Token }

Token ::= SIGNED { SEQUENCE {
    algorithm               [0]     AlgorithmIdentifier,
    name                    [1]     DistinguishedName,
    time                    [2]     UTCTime,
    random                  [3]     BIT STRING }}
```

Figure 14-11: ASN.1 Construct for Entity Authentication

Signed Operations

In order to provide data origin authentication and integrity protection, the arguments or results of any Directory remote operation may, depending upon applicable security policy requirements, be signed by that sender.

The requestor of an operation may, depending upon applicable security policy requirements, sign the arguments. It may also request, via a *protection-request* indicator, that the results of the operation be signed by the system that generates those results. However, recognizing the varying capabilities of different systems, the signing of results is not mandatory, even when requested.

The signing protocol employs an *OPTIONALLY-SIGNED* ASN.1 construct which translates to a choice between an unprotected representation of the field or a representation which is protected using the *SIGNED* ASN.1 construct (see Section 12.6). Supporting protocol information is conveyed in an accompanying *security-parameters* field, which contains any of the following optional components:

- *Certification-path*: A certificate containing a public key for the sender, for use in verifying the signature on arguments or results. Other supporting certificates, forming a certificate chain, may also be included.
- *Name*: The distinguished name of the first intended recipient of the arguments or results.
- *Time*: The intended expiry time for the validity of a signature (to reduce vulnerability to replay attacks).
- *Random*: A non-repeating value (to limit vulnerability to replay attacks).
- *Protection-request*: The requestor's indication as to whether results of an operation should be signed.

Access Control

Support for access control places significant procedural requirements on the operation of DSAs. These requirements are described in ISO/IEC 9594-3 (ITU-T X.511) and ISO/IEC 9594-4 (ITU-T X.518). However, access control support does not generally require special fields or values in PDUs (exceptions are the *authentication-level* field discussed in Section 14.4, and error indications resulting from access control denials).

There is a substantial requirement to query and manipulate access control information associated with Directory entries or subentries. This can be accommodated using the standard Directory operations in conjunction with appropriate object class and attribute type definitions. Access control information itself needs to be carefully protected. This protection can be provided through sufficiently careful application of the Directory security features, in conjunction with appropriate conventional security controls.

Summary

The Directory is an important open-system network application which can play a valuable role in supporting information retrieval needs of other applications. Because of the diversity of the user and information-owner populations, and requirements for confidentiality and integrity of the information, the Directory application incorporates substantial security features. The Directory is also significant to network security because of the role it can play as a distributor of public-key certificates for use by any network protocol or application which employs public-key techniques.

The Directory Authentication Framework (X.509) describes authentication and digital signature techniques, certificate formats, certificate management procedures, and supporting ASN.1 constructs. All of these are targeted for use both by the Directory application and by other applications which may use the Directory as a public-key certificate distributor.

The other major security topic in the Directory standards is access control to information held in the Directory. A Basic Access Control scheme is defined, together with a subset called the Simplified Access Control Scheme. These schemes use an access control list mechanism. Access to an entry or its contents is controlled by one or more access control statements, each of which identifies the parts of an entry to which it applies, the class of users covered by the statement, a list of permissions granted and permissions denied, a precedence indicator, and an authentication level requirement. A decision procedure is defined for use when multiple statements apply to one entry.

An access control statement may be associated with a single Directory entry or may be used by a Security Authority to govern multiple entries. The latter case is called a prescriptive-ACI statement and is associated with a DIT subtree known as either an Access Control Specific Area or an Access Control Inner Area. Access Control Specific Areas are non-overlapping partitions which solidly bound the scopes of access control statements. Access Control Inner Areas are nested within Access Control Specific Areas and support partial delegation of access control authority. Every prescriptive-ACI statement also has attached a Directory Access Control Domain descriptor which identifies the precise set of entries within the corresponding area to which the statement applies.

The Directory protocols provide for entity authentication at association establishment, for optional entity authentication and data origin authentication via signing of remote operation arguments and results, and for communication of access control information.

Exercises

1. Briefly explain the meanings of the following terms, as defined and used in the Directory standards:

   (a)   Directory Information Tree (DIT);
   (b)   distinguished name;
   (c)   Directory System protocol (DSP);
   (d)   algorithm identifier; and
   (e)   certificate revocation list.

2. Discuss the comparative advantages and disadvantages of the following types of authentication exchange: (a) simple authentication with protection function;   (b) strong authentication with two-way exchange;   (c) strong authentication with three-way exchange.

3. Explain the use of authentication levels in Directory access control. What role can the referral mechanism play in ensuring that authentication level requirements are met when making an access control decision?

4-6. User *u* is requesting read access to the value of attribute *a* of Directory entry *e*, with an authentication level of *simple*. Each of the tables below gives a set of access control statements applying simultaneously to entry *e*. In each of the three cases, state whether or not access should be granted and identify the decision rule(s) used in making the decision.

Protected Items	User Classes	Per- missions	Prece- dence	Authenti- cation Level
entry (*e*), all-attri- bute-values (*a*)	name (*u*)	grant-read	10	none
entry (*e*), all-attri- bute-values (*a*)	name (*u*)	deny-read	20	simple
entry (*e*), all-attri- bute-types-and-values	all-users	grant-read	20	strong

Protected Items	User Classes	Per- missions	Prece- dence	Authenti- cation Level
entry (*e*), all-attri- bute-values (*a*)	name (*w*)	deny-read	10	strong
entry (*e*), all-attri- bute-values (*a*)	name (*u*)	grant-read	10	none
entry (*e*), all-attri- bute-types-and-values	all-users	grant-read	10	simple

Protected Items	User Classes	Per- missions	Prece- dence	Authenti- cation Level
entry (*e*), all-attri- bute-values (*a*)	name (*u*)	deny-read	10	simple
entry (*e*), all-attri- bute-types-and-values	name (*u*)	grant-read	10	simple
entry (*e*), all-attri- bute-types-and-values	all-users	deny-read	10	none

7. Describe the differences between the basic and simplified access control schemes.

8. In the diagram below, which administrative entries have to be considered in determining the access control statements applying to each of the entries *P*, *Q*, *R*, and *S*, respectively?

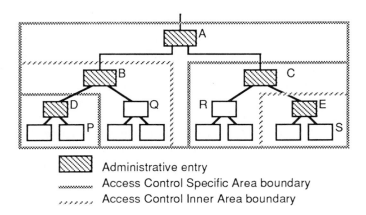

    ▨   Administrative entry
    〰   Access Control Specific Area boundary
    ∕∕∕∕   Access Control Inner Area boundary

REFERENCES

[BOE1] S. Boeyen, "Enhancements to Directory Standards," in *Handbook of Local Area Networks — 1992 Supplement*, Auerbach, New York, 1992.

[DIC1] G. Dickson and A. Lloyd, *Open Systems Interconnection*, Prentice Hall, Englewood Cliffs, NJ, 1991.

[IAN1] C. I'Anson and C. Mitchell, "Security Defects in CCITT Recommendation X.509 — The Directory Authentication Framework," *Computer Communications Review*, vol. 20, no. 2 (April 1990), pp. 30-34.

[MUL1] M. Müller and B. Plattner, "Security Capabilities of X.509: Evaluation and Constructive Criticism," in *Message Handling Systems and Application Layer Communication Protocols*, North-Holland, Amsterdam, 1991, pp. 521-536.

[NIS1] U.S. Department of Commerce, National Institute of Standards and Technology, *Stable Implementation Agreements for Open Systems Interconnection Protocols Version 6 Edition 1 December 1992*, NIST Special Publication 500-206, 1993 (or latest revision thereof).

[RAN1] M. Ransom, "Standardized Access Control for the OSI Directory," in *Handbook of Local Area Networks — 1992 Supplement*, Auerbach, New York, 1992.

[ROS1] M.T. Rose, *The Little Black Book: Mail-Bonding with OSI Directory Services*, Prentice Hall, Englewood Cliffs, NJ, 1991.

Standards

ISO/IEC 9594-1: *Information Technology — Open Systems Interconnection — The Directory: Overview of Concepts, Models, and Services* (Also ITU-T Recommendation X.500).

ISO/IEC 9594-2: *Information Technology — Open Systems Interconnection — The Directory: Models* (Also ITU-T Recommendation X.501).

ISO/IEC 9594-3: *Information Technology — Open Systems Interconnection — The Directory: Abstract Service Definition* (Also ITU-T Recommendation X.511).

ISO/IEC 9594-4: *Information Technology — Open Systems Interconnection — The Directory: Procedures for Distributed Operation* (Also ITU-T Recommendation X.518).

ISO/IEC 9594-5: *Information Technology — Open Systems Interconnection — The Directory: Protocol Specifications* (Also ITU-T Recommendation X.519).

ISO/IEC 9594-6: *Information Technology — Open Systems Interconnection — The Directory: Selected Attribute Types* (Also ITU-T Recommendation X.520).

ISO/IEC 9594-7: *Information Technology — Open Systems Interconnection — The Directory: Selected Object Classes* (Also ITU-T Recommendation X.521).

ISO/IEC 9594-8: *Information Technology — Open Systems Interconnection — The Directory: Authentication Framework* (Also ITU-T Recommendation X.509).

ISO/IEC 9594-9: *Information Technology — Open Systems Interconnection — The Directory: Replication* (Also ITU-T Recommendation X.525).

15 **Network Management**

Network management protocols provide the means for managing systems, networks, and network components. They support administrative functions such as configuration management, accounting, and event logging, and they provide facilities to assist in diagnosing network problems. Network management protocols are themselves application protocols, which use lower-layer communication facilities the same way as other applications.

There are two main families of open-system network management standards — the international standards for OSI management, which define the *Common Management Information Protocol* (CMIP), and the Internet network management standards, which define the *Simple Network Management Protocol* (SNMP).

This chapter deals with security-related aspects of OSI and Internet network management protocols. Two distinct sides of the subject are covered:

- the support provided by network management protocols towards the provision of security services (sometimes known as "management of security"); and
- the means for protecting network management communications (sometimes known as "security of management").

The chapter is organized into four sections:

(1) an overview of the OSI management architecture and standards;
(2) a discussion of security aspects of OSI management, including the security alarm reporting and audit trail functions, access control provisions, and CMIP security;
(3) an overview of SNMP and associated Internet network management standards; and
(4) a description of the security protocols defined for SNMP.

15.1 OSI Management Overview

The OSI management standards were developed by the ISO/IEC JTC1/SC21 subcommittee, in collaboration with the ITU. They comprise several "frame-

411

work" standards in addition to the CMIP specification. For detailed tutorials, see [KLE1, RAM1, YEM1]. Following is a brief overview.

Framework Standards

The first OSI management standard, published in 1989, defines a Management Framework for OSI (ISO/IEC 7498-4). Two types of management are identified — *OSI Systems Management* supports the management of systems generally, while *OSI Layer Management* relates to management of particular OSI layer entities. The Management Framework further defines five management functional areas: configuration management, fault management, accounting management, performance management, and security management. The Management Framework was later augmented by the Systems Management Overview (ISO/IEC 10040). This standard defines terms used throughout the OSI management standards, explains the basic OSI management concepts, describes relationships between the various standards, and establishes rules for conformance to these standards.

The OSI management standards employ an object-oriented information modeling technique. Resources to be managed are modeled in terms of *managed objects*. Managed objects are characterized by the *actions* they accept, the *notifications* they emit, the *attributes* they make visible, and the *behavior* they exhibit. The range of managed object types in practical networks is virtually unbounded, and managed object definitions can be produced by different organizations. Managed objects are arranged in a hierarchy based on containment. For example, a file may contain records which, in turn, contain fields. The containment tree for each system has, at the top, a System Managed Object. The full information model is described in the Structure of Management Information standard (ISO/IEC 10165), which comprises multiple parts as follows:

- The *Management Information Model* describes concepts such as managed objects, operations and notifications, filters, inheritance and allomorphism, containment, and naming.
- The *Definition of Management Information*: defines certain generally useful managed object classes, attributes, actions, and events.
- The *Guidelines for the Definition of Managed Objects* specify techniques and guidelines for users of these standards to define their own managed object classes;
- The *Generic Management Information* part defines generic superclasses (e.g., *connection*) from which OSI layer-specific or resource-specific class definitions (e.g., *transport-connection*) can be derived.

A further standard, ISO/IEC 10164, defines a number of systems management functions in the five management functional areas of accounting management, configuration management, fault management, performance management, and security management (functions in the latter area are discussed in the next section).

Protocol

The architectural framework for OSI management is shown in Figure 15-1. It consists of a *managing system* and a *managed system* which contains one or more managed objects. The two systems communicate using the CMIP Application Layer protocol.

CMIP is specified in ISO/IEC 9596. The service provided by CMIP, known as the *Common Management Information Service* (CMIS), is described in ISO/IEC 9595. CMIP is a request/reply protocol which employs the remote operations model (see Section 3.2). Two types of services are provided:

- the carriage of event notifications generated by managed objects (the *M-EVENT-REPORT* service); and
- the carriage of operations invoked by the managing system and targeted at managed objects.

The latter operations include:

- *M-GET*: Obtain information as to attribute values of a managed object or collection thereof.
- *M-SET*: Change the value(s) of one or more attributes of one or more managed objects.

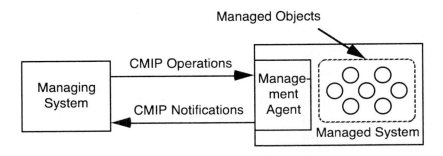

Figure 15-1: OSI Management Architecture

- *M-CREATE*: Cause an instance of a managed object to be created.
- *M-DELETE*: Remove one or more managed objects from the environment.
- *M-ACTION*: Invoke a pre-defined action procedure specified as part of a managed object.
- *M-CANCELGET*: Stop the operation of a lengthy *GET* operation.

15.2 OSI Management Security

The OSI management standards do not comprehensively address either "management of security" or "security of management." However, they have elements which contribute to both topics. To support "management of security," two important *security functions* are defined in the security management area — the Security Alarm Reporting Function and the Security Audit Trail Function. To support "security of management," an access control model and supporting access control information definitions are provided, and provision is made for limited security features in the CMIP protocol.

Security Alarm Reporting Function

The security services of authentication, access control, confidentiality, and integrity all aim to prevent security compromises from occurring. However, it should not be assumed that these services will always function perfectly. There is always a risk of security compromises occurring, due to inadequate or malfunctioning protection mechanisms, exceptionally ingenious or persistent attacks, or circumstances with which the mechanisms cannot cope (e.g., stolen passwords). There is therefore a need for facilities which detect security compromises or suspicious events and report them to a human operator, administrator, or manager. These *security alarms* can result in such follow-up actions as initiating surveillance of a suspicious user, overriding the privileges of a suspicious user, invoking stronger protection mechanisms, or disabling or repairing a faulty network or system component.

A security alarm is triggered by a security-related event which can, in principle, be detected by any network or system component. In terms of the management model, the component detecting the event is a managed object. The security alarm is advised to the managing system via an M-EVENT-REPORT, as illustrated in Figure 15-2.

The Security Alarm Reporting Function standard (ISO/IEC 10164-7) describes the information conveyed in the M-EVENT-REPORT invocation. The precise abstract syntax used in the exchange is specified in the Definition of Managed Information (ISO/IEC 10165-2).

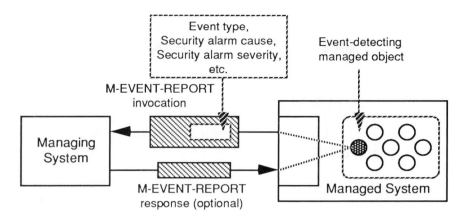

Figure 15-2: Security Alarm Report

The parameters conveyed in a security alarm report fall into three categories:

(a) parameters common to any M-EVENT-REPORT, defined in ISO/IEC 9595 (*invoke identifier*, *mode*, *managed object class*, *managed object instance*, *event type*, *event time*, and *current time*);

(b) parameters common to any management alarm, defined in ISO/IEC 10164-4 (*notification identifier*, *correlated notifications*, *additional information*, and *additional text*); and

(c) parameters specific to security alarms (*security alarm cause*, *security alarm severity, security alarm detector*, *service user*, and *service provider*).

The combination of event type and security alarm cause indicates the reason for the alarm. The possible values for event type and the corresponding options for security alarm cause are:

• *Integrity violation*: An event indicating unauthorized modification, insertion, or deletion of data. Possible values for security alarm cause are *duplicate information*, *information missing*, *information modification detected*, *information out of sequence*, and *unexpected information*.

• *Operational violation*: An event indicating unavailability, malfunction, or incorrect invocation of some service. Possible values for security alarm cause are *denial of service* (suspected deliberate prevention of legitimate use of a service), *out of service*, *procedural error*, and *unspecified reason*.

- *Physical violation*: An event indicating a suspected attack on a physical resource. Possible values for security alarm cause are *cable tamper* (physical damage to a communications medium), *intrusion detection* (suspected illegal entry to a site or tampering with equipment), and *unspecified reason*.
- *Security service or mechanism violation*: An event indicating that an implemented security service or mechanism has detected a potential attack. Possible values for security alarm cause are *authentication failure*, *breach of confidentiality*, *non-repudiation failure*, *unauthorized access attempt*, and *unspecified reason*.
- *Time domain violation*: An event indicating that something has happened at an unexpected or prohibited time. Possible values for security alarm cause are *delayed information* (information was received later than expected), *key expired* (an out-of-date encryption key was presented or used), and *out of hours activity* (a resource was utilized at an unexpected time).

The security alarm severity parameter indicates the significance of the alarm as perceived by the initiating managed object. Possible values are:

- *Indeterminate*: The integrity of the system is unknown.
- *Critical*: A breach of security has occurred that has compromised the system. The system may no longer be assumed to be operating correctly in support of the security policy. Examples are unauthorized modification or disclosure of sensitive security-related information, such as system passwords, or breaches of physical security.
- *Major*: A breach of security has been detected, and significant information or mechanisms have been compromised.
- *Minor*: A breach of security has been detected, and less significant information or mechanisms have been compromised.
- *Warning*: the security of the system is not believed to be compromised.

The security alarm detector parameter identifies the entity which detected the alarm condition. The service user parameter identifies the entity whose request for service led to the generaton of the alarm. The service provider parameter identifies the entity providing the service that led to the generation of the alarm.

The standards do not specify the semantics of the values used in alarm indications in any more detail than that given above. The precise interpretation of these fields is therefore left to the specifiers of managed object classes which generate alarms, and/or to local security policy.

Security Audit Trail Function

As discussed in Chapter 2, a security audit trail plays an important role in securing any network. It can be used for such purposes as testing the adequacy of a security policy, confirming compliance with security policy, assisting in the analysis of attacks, and gathering evidence for use in prosecuting an attacker. Security audit trails record any suspicious events (as might generate a security alarm); they also record many routine events such as connection establishment and termination, security mechanism utilization and accesses to sensitive resources. Auditable events may be detected in the same or a different system to that in which the security audit trail log is maintained. The security audit trail function provides the necessary support for conveying event information to a system in which the log is maintained and for creating and retrieving log entries.

The main standard addressing this area is the Security Audit Trail Function (ISO/IEC 10164-8). Because the mechanisms for managing a security audit trail log are virtually the same as those for managing any other kind of event log used in network management, this standard leans heavily upon two other standards — the Event Report Management Function (ISO/IEC 10164-5) and the Log Control Function (ISO/IEC 10164-6).

The process of notifying an event for a security audit trail is similar to that of generating a security alarm report. It involves an M-EVENT-REPORT invocation initiated by some managed object. Management notifications of virtually any type, as indicated by the event type parameter, may be recorded in a security audit trail log. These include the security alarm report notifications as defined in ISO/IEC 10164-7.

The Security Audit Trail Function standard additionally defines two specific types of notification, corresponding to event type values of *service report* and *usage report*, respectively. A service report indicates an event associated with the provision, denial, or recovery of some service. A usage report is used to log statistical information which has security significance. With these event types, the parameters conveyed are mainly the same as those for security alarm reports, including the parameters common to any M-EVENT-REPORT and parameters common to any management alarm. One additional parameter, *service report cause*, is defined for use with the service report event type, to indicate the reason for the report. This parameter is an ASN.1 object identifier, which means that virtually anyone can define and register values for it. The standard defines some values which are of general applicability: *request for service*, *denial of service*, *response from service*, *service failure*, *service recovery*, and *other reason*.

Control of the audit trail process and retrieval of entries from a security audit trail are independent of the above notification procedure. They employ general procedures defined in other standards. The Event Report Management

Function (ISO/IEC 10164-5) provides for the setting-up of a long term event reporting relationship between two systems. The decision as to which event reports are sent to which system is controlled by (conceptual) filtering mechanisms called *event forwarding discriminators*. These discriminators are themselves modeled as managed objects; hence their characteristics and operational states can be set up and maintained remotely.

The Log Control Function (ISO/IEC 10164-6) supports the creation and deletion of logs used for security audit trail and other purposes, as well as the retrieval of records from such logs. To achieve this, it defines managed object classes to model logs and log records respectively. Instances of log and log record objects can be manipulated remotely using the management procedures in ISO/IEC 10164-1.

Access Control to Management Resources

Network management has its own access control requirements. It is necessary to control who can invoke management actions and who can create, delete, modify, or read management information. Such access control is of critical importance in any network which uses network management protocols, as compromise of a network management resource can easily equate to compromise of the complete network.

This type of access control is addressed in standard ISO/IEC 10164-9 (entitled *Objects and Attributes for Access Control*). This standard presents an access control model, together with required information object definitions to support communication of access control information between systems. The terminology and the conceptual model from the Access Control Framework standard (ISO/IEC 10181-3) are employed[1]. Various access control policies are accommodated, and various access control mechanisms may be used, including access control lists, capabilities, security labels, and context-based controls.

Access control decisions apply to the invocation of management operations such as M-GET or M-SET. The architectural components involved are shown in Figure 15-3. The initiator is the managing system (or the managing user at that system), and the target is an information resource in a managed system. Different target granularities are possible — a target could be a managed object, an attribute of a managed object, a managed object attribute value, or a managed object action. It is therefore possible to provide a very fine level of control over precisely which management user can access what management information and for what purpose.

---

[1] The terminology and concepts are generally in line with those used in Chapter 6 of this book.

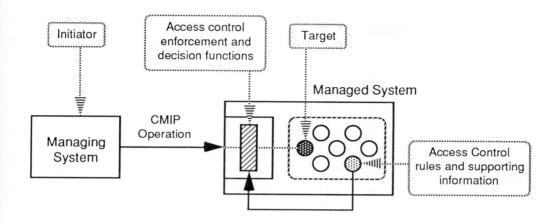

Figure 15-3: Access Control to Management Resources

Decisions whether to grant or deny access requests are based on *access control rules*. Access control rules can themselves be expressed as management information items and be manipulated (e.g., read or modified) using the CMIP protocol.

Three different types of access control rule are differentiated. *Global rules* are used by a security domain authority to protect all targets in that domain with respect to particular initiators or classes of initiator (e.g., particular roles recognized within the domain). *Item rules* are specific rules applying to specific targets. *Default rules* are used for making access decisions when no global or item rules apply.

When multiple rules apply to a particular access request, the different types of rules take precedence in the following order:

(1) global rules that deny access;
(2) item rules that deny access;
(3) global rules that grant access;
(4) item rules that grant access; and
(5) default rules.

An access control rule can be based on virtually any decision process a security policy demands. A specification of a rule can contain multiple elements, such as:

- *Access permission*: An indication whether the rule relates to denial or granting of access.
- *Initiators list*: A list of applicable initiators, expressed in terms of access control lists, capabilities, or security labels.
- *Targets list* (item rules only): A list of applicable targets (e.g., managed objects, attributes, and/or attribute values) and applicable operations on those targets.
- *Scheduling conditions*: An indication of times at which the rule applies (e.g., only during regular business hours, or only from Monday to Friday).
- *State conditions*: An indication of required states of the attributes of a managed object for the rule to apply (e.g., only applicable while the system is in diagnostic mode).
- *Authentication context*: An indication of the authentication level required, when authenticating initiators.

The access control decision procedure is as follows. First, any access control information presented with the access request (e.g., a presented access control certificate or token) may need to be validated. All access rules that apply to the initiator and target are then identified and grouped according to their global/item/default significance. These rules are then applied, taking into account the precedence constraints.

The method of applying a rule depends on the particular access control mechanism used. With an access control list mechanism, the initiator's identity is compared with the applicable access control list. With a capability mechanism, capabilities presented by the initiator are compared with capabilities stated in the rule. With a label-based mechanism, a label associated with the initiator is compared with the set of labels recognized by the rule. Context-based checks, e.g., for scheduling conditions, state conditions, or authentication level may also need to be applied.

After making an access decision, other actions may need to occur. Information used in making the decision may need to be temporarily stored to assist in making future decisions involving the same initiator (such information is called *retained access control decision information*, or *retained ADI*). Access control information associated with the target may need to modified, e.g., if the management operation caused a managed object to be created or deleted. Dependent upon security policy, it may also be necessary to generate a security alarm report and/or security audit trail notification.

In the event of access being denied, there are various ways of responding to the initiator. Security policy may stipulate any of the following types of response: an access-denied error indication, no response, a false response (i.e., it appears to the initiator that access has been granted), or aborting of the application-association.

To support the above procedures, there is a need to remotely manage (e.g., create, update) the stored information used in making access control decisions. For this purpose, the standard provides several managed object class and attribute type definitions, for representing access control rules and supporting information structures. These definitions enable access control information to be manipulated remotely using the procedures defined in ISO/IEC 10164-1.

CMIP Security

The CMIP protocol specification includes minimal security features. In fact, the only built-in security feature is provision for conveying an access control certificate with relevant operation invocations. No particular certificate format is mandated, but a possible certificate definition, based on the work of the European ECMA group, is attached to ISO/IEC 10164-9.

This does not necessarily mean that CMIP communications cannot be protected, as the OSI modular approach to security enables protection to be added in other places. For example, the OIW Network Management agreements [NIS1] provide for an authentication exchange, derived from the Directory protocol, to be conveyed in the ACSE authentication fields when establishing a CMIP application-association. This can support unilateral or mutual authentication using any of: passwords, transformed passwords, or public-key signed tokens (see Section 12.3).

Overall data integrity and/or confidentiality of CMIP sessions can be provided using end-system level security services, such as those provided by TLSP or NLSP (see Chapter 11). More comprehensive application level security services can be added using the generic upper layers security facilities described in Chapter 12.

15.3 Internet SNMP Overview

The Simple Network Management Protocol (SNMP) is part of a group of Internet standards which collectively support the management of TCP/IP-based systems. Version 1 of SNMP [ROS2 ROS3, CAS1] has been stable since 1990, and has been widely implemented. Version 2, which incorporates substantial security facilities, was released in 1993 [CAS2, CAS3, CAS4, CAS5, GAL1, GAL2, MCC1]. For a general tutorial on SNMP and the Internet management framework, see [ROS1]. Following is a brief overview of the main concepts.

Architectural Model

The SNMP architectural model is illustrated in Figure 15-4 The main
components are at least one *network management station* and a number of
network elements. A network management station is a host system which runs
SNMP plus network management applications. Network elements are
managed systems, such as hosts, routers, gateways, or servers. A network
element contains a management *agent*. The agent implements SNMP and gives
access to management information which is the network element's view of a
Management Information Base (MIB).

Network Management Station   Network Element

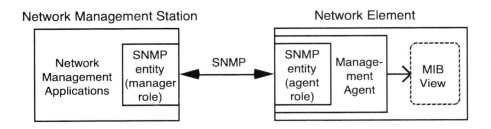

Figure 15-4: SNMP Architecture

The entities which implement the SNMP in communicating management
stations and network elements are called *SNMP protocol entities* or simply
SNMP entities. An SNMP entity operates in either a *manager role* or an *agent
role*.
SNMP also provides for the management of a device via a *proxy agent*.
A proxy agent acts in an agent role with respect to a management station but, in
order to process a management request, needs to communicate further with a
remote managed system. The latter communication can be either SNMP-based
(native proxy configuration) or can use another protocol (foreign proxy
configuration). Foreign proxy configurations enable an SNMP manager to
manage a non-SNMP device.
Version 2 of SNMP also added support for protocol interactions between
two SNMP entities operating in the manager role, for purposes of transferring
management information.
The communication needs of SNMP entities are satisfied by underlying
protocol layers, typically the Internet UDP and IP protocols plus lower-layer
protocols.

Information Model

Management information in a network element is modeled by a collection of *managed objects*, which form part of the MIB database. The Internet Structure of Management Information (SMI) [CAS3, ROS2, ROS3] defines a set of rules which constitute the schema for the MIB database.

Internet managed objects differ from OSI managed objects in that the former do not directly model behavior (i.e., there is no direct equivalent of the OSI M-ACTION operation)[2]. An Internet managed object is essentially a particular type of data variable which forms part of the MIB. The main elements of a managed object definition are a *syntax* (an ASN.1 type) and an *object name* (an ASN.1 object identifier).

There may be multiple instances of a managed object recognized by one agent. A managed object instance is identified by a *variable name*, obtained by appending an *instance identifier* suffix to the object name.

A collection of related managed objects is defined in a *MIB module*. Various MIB modules, for such purposes as managing the configuration and state information of Internet protocol entities, are defined in the RFC series.

For a user performing an operation on a network element, in general, only a subset of variables (managed object instances) in the MIB are visible. Such a subset is called an SNMP *MIB view*. An SNMP agent may partition its MIB into several (potentially overlapping) MIB views. Access policy determines which MIB view is available for a given user and operation.

Protocol

The protocol specifications for SNMP Versions 1 and 2 respectively are in [CAS1, CAS5]. In comparison with the OSI management protocol, SNMP is simpler and less costly to implement. In particular, it is suitable for implementation in comparatively small network systems.

SNMP models all management agent functions as alterations or inspections of variables (managed object instances). Hence the primary protocol operations are read and write operations issued by a network management station. The only additional functions are *traversal*, which allows a management station to determine which variables a network element supports, and *traps*, which allow a network element to report an extraordinary event to a management station. A trap does not itself convey substantial information to a management station — it is a signal that the management station should poll the network element to read any required information.

---

[2] An Internet managed object action can be invoked as a consequence of setting a variable. The definition of an object indicates what action occurs based on the new value.

There are six basic SNMP protocol interactions, which involve seven types of PDU:

- *Get*: A management station requests specific management information from an agent via a *GetRequest* PDU. The agent responds via a *Response* PDU.
- *Get Next* A management station can traverse the variables of an agent on the basis of the tree structure resulting from the object-identifier-based identification scheme for managed object instances. The GetNext operation requests the return of management information regarding the next variable after that identified by the requestor. The request employs a *GetNextRequest* PDU. The agent responds via a *Response* PDU.
- *Set*: A management station stores management information with an agent, via a *SetRequest* PDU. The agent responds via a *Response* PDU.
- *Get Bulk* (added in Version 2): A management station requests the transfer of a potentially large amount of data (e.g., a large table) via a *GetBulkRequest* PDU. The agent responds with a *Response* PDU.
- *Inform* (added in Version 2): A management station conveys management information to another management station via an *InformRequest* PDU. The latter responds with a *Response* PDU.
- *Trap*: An agent reports an extraordinary event to a management station via a *Trap* PDU.

PDUs contain *request identifiers*, which are used to associate responses with requests. This allows several requests to in transit in parallel, and also provides a means for gauging round-trip time. SNMP PDUs are specified using ASN.1 notation.

An SNMP PDU is conveyed in an *SNMP message*. The way the PDU is incorporated into the message depends upon the *administrative model* (and corresponding security provisions) in use.

Administrative Models

In SNMP Version 1, a *community-based* administrative model was employed. An *SNMP community* is defined to be a relationship between an SNMP agent and one or more management stations. Each SNMP community has a community name which is an octet string (usually a string of printable characters). An SNMP *access mode* is defined to be an element taking the value *read-only* or *read-write*. A pairing of an SNMP access mode with an SNMP MIB view is called an SNMP *community profile*. Hence, a community profile represents specific access rights to the variables in a particular MIB view.

Using the community-based administrative model, an SNMP message comprises a version number, a community name, and an unprotected SNMP PDU. An agent receiving such a message uses the community name as the basis for determining the legitimacy of the request and the applicable access rights. The term "trivial authentication protocol" is sometimes used to refer to this approach.

In SNMP Version 2, an enhanced administrative model was defined [GAL1]. A basic change in this new model is provision for the source and intended recipient of each SNMP message to be unambiguously identified. This provides the necessary foundation on which to build identity-based access control, and authentication on an individual system basis.

The enhanced administrative model introduces the concept of an *SNMP party*. (This concept serves a purpose similar to the security association concept used in the security protocols described in Chapters 11 and 12.) An SNMP message has one SNMP party as its source and one as its destination. An SNMP party corresponds to an SNMP entity, operating under a particular set of constraints which are consistently understood by another SNMP entity with which SNMP communication occurs. A particular SNMP entity may need to know of multiple SNMP parties with which it communicates — for each of these SNMP parties it will recognize a party identity and will maintain certain attribute and state information. Furthermore, a particular SNMP entity may constitute multiple SNMP parties, as seen by other SNMP entities.

An SNMP Version 2 message conveys a construct, called an *SNMP management communication*, which comprises the following components:

- *Destination party*: An ASN.1 object identifier identifying the destination SNMP party.
- *Source party*: An ASN.1 object identifier identifying the source SNMP party.
- *Context*: An ASN.1 object identifier identifying the collection of managed object resources referenced by the communication.
- *PDU*: The SNMP PDU transferred.

The way the SNMP management communication is incorporated into an SNMP message depends upon the security options in use.

15.4 SNMP Security

Security protocols for SNMP Version 2 are defined in [GAL2]. This RFC includes a discussion of required security services, together with specifications of two security protocols and supporting security techniques for use in protecting SNMP PDUs.

Security Services

The two primary threats in the SNMP environment are considered to be:

- *Data modification*: Somebody may alter an in-transit SNMP message so as to cause an unauthorized management operation to occur (e.g., a managed object is set to the wrong value).
- *Masquerade*: An unauthorized party, assuming the identity of another party, generates a SNMP message which causes an unauthorized management operation to occur.

Two secondary threats are:

- *Message stream modification*: SNMP messages may be reordered, delayed, or replayed, so as to effect an unauthorized management operation (this may be very easy to do, as messages are usually conveyed over connectionless underlying services).
- *Eavesdropping*: Disclosure of management information may sometimes be a concern (it is always a concern when managing the security facilities themselves).

Consequently the required security services are:

(1) a combination of the services of data integrity and data origin authentication;
(2) sequence integrity; and
(3) (optionally, in addition) data confidentiality.

This results in the definition of two SNMP security protocols. The *Digest Authentication Protocol* provides for data integrity, data origin authentication, and sequence integrity protection. The *Symmetric Privacy Protocol* provides for data confidentiality protection. When the latter protocol is used, the former must also be used, thereby providing all of the services (1), (2), and (3).

Digest Authentication Protocol

The Digest Authentication Protocol provides its protection via an *authentication information* data item. This item is incorporated into an SNMP authenticated

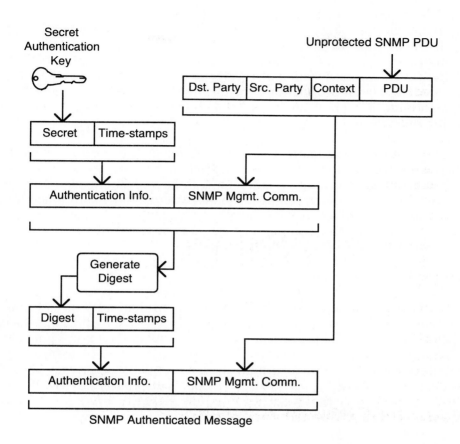

Figure 15-5: Message Generation with Digest Authentication Protocol

message, along with a regular SNMP PDU. The process at the sending end is shown in Figure 15-5. (The corresponding process at the receiving end can be readily deduced.)

The authentication information item comprises the following fields:

- *Source authentication time-stamp*: This field conveys the time of generation of the message, according to the source party's clock. The main purpose of this field is to protect against message reordering or replay, thereby supporting a sequence integrity service.
- *Destination authentication time-stamp*: This field conveys the time of generation of the message, according to the destination party's clock.

(Every party maintains clock values for all other parties with which it communicates.) This field is mainly to facilitate clock synchronization.

- *Authentication digest*: This field conveys a seal, calculated over the message. The sealing process effectively involves applying a hash function to a concatenation of a secret authentication key and the message content. The hash function recommended is the MD5 message digest algorithm [RIV1]. Both the secret authentication key and the digest are 128 bits in length.

The method of generating the digest is particularly interesting (it has been cleverly designed for simple and efficient implementation). First, the complete SNMP authenticated message is assembled, in its ASN.1-encoded form, with the value of the 128-bit secret authentication key temporarily substituted for the 128-bit digest. The digest is then calculated by applying the hash function to this string of octets. The resultant 128-bit value is then written back into the string, overwriting the secret authentication key.

Symmetric Privacy Protocol

The Symmetric Privacy Protocol provides confidentiality protection by encrypting an SNMP authenticated message, as generated by the Digest Authentication Protocol. The process at the sending end is shown in Figure 15-6. (The corresponding process at the receiving end can be readily deduced.) The encryption uses a symmetric algorithm and a pre-established privacy key. The algorithm recommended is DES in CBC mode. The privacy key is 128 bits in length, comprising a 56-bit DES key (plus 8 parity bits) plus a 64-bit initialization vector. Messages must be padded out to an integral number of 8-octet blocks for encryption.

Management of SNMP Security

Use of the above security protocols depends upon the following management functions:

- key management, with respect to both the authentication keys and the privacy keys;
- ensuring that clocks in all systems are kept loosely synchronized (as correct functioning of the sequence integrity mechanism depends upon such synchronization)[3]; and

---

[3] Note that protection against replay in SNMP security protocols depends solely upon time-stamps, therefore upon secure clock synchronization. As secure maintenance of clock values can be difficult in practice, there are possible vulnerabilities in this area.

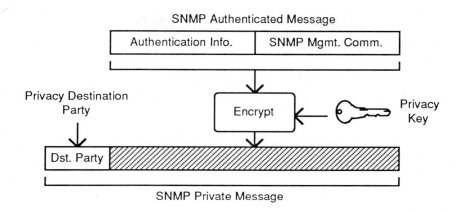

Figure 15-6: Message Generation with Symmetric Privacy Protocol

- establishment and maintenance of information in each system regarding other SNMP parties with which communication occurs.

The SNMP security protocol RFC describes procedures whereby a central management station can use SNMP to perform both key management and clock synchronization over a set of other SNMP implementations. Alternatively, there is nothing precluding the use of more robust (e.g., public-key-based) key management systems, using other protocols.

To establish and maintain SNMP party information, an initial configuration of a small number of parties needs to be manually set up in an SNMP protocol entity at the time of its initial installation. Thereafter, party information can be maintained from a central management station using SNMP itself. The managed object definitions needed to support such maintenance are provided in [MCC1].

Access Control

The SNMP Version 2 administrative model includes an access control model, to govern which SNMP PDUs can be legitimately sent between a pair of parties, with reference to a particular set of managed object resources. Access control information is considered to exist in the form of access control lists. An access control list entry has the following components:

- *acl Target*: Identifier of a party to which access is permitted.
- *acl Subject*: Identifier of a party to which access privileges are granted (i.e., an initiator, in the terminology of ISO/IEC 10181-3).
- *acl Resources*: Identifier of an SNMP context, i.e., a collection of managed object resources.
- *acl Privileges*: A set of flags, one for each SNMP operation, indicating whether or not that operation is permitted.

On receipt of any PDU, the receiving system checks the applicable (locally-stored) access control list to ensure that the communication is permitted.

The necessary managed object definitions for specifying access control lists are defined in [MCC1]. This enables access control information stored in remote systems to be managed using SNMP itself.

Summary

Network management protocols provide the means for managing systems, networks, and network components. They support administrative functions and provide facilities to assist in diagnosing network problems. There are two major families of open-system network management standards — OSI management standards, which define the *Common Management Information Protocol* (CMIP), and Internet network management standards, which define the *Simple Network Management Protocol* (SNMP).

The OSI management standards define two important security functions — the Security Alarm Reporting Function and the Security Audit Trail Function. Security alarms are used to report security compromises or suspicious events to a human operator, administrator, or manager. Security audit trails record suspicious events plus routine events which may later have security significance. The security audit trail function supports the transfer of event information to a system in which an audit trail log is maintained, and the creation and retrieval of log entries. Both functions use CMIP operations for conveying information, in a standard format, between managed system and managing system.

The OSI management standards also include a model and accompanying information object definitions, to support access control for OSI management operations. The CMIP protocol has minimal built-in security, but protection can be added using the standard OSI lower layers or upper layers security protocols.

The Internet management standards include optional security protocol extensions for protecting SNMP communications. The Digest Authentication

Protocol provides for data integrity, data origin authentication, and sequence integrity protection by adding an authentication information data item to an SNMP message. The Symmetric Privacy Protocol provides additionally for confidentiality protection, by encrypting an SNMP authenticated message generated by the Digest Authentication Protocol. Symmetric encryption (typically DES) is used.

Use of these SNMP security protocols depends upon management functions for key management, clock synchronization, and establishment and maintenance of information regarding other SNMP parties. Procedures are specified whereby SNMP can itself be used for these management purposes.

SNMP also includes an access control model, which supports the definition of access control lists. These lists govern which SNMP PDUs can legitimately be sent between any pair of parties, with reference to a particular set of managed resources. Necessary definitions are provided to enable management of access control information in a remote system using SNMP itself.

Exercises

1. Describe how the OSI Security Alarm Reporting Function and Security Audit Trail Function might be employed in a centrally managed enterprise network. How important is it to have standardized definitions of these functions?

2. Figure 15-5 illustrates the SNMP Digest Authentication Protocol procedure at the sending end. Describe, with the aid of an illustration if desired, the corresponding procedure at the receiving end.

3. Why is clock synchronization important when using the SNMP Digest Authentication Protocol? If the clock used by an SNMP agent is (accidentally or deliberately) set back, what type of attack can be easily perpetrated? Describe such an attack scenario.

REFERENCES

[CAS1] J. Case, M. Fedor, M. Schoffstall, and J. Davin, *A Simple Network Management Protocol (SNMP)*, Request for Comments (RFC) 1157, Internet Activities Board, 1990.

[CAS2] J. Case, K. McCloghrie, M. Rose, and S. Waldbusser, *Introduction to Version 2 of the Internet-standard Network Management Framework*, Request for Comments (RFC) 1441, Internet Activities Board, 1993.

[CAS3] J. Case, K. McCloghrie, M. Rose, and S. Waldbusser, *Structure of Management Information for Version 2 of the Simple Network Management Protocol (SNMPv2)*, Request for Comments (RFC) 1442, Internet Activities Board, 1993.

[CAS4] J. Case, K. McCloghrie, M. Rose, and S. Waldbusser, *Textual Conventions for Version 2 of the Simple Network Management Protocol (SNMPv2)*, Request for Comments (RFC) 1443, Internet Activities Board, 1993.

[CAS5] J. Case, K. McCloghrie, M. Rose, and S. Waldbusser, *Protocol Operations for Version 2 of the Simple Network Management Protocol (SNMPv2)*, Request for Comments (RFC) 1448, Internet Activities Board, 1993.

[GAL1] J. Galvin and K. McCloghrie, *Administrative Model for Version 2 of the Simple Network Management Protocol (SNMPv2)*, Request for Comments (RFC) 1445, Internet Activities Board, 1993.

[GAL2] J. Galvin and K. McCloghrie, *Security Protocols for Version 2 of the Simple Network Management Protocol (SNMPv2)*, Request for Comments (RFC) 1446, Internet Activities Board, 1993.

[KLE1] S.M. Klerer, "System Management Information Modelling," *IEEE Communications Magazine*, vol. 31, no. 5 (May 1993), pp. 38-44.

[MCC1] K. McCloghrie and J. Galvin, *Party MIB for Version 2 of the Simple Network Management Protocol (SNMPv2)*, Request for Comments (RFC) 1447, Internet Activities Board, 1993.

[NIS1] U.S. Department of Commerce, National Institute of Standards and Technology, *Stable Implementation Agreements for Open Systems Interconnection Protocols Version 6 Edition 1 December 1992*, NIST Special Publication 500-206, 1993 (or latest revision thereof).

[RAM1] L. Raman, "CMISE Functions and Services," *IEEE Communications Magazine*, vol. 31, no. 5 (May 1993), pp. 46-51.

[RIV1] R. Rivest, *The MD5 Message-Digest Algorithm*, Request for Comments (RFC) 1321, Internet Activities Board, 1992.

[ROS1] M.T. Rose, *The Simple Book*, Prentice Hall, Englewood Cliffs, NJ, 1991.

[ROS2] M.T. Rose and K. McCloghrie, *Structure and Identification of Management Information for TCP/IP-based Internets*, Request for Comments (RFC) 1155, Internet Activities Board, 1990.

[ROS3] M.T. Rose and K. McCloghrie, *Concise MIB Definitions*, Request for Comments (RFC) 1212, Internet Activities Board, 1991.

[YEM1] Y. Yemini, "The OSI Network Management Model," *IEEE Communications Magazine*, vol. 31, no. 5 (May 1993), pp. 20-29.

Standards

ISO/IEC 7498-4: *Information Technology — Open Systems Interconnection — Basic Reference Model — Part 4: Management Framework* (Also ITU-T Recommendation X.700).

ISO/IEC 9595: *Information Technology — Open Systems Interconnection — Common Management Information Service Definition* (Also ITU-T Recommendation X.710).

ISO/IEC 9596: *Information Technology — Open Systems Interconnection — Common Management Information Protocol Specification* (Also ITU-T Recommendations X.711, X.712).

ISO/IEC 10040: *Information Technology — Open Systems Interconnection — Systems Management Overview* (Also ITU-T Recommendation X.701).

ISO/IEC 10164-1: *Information Technology — Open Systems Interconnection — Systems Management: Object Management Function* (Also ITU-T Recommendation X.730).

ISO/IEC 10164-4: *Information Technology — Open Systems Interconnection — Systems Management: Alarm Reporting Function* (Also ITU-T Recommendation X.733).

ISO/IEC 10164-5: *Information Technology — Open Systems Interconnection — Systems Management: Event Report Management Function* (Also ITU-T Recommendation X.734).

ISO/IEC 10164-6: *Information Technology — Open Systems Interconnection — Systems Management: Log Control Function* (Also ITU-T Recommendation X.735).

ISO/IEC 10164-7: *Information Technology — Open Systems Interconnection — Systems Management: Security Alarm Reporting Function* (Also ITU-T Recommendation X.736).

ISO/IEC 10164-8: *Information Technology — Open Systems Interconnection — Systems Management: Security Audit Trail Function* (Also ITU-T Recommendation X.740).

ISO/IEC 10164-9: *Information Technology — Open Systems Interconnection — Systems Management: Objects and Attributes for Access Control* (Also ITU-T Recommendation X.741) (Draft).

ISO/IEC 10165-1: *Information Technology — Open Systems Interconnection — Structure of Management Information: Management Information Model* (Also ITU-T Recommendation X.720).

ISO/IEC 10165-2: *Information Technology — Open Systems Interconnection — Structure of Management Information: Definition of Management Information* (Also ITU-T Recommendation X.721).

ISO/IEC 10165-4: *Information Technology — Open Systems Interconnection — Structure of Management Information: Guidelines for the Definition of Managed Objects* (Also ITU-T Recommendation X.722).

ISO/IEC 10165-5: *Information Technology — Open Systems Interconnection — Structure of Management Information: Generic Management Information* (Also ITU-T Recommendation X.723).

ISO/IEC 10181-3: *Information Technology — Security Frameworks in Open Systems — Access Control Framework* (Also ITU-T Recommendation X.812) (Draft).

16 Security Evaluation Criteria

The main focus of this book has been on standard security protocols and techniques for use in the design of network security solutions. However, when it comes to *implementing* such security solutions, new issues become apparent.

A major issue is: *How can a purchaser of a security product be assured that the product provides the protection required?* This includes being assured that the product design is adequate and appropriate, and being assured that the design is correctly implemented. A purchaser also needs to be assured that the product does not perform any additional function(s) which could be deleterious to the purchaser's or user's needs (e.g., the possible existence of a virus, Trojan horse, or undocumented back door in the product).

While such assurances might be obtainable by ad hoc means, purchasers can best be served by having a standard metric for comparing the security provisions in different products being considered for purchase. This raises a demand for independent assessments of products by impartial organizations which *evaluate* products. Such evaluations may lead to *endorsement* or *certification* of products. As evaluation processes need to be commonly understood by many different organizations, including product developers, purchasers and evaluators, there is a need for objective and well-defined evaluation criteria to be standardized. The subject area of *security evaluation criteria* addresses these needs.

This chapter introduces this subject area and the published documents which provide the foundation for ongoing work in the field. The chapter is organized into four sections, which provide overviews of:

(1) the U.S. Department of Defense *Orange Book* and related publications, which constitute the starting point for virtually all work in the field;
(2) the European Information Technology Security Evaluation Criteria (ITSEC);
(3) other security evaluation criteria development initiatives, including the Canadian Criteria, the U.S. Federal Criteria, and the ISO/IEC international criteria; and
(4) the related topic of standards for the implementation and validation of cryptographic devices.

16.1 U.S. Department of Defense Criteria

Throughout the 1970s and 1980s, the U.S. Department of Defense (DoD) and the National Bureau of Standards (now NIST) conducted various programs addressing the building, evaluating, and auditing of secure computer systems. The systems of primary concern were those to be used in handling classified or other sensitive government information. This work led to the publication, in 1983, of the landmark *Orange Book* — a Department of Defense standard on security evaluation criteria for computer systems. The *Orange Book* was subsequently augmented by further publications, notably the *Red Book* which extended its applicability to network environments. The *Orange Book* and related publications became the starting point for a variety of national security evaluation criteria development activities in several countries.

The Orange Book

The Trusted Computer System Evaluation Criteria (TCSEC) was first published in 1983 and revised in 1985 [DOD1]. Because of its distinctive cover, it has since become well known as the *Orange Book*.
    The stated purposes of this document are[1]:

- To provide a standard to manufacturers as to what security features to build into their new and planned commercial products in order to provide widely available systems that satisfy trust requirements (with particular emphasis on preventing the disclosure of data) for sensitive applications.

- To provide DoD Components[2] with a metric with which to evaluate the degree of trust that can be placed in computer systems for the secure processing of classified and other sensitive information.

- To provide a basis for specifying security requirements in acquisition specifications.

The products addressed include computer operating systems and other computer system components.
    The *Orange Book* focuses on providing confidentiality protection of sensitive information. The fundamental requirements assumed are:

(1) *Security policy*: There must be an explicit and well-defined security policy enforced by the system.
(2) *Marking*: Access control labels must be associated with objects.
(3) *Identification*: Individual subjects (users) must be identified.

---

[1] Source [DOD1], page 2.

[2] Refers to the various organizational arms of the U.S. Department of Defense.

(4) *Accountability*: Audit information must be selectively kept and protected so that actions affecting security can be traced to the responsible party.

(5) *Assurance*: The computer system must contain hardware/software mechanisms that can be independently evaluated to provide sufficient assurance that the system enforces requirements (1) to (4) above.

(6) *Continuous protection*: The trusted mechanisms that enforce these basic requirements must be continuously protected against tampering and/or unauthorized changes.

The document comprises two main parts. The first part specifies detailed criteria whereby a computer system can be assigned to a particular class, according to the overall confidence one can place in the system for the protection of sensitive information. The second part provides a discussion of basic objectives, rationale, and U.S. government policy behind the development of the criteria. It also provides guidelines for developers pertaining to covert channels, security testing, and the implementation of mandatory (multilevel) access controls.

The criteria define a four-level hierarchy — divisions *A*, *B*, *C*, and *D*— with *A* indicating systems providing the most comprehensive security and *D* indicating those with minimal security. Divisions can be further subdivided into classes.

The various classes differ in both requirements for specific security features and requirements for mechanisms/methods needed to evaluate assurance levels. The specific classes identified and their main characteristics are summarized below. The classes form a hierarchy of progressively more trusted systems (each adds requirements to those of earlier classes). The term *Trusted Computing Base* (TCB) is used to indicate security-critical hardware/software components of the system under evaluation.

- *Class D (Minimal Protection)*: A system which has been evaluated but failed to reach a higher class.
- *Class C1 (Discretionary Security Protection)*: Satisfies discretionary (need-to-know) requirements by providing separation of users and data. It incorporates controls capable of enforcing access limitations on an individual basis; users can protect project or private information and keep other users from accidentally reading or destroying their data. The class *C1* environment is intended for cooperating users processing data at the same level(s) of sensitivity. The criteria include certain system documentation requirements.
- *Class C2: (Controlled Access Protection)*: Systems in this class enforce a more finely grained discretionary access control than *C1* systems, making users individually accountable for their actions through login procedures,

auditing of security-relevant events, and resource isolation. It includes provisions regarding object reuse, to ensure that information in a storage object (e.g., data buffer) cannot be disclosed to a new user of that object when it is reassigned.

- *Class B1 (Labeled Security Protection)*: This is the first class requiring support of mandatory access controls. Systems must carry sensitivity labels with major data structures in the system. An informal statement of the security policy model, data labeling, and mandatory access control over named subjects and objects must be present. The capability must exist for accurately labeling exported information.

- *Class B2 (Structured Protection)*: The Trusted Computing Base (TCB) must be based on a formal security policy model. The discretionary and mandatory access control enforcement found in class *B1* systems is extended to all subjects and objects in the system. In addition, covert channels are addressed. The TCB must be specially structured. Authentication mechanisms are strengthened. Specialized system administrator and operator functions are required, and stringent configuration management controls are imposed.

- *Class B3 (Security Domains)*: The TCB must mediate all accesses of subjects to objects, be tamperproof, and be small enough to be subjected to analysis and tests. Further structuring restrictions apply. A security administrator is supported, audit mechanisms are expanded to signal security-relevant events, trusted system recovery procedures are required.

- *Class A1 (Verified Design)*: Functionally equivalent to Class *B3*; however, formal design specification and verification techniques must have been employed throughout its development. A trusted distribution system must exist.

The *Orange Book* is used as the basis of an evaluation program operated by the U.S. National Computer Security Center and the Canadian Communications Security Establishment. This program evaluates commercial products submitted by vendors and assigns an appropriate rating (class) to each. The results are published in an Evaluated Products List, which is used by government departments and agencies in the procurement of computer products for classified or sensitive applications. Additional publications have been produced to enable a government procurer to determine which class is appropriate for a given secure application [DOD2, DOD3]. This decision is based on a *risk index*, which is a function of the minimum clearance or authorization of system users and the maximum sensitivity (i.e., classification) of data processed by the system.

Orange Book ratings are also recognized by some commercial buyers. For example, some commercial acquisitions demand a rating of at least Class

$C2$, the class generally required for unclassified but sensitive government applications.

The Red Book

The Trusted Network Interpretation (TNI) of the Trusted Computer System Evaluation Criteria (the *Red Book*) was published in 1987 [DOD4]. Its purpose is to provide subsidiary information to enable *Orange Book* principles to be applied to a network environment.

The *Red Book* has two main parts. The first part is an extension of the *Orange Book*, addressing the same security features, assurance requirements, and rating structure. It provides detailed guidance as to how the *Orange Book* should be interpreted in a network environment. It therefore constitutes a basis for assigning ratings to network products, ranging from isolated LANs to wide-area internetworked computers.

The second part of the *Red Book* describes a number of additional security services, e.g., authentication, non-repudiation, and network management, that arise in network environments. These services are considered inappropriate for the rigorous *Orange Book* style of evaluation, but a product may be given an additional qualitative rating on the basis of each such service. The additional services are, at a general level, aligned with the security services defined in the OSI Security Architecture (ISO/IEC 7498-2) and discussed in Part I of this book.

16.2 European Criteria

Following the publication of the U.S. *Orange Book*, several European countries produced their own security evaluation criteria specifications. These included United Kingdom criteria for government use [UKG1], the United Kingdom *Green Book* for commercial security products [UKG2], the French *Blue-White-Red Book* [FRA1], and the German National Criteria [GER1].

As the formation of the European Community progressed, the need for harmonized security evaluation criteria became apparent, so that product evaluations performed in one country would be applicable in another. Consequently, a cooperative activity was established between the governments of France, Germany, the Netherlands, and the United Kingdom to develop a harmonized criteria document called the Information Technology Security Evaluation Criteria (ITSEC). The resultant specification was published by the Commission of the European Communities [EUR1].

The ITSEC is less rigid than the *Orange Book*, aiming to be adaptable across a variety of products, applications, and environments. It provides a consistent approach to the evaluation of both products and systems. This makes it both easy and economical to evaluate systems containing products which have previously been evaluated.

The ITSEC also provides a clear separation between security features and security assurance. It does not specify precise functionality requirements, but permits different functionality profiles to be defined and used. The security functionality for a product or system under evaluation may be either specially defined or defined by reference to a pre-defined *functionality class*.

The ITSEC includes a number of example functionality classes, based upon classes defined in the German National Criteria. These include five classes (denoted *F-C1*, *F-C2*, *F-B1*, *F-B2*, and *F-B3*) that align closely with the functional requirements of the *Orange Book* classes *C1*, *C2*, *B1*, *B2*, and *B3*, respectively.

Assurance is dealt with separately, by the assignment of an *evaluation level* (one of seven levels, designated *E0* through *E6*) which indicates the confidence the procurer of a product or system can have that the stated security functionality is both appropriate and implemented correctly.

The evaluation process starts by having the product or system *sponsor* (typically the vendor) state a *security target*, which includes an assessment of security objectives and threats, a specification and justification of the security enforcing functions and mechanisms employed, and a *target evaluation level*. The product or system is subject to assessment as to both the effectiveness of the security design and the correctness of the implementation. The evaluation process involves having an independent evaluator confirm the evaluation level, following a process not unlike a financial auditing process.

The evaluation levels can be characterized as follows:

- *Level E0*: This level represents inadequate assurance.
- *Level E1*: At this level, there must be a security target and an informal description of the architectural design of the product/system. Functional testing is used to show that the security target is met.
- *Level E2*: In addition to *E1* requirements, there must be an informal description of the detailed design. Evidence of functional testing must be evaluated. There must be a configuration control system and an approved distribution procedure.
- *Level E3*: In addition to *E2* requirements, the source code and/or hardware drawings corresponding to the security mechanisms must be evaluated. Evidence of testing of those mechanisms must be evaluated.
- *Level E4*: In addition to *E3* requirements, there must be an underlying formal model of security policy supporting the security target. The security enforcing functions, the architectural design, and the detailed design must be specified in a semi-formal style.

- *Level E5*: In addition to *E4* requirements, there must be a close correspondence between the detailed design and the source code and/or hardware drawings.
- *Level E6*: In addition to *E5* requirements, the security enforcing functions and the architectural design must be specified formally, consistent with the specified underlying formal model of security policy.

Each *Orange Book* class can be mapped to a specific combination of an ITSEC functionality class and an evaluation level, as shown in Table 16-1. However, the ITSEC permits other many other combinations beyond those mapping to the *Orange Book* classes.

Orange Book *Class*	ITSEC Equivalent *{functionality class, evaluation level}*
D	{ − , E0}
C1	{F-C1, E1}
C2	{F-C2, E2}
B1	{F-B1, E3}
B2	{F-B2, E4}
B3	{F-B3, E5}
A1	{F-B3, E6}

Table 16-1: Mapping Between Orange Book and ITSEC

16.3 Other Criteria Projects

The following security evaluation criteria development activities are also significant:

- the Canadian Criteria;
- the U.S. Federal Criteria; and
- the ISO/IEC international criteria.

In Canada, the Canadian System Security Centre (CSSC) of the Communications Security Establishment (CSE) is responsible for the Canadian Trusted Computer Product Evaluation Criteria (TCPEC) [CAN1]. The Canadian Criteria aim to serve two purposes: they provide a comparative scale for the evaluation of commercial products, and they provide a guide to manufacturers as to what security features to build into their products. The Canadian Criteria go even further than the ITSEC in separating security functionality from assurance. Distinct criteria are defined for each of four functionality categories — *confidentiality*, *integrity*, *availability*, and *accountability* — plus an *assurance* category for evaluating trust. Each category may be divided into multiple divisions, and multiple evaluation levels are defined for each division.

In the United States, NIST and the National Security Agency (NSA) established a joint project to develop a series of Federal Information Processing Standards (FIPS), collectively called the *Federal Criteria*. These criteria serve to update the *Orange Book* and move towards alignment with other criteria developments such as the ITSEC and the Canadian Criteria. The scope is being expanded significantly beyond that of the *Orange Book*, especially with respect to access control (models other than the multi-level model), integrity and availability. The initial version of the Federal Criteria provides for the definition of different *protection profiles* to accommodate the security requirements of different environments. It specifically includes protection profiles for commercial environments, i.e., the environments not well served by the *Orange Book*.

At the international level, ISO/IEC JTC1/SC27 has an active project to develop internationally harmonized security evaluation criteria. The main contributions to this work are the *Orange Book,* the U.S. Federal Criteria, the ITSEC, and the Canadian Criteria.

In summary, a steady evolution of security evaluation criteria is currently in progress, building upon what the *Orange Book* started, and taking into account contributions from a number of countries around the world. An important outcome of this work will be criteria for use in non-government environments. International alignment of the results of the various national and regional criteria projects is anticipated.

16.4 Cryptographic Devices

The above work on security evaluation criteria expressly excludes the evaluation of cryptographic devices which form part of a computer/communications security solution. This is a more specialized and sensitive topic, and is much less amenable to international agreement. We shall limit coverage of this topic to U.S. government standards which define requirements for cryptographic modules used for the protection of unclassified data, and which form the basis of validation programs for such equipment. In general, acquisition of such equipment for use in government applications depends upon such a validation.

U.S. Federal Standard 1027, issued in 1982, provided the basis for evaluating DES-based cryptographic equipment. Subsequent to the Computer Security Act of 1987, responsibility for this standard moved to NIST, and it was redesignated FIPS PUB 140. Federal Standard 1027 had formed the basis of a validation program for DES-based equipment operated by the National Security Agency.

In 1993, NIST issued a complete replacement for FIPS PUB 140, designated FIPS PUB 140-1. This is a much more comprehensive standard than its predecessor, and it eliminates the links to DES technology.

FIPS PUB 140-1 defines four levels which embrace functionality and assurance requirements for cryptographic devices:

- *Level 1*: This is the lowest level, with only certain basic security requirements (e.g., the encryption algorithm must be a NIST-approved algorithm). No physical security mechanisms are required. Software cryptographic functions may be performed in a general-purpose personal computer. Typical systems validated at this level are low-cost, add-on personal computer encryption boards.

- *Level 2*: This level adds a requirement for low-cost, tamper evident coatings or seals, or for pick-resistant locks, to protect against access to cryptographic keys or other sensitive parameters stored within the module. A module must authenticate an operator on a role basis and apply role-based access control to check for authorization to perform any function. Software cryptographic functions can be implemented in a multi-user time-sharing system with an *Orange Book C2* rating.

- *Level 3*: This level is comparable to that specified in the earlier FIPS 140 (Federal Standard 1027). It requires enhanced physical security, e.g., by having sensitive components in a strong enclosure, with critical security parameters being zeroized if an attempt is made to penetrate the enclosure. A module must authenticate operators individually. There are stronger requirements for entering and outputting critical security parameters — data ports for this purpose must be physically separate from other ports, and parameters must be entered/output either in encrypted form or in a manner which uses split knowledge procedures. To provide adequate software or firmware assurance, the manufacturer must provide a specification of a formal model of the cryptographic module security policy, and automated tools should be used to verify that the software design is consistent with the formal model. If software cryptographic functions are implemented in a multi-user, time-sharing system, an *Orange Book B1* rating is required. This protects cryptographic software and critical security parameters from other software that may run on the system, prevents plaintext from being mixed with ciphertext, and prevents unintentional transmission of critical information (e.g., plaintext keys).

- *Level 4*: The highest level, with more stringent physical security requirements, which permit operation in physically unprotected environments where an intruder may have ready access to the device. The module must be protected against a compromise of its security due to environmental conditions or fluctuations outside its normal operating ranges for voltage and temperature. A module is required to either include special environmental protection features designed to detect fluctuations and zeroize critical security parameters, or to undergo rigorous environmental failure testing. If software cryptographic functions are implemented in a multi-user, time-sharing system, an *Orange Book B2* rating is required.

Summary

Security evaluation criteria are standards which respond to the question: *How can a purchaser of a security product be assured that the product provides the protection required?* This includes being assured that the product design is adequate and appropriate, being assured that the design is correctly implemented, and being assured that the product does not perform any additional unwanted functions. To give a purchaser a metric to compare the security provisions in different products, products are evaluated by impartial organizations. Security evaluation criteria standards provide the basis for a common understanding between product developers, purchasers, and evaluators as to the evaluation process.

The starting point for virtually all work in this field was the U.S. Department of Defense Trusted Computer System Evaluation Criteria — the TCSEC or *Orange Book*. This standard defines detailed criteria whereby a computer system, or component thereof, can be classified according to the overall confidence one can place in the system for the protection of sensitive information. The classes are: Class *D* (Minimal Protection), Class *C1* (Discretionary Security Protection), Class *C2* (Controlled Access Protection), Class *B1* (Labeled Security Protection), Class *B2* (Structured Protection), Class *B3* (Security Domains), and Class *A1* (Verified Design). Each class provides for progressively more security features and a higher level of product assurance than the preceding class. The *Red Book* provides guidance as to how the *Orange Book* should be interpreted in a network environment, and also provides for qualitative product ratings for network security services not covered by the *Orange Book*.

The European Information Technology Security Evaluation Criteria (ITSEC) separates the aspects of security functionality and security assurance.

A product or system has a recognized functionality class which is pre-defined, e.g., in the standard or by a registration procedure. Assurance is dealt with separately, by the assignment of an evaluation level. The evaluation level indicates the confidence the procurer of a product or system can have that the stated security functionality is both appropriate and implemented correctly. Each *Orange Book* class can be mapped to a specific combination of an ITSEC functionality class and an evaluation level.

Other significant security evaluation criteria developments include the Canadian criteria, the U.S. Federal Criteria, and the international criteria being developed by ISO/IEC.

Cryptographic devices are not considered in the above processes because they represent a more specialized and sensitive topic. Separate standards covering the implementation and validation of such devices have been produced by the U.S. federal government.

REFERENCES

[CAN1] Canadian System Security Centre, *The Canadian Trusted Computer Product Evaluation Criteria*, Version 3.0e, April 1992 (Draft).

[DOD1] U.S. Department of Defense, *Department of Defense Trusted Computer System Evaluation Criteria*, DOD 5200.28-STD, National Computer Security Center, Fort Meade, MD, December 1985.

[DOD2] U.S. Department of Defense, *Computer Security Requirements — Guidance for Applying the Department of Defense Trusted Computer System Evaluation Criteria in Specific Environments*, CSC-STD-003-85, DoD Computer Security Center, Fort Meade, MD, June 1985.

[DOD3] U.S. Department of Defense, *Technical Rationale Behind CSC-STD-003-85: Computer Security Requirements — Guidance for Applying the Department of Defense Trusted Computer System Evaluation Criteria in Specific Environments*, CSC-STD-004-85, DoD Computer Security Center, Fort Meade, MD, June 1985.

[DOD4] U.S. National Computer Security Center, *Trusted Network Interpretation of the Trusted Computer System Evaluation Criteria*, NCSC-TG-005 Version 1, July 1987.

[EUR1] Commision of the European Communities, *Information Technology Security Evaluation Criteria (ITSEC): Provisional Harmonised Criteria*, ISBN 92-826-3004-8, Brussels, Belgium, 1991.

[FRA1] Service Central de la Sécurité des Systèmes d'Information, France, *Catalogue de Critères Destinés à évaluer le Degré de Confiance des Systèmes d'Information*, 692/SGDN/DISSI/SCSSI, 1989.

[GER1] German Information Security Agency, *Criteria for the Evaluation of Trustworthiness of Information Technology (IT) Systems*, ISBN 3-88784-200-6, 1989.

[UKG1] Communications-Electronics Security Group, United Kingdom, *U.K. Systems Security Confidence Levels*, CESG Memorandum No. 3, 1989.

[UKG2] Department of Trade and Industry, United Kingdom, *DTI Commercial Computer Security Centre Evaluation Levels Manual*, V22 DTI, 1989.

Standards

FIPS PUB 140-1: *Security Requirements for Cryptographic Modules*, Federal Information Processing Standards Publication 140-1, 1993 (Draft).

ISO/IEC 7498-2: *Information Technology — Open Systems Interconnection — Basic Reference Model — Part 2: Security Architecture*.

17   **Planning Considerations**

This book has described a range of security techniques and security protocols for use in protecting computer networks. Application of these techniques and protocols will have various impacts upon network system and product planning. This, the final, chapter aims to highlight the major impacts.

The planning process is addressed in terms of four broad areas:

- requirements analysis;
- overall solution;
- supporting infrastructure; and
- product planning.

Note that the impacts identified span a variety of planning roles, such as policy-maker, specification-writer, network architect, and product designer.

17.1 Requirements Analysis

Policy and Environment

Development of a network security requirements statement depends upon having a clear understanding, in general terms, of the security policy to apply to the resultant (protected) network. Questions which need to be addressed early include: What categories of resource need to be protected? From whom does each category require protection? Which basic security objective(s) (confidentiality, integrity, availability, legitimate use) relate to the protection? Policy consideration also needs to take into account any issues of legal liability (e.g., as to the binding nature of digital signatures), and issues of accountability of individuals and organizations.

Another aspect needing to be understood early (at a broad level) is that of network environment. For example, what types of communications paths will be involved, e.g., corporate premises, physically unprotected premises, public networks, radio links, and/or gateways to other networks? Is access from public networks possible?

Security Functionality

A threat assessment takes into account the above policy and environment information plus other relevant factors. A quantitative risk analysis involves estimating the likelihood of the various threats being realized and the impact (cost) of such realizations. This analysis can assist in determining which safeguards are warranted. Note that a security system is only as strong as its weakest link. Note also that communications security is only one part of a security solution — it is necessary to simultaneously specify requirements for physical security, personnel security, administrative security, media security, and hardware/software security. From the above, the required security services should be determinable. (See Chapter 2 for further discussion.)

The functionality profiles in the new generation of security evaluation criteria standards should be considered, with a view to aligning network requirements with one of these profiles (see Chapter 16). From the purchaser perspective, such alignment will facilitate subsequent product comparisons. From the vendor perspective, such alignment will better position a product for future market opportunities. Because these standards are in active development as this book goes to print, detailed guidance is not possible.

Required assurance level (in terms of one of the security evaluation criteria standards) should also be assessed.

Performance

Performance requirements need to be assessed carefully, as they may have a major impact on the selection of a security solution. Throughput and delay figures for data requiring confidentiality protection are particularly important. Bulk encryption is likely to apply to such data, introducing significant processing overheads. It may be necessary to trade off performance against strength of protection (e.g., choice of algorithm or key length) and cost (e.g., choice of hardware versus software implementation). Performance overheads for functions which involve authentication or key management should be treated separately. Because these functions occur sporadically, delay figures are generally much more important than throughput.

Operational Cost

The inclusion of security equipment in a network may imply much higher operational costs than for a network without such equipment. Contributing factors to higher operational costs include:

   (a) the need to maintain physically secured equipment enclosures or sites;

(b) the need to dispatch trusted personnel to equipment sites periodically, for such purposes as manual key updating;

(c) the need for higher-integrity network management facilities (e.g., more training, better personnel screening); and

(d) infrastructure costs (see Section 17.3).

Well-designed, modern security equipment can minimize such costs. For example, with respect to (a), critical security functions can be housed in electronically monitored, tamperproofed housings which require no further external protection. With respect to (b), the use of public-key cryptosystems in key management can greatly reduce this cost in comparison with symmetric cryptosystems.

Trade-offs will arise in this area, so it is necessary to identify any constraints at the requirements stage.

International Considerations

The potential need for a network to span international boundaries should be considered at an early stage, as it may imply constraints on the security techniques that may be employed. This results from export and import restrictions placed upon cryptographic equipment.

The most sensitive area is that of cryptographic algorithms used for confidentiality purposes. Many nations place constraints on the export and/or import of such algorithms. For example, while DES can be used freely for confidentiality purposes within the United States and Canada, it cannot be exported without a government-approved license. Granting of such a license depends upon the destination country and upon the purpose for which the algorithm will be used. Usually, such licenses can be obtained for protecting banking communications and for protecting the proprietary information of U.S. and Canadian corporations, but license applications for other purposes may not be approved. Licenses may be granted more freely for other (non-standard) algorithms, depending upon an assessment of the algorithm by applicable national security agencies.

Cryptographic algorithms not used for confidentiality purposes, e.g., algorithms for authentication, integrity, or non-repudiation, also require export and import licenses, but licenses are more freely granted.

Network geography can therefore have a major impact on the technical security solution that can be employed. It is also necessary to consider prospects for future network expansion across international boundaries, to avoid the possibility of not being able to extend existing security mechanisms across such boundaries.

User Acceptability

A requirements study should consider user acceptability criteria. If security features are deemed overly burdensome or unfriendly to users, there is a serious risk they will not be used or they will be misused. Either can defeat the entire purpose of providing the feature. The ideal security feature is transparent to the user community. Security features which require users to perform complex procedures or remember lengthy data strings, or which introduce excessive performance overheads, are at risk of proving ineffective through user rejection.

17.2 Overall Solution

Standards and Profiles

Given a sound understanding of requirements, standards become a major factor in determining a network security solution. Neither purchaser nor vendor gains by the provision of a non-standard solution, when a feasible standard alternative exists. For a purchaser, non-standard systems limit future vendor choice. For a vendor, non-standard systems limit future market opportunities. For both purchaser and vendor, non-standard systems are also at risk of becoming a support burden. Standards are of various types, such as international and national standards, industry standards (e.g., banking standards) and community standards (e.g., Internet standards). Chapters 9 through 16 of this book describe the range of standards available.

Standard profiles also play an important role in deciding which standards and which features of those standards to employ to achieve interworking between equipment of different vendors in a particular application environment. The profiles most likely to apply to network security are government OSI profiles (e.g., U.S. GOSIP, U.K. GOSIP, and Canadian COSAC), regional workshop profiles (e.g., OIW, EWOS, and AOW agreements), ISO/IEC ISPs, and IGOSS (see Appendix A for further details).

Architectural Placement

Chapter 3 described the possible need to decide the architectural level (application level, end-system level, subnetwork level, or direct-link level) at which any security service should be placed. In some cases it may also be necessary to decide upon an architectural layer within a level (e.g., the choice of placing an end-system level service at the Transport Layer or Network Layer). The criteria for making such decisions are discussed in Chapter 3.

Security Techniques and Algorithms

The decisions as to appropriate security techniques and algorithms are generally independent of communications architectural issues. Security techniques and algorithms are also, to a large extent, separable from each other. For example, one can decide to use a two-way authentication exchange with public-key signed tokens, and independently decide which digital signature algorithm to use.

Information to support the selection of security techniques is provided in Chapters 5, 6, 7, 8, and 10 of this book.

The selection of algorithm will be governed by a variety of factors such as cryptographic strength, performance, exportability, and licensing provisions. It is important to realize that different user environments will have different algorithm requirements. Furthermore, algorithm requirements will change with time, due to cryptographic advances, technological advances, and political change. It is therefore recommended that system and product designers not tie their designs to particular algorithms, but take a "plug-in" approach to cryptographic algorithms. In some cases, simultaneous support for multiple algorithms may be warranted to enable a product to communicate securely with multiple environments.

Governments typically recognize a range of algorithm types and corresponding cryptographic device types, like the following (used by the U.S. government):

- *Type 1*: Classified algorithms approved by the NSA for securing classified information. Corresponding cryptographic devices are endorsed by the NSA.

- *Type 2*: Classified algorithms approved by the NSA for protecting Department of Defense unclassified information covered by the Warner Amendment (10 USC 2315). Corresponding cryptographic devices are endorsed by NSA.

- *Type 3*: NIST standard algorithms to be used for protecting unclassified, sensitive, non-Warner Amendment government information or commercial information. DES was the primary Type 3 algorithm for many years.

- *Type 4*: Commercial algorithms that are not government standards. Such an algorithm may be proprietary to a particular vendor.

A security product may implement more than one type of algorithm, e.g., a Type 2 algorithm and a Type 3 algorithm, or a Type 3 algorithm and a Type 4 algorithm.

Registration

Various aspects of a security solution may depend upon registration rather than standardization. For example, cryptographic algorithms, security exchanges, security transformations, and security labels are frequently registered rather than standardized. See Section 10.1 and Appendix B for further discussion.

Failure/Recovery Strategies

Failure/recovery strategies constitute a critical part of a security solution. Because such strategies are not fully addressed by security standards, it is essential that they be given careful attention in the planning of any overall network security solution.

It should generally be recognized that security components, like any electronic device, can be subject to failure. However, it is essential to ensure that such failures do not lead to major security exposures. For example:

- failure of an encryption device should not result in sensitive traffic continuing to flow but with inadequate protection;
- failure of a secure communications channel should not result in sensitive traffic being diverted via an insecure channel; and
- failure of an authentication system should not result in users being granted access to a system without being properly authenticated.

Also, when corrective action is performed following a failure, e.g., by restoration or replacement of a faulty component, care must be taken to ensure that the recovery process does not introduce major security exposures.

In some circumstances, response to a failure may be to continue network operation with an increased risk of exposure. For example, in the event of failure of a key management system, a decision may be made to continue to operate the dependent cryptographic systems for a limited time without key updating, i.e., with extended cryptoperiods. Any such decision should be made only after a complete anaysis of the risk. Particular consideration should be given to the prospect of an attacker deliberately inducing a system failure, in order to invoke the state of heightened exposure in which a planned attack may be perpetrated.

17.3 Supporting Infrastructure

Virtually any network security solution, in an operational environment, has infrastructural support requirements. Planning for the establishment and maintenance of this infrastructure can be a major task.

Naming and Name Management

Several aspects of security, including access control, accountability, and non-repudiation depend upon the recognition of unique names for human users (and sometimes system components). In general, all individuals who potentially wish to communicate securely with each other need to have names assigned from a common name space. Given the uncertainty that commonly exists as to potential future needs to interconnect with other networks, a wise decision is to provide for a *globally unique* naming scheme from day one. This can typically be achieved, say, for members or staff of a large organization, by considering each name to comprise two components: a globally unique organization name, plus an intra-organization name assigned by the administration of the organization.

The naming scheme which is becoming widely adopted for this purpose is that of *directory distinguished names*, defined in the ISO/IEC 9594 standard (see Chapter 14). This naming scheme is now supported by the necessary registration authority structures at the international and national levels, to the extent that an organization can obtain an assured globally unique organization name.

Ongoing name management requires a certain amount of care, in ensuring that uniqueness is maintained and also in dealing with name reuse. If a name is de-assigned from one person, e.g., because that person ceases employment with the organization, and the same name is then assigned to another person, care must be taken to ensure that the new assignee does not inadvertently acquire the access rights of the original assignee. For example, if the name is referenced in access control lists in systems distributed across a network, and if there is no system for systematically purging deassigned names from such access control lists, this can have the effect of passing the access rights to the new assignee. This can be a difficult problem to deal with when authorization responsibilities are widely distributed.

Security Management Infrastructures

In a network environment, network-wide infrastructures are commonly required to support a range of security management functions:

- *Authentication management*: Authentication decisions typically need to be made at many different systems, on the basis of a common database of authentication information. The form of this infrastructure will vary depending upon the type of authentication mechanism employed (see Chapter 5). In general, either a system of on-line servers or a certificate management system will be required. A large distributed database system may be necessary.

- *Access control management*: Authorization and access control can range from being fully distributed to being fully centralized. Except for the fully distributed case, an infrastructure will be required for distributing authorization or privilege information to the points at which access control decisions are made.
- *Key management*: Keys for use in confidentiality or integrity services may or may not require a special key management infrastructure, depending upon the techniques employed. For example, symmetric key management techniques (e.g., ANSI X9.17) require an infrastructure of key distribution or key translation servers (see Chapter 4). For infrastructural purposes, key management can often be integrated with authentication management.
- *Certificate management*: Certificate management is required to support digital signatures and can also provide the infrastructure needed for authentication. The main functions needed are public-key certificate distribution and revocation certificate distribution.
- *Security audit trail accumulation*: Audit trails can be handled on a distributed basis or a centralized basis. If centralized, an infrastructure for accumulating audit trail information from multiple distributed systems is required.
- *Security alarm reporting*: As with audit trails, an infrastructure is required if a centralized security alarm system is employed.
- *Configuration management*: For network components with configurable security software (e.g., user workstations, routers, servers), the software configuration for each system may need to be securely managed. This allows a security administrator to restrict the capabilities and privileges of different systems, based on such factors as operational role and physical environment. Such configuration control may be another function for a security management infrastructure.
- *Remote monitoring*: There may be a requirement to regularly monitor the state or configuration of a remote system. This might even apply to user workstations; for example, an organization might install a capability to regularly execute virus scans on remote systems or to check for the presence of unauthorized software.

When considering the need for and scope of security management infrastructures, a general issue which arises is the extent to which security mechanisms should be integrated and centralized. It is certainly possible to put in place multiple security protective features which operate independently and are locally controlled, thereby obviating the need for any security management infrastructure. However, such approaches are not encouraged because of the difficulty of analyzing the resultant risk scenario and the likelihood of hidden security vulnerabilities existing. In general, comprehensive, integrated approaches to network security provide superior protection over independent locally controlled countermeasures.

17.4 Product Planning

The main aspect of planning a security product, which is different from that of any other product, is the *trust* requirement. The customer needs a high level of assurance that the product correctly performs the functions it claims to perform, and that it does not perform any unwanted functions. This is a complex subject, which this book does not attempt to cover in depth. Some of the issues a product planner may encounter are identified in the following subsections.

Product Life Cycle

Assurance of product trust can depend upon the application of special controls at all stages of the product life cycle. Examples of such special controls are:

- *Design*: A product design requires special review to ensure its correctness; formal proofs of correctness may be warranted, to ensure the absence of design flaws.
- *Manufacturing*: Stringent quality controls are required to ensure that no faults with a potential trust impact are introduced (accidentally or deliberately) into the product.
- *Shipping*: Special controls may be needed to ensure that a product is not modified or substituted in this potentially vulnerable environment (i.e., when it is out of the direct control of both supplier and customer). Product tamperproofing and/or special packaging may be warranted.
- *Installation*: Controls at this stage ensure that the correct product is installed, and that it is initialized correctly within its operational environment.
- *Operation*: It is necessary to ensure that a product can continue to be trusted throughout a long operational life; features such as tamperproofing, remote monitoring, and self-testing may be required.
- *Maintenance*: Controls are needed to ensure that product trust cannot be compromised in situations of preventative, diagnostic, or corrective maintenance; software upgrading or modification requires strict controls over media handling and installation procedures.
- *Decommissioning*: It may be necessary to securely decommission a product to ensure that residual sensitive information held internally is not

compromised, and/or that the product or its components cannot be adapted to form part of a future attack vehicle.

Evaluation and Endorsement

Subjecting a product to a third party evaluation and obtaining a corresponding endorsement is increasingly becoming a firm customer requirement. Chapter 16 discusses the standard criteria being developed to support such evaluations and endorsements. Product planners should note that this issue needs to be addressed very early in the product planning process, because it can potentially impact all phases of the product life cycle. Attempts to deal with product evaluation and endorsement at a late planning stage are likely to prove particularly costly and result in a lower evaluation level than desired.

Summary

Application of the security techniques and security protocols described in this book may have several impacts upon network system and product planning.

In the requirements analysis phase, aspects requiring special consideration include security policy, vulnerabilities of network environments, threats and required security functionality, performance, operational costs, international export/import considerations, and user acceptability.

In planning the overall solution, issues to consider include use of standards and profiles, architectural placement of security services, choice of security techniques and algorithms, registration of specifications, and failure/recovery strategies.

Virtually any network security solution, in an operational environment, has infrastructural support requirements. Several aspects of security depend upon the recognition of unique names. Provision for a globally unique naming scheme, such as the directory distinguished name scheme, can accommodate all potential future interconnection needs. Network-wide operational infrastructures are commonly required to support security management functions, including authentication management, access control management, key management, certificate management, security audit trail accumulation, and security alarm reporting. In general, comprehensive, integrated approaches to network security provide better protection than independent, local countermeasures.

In planning security products, the main aspect which is different from that of other products is the trust requirement. Assurance of product trust can depend upon the application of special controls at all stages of the product life cycle, including design, manufacturing, shipping, installation, operation, maintenance, and decommissioning. Product evaluation may be a customer requirement, and needs to be addressed very early in the planning process.

APPENDIX A

The Standardization Process

There are many categories of standards, including international, regional, and national standards, government standards, functional standards, and community standards. The significance of any standard depends entirely upon the extent to which it is recognized and used. This book addresses security techniques and protocols drawn from many standards, spanning all of the above categories.

The development of standards can be a surprisingly lengthy process. For an international standard, the elapsed time from conception to formal publication is typically three years, and often five or six years. It is frequently necessary to start using standards prior to completion of their formal publishing process, provided their contents have reached an acceptable level of stability.

This appendix explains the roles and interrelationships of the various international, regional, national, and community organizations that develop standards relevant to computer network security. The procedures followed by these organizations are also summarized. This will assist readers in assessing the significance and stability of the many standards and draft standards referenced in this book. It also provides background for those readers interested in becoming directly involved in the standardization process.

Attention is drawn to Appendix C, which describes the conventions used in naming standards in the references throughout this book and which provides information on how to obtain copies of the referenced standards.

A.1 ISO and IEC

The main international standards applying to open system security are developed by the International Organization for Standardization (ISO) and the International Electrotechnical Commission (IEC).

ISO, which was founded in 1946, is a worldwide federation of national standards bodies. The *ISO Memento* [ISO1] states:

> The object of ISO is to promote the development of standardization and related activities in the world with a view to facilitating international exchange of goods and services, and to developing cooperation in the sphere of intellectual, scientific, technological and economic activity. The scope of ISO covers standardization in all fields except electrical and electronic engineering standards which are the responsibility of IEC. ISO brings together the interests of

producers, users (including consumers), governments and the scientific community, in the preparation of International Standards.

A member body of ISO is the national body "most representative of standardization in its country." Member bodies are "entitled to participate and exercise full voting rights on any technical committee of ISO, are eligible for Council membership and have seats in General Assembly." Examples of ISO member bodies are the American National Standards Institute (ANSI), the British Standards Institute (BSI), and the Standards Council of Canada (SCC).

IEC, which was founded in 1906, is another non-governmental organization which develops international standards. IEC is devoted to the preparation and publication of standards for the electrical and electronics fields.

ISO and IEC are closely related organizations, with the main distinction between them lying in the scope of topics covered. Both organizations are headquartered in Geneva, Switzerland.

With the emergence in the 1970s and 1980s of information technology as a major standardization field, the appropriate division of scope between ISO and IEC became unclear. This was resolved pragmatically in 1987 with the formation of the first ISO/IEC Joint Technical Committee (*JTC1*) responsible for international standards on Information Technology and reporting jointly to both ISO and IEC. ISO/IEC JTC1 now carries responsibility for most of the international standards relevant to open system security. The national member organizations of JTC1 are a subset of the ISO member bodies.[1] JTC1 also works in collaboration with certain *liaison organizations* such as the ITU and ECMA (discussed later).

Committee Structures

ISO and IEC assign responsibility for the development of standards in particular areas to *technical committees* (TCs). A technical committee determines its own program of work, within a broad scope approved by overseeing ISO and/or IEC technical boards. The technical committees (as existing in 1993) responsible for standards referenced in this book are:

- *ISO/IEC JTC1*: Information technology; and
- *ISO TC68*: Banking and related financial services.

Technical committees establish subcommittees (SCs) to cover different aspects of their work. Subcommittees, in turn, establish working groups

---

[1] The term *national body* is used in JTC1, to subsume the concepts of IEC *National Committee* and ISO *Member Body*. The latter terms denote the national organizations which hold formal IEC and ISO membership, respectively.

(WGs) to deal with specific topics. While the structures of TCs, SCs, and WGs evolve over time, the evolution is not rapid and these groups are typically in existence for several years. Figure A-1 shows the JTC1 subcommittees with security-related projects in 1993.

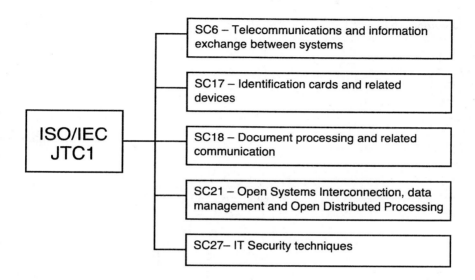

Figure A-1: Security-Relevant ISO/IEC JTC1 Subcommittees

Procedures

Development of an international standard involves a complex process of contributing, reviewing, negotiating, and balloting. The JTC1 process [ISO2] is illustrated in Figure A-2. It commences with the generation of a New Work Item proposal (NP) by either a subcommittee or an individual national body. The NP is subjected to a three-month letter ballot at the technical committee level. The project can proceed only if a majority of the national bodies supports its intent, and at least five national bodies agree to work on its development. If approved, the project is assigned to a subcommittee which, in turn, assigns it to one of its working groups.

Large working groups typically introduce another level to the organiz-ational hierarchy for progressing specific projects, often known as Rapporteur groups or Editor groups (Rapporteurs and Editors are formal individual appointments at the subcommittee level).

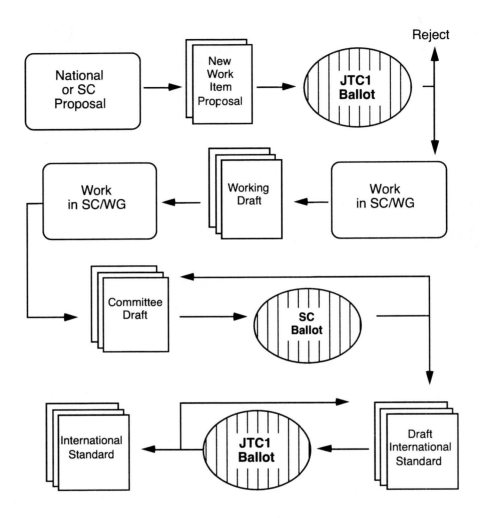

Figure A-2: ISO/IEC JTC1 Standard Development Process

On the basis of national body contributions, a Working Draft document is produced; this often spans several meetings, which are typically six months apart. When the Working Draft is considered stable, it is registered as a Committee Draft (CD). The CD is issued for a three-month letter ballot (by the national bodies participating in the subcommittee) for progression to the status of Draft International Standard (DIS). Responses to this ballot are typically accompanied by detailed technical criticism, which needs to be resolved through negotiation between technical experts of the national bodies involved.

If the comments are not major or if they can be accommodated by readily agreed modifications, the document can progress to DIS status. Otherwise, the document will be revised and reballoted at the CD level. A full round of balloting at this level typically takes six to nine months.

After progression to DIS, there is a further letter ballot, at the technical committee level, to advance the document to the final status of International Standard (IS). In principle, this stage should be nothing more than final editorial review. However, further negotiations as to technical details are not uncommon. As with CD balloting, multiple rounds of balloting and comment resolution may occur. A full balloting round at this stage typically takes twelve months.

Many equipment vendors and buyers cannot afford to wait for formal publication of a standard before taking notice of it. Product development and purchase planning lead times require them to start following standards earlier. Documents at CD or DIS stage assume considerable importance. At CD stage, it can be assumed that the overall approach taken by the standard has been internationally agreed, although details are still subject to change. At DIS stage, it can be assumed that the full technical solution is agreed, although the documentation may still need some refinement.[2]

Revision and Amendment

A published international standard is intended to be a stable document that its user community can confidently buy and use over a period of several years. Each international standard is automatically reviewed after five years, at which time it may be re-endorsed, withdrawn, or, more commonly, updated using basically the same procedures as for its original development.

Independently of this automatic *revision* process, an international standard is frequently *amended*. There are two types of amendment process — standard amendment and rapid amendment. The standard amendment process employs essentially the same committee procedures as a new standard (an amendment at CD stage is known as a Proposed Draft Amendment or *PDAM*, and one at DIS stage is known as a Draft Amendment or *DAM*). Frequently, in developing a new standard, agreement can be reached early on a basic form of the standard, but agreement on more sophisticated features requires further negotiation. In such cases, a basic standard is progressed to International Standard status, while work continues on amendments that will later add the more sophisticated features.

---

[2] Nevertheless, readers need to recognize that all standards in their development stages (including CD and DIS) are subject to change and should not be formally cited in product requirement or conformance specifications.

The rapid amendment process (also known as *defect correction*) is directed more towards correcting errors in or clarifying standards. It employs streamlined committee procedures and leads to the publication of corrigenda to standards.[3]

Security Projects

Active standardization projects and their assignments to working groups change dynamically. Following is a snapshot of active ISO/IEC projects relating to computer communications security in the 1993 timeframe. The five primary projects are spread across three JTC1 subcommittees:

- OSI security architecture and security frameworks, in SC21/WG1;
- OSI upper layers security, in SC21/WG8;
- OSI lower layers security, in SC6;
- information technology security techniques, in SC27/WG2; and
- security evaluation criteria, in SC27/WG3.

In addition, there are several more specialized, security-related standardization activities, which include:

- integrated circuit cards, in JTC1/SC17;
- Message Handling Systems security, in JTC1/SC18/WG4;
- Directory and OSI Management security, in JTC1/SC21/WG4;
- security requirements and guidelines, in JTC1/SC27/WG1;
- wholesale banking security, in TC68/SC2;
- retail banking security, in TC68/SC6/WG6; and
- security architecture of banking systems using integrated circuit cards, in TC68/SC6/WG7.

National Bodies

The technical work behind the development of all international standards falls ultimately upon the national committees, and their individual members, who contribute to the work. Generally, national standardization bodies benefit by simply adopting the resultant international standards as national standards.

---

[3] Readers should note that publication of corrigenda typically takes at least a year, and standards users are not necessarily automatically advised of such corrigenda. Hence, concerned standards users are advised to establish their own links with their national standards committees to maintain awareness of forthcoming amendments.

Some national standardization organizations develop their own national standards which address needs not covered by international standards. These national standards may subsequently become or may heavily influence new international standards. Some of the more prominent national organizations are noted in discussion of regional activities in later sections.

A.2 International Telecommunication Union Standards

The International Telecommunication Union (ITU) is an intergovernmental organization established in 1865, i.e., in the early days of international telegraphy. With the formation of the United Nations in 1947, the ITU became the *specialized agency* of the UN responsible for telecommunications.

In practical terms, the ITU represents the public telecommunications interests of over 170 countries, in support of international public terrestrial networks and radio communications. ITU activities include the establishment of standards (called *Recommendations*) relating to technical, operating, and tariff issues. While these Recommendations are not binding on ITU members, they form the basis of international telecommunications agreements in many areas, including network addressing and interconnection protocols.

Until 1993, standardization activities were dealt with in two arms of the ITU called the International Telegraph and Telephone Consultative Committee (CCITT) and the International Radio Consultative Committee (CCIR). In 1993, changes to the internal organization of ITU resulted in the termination of those groups and the establishment of the ITU Telecommunication Standardization Sector (ITU-TS), to take over their standardization activities. Many standards relevant to computer communications were developed by CCITT, and their maintenance and follow-up development continues in the ITU-TS.[4]

Within a member country, the national government determines who will represent it in the ITU standardization sector. In many countries it is a government public telecommunications agency (or PTT). In others (such as the U.S. and Canada), a government-convened committee is formed to represent the common interests of public carriers and their users.

Committee Structures and Procedures

In the ITU standardization sector, the technical work is spread across a set of *study groups* (SGs). The study group responsible for data communications is

---

[4] ITU Recommendations published prior to April 1993 are called *CCITT Recommendations* and those published subsequently are called *ITU-T Recommendations*. For simplicity and forward compatibility, references in this book use the term *ITU-T Recommendation* for all of these standards.

Study Group 7 — *Data Networks and Open System Communications*. Within a study group, work is assigned to *working parties* (WPs).

The work program is based on a four-year cycle, called a *study period*. At the start of a study period, a set of *Questions* for each study group is established. These Questions define the scope of new Recommendations to be developed or existing Recommendations to be revised during the study period. A Question is assigned to a Rapporteur, who works by correspondence and/or meetings as necessary throughout the study period to develop the necessary draft Recommendations.

Historically, publication of CCITT Recommendations was synchronized with this four-year cycle, resulting in the publication of major compendia of Recommendations such as the 1984 *Red Book* and the 1988 *Blue Book*. However, in 1988, the tight linkage of Recommendation publication to the four-year cycle was broken. Study groups were given authority to approve Recommendations as they became mature and stable, subject to certain review and balloting procedures.

The ITU has a general policy of aligning its Recommendations with ISO/IEC International Standards where practical. In the 1981–1984 study period, close collaboration was established with ISO TC97 (the forerunner of ISO/IEC JTC1), leading to the publication of *aligned* publications on the OSI reference model and the early OSI layer service and protocol specifications. This meant that ISO published an international standard while the ITU published a Recommendation on the same subject. The technical details of the two documents were generally the same; there were stylistic differences and, in some cases, small technical differences (on issues where the two organizations could not reach full agreement). By 1992, the collaborative links had tightened to the extent that the JTC1 and ITU organizations agreed to a procedure for producing *common text* for publications whenever possible.

Security Projects

ITU involvement in OSI security commenced in the 1985–1988 study period, with security extensions to the Message Handling Systems standards and security features in the new Directory standards (Chapters 13 and 14 describe the results).

ITU involvement in general-purpose security standards did not commence until the 1989–1992 study period, when a fledgling security group worked collaboratively with JTC1/SC21 on several security topics, and initiated the publication of the OSI Security Architecture as ITU-T Recommendation X.800. Collaboration on general-purpose security standards is continuing subsequently.

A.3 Profiles

International standards often contain many optional features. This results from such factors as:

- incomplete knowledge of the full range of potential user requirements;
- varying requirements for particular user sectors; and
- inability to agree on the selection of a specific technical solution from a range of alternatives.

Consequently, the users of a standard may be faced with choices from a vast range of options, and with the prospect that separate implementations of the same standard may not interwork if compatible sets of options are not chosen. It is here that *profiles* (sometimes known as *functional standards*) play an important role.

A profile defines a limited set of options, plus other constraints, which facilitate the building of interworking implementations of an international standard. Profiles are developed in forums separate from those developing the base standards. Working close to the implementors and end users, and with less rigid procedural constraints, the profilers produce results which are unattainable in the base standard development process.

The main developers of profiles are:

- regional workshops (discussed below);
- national governments, which develop profiles for use for government procurement purposes, e.g., the *Government Open Systems Interconnection Profile* (GOSIP) specifications of the U.S. and U.K. governments; and
- industry groups.

ISO/IEC JTC1 also produces profiles, known as *International Standardized Profiles* (ISPs), with the goal of minimizing duplication of effort among different profiling groups. ISPs are not developed by standards committees, but by other profiling groups such as the regional workshops. They are processed according to expedited procedures in ISO/IEC. They do not have the formal status of International Standards but are widely recognized.

A.4 Standardization in North America

The principal ISO/IEC national bodies in North America are the American National Standards Institute (ANSI) and the Standards Council of Canada

(SCC). The former warrants special consideration, because of the major influence many U.S. national standards have upon international standards developments in the security arena.

American National Standards Institute (ANSI)

Founded in 1918, ANSI is a not-for-profit, privately funded membership organization which coordinates the development of U.S. voluntary national standards and which is the U.S. member body of ISO and IEC.

The ANSI Information Systems Standards board (ISSB) manages the development of standards for interfaces between information system components, human-machine interfaces, and information processing techniques. Under the ISSB are several Accredited Standards Committees addressing specific work areas. These committees generally conduct technical work in multiple technical committees and subgroups. The committees of most relevance to computer network security are:

- X3 *Information Processing Systems*: Standards in the areas of computers, information processing and peripheral equipment, devices, and media. X3 provides the U.S. representation in JTC1, hence represents U.S. interests in the majority of the international standards addressed in this book. In the security area, this committee generally operates by contributing to international standards developments then adopting the result as a national standard, rather than by producing national standards in advance of international standards.[5]

- X9 *Financial Services*: Standardization for facilitating financial services operations. This committee has been a long time leader in the establishment of financial industry standards, including security-related standards. Several security standards were developed by X9 as national standards, and subsequently formed the basis for international standards.

- X12 *Electronic Business Data Interchange*: Standardization to facilitate electronic interchange between businesses and institutions, relating to such business transactions as order placement and processing, shipment, receiving, and payment. X12 has developed a full suite of EDI standards, which includes standards for EDI security. These standards are discussed in Chapter 13.

Full participation in any of these committees is open to any U.S. organization which takes out membership. Non-members can participate as

---

[5] The notable exceptions are the ANSI X3.92 standard (Data Encryption Algorithm) and related standards X3.105 and X3.106.

observers at meetings, but do not have an entitlement to vote on the contents of standards.

The Institute of Electrical and Electronics Engineers (IEEE)

IEEE is an independent organization of engineering professionals, which includes among its many activities the development of certain standards in the electrotechnical field. While IEEE is international by charter, its standards activities are predominantly U.S.-based. Some IEEE standards are adopted by ANSI as U.S. national standards.

In the field of local area networks (LANs), IEEE has assumed the role of the leading standards development forum internationally. Many of the IEEE 802 series of LAN standards have been adopted by ISO/IEC (the ISO/IEC 8802 series) as well as by ANSI (the ANSI/IEEE 802 series).

To address LAN security, IEEE established committee 802.10 to develop a *Standard for Interoperable LAN Security* (SILS). The plan for this standard calls for several parts including a model, a secure data exchange specification, a key management specification, and a security management specification. This work is discussed in Chapter 11.

U.S. Federal Government Standards

U.S. Federal Information Processing Standards publications (FIPS PUB) are developed by the National Institute of Standards and Technology (NIST)[6] which is responsible to the U.S. Department of Commerce. These official standards and guidelines are developed for use by Federal Government departments and agencies, and organizations which communicate with these departments or agencies. Because of the immensity of this marketplace, the FIPS PUBs can be as important to equipment vendors as national standards. Furthermore, conformance to FIPS PUBs is usually a mandatory requirement in Federal Government procurements. Each standard contains information about its applicability and implementation requirements.

The procedure for issuing a FIPS PUB is as follows. NIST, usually in consultation with other government agencies and industry, generates a draft FIPS. This is distributed for a period of public review and comment, as announced in the *Federal Register*. Comment received is taken into account in deciding whether to proceed with publication of the FIPS and in determining any changes to be made to the document prior to final publication.

FIPS PUB 146, the *Government Open Systems Interconnection Profile* (*GOSIP*), is particularly important in the open system communications field [LIN1, OHL1]. It specifies profiles for OSI protocols at all layers, and for key

---

[6] Formerly the National Bureau of Standards (NBS).

OSI applications, including Message Handling Systems and Directory. U.S. GOSIP Version 1 was issued in 1988, and mandated for use in government procurements in 1990. Revisions are issued periodically (e.g., the first revision, FIPS PUB 146-1, was issued in 1991). The GOSIP specifications make heavy reference to both the OIW agreements and the IGOSS (discussed in the following subsections).

The Open Systems Environment Implementors' Workshop (OIW)

The OIW commenced operation in 1983, when NIST (then NBS) organized a public international workshop at the request of implementors, users, and suppliers of OSI protocols.[7] This led to the establishment of a recurrent workshop activity, sponsored by NIST and meeting four times annually at NIST headquarters in Gaithersburg, Maryland. The workshop series provides a technical forum for the timely development of implementation agreements based on emerging international open-systems standards or specifications. The workshop uses, as input, the standards or other specifications and produces, as output, implementation agreements and testing details for these protocols or specifications. The stable outputs of the workshop are published periodically by NIST (e.g., [NIS1]).

While the OIW is hosted by NIST, it is not formally linked with the U.S. government. It has its own charter, which declares it to be an open public assembly; any organization may participate and may send as many representatives as it wishes. It is international in nature; while participation is predominantly U.S.-based, there is significant participation by organizations and individuals from Canada and other countries. The contents of the formal workshop outputs, and all decisions as to the workshop's organization and program of work, are made on the basis of voting in the workshop Plenary meeting. Only organizations that regularly attend and are knowledgeable of the issues may vote, and only organizations that plan to sell, buy, test, certify, or register related products may vote on implementation decisions.

The technical work of the OIW is conducted in Special Interest Groups (SIGs). The Security SIG assists other SIGs (e.g., the X.400 SIG, the Network Management SIG) on security-related aspects of their implementation agreements. The Security SIG also maintains its own implementation agreements. These agreements identify security-related algorithms which are of general applicability. They also serve to register algorithms if necessary, i.e., they assign ASN.1 object identifiers to algorithms to permit their use in network protocols.

---

[7] The workshop was known as the OSI Implementors' Workshop until 1992, when its scope was broadened to cover other open-systems topics beyond OSI.

Industry/Government Open Systems Specification (IGOSS)

The *Industry/Government Open Systems Specification* (IGOSS) is developed and maintained by a group of organizations, each of which originally developed its own open-systems profile specification. The goal of IGOSS is to maximize the degree of commonality between the different organizations' profiles, by having a common document which the individual profiles can all reference. Organizations involved (and their respective profile specifications) include NIST (U.S. GOSIP), the World Federation of MAP/TOP Users Groups (Manufacturing Automation Profile/Technical Office Protocol specifications), the Electric Power Research Institute (Utilities Communication Architecture), and the Canadian government (Canadian Open Systems Application Criteria).

A.5 Standardization in Europe

European countries have their own national standards organizations which participate in the work of ISO and IEC. These include:

Belgium:	Institut belge de normalisation (IBN)
Denmark:	Dansk Standardiseringsraad (DS)
Finland:	Suomen Standardisoimisliitto (SFS)
France:	Association française de normalisation (AFNOR)
Germany:	Deutsches Institut für Normung (DIN)
Italy:	Ente Nazionale Italiano di Unificazione (UNI)
Netherlands:	Nederlands Normalisatie-instituut (NNI)
Norway:	Norges Standardiseringsforbund (NSF)
Portugal:	Instituto Português da Qualidade (IPQ)
Spain:	Asociación Española de Normalización y Certificación (AENOR)
Sweden:	Standardiseringskommissionen i Sverige (SIS)
Switzerland:	Swiss Association for Standardization (SNV)
United Kingdom:	British Standards Institution (BSI)

European national governments also have distinct government standards programs. For example, the U.K. Government Open Systems Interconnection Profile (GOSIP) program is the British counterpart of U.S. GOSIP.

However, in Europe, a further standardization level has assumed great importance — European regional standardization. This followed on from the passage of the European Community (EC) Council of Ministers Resolution of 1985 on the "New Approach to technical harmonization and standardization."

Under the "new approach," EC Directives establish "essential requirements" (written in general terms) which must be satisfied before products may be sold in the EC. Conformance to European Standards will be the main way for businesses to demonstrate that these "essential requirements" have been met. The body with primary responsibility for ensuring that appropriate standards are in place is the *Commission of the EC*.

A 1990 Draft Commission Green Paper on the Development of European Standardization recognized the critical stage reached by European standardization and noted the priority attention needed from European industry and from standards users. Many EC-funded activities contributing to the development of voluntary standards for information technology have been established, and security is one topic on the agenda. The key organizations are described in the following subsections.

CEN and CENELEC

The European Committee for Standardization (CEN) develops voluntary European Standards (EN) in building, machine tools, information technology, and other fields, excluding electrotechnical fields. The latter are covered by the sister organization, the European Committee for Electrotechnical Standardization (CENELEC). In 1984, the Commission of the EC signed a cooperation agreement with CEN and CENELEC, whereby these organizations would prepare standards for EC adoption.

In addition to European Standards, CEN produces other specifications with various standing, such as:

- *Harmonization Documents* (HD): A specification applied with greater flexibility than a European Standard, so that the technical, historical, or legal circumstances pertaining to each country can be taken into account.
- *European Prestandard* (ENV): A prospective standard for provisional application in areas of technology in which there is a high level of innovation or when there is felt to be an urgent need for guidance.
- *Normes Europeennes de Telecommunications* (NET): Common technical specifications covering access to networks, and equipment for attachment to networks.

CEN and CENELEC sponsor a joint Information Technology Steering Committee (ITSTC). European-specific work on open-systems security standards falls under this committee. Participation in such committee activities is restricted to official representatives of member countries.

European Telecommunications Standards Institute (ETSI)

The European Telecommunications Standards Institute (ETSI) was founded in 1988 as a private, not-for-profit organization to produce standards needed to achieve a unified European telecommunications network and telecommunications equipment market. ETSI membership is open to any interested European organization. The membership includes postal/telecommunications administrations, private corporations, and trade associations in European-region countries (not limited to the EC). By invitation, non-Europeans may participate in ETSI work as observers. In 1992, ETSI became recognized as a formal European standards-making body (along with CEN and CENELEC). For further information on ETSI, see [TEM1].

ETSI is conducting work related to communications security, including work on security algorithms and techniques.

European Workshop on Open Systems (EWOS)

EWOS is, in most respects, a European counterpart of the North American OIW. It is an informal association of many organizations, established in 1987 within the CEN/CENELEC framework, for the purpose of drawing up documents for incorporation in the standardization process at international or European levels. EWOS is a focal point in Europe for the study and development of OSI profiles and corresponding conformance test specifications. EWOS has status which allows it to draft documents which have only to be submitted to public inquiry by CEN and CENELEC before becoming European Standards.

In the security area, EWOS (working with the OIW) played a major role in developing the security profiles for Message Handling Systems (see Chapter 14). In 1991, EWOS established an expert group on security to address general security topics.

European Computer Manufacturers Association (ECMA)

ECMA is a not-for-profit organization whose membership comprises European companies which develop, manufacture, and market hardware or software products or services in the field of information technology or telecommunications [ECM1]. ECMA's activities include the development of ECMA standards and technical reports. These documents have frequently constituted major inputs to the work of ISO/IEC and ITU. ECMA has formal status as a Liaison Organization in ISO/IEC JTC1.

ECMA has been very active in the formative stages of work on OSI and other open-systems topics, including open-systems security. ECMA Technical Committee TC36 is dedicated to the Information Technology Security field.

ECMA has published some significant security-related standards [ECM2, ECM3].

A.6 Standardization in Asia and the Pacific Region

In the Asian and Pacific regions, national standards organizations which actively participate in ISO and IEC work on open-systems security include:

Australia:	Standards Australia (SAA)
Japan:	Japanese Industrial Standards Committee (JISC)
Korea:	Korean Bureau of Standards (KBS)
New Zealand:	Standards Association of New Zealand (SANZ)

The Asia-Oceania Workshop (AOW) was established to develop profiles for OSI standards and can be considered a regional counterpart of the OIW in North America and of EWOS in Europe. These three workshops now work together to develop harmonized profiles for OSI standards. A Regional Workshop Coordination Committee (RWCC) was established in 1991 to monitor harmonization activities between the three workshops.

A.7 Internet Standards

The Internet is the result of interconnecting an unbounded community of government, academic, and private computer networks worldwide. It started as a project sponsored by the U.S. government, and it has a traditional base in research and educational institutions. However, the Internet environment has since expanded to equally embrace private organizations desiring open inter-connectability on a cooperative basis.

The operation of the Internet depends heavily upon interconnection standards. Some international standards are employed in the Internet, but many community standards are established as well. These *Internet standards* satisfy needs not met by existing formal standards.

The body responsible for coordinating Internet design, engineering, and management is the Internet Activities Board (IAB) [CER1]. The IAB delegates to a subsidiary task force, the Internet Engineering Task Force (IETF), the primary responsibility for the development and review of potential Internet standards from all sources. Final decisions on Internet standardization are made by the IAB, based on recommendations from the Internet Engineering Steering Group (IESG), the leadership body of the IETF. Participation in the IETF is on the basis of individual technical contributors, rather than formal representatives of organizations. The process depends greatly upon a spirit of cooperation between participants.

Specifications that are destined to become Internet standards evolve through a set of maturity levels or states known as the "standards track." All standards track specifications are published in the Internet Request for Comment (RFC) document series.[8]

The maturity levels of standards track specifications are:

- *Proposed Standard*: A specification entering the standards track. It must be generally stable, have resolved known design choices, be believed to be well understood, have received significant community review, and appear to enjoy enough community interest to be considered valuable. A specification must remain at proposed standard level for at least six months.

- *Draft Standard*: A specification from which at least two independent and interoperable implementations have been developed, and for which adequate operational experience has been obtained. It must be well understood and known to be quite stable, both in its semantics and as a basis for developing an implementation. A standard must remain at the draft standard level for at least four months.

- *Standard*: A specification characterized by a high degree of technical maturity and by a generally held belief that the specified protocol or service provides significant benefit to the Internet community.

For further details of the standards track process, see [CHA1]. For up-to-date information on the current status of all Internet standards, see the latest version of the RFC entitled *IAB Official Protocol Standards*, which is reissued periodically.

REFERENCES

[CER1] V. Cerf, *The Internet Activities Board*, Request for Comments (RFC) 1160, Internet Activities Board, 1990.

[CHA1] L. Chapin, *The Internet Standards Process*, Request for Comments (RFC) 1310, Internet Activities Board, 1992.

[ECM1] European Computer Manufacturers Association, *ECMA Memento*, (published annually).

---

[8] As well as standards, the RFC series contains documents for general information and documents intended to stimulate comment and discussion. RFCs are publicly available on-line free-of-charge. See Appendix A for details of obtaining copies of RFCs.

[ECM2] European Computer Manufacturers Association, *Security in Open Systems — A Security Framework*, ECMA Technical Report TR/46, July 1988.

[ECM3] European Computer Manufacturers Association, *Security in Open Systems — Data Elements and Service Definitions*, ECMA-138, December 1989.

[ISO1] ISO, *ISO Memento*, (published annually).

[ISO2] ISO/IEC, *ISO/IEC Directives — Procedures for the technical work of ISO/IEC JTC1 on Information Technology*, Second Edition, 1992.

[LIN1] K.F. Lini and J.Y. Moore, *GOSIP Made Easy: The Complete Procurement Guide*, The Corporation for Open Systems, McLean, VA, 1990.

[NIS1] U.S. Department of Commerce, National Institute of Standards and Technology, *Stable Implementation Agreements for Open Systems Interconnection Protocols Version 6 Edition 1 December 1992*, NIST Special Publication 500-206, 1993.

[OHL1] W. Ohle, F. Ferrante, V. Hsin, and E. Gardner, "U.S. Government Open Systems Interconnection Profile (GOSIP) Status and Registration Implementation," in *Message Handling Systems and Application Layer Communication Protocols*, North-Holland, Amersterdam, 1991, pp. 3-13.

[TEM1] S.R. Temple, "The European Telecommunications Standards Institute — Four Years On," *Electronics & Communication Engineering Journal* (August 1992), pp. 177-181.

APPENDIX B

ASN.1 and Registration

B.1 Introduction to Abstract Syntax Notation One (ASN.1)

Application Layer protocol-data-unit formats are defined in terms of abstract syntaxes. ASN.1 is a data-typing language, designed for specifying abstract syntaxes. What makes ASN.1 special, in terms of data-typing languages, is that it has accompanying rules for encoding data-type values into bit string representations, suitable for transfer by lower-layer protocols. The ASN.1 notation is defined in standard ISO/IEC 8824.

ASN.1 provides a way to specify data types and values of those types. Types may be arbitrarily complex, because ASN.1 includes features for constructing new types out of simpler types already defined. ASN.1 also has extensive features to support the modularization of specifications, such that pieces of specification can be readily reused for different purposes.

Following is a simplified introduction to ASN.1's basic features, aimed at making the unfamiliar reader sufficiently comfortable to follow the limited use of ASN.1 notation in this book. For a full tutorial, see [STE1].

The Basic Notation

The main elements of the notation are:

- *Keywords*: Defined in the standard, and generally distinguishable by being all upper-case alphabetics, e.g., `INTEGER`.
- *Type-references*: Used to name a type; the first letter must be an upper-case alphabetic, and usually at least some of the remaining characters are lower-case alphabetics, e.g., `CurrentMonth`.
- *Value-references*: Used to name a value of a type; the first letter must be a lower-case alphabetic, e.g., `december`.
- *Identifiers*: Used to name various items in an ASN.1 specification, including a component of a structured type; the first letter must be a lower-case alphabetic, e.g., `dateField`. (A value-reference and an identifier can always be differentiated by virtue of the context in which the string occurs.)
- *Various special items*: The assignment item `::=`, bracketing items for different contexts (e.g., `{`, `}`, `[`, `]`), and others.

- *Comments*: The start of a comment field is signaled by two hyphens --; the end of the field by a further two hyphens or the end-of-line.

Certain basic (or unstructured) types are defined in the ASN.1 standard. They are known as either *simple types* or *useful types*. Simple types include:

- BIT STRING: Each value is an ordered sequence of bits.
- BOOLEAN: Takes two possible values, TRUE and FALSE.
- CHARACTER STRING: Each value is a string of characters from some defined character set.
- ENUMERATED: A set of values, each with a distinct identifier (e.g., the set of 12 months in a year).
- INTEGER: Takes any integer value.
- OBJECT IDENTIFIER: (See *Object Identifiers and Registration* below).
- OCTET STRING: Each value is an ordered sequence of 8-bit values.
- NULL: Used where several alternatives are possible, but none apply.
- REAL: Takes any real-number value.

Useful types defined in the standard include:

- GeneralizedTime: Local date/time, plus local time differential factor.
- UTCTime: Coordinated Universal Time (GMT).

Additionally, several special cases of character strings are defined, including NumericString, PrintableString, TeletexString, VideotexString, VisibleString, IA5String, and GraphicString.

Constructed Types

The main constructed types are SEQUENCE, SET, and CHOICE.

A value for a SEQUENCE type is a concatenation of values from other types. A SEQUENCE type is defined by referencing a fixed ordered list of existing types (some of which may be designated optional). Each value of the new type is an ordered list of values, one from each component type. An illustration of the notation is as follows:

```
NewType ::= SEQUENCE
{
    component1    [0]   Component1Type,
    component2    [1]   Component2Type,
    component3    [2]   Component3Type
}
```

Here, NewType identifies the new type being defined. The fields component1, component2, and component3 are identifiers for the three components. The fields Component1Type, Component2Type and Component3Type are type specifications or type-references. Any of these could be optionally followed by the keyword OPTIONAL, or the keyword DEFAULT and a value, which indicates that this component may be omitted. The fields [0], [1], and [2] are tags, which may be required to ensure that the different components can be distinguished in an encoding. They can be omitted, if the encoding would be unambiguous anyway (e.g., if no components are optional).

A SET type is essentially the same as a SEQUENCE type, except that the ordering of the components is insignificant and need not be preserved. The notation is the same as for the SEQUENCE type, but the keyword SET replaces SEQUENCE.

A CHOICE type is defined by referencing a fixed list of existing types; each value of the new type is a value of one of the component types. The notation for CHOICE is also the same as for SEQUENCE, with the keyword CHOICE replacing SEQUENCE and without the OPTIONAL or DEFAULT options.

Example of ASN.1 Usage

Following is an example of the use of ASN.1 to define a structured type which could constitute a complete abstract syntax specification. This abstract syntax contains two Application Layer protocol-data-units, for use in accessing a (simplified) time server. The first protocol-data-unit is used for a client-to-server request; the second for the server-to-client response.

```
TimeServerAbstractSyntax ::= CHOICE
{
    requestPDU          [0]  RequestPDU,
                             -- From client to server
    responsePDU         [1]  ResponsePDU
}                            -- From server to client
RequestPDU ::= SEQUENCE
{
    clientName          [0]  GraphicString,
                             -- The server checks this
    requestRefNumber    [1]  INTEGER OPTIONAL
}            -- This number is used by the client
             -- to correlate a response with a request
```

```
ResponsePDU ::= SEQUENCE
{
    resultCode          [0]  ResultCode DEFAULT success,
    requestRefNumber    [1]  INTEGER OPTIONAL,
    time                [2]  UTCTime  -- GMT time returned
}
ResultCode ::= ENUMERATED
  { success (0), formatError (1), unrecognizedClient (2) }
```

B.2   The 1993 Revision to ASN.1 Notation

The 1993 revision of the ASN.1 standards introduced some major extensions
to the original notation. These are reflected in new parts (Parts 2, 3, and 4) to
what is now a multi-part ASN.1 standard (ISO/IEC 8824). A major impact of
the 1993 revision is to provide a functional replacement for the *macro* feature in
the 1988 notation. That feature allowed an ASN.1 user to construct his own
type or value notation, but was not amenable to automated code generation.
     New features in the 1993 extensions include:

*   *Information object classes*: A facility to support the definition of
    conglomerates of ASN.1 types and/or values, which relate to some
    particular application concept. Examples of information object classes
    arising in this book include security exchanges and security transform-
    ations.
*   *Constraints*: Notation to constrain values of any type in any particular
    instance of use.
*   *Parameterized types*: Notation to support partial specification of ASN.1
    types in different specification modules. The definition of a
    parameterized type may include types and/or values in the form of dummy
    parameters. Specific types and/or values are substituted for these
    parameters when the parameterized type is referenced from another
    specification.
*   EMBEDDED PDV: Notation for a type that implies that a presentation data
    value from another abstract syntax is embedded at a particular point. A
    similar function is provided by the EXTERNAL notation, which is being
    phased out as of the 1993 ASN.1 revision.

B.3 ASN.1 Encoding Rules

Standard ISO/IEC 8825 specifies encoding rules that may be applied to any data item defined using ASN.1, giving a straightforward method of deriving a transfer syntax (i.e., representation bit-string) for that abstract syntax item. The original version of ISO/IEC 8825 defined the Basic Encoding Rules (BER) for ASN.1. These rules generate encodings using a simple tag-length-value scheme.

One shortcoming of the BER is that they permit multiple different representations for some values. The 1993 extensions to ISO/IEC 8825 added a new encoding alternative, the Distinguished Canonical Encoding Rules, which generate a unique encoding for every data value (see discussion relating to security trensformations in Section 12.5).

B.4 Object Identifiers and Registration

Object Identifiers

There are many items in OSI which need to be uniquely identified with respect to other items of similar type. Some non-security-related examples are application-contexts, abstract syntaxes, and transfer syntaxes (see Chapter 3). Examples in the security arena are cryptographic algorithms and security exchanges. To support unique identification of such items on a universal scale, the *object identifier* type was included in ASN.1.

An object identifier is a value, comprising a sequence of integer components, which can be conveniently assigned for some specific purpose, and which has the property of being unique within the space of all object identifiers. The object identifier works on the basis of a hierarchical structure of distinct value-assigning authorities, with each level of the hierarchy having responsibility for one integer component of the value. Rules for the upper levels of the hierarchy are defined in annexes to the ASN.1 standard and in the Registration Authority Procedures Standard ISO/IEC 9834-1. The values assigned at the top-most level are 0 (for ITU use), 1 (for ISO use), and 2 (for joint ISO-ITU use). The next level is assigned by the identified organization.

Under the ISO arc, the second level takes the values 0 (for use in ISO standards), 1 (for special-purpose registration authorities), 2 (for ISO-recognized countries), and 3 (for recognized international organizations).

The countries arc (arc 2) is particularly important. At the next level down, it uses ISO 3166 3-digit country codes to identify individual countries. A nominated organization in each country acts as a national registration authority. For example, the ISO 3166 code for the United States is 840. This points to the organization ANSI which acts as a U.S. national registration authority. ANSI, in turn, allocates the next level down to U.S. organizations which register with it. ANSI might, for instance, assign value 678 to the Acme Corporation. Putting all the components together, this now means that the Acme Corporation has unique assignment of the object identifier with components {1, 2, 840, 678}. The Acme Corporation then has the right to assign component values at lower levels for its own purposes, e.g., the value {1, 2, 840, 678, 66} for its own private cryptographic algorithm specification.

Registration Procedures

The three main objectives of registration procedures are:

(a) assignment of a globally unique identifier (an ASN.1 object identifier) to a specification;
(b) encouraging common use of previously registered specifications (in general, the same specification should be registered only once); and
(c) providing a generally available listing of registered items.

From the technical viewpoint, the only essential objective is (a). Almost anyone can register specifications which satisfy this objective. All that is needed is an object identifier subtree root, which can be obtained from a national registration authority, in accordance with ISO/IEC 9834-1. However, in the interests of (b) and (c), it may be desirable to register specifications in a way that makes them most publicly visible. Also, a new specification should not be registered unless it is reasonably certain that a suitable specification has not already been registered by someone else.

Specific registration for cryptographic algorithms is provided through an international registration authority assigned in accordance with ISO/IEC 9979. This facilitates meeting objectives (b) and (c).

Registration of a specification does not necessarily imply anything about the correctness or usefulness of the contents of the specification. In the case of ISO/IEC 9979, it does not even require that all details of the specification be made public.

REFERENCES

[STE1] D. Steedman, *Abstract Syntax Notation One (ASN.1): The Tutorial and Reference*, Technical Appraisals Ltd., Isleworth, U.K., 1990.

Standards

ISO 3166: *Codes for the Representation of Names of Countries.*

ISO/IEC 8824-1: *Information Technology — Open Systems Interconnection — Abstract Syntax Notation One (ASN.1) — Part 1: Specification of Basic Notation* (Also ITU Recommendation X.680).

ISO/IEC 8824-2: *Information Technology — Open Systems Interconnection — Abstract Syntax Notation One (ASN.1) — Part 2: Information Object Specification* (Also ITU Recommendation X.681).

ISO/IEC 8824-3: *Information Technology — Open Systems Interconnection — Abstract Syntax Notation One (ASN.1) — Part 3: Constraint Specification* (Also ITU Recommendation X.682).

ISO/IEC 8824-4: *Information Technology — Open Systems Interconnection — Abstract Syntax Notation One (ASN.1) — Part 4: Parameterization of ASN.1 Specifications* (Also ITU Recommendation X.683).

ISO/IEC 8825-1: *Information Technology — Open Systems Interconnection — Specification of ASN.1 Encoding Rules — Part 1: Basic Encoding Rules (BER)* (Also ITU Recommendation X.690).

ISO/IEC 8825-3: *Information Technology — Open Systems Interconnection — Specification of ASN.1 Encoding Rules — Part 3: Distinguished Canonical Encoding Rules* (Also ITU Recommendation X.692).

ISO/IEC 9834-1: *Information Technology — Open Systems Interconnection — Procedures for the Operation of OSI Registration Authorities — Part 1: General Procedures* (Also ITU Recommendation X.660).

ISO/IEC 9979: *Data Cryptographic Techniques — Procedures for the Registration of Cryptographic Algorithms.*

How to Obtain Standards Documents

In general, standards referenced in this book have been formally published by the organization identified. In some instances, formal publication has not been completed at the publication date of this book. In such cases, the standard reference is followed by the indication *(Draft)*. While all standards with the *(Draft)* designation can be assumed to be reasonably mature, they are still subject to change in detail.

C.1 ISO and ISO/IEC Standards

In the references to international standards in this book, dates are not stated. All standards are revised regularly, and the reader is always referred to the latest version (as advised by ISO or its sales agents). Note that many standards for which ISO was originally responsible are now the joint responsibility of ISO and IEC. All such standards are designated *ISO/IEC nnnn* in this book, even though the version currently on sale may be designated *ISO nnnn*.

Various standards prefixes have also changed through time, and this book generally uses the latest prefix (even though other prefixes may be encountered on some standards still on sale). Some equivalent prefixes are:

- *Information Technology* and *Information Processing Systems*;
- *Banking and Related Financial Services* and *Banking*;
- *Data Communications* and *Telecommunications and Information Exchange Between Systems*; and
- *Data Cryptographic Techniques* and *Security Techniques*.

Also note that some standards are multi-part, e.g., a standard may comprise parts *ISO/IEC nnnn-1* and *ISO/IEC nnnn-2*. In this book, the convention *ISO/IEC nnnn* is used for a multi-part standard when referring to the collection of all parts, and *ISO/IEC nnnn-p* when referring to part *p* only.

Standards not yet published [i.e., those with the *(Draft)* designation] can be obtained in the interim as *DIS* (Draft International Standard) or *CD* (Committee Draft) documents. These documents may not be obtainable through the normal sales channels, but can usually be obtained through national standards organizations or corporations or individuals who participate in the standardization activities.

Published standards can be purchased from ISO sales agencies, most of which are national standards organizations. Agencies include:

Australia:	Standards Australia, Sydney
Belgium:	Institut belge de normalisation, Bruxelles
Canada:	Standards Council of Canada, Ottawa
Denmark:	Dansk Standardiseringsraad, Hellerup
France:	Association française de normalisation, Paris
Germany:	Deutsches Institut für Normung, Berlin
Italy:	Ente Nazionale Italiano di Unificazione, Milano
Japan:	Japanese Industrial Standards Committee, Tokyo
Netherlands:	Nederlands Normalisatie-instituut, Delft
New Zealand:	Standards Association of New Zealand, Wellington
Norway:	Norges Standardiseringsforbund, Oslo
Portugal:	Instituto Português da Qualidade, Lisboa
Spain:	Asociación Española de Normalización y Certificación, Madrid
Sweden:	Standardiseringskommissionen i Sverige, Stockholm
Switzerland:	Swiss Association for Standardization, Zurich
United Kingdom:	British Standards Institution, London
United States:	American National Standards Institute, New York

In other countries, contact your national standards organization, or:

ISO Central Secretariat,
Case postale 56
CH-1211 Geneva 20
Switzerland
Tel: +41 22 749 01 11

International standards are sometimes republished as national standards in some countries and become known under a national standard reference number. For details, contact your national standards organization, quoting the ISO or ISO/IEC standard number.

C.2 ITU Standards

ITU Recommendations published prior to April 1993 are called *CCITT Recommendations* and those published subsequently are called *ITU-T Recommendations*. For simplicity and forward compatibility, references in this book use the term *ITU-T Recommendation* for all of these standards.

ITU Recommendations are available both in hardcopy form and on-line. For further information, contact:

> International Telecommunication Union,
> General Secretariat — Sales Section,
> Place des Nations, CH-1211
> Geneva 20, Switzerland
>
> Tel: +41 22 730 51 11 (general inquiries)
>   +41 22 730 5554/5338 (on-line system inquiries)

C.3 ANSI Standards

ANSI standards can be obtained from:

> American National Standards Institute,
> 11 West 42nd Street,
> New York, NY 10036, U.S.A.
> Tel: +1 (212) 642 4900

C.4 IEEE Standards

IEEE standards can be obtained from:

> IEEE Customer Service,
> 445 Hoes Lane, PO Box 1331
> Piscataway, NJ 08855-1331, U.S.A.
> Tel: +1 (908) 981-1392

C.5 U.S. Federal Government Publications

U.S. Federal Information Processing Standards Publications (FIPS PUB) and most other NIST publications can be obtained from:

> National Technical Information Service,
> U.S. Department of Commerce,
> Springfield, VA 22161, U.S.A.
> Tel: +1 (703) 487 4650

Many NIST publications in the OIW and GOSIP series can be obtained on-line. For information send an e-mail message containing the line "send help" to "oiw@nemo.ncsl.nist.gov", or contact:

> Standards Processing Coordinator (ADP),
> National Institute of Standards and Technology,
> Technology Building, Room B-64,
> Gaithersburg, MD 20899, U.S.A.
> Tel: +1 (301) 975 2816

C.6 Internet Publications

Internet standards and other Internet documents in the *Request for Comments* (RFC) series can be obtained on-line or on paper.

Paper copies are available, either individually or on a subscription basis, from:

> SRI International,
> Network Information Systems Center
> 333 Ravenswood Ave.,
> Menlo Park, CA 94025, U.S.A.
> Tel: +1 (415) 859 6387

Full details on obtaining RFCs via FTP or Internet e-mail can be obtained by sending an e-mail message to "rfc-info@ISI.EDU" with the message body "help: ways_to_get_rfcs". For example:

> To: rfc-info@ISI.EDU
> Subject: getting rfcs
>
> help: ways_to_get_rfcs

Most RFCs are available on-line from various Internet servers throughout the world. In North America, copies are available via FTP from "ftp.nisc.sri.com" as "rfc/rfc*NNNN*.txt" or "rfc/rfc*NNNN*.ps" (*NNNN* is the RFC number without leading zeroes; use "txt" for ASCII text or "ps" for PostScript format).

RFCs may also be requested through e-mail from SRI's automated mail server by sending a message to "mail-server@nisc.sri.com". In the body of the message, indicate the RFC requested, in the form "send rfc*NNNN*.txt" for an RFC in ASCII text format or "send rfc*NNNN*.ps" for PostScript format. A full list of RFCs can be requested by specifying "send rfc-index".

Index

*-Property, 155

Abstract syntax, 297
Abstract Syntax Notation One (ASN.1),
   45, 299, 475
Access control, 149
   certificate, 169
   decision function (ADF), 164
   enforcement function (AEF), 164
   Framework, 235
   forwarding, 168
   inner area, 401
   list, 158, 391
   (for) network management, 419, 429
   policy, 15
   service, 25
   specific area, 399
Access:
   enforcement key server, 90
   matrix, 150
   permissions, 150
   request filtering, 149
Accountability, 16
ACSE, see Association Control Service
   Element
Active threat, 16
Address-hiding, 183
Administrative security, 21
Agreed set of security rules (ASSR), 266
Algorithm identifier, 387
American National Standards Institute
   (ANSI), 466
ANSI X9.17, 87, 249
Appendix, 75
Application:
   -service-element (ASE), 44
   -service-object (ASO), 44
   -association, 44

   -context, 44
   level, 53
   relay, 56
   -service-element (ASE), 295
   -service-object (ASO), 295
   Layer, 40, 44, 50
   Layer structure, 295
Arbitrator, 202
ASE, see Application service element
Asia-Oceania Workshop (AOW), 472
ASN.1, see Abstract Syntax Notation One
ASO, see Application-service-object
Association Control Service Element
   (ACSE), 44, 296, 303, 421
Attack, 16
Authenticated Diffie-Hellman exchange,
   137
Authenticated key exchange, 131
Authentication, 109
   address-based mechanism, 121
   exchange, 140, 386
   Framework, 231
   level, 156, 396
   off-line server, 125
   on-line server, 123
   replay and interception attacks, 128
   service, 23
   use of cryptographic techniques, 122
Authenticator, 134
Authority, 14, 149
Authorization, 15, 149
Authorization violation, 18
Availability objective, 13

Banking standards, 252, 255
Basic Encoding Rules (BER), 479
Bell LaPadula model, 155
Block cipher, 68

487